THE BIRTH OF BRITAIN

THE BIRTH OF BRITAIN

A History of the
English-Speaking Peoples

Volume I

WINSTON S. CHURCHILL, KG

INTRODUCTION BY MICHAEL FRASSETTO

BARNES & NOBLE
NEW YORK

THE BARNES & NOBLE
LIBRARY OF ESSENTIAL READING

This edition published by Barnes & Noble, Inc., by arrangement with
Dodd, Mead & Company, Inc.

Introduction and Suggested Reading
© 2005 by Barnes & Noble, Inc.

This 2005 edition published by Barnes & Noble, Inc.

Maps by James Macdonald

ISBN: 978-0-7607-6857-0

Printed and bound in Canada

17 19 21 23 24 22 20 18 16

CONTENTS

BOOK II
THE MAKING OF THE NATION

BOOK III
THE END OF THE FEUDAL AGE

MAPS AND GENEALOGICAL TABLES

Acknowledgments

I DESIRE TO RECORD MY THANKS TO MR. F. W. DEAKIN AND MR. G. M. Young for their assistance before the Second World War in the preparation of this work, to Mr. Alan Hodge, to Mr. A. R. Myers of Liverpool University, who has scrutinised the text in the light of subsequent advances in historical knowledge, and to Mr. Denis Kelly and Mr. C. C. Wood. I have also to thank many others who have read these pages and commented on them.

INTRODUCTION

THE BIRTH OF BRITAIN IS THE FIRST VOLUME OF *A HISTORY OF THE English-Speaking Peoples*, the immensely popular and eminently readable four-volume work of history by Winston Churchill. Written by one of the masters of the English language, it is a grand and sweeping story that captures the drama of history. A rousing account of the early history of Britain, the work describes the great men and women of the past and their impact on the development of the legal and political institutions of the English. Indeed, Churchill celebrates the creation of the constitutional monarchy and parliamentary system and the kings, queens, and leading nobles who helped create English democracy in *The Birth of Britain*, which was first written at a time when that great achievement faced its darkest hour.

One of the greatest figures of the twentieth century, Winston Churchill is best known for his leadership of Britain during the Second World War. After a period of political exile that was part of a storied career in public life that included great successes and dramatic failures, Churchill was called to power and led Britain during its finest hour. As prime minister, Churchill joined with Franklin D. Roosevelt and Joseph Stalin to defeat Hitler and the Axis powers of Italy and Japan. Although voted out of office following the end of World War II, Churchill helped shape the post-war world and returned to the prime minister's office in 1951. His famed "Iron Curtain" speech offered the best description of the world order following the defeat of the Nazis and the subsequent spread of communism. But Churchill was not simply one of the most important political leaders of his time. He was also the winner of the Nobel Prize for Literature in 1953, and his many works include fiction, biography, and history as well as collections of essays and speeches. His memoirs, speeches, and other works during his long career remain essential documents for the history of his time. More popular with non-scholars than with academic historians, Churchill's works of history, nonetheless, reveal the keen grasp of history by an author who not only witnessed history but made it himself.

The Birth of Britain was not Churchill's only written work, but was one of the last of many works of fiction and nonfiction. Despite his role as one of the great political leaders of his county throughout the first half of the twentieth century—he was a member of Parliament, first lord of the admiralty on two occasions, and prime minister in World War II and again from 1951 to 1955—Churchill compiled a large literary corpus. While still a young man, Churchill was a newspaper correspondent and prior to that served a tour of duty in the military, which formed the core of his first book, *The Story of the Malakand Field Force*. In 1900, he published his only work of fiction, the novel *Savrola*, a modern political drama in which Churchill reveals his political philosophy. Churchill's true talents, however, rested in the writing of nonfiction, and many of his works proclaimed his devotion to democratic principles and praised figures of the past who embodied the virtues of honour and decency or who provided a political education for Churchill and others. His interest in political biography was most clearly demonstrated in his biography of his father, *Lord Randolph Churchill* (1906). This work defended his father's legacy and also provided Churchill a model for his own political beliefs and practices. A second biography, which also served to vindicate one of his ancestors and to provide a model of statesmanship, was *Marlborough: His Life and Times* (1933–38). The biography examines the life of John Churchill, duke of Marlborough, whose place in government and leadership against the absolute monarch Louis XIV may be seen to prefigure his descendant's career in the twentieth century. A talented biographer, Churchill's greatest literary achievement came in the field of history, particularly his *The Second World War* (6 vols. 1948–54).

In this history, Churchill, like a twentieth-century Thucydides, presents his personal memoir of the war effort. It was in recognition of this work of history that Churchill was awarded the Nobel Prize for Literature in 1953.

Churchill began *The Birth of Britain* and his history of the English peoples more than two decades before its final publication. He accepted the commission to write the history in 1932, at a time when he needed the money and was lost in the middle of what he called his "political wilderness"; he was a member of the opposition to the policies and leadership of his own party. Although he had no illusions about writing a history that would compete with those of the professional historians, Churchill proposed a work that would demonstrate the importance to world history of the shared heritage of the British and American peoples. He defined the English-speaking peoples as those who lived in the British Isles and all the peoples throughout the world whose institutions derived from those of England, and in the first volume of the work focused on England itself from the time of Julius Caesar's invasion of the island to the triumph of Henry VII, the first Tudor king. He planned to deliver some half million words to the publisher in 1939 and nearly completed his task when he was interrupted by events on the continent. The rise of Hitler and his threat to world peace brought Churchill back into the government, ultimately to the prime minister's office, and away from his writing. His work would be completed only after the war and after he wrote his personal history of World War II. After all that had been completed, he turned once again to his history of the English-speaking peoples in the early 1950s, finishing it after revising it in light of his own experiences and changes in scholarship since the 1930s. And once it appeared, the work was a best seller that has gone through numerous printings and even received warm reviews from professional scholars such as A. J. P. Taylor.

Churchill recognised that his was not the work of a professional historian, but that did not prevent him from turning to the same sources that scholars used and employing the best contemporary scholars as research assistants. Along with the advice of his researchers, Churchill drew from the most important works of his day and from his own broad reading. One of the most important influences on Churchill in the writing of his history was the monumental work by Edward Gibbon, *The Decline and Fall of the Roman Empire*, which Churchill admired and sought to emulate. Among the contemporary historians Churchill cites are G. M. Trevelyan, one of the leading social historians whose literary style matched that of Churchill's, and Leopold von Ranke, the founder of modern historiography. He also cites the English Roman historian and philosopher of history, R. G. Collingwood, and the eminent historian of the English constitution, William Stubbs. Although he was not a professional historian himself, Churchill's use of the works of the leading scholars of his day allowed *The Birth of Britain* to reflect the main scholarly currents of his time.

More important, perhaps, than the modern works that Churchill used in his history are the primary documents he cites throughout *The Birth of Britain*. Churchill's skillful use of primary sources, the essential building blocks of any work of history, adds colour to his narrative. At many places throughout the work, Churchill quotes directly from a wide variety of ancient and medieval documents to great dramatic effect. These quotations reveal important insights from contemporaries on the character of many of the figures under consideration or of the great events Churchill recorded. He quotes from biographies of kings Stephen and Henry V as well as the great ancient historians Tacitus and Dio Cassius. He refers to Gildas, Bede, and Nennius for the history of early medieval Britain and for the shadowy figure of England's greatest hero King Arthur, whose existence is now doubted but which Churchill confirmed, although not the Arthur of later legends. Churchill also cites the *Anglo-Saxon Chronicle*, a letter from King Alfred, and the sagas of Snorre Sturlason, and thereby reveals his command of a broad range of historical sources. For events in later medieval Britain, Churchill again turns to the most important contemporary documents to provide insights and firsthand evidence of the people and events of the time. Churchill turns to the Paston letters for evidence concerning social change from the perspective of a noble family, and he uses Jean Froissart's chronicle to depict the events of the 100 Years' War. And, with a healthy dose of skepticism, he quotes from the biography of Richard III by the Tudor historian Thomas

More. Although not a work to which most historians turn, *The Birth of Britain* is based on the type of historical research, in both primary and secondary sources, admired by most professional scholars.

Churchill not only revealed great command of the historical literature but mastery of the English language. It is his brilliance as a literary stylist that gives the book, at least in part, its enduring value. This is no dry as dust academic history or a work of names and dates and events but a literary tour de force in which the passions of the figures involved are clearly captured in Churchill's stunning prose. Better than most, Churchill expresses the drama and pathos of history throughout *The Birth of Britain*. His sense that history is one grand narrative makes reading his work an exhilarating experience and places Churchill's work among the ranks of the great English literary historians Thomas Babington Macaulay and G. M. Trevelyan as well as the greatest of all English historians, Edward Gibbon. In one of many notable passages, which comments on the career of King Arthur but offers a statement on both the past and Churchill's own age, he notes that "wherever men are fighting against barbarism, tyranny, and massacre, for freedom, law, and honour, let them remember that the fame of their deeds, even though they themselves be exterminated, may perhaps be celebrated as long as the world rolls round." His brilliant prose echoes throughout *The Birth of Britain* and perhaps no place better than in his discussion of the many battles and wars fought during England's medieval history. His treatment of the battle of Hastings, the crusade of Richard I, the great English victories in the one hundred Years' War, and the tragedy of the Wars of the Roses reveals Churchill's appreciation for the military arts and brings the reader into the heart of the battle.

Although it no longer reflects the major trends in historiography, Churchill's *The Birth of Britain* is unabashedly political, focusing on the leaders of English political society and the formation of the constitution. Even though the published version of the work toned down the emphasis on individual kings, which is most evident in new chapter headings such as Magna Carta, the work focuses primarily on the leading figures of ancient and medieval Britain. Churchill, however, recognised that it was not only the successful kings who shaped the institutions and history of Britain but also the failed or incompetent kings who left a mark on English history. In fact, he notes that "the English-speaking people owe far more to the vices of John than to the labours of the virtuous sovereigns," because it was during the reign of King John that the barons joined together to impose limits on the monarchy, one of the signal achievements of the English, and forced him to sign the Magna Carta. The deeds of far worse kings fill the pages of *The Birth of Britain*, and perhaps the most notorious was Richard III. Churchill recognised Richard was not the monster depicted in the works of the Tudor historians but also argued that Richard's seizure of the crown alienated his allies and opened the way for the triumph of Henry VII and the Tudor dictatorship. Aware that the malevolent and incompetent left an important legacy, Churchill nonetheless filled the pages of *The Birth of Britain* with the actions in war and peace of the truly great kings and nobles of England. He charts the development of English institutions through the activities of Alfred the Great, William the Conqueror, Henry II, Henry V, and others. Churchill also turned to great leaders outside England, such as William Wallace, who helped forge the kingdom of the Scots.

Although much of *The Birth of Britain* focuses on the deeds of great men, Churchill does recognise the importance of the average person in history and does address the impact of the deeds of the great on them. He also recognises the role of the great women of history, even though few mentions of them are made in the work and most of the women who are discussed are done so in relation to their husbands or fathers. He does, of course, describe the accomplishments of Queen Maud, Eleanor of Aquitaine, and Joan of Arc as well as those of the heroine of the opposition to Rome's invasion, Boadicea. And in all cases, men or women, Churchill cast his own judgment on their political and personal actions.

The central theme of *The Birth of Britain*, however, is the evolution of the English constitutional system and its democratic principles, in which Churchill took obvious pride as prime minister. Indeed, the creation of the constitutional monarchy and the concept of limited government is rightly identified as Britain's lasting legacy to the world, and writing the history of that development offered Churchill the opportunity to defend freedom at a time when tyranny seemed on the verge of triumph. The struggles of the great figures of ancient and, especially, medieval Britain invariably shaped the political system that Churchill himself headed twice. Although *The Birth of Britain* ends with the establishment of what Churchill termed the Tudor dicta-torship, the work charts the evolution of the central institutions of English government, which would guarantee the freedom and well being of the English people. It was during the formative period of English history, explored in *The Birth of Britain*, that the main outlines of the English system were set and institutions such as Parliament, jury trials, and the structures of local government appeared. Both the virtuous and the flawed figures that fill the pages of this volume all contributed in some fashion to the development of democratic prin-ciples and a limited constitutional monarchy. Even the tyrannical John and the tragic Richard II, albeit unintentionally, furthered the devel-opment of the English legal and constitutional system. Churchill's narrative in *The Birth of Britain* thus traces the triumphs and tragedies of the English people as they laid the foundation for one of the great-est political systems in world history.

Michael Frassetto is religion editor at Encyclopaedia Britannica. He holds a Ph.D. in history from the University of Delaware and has taught at several colleges and written extensively on European reli-gious and cultural history.

PREFACE

IT IS NEARLY TWENTY YEARS AGO THAT I MADE THE ARRANGEMENTS which resulted in this book. At the outbreak of the war about half a million words were duly delivered. Of course, there was still much to be done in proof-reading when I went to the Admiralty on September 3, 1939. All this was set aside. During six years of war, and an even longer period in which I was occupied with my war memoirs, the book slumbered peacefully. It is only now when things have quietened down that I present to the public *A HISTORY OF THE ENGLISH-SPEAKING PEOPLES.*

If there was need for it before, that has certainly not passed away. For the second time in the present century the British Empire and the United States have stood together facing the perils of war on the largest scale known among men, and since the cannons ceased to fire and the bombs to burst we have become more conscious of our common duty to the human race. Language, law, and the processes by which we have come into being already afforded a unique foundation for drawing together and portraying a concerted task. I thought when I began that such a unity might well notably influence the destiny of the world. Certainly I do not feel that the need for this has diminished in any way in the twenty years that have passed.

On the contrary, the theme of the work has grown in strength and reality and human thought is broadened. Vast numbers of people on both sides of the Atlantic and throughout the British Commonwealth of Nations have felt a sense of brotherhood. A new generation is at hand. Many practical steps have been taken which carry us far. Thinking primarily of the English-speaking peoples in no way implies any sense of restriction. It does not mean canalising the development of world affairs, nor does it prevent the erection of structures like United Europe or other similar groupings which may all find their place in the world organisation we have set on foot. It rather helps to invest them with life and truth. There is a growing feeling that the English-speaking peoples might point a finger showing the way if things went right, and could of course defend themselves, so far as any of us have the power, if things went wrong.

This book does not seek to rival the works of professional historians. It aims rather to present a personal view on the processes whereby English-speaking peoples throughout the world have achieved their distinctive position and character. I write about the things in our past that appear significant to me and I do so as one not without some experience of historical and violent events in our own time. I use the term "English-speaking peoples" because there is no other that applies both to the inhabitants of the British Isles and to those independent nations who derive their beginnings, their speech, and many of their institutions from England, and who now preserve, nourish, and develop them in their own ways.

This first volume traces the story of the English-speaking peoples from the earliest times to the eve of the European discovery of the New World. It concludes upon the field of Bosworth, the last battle of the tumultuous English Middle Ages. The year is 1485, and a new dynasty has just mounted the English throne. Seven years later Columbus landed in the Americas, and from this date, 1492, a new era in the history of mankind takes its beginnings.

* * * * *

Our story centres in an island, not widely sundered from the Continent, and so tilted that its mountains lie all to the west and north, while south and east is a gently undulating landscape of wooded valleys, open downs, and slow rivers. It is very accessible to the invader, whether he comes in peace or war, as pirate or merchant, conqueror or missionary. Those who dwell there are not insensitive to any shift of power, any change of faith, or even fashion, on the mainland, but they give to every practice, every doctrine that comes to it from abroad, its own peculiar turn and imprint. A province of the Roman Empire, cut off and left to sink or swim in the great convulsion of the Dark Ages; reunited to Christendom, and almost torn away from it once more by the heathen Dane; victorious, united, but exhausted, yielding, almost without resistance, to the Norman Conqueror; submerged, it might seem, within the august framework of Catholic feudalism, was yet capable of reappearing with an individuality of its own. Neither its civilisation nor its speech is quite Latin nor quite Germanic. It possesses a body of custom which, whatever its ultimate sources may be—folkright brought from beyond the seas by Danes, and by Saxons before them, maxims of civil jurisprudence culled from Roman codes—is being welded into one Common Law. This is England in the thirteenth century, the century of Magna Carta, and of the first Parliament.

As we gaze back into the mists of time we can very faintly discern the men of the Old Stone Age, and the New Stone Age; the builders of the great megalithic monuments; the newcomers from the Rhineland, with their beakers and tools of bronze. Standing on a grassy down where Dover now is, and pointing to the valley at his feet, one of them might have said to his grandson, "The sea comes farther up that creek than it did when I was a boy," and the grandson might have lived to watch a flood-tide, a roaring swirl of white water, sweeping the valley from end to end, carving its grassy sides into steep chalk edges, and linking the North Sea with the Channel. No wanderings, henceforth, of little clans, in search of game or food-yielding plants, from the plains of France or Belgium, to the wooded valleys and downs of Southern England; no small ventures in dugout canoes across narrow inlets at slack water. Those who come now must come in ships, and bold and wary they must be to face and master the Channel fogs and the Channel tides, and all that may lie beyond them.

Suddenly the mist clears. For a moment the Island stands in the full light of historic day. In itself the invasion of Britain by Julius Cæsar was an episode that had no sequel; but it showed that the power of Rome and the civilisation of the Mediterranean world were not necessarily bounded by the Atlantic coast. Cæsar's landing at Deal bridged the chasm which nature had cloven. For a century, while the Roman world was tearing itself to pieces in civil war, or slowly recovering under a new imperial form, Britain remained uneasily poised between isolation and union with the Continent, but absorbing, by way of trade and peaceful intercourse, something of the common culture of the West. In the end Rome gave the word and the legions sailed. For nearly four hundred years Britain became a Roman province. This considerable period was characterised for a great part of the time by that profound tranquillity which leaves little for history to record. It stands forth sedate, luminous, and calm. And what remained? Noble roads, some-times overgrown with woodland; the stupendous work of the Roman Wall, breached and crumbling; fortresses, market towns, country houses, whose very ruins the next comers contemplated with awe. But of Roman speech, Roman law, Roman institutions, hardly a vestige. Yet we should be mistaken if we therefore supposed that the Roman occupation could be dismissed as an incident without consequence. It had given time for the Christian faith to plant itself. Far in the West, though severed from the world by the broad flood of barbarism, there remained, sorely beset, but defended by its mountains, a tiny Christian realm. British Christianity converted Ireland. From Ireland the faith recrossed the seas to Scotland. Thus the newcomers were enveloped in the old civilisation; while at Rome men remembered that Britain had been Christian once, and might be Christian again.

This island world was not wholly cut off from the mainland. The south-east at all events kept up a certain intercourse with its Frankish cousins across the straits, and hence came the Roman missionaries. They brought with them a new set of beliefs, which, with some brief, if obstinate, resistance here and there, were accepted with surprising readiness. They brought a new political order, a Church which was to have its own rulers, its own officers, its own assemblies, and make its own laws, all of which had somehow or other to be fitted into the ancient customs of the English people. They planted the seed of a great problem, the problem of Church and State, which will grow until a thousand years later it almost rives the foundations of both asunder. But all this lies in the future. What mattered at the moment was that with her conversion England became once more part of the Western World. Very soon English missionaries would be at work on the Continent; English pilgrims would be making their way across the Alps to see the wonders of Rome, among them English princes, who, their work in this world being done, desired that their bones should rest near the tomb of the Apostles.

Nor was this all, because the English people now have an institution which overrode all local distinctions of speech, or custom, or even sovereignty. Whatever dynastic quarrels might go on between the kingdoms, the Church was one and indivisible; its rites are everywhere the same, its ministers are sacred. The Kingdom of Kent may lose its ancient primacy, Northumbria make way for Mercia; but Canterbury and York remain. The contrast is startling between the secular annals of these generations, with their meagre and tedious records of forays and slaughter, and the brilliant achievements of the English Church. The greatest scholar in Christendom was a Northumbrian monk. The most popular stylist was a West Saxon abbot. The Apostle of Germany was Boniface from Devon. The revival of learning in the Empire of Charlemagne was directed by Alcuin of York.

But this youthful, flourishing, immature civilisation lacked any solid military defence. The North was stirring again: from Denmark up the Baltic, up the Norwegian fiords, the pirate galleys were once more pushing forth in search of plunder, and of new homes for a crowded people. An island without a fleet, without a sovereign to command its scattered strength, rich in gold pieces, in cunning metal-work, and rare embroideries, stored in defenceless churches and monasteries, was a prize which the heathen men might think reserved for them whenever they chose to lay hands on it. Those broad, slow rivers of the English plain invited their galleys into the very heart of the country, and once on land how were rustics hurriedly summoned from the plough to resist the swift and disciplined march of armed bands, mounted or on foot? When the storm broke the North, the Midlands, the East, went down under its fury. If Wessex had succumbed all would have been lost. Gradually however it became manifest that the invaders had come not only to ravage but to settle.

At last the hurricane abated and men could take count of their losses. A broad strip of land along the middle of the eastern coast and stretching inland as far as Derby was in Danish hands; seafarers turned farmers were still holding together as an army. But London, already one of the great ports of Northern Europe, had been saved, and all the South, and here was the seat and strength of the royal house. The tie with the mainland had not been severed. Year by year, sometimes by treaty, sometimes by hard fighting, King Alfred's dynasty laboured to establish its ascendancy and reunite the land; so successfully that the temporary substitution of a Danish for an English king made little mark on history. He too was a Christian; he too made the pilgrimage to Rome. After this brief interlude the old line returned to the throne, and might have remained there from one generation to another. Yet in three short winter months, between October and Christmas Day in 1066, the astounding event had happened. The ruler of one French province—and that not the largest or most powerful—had crossed the Channel and made himself King of England.

*　　*　　*　　*　　*

The structure into which the Norman enters with the strong hand was a kingdom, acknowledged by all who spoke the King's English, and claiming some vague sovereignty over the Welsh and the Scots as well. It was governed, we may say, by the King in Council, and the Council consisted of his wise men, laymen and clerics; in other words, bishops and abbots, great landowners, officers of the Household. In all this it departed in no way from the common pattern of all kingdoms which had been built out of fragments of the Roman Empire. It had also been showing, since the last of the strong kings died, a dangerous tendency to split up into provinces, or earldoms, at the expense of the Crown and the unity of the nation; a tendency only, because the notion still persisted that the kingdom was one and indivisible, and that the King's Peace was over all men alike. Within this peace man was bound to man by a most intricate network of rights and duties, which might vary almost indefinitely from shire to shire, and even from village to village. But on the whole the English doctrine was that a free man might choose his lord, following him in war, working for him in peace, and in return the lord must protect him against encroaching neighbours and back him in the courts of law. What is more, the man might go from one lord to another, and hold his land from his new lord. And these lords, taken together, were the ruling class. The greatest of them, as we have seen, sat in the King's Council. The lesser of them are the local magnates, who took the lead in shire or hundred, and when the free men met in the shire or hundred court to decide the rights and wrongs of a matter it was their voice which carried weight. We cannot yet speak of a nobility and gentry, because the Saxons distinguished sharply between nobles and peasants and there was no room for any middle rank. But there were the makings of a gentry, to be realised hereafter.

Such was the state of England when the new Norman order was imposed on it. The Conqueror succeeded to all the rights of the old kings, but his Council now is mainly French-born, and French-speaking. The tendency to provincialisation is arrested; the King's Peace is everywhere. But the shifting pattern of relationships is drastically simplified to suit the more advanced, or more logical, Norman doctrine, that the tie of man to lord is not only moral and legal, but material, so that the status of every man can be fixed by the land he owns, and the services he does for it, if he is a tenant, or can demand, if he is a lord. In Norman days far more definitely than in Saxon the governing class is a landowning class.

In spite of its violent reannexation to the Continent, and its merger in the common feudalism of the West, England retained a positive individuality, expressed in institutions gradually shaped in the five or six hundred years that had passed since its severance, and predestined to a most remarkable development. The old English nobility of office made way for the Norman nobility of faith and landed wealth. The lesser folk throve in a peaceful but busy obscurity, in which English and Norman soon blended, and from them will issue in due course the Grand Jurors, the Justices of the Peace, the knights of the shire; ultimately overshadowing, in power if not in dignity, the nobility, and even the Crown itself. These days are far off. In the meantime we may picture the Government of England in the reign of Henry II, let us say, somehow thus. A strong monarchy, reaching by means of its judges and sheriffs into every corner of the land; a powerful Church that has come to a settlement with the Crown, in which the rights of both sides are acknowledged; a rich and self-willed nobility, which the Crown is bound by custom to consult in all matters of State; a larger body of gentry by whom the local administration is carried on; and the king's Household, his personal staff, of men experienced in the law and in finance. To these we must add the boroughs, which are growing in wealth and consequence now that the peace is well kept, the roads and seaways safe, and trade is flourishing.

＊　　＊　　＊　　＊　　＊

Standing at this point, and peering forward into the future, we see how much depends on the personality of the sovereign. In the period after the Conquest we have had three powerful rulers: in William a ruthless and determined soldier-prince who stamped the Norman pattern on the land; in his son Henry I a far-sighted, patient administrator; in Henry's grandson, the second Henry, a great states-man who had seen that national unity and the power of the Crown hung together, and that both could only be served by offering, for a price, even justice to all men, and enforcing it by the royal authority. Certain strains are developing in that compact fabric of Plantagenet England. The Crown is pressing rather hard on the nobility; the king's Household is beginning to oust the ancient counsellors of the kingdom. We need a strong king who will maintain the law, but a just king who will maintain it for the good of all, and not only for his private emolument or aggrandisement. With King John we enter on a century of political experiment.

Anyone who has heard from childhood of Magna Carta, who has read with what interest and reverence one copy of it was lately received in New York, and takes it up for the first time, will be strangely disappointed, and may find himself agreeing with the historian who proposed to translate its title not as the Great Charter of Liberties, but the Long List of Privileges—privileges of the nobility at the expense of the State. The reason is that our notion of law is wholly different from that of our ancestors. We think of it as something constantly changing to meet new circumstances; we reproach a Government if it is slow to pass new legislation. In the Middle Ages circumstances changed very gradually; the pattern of society was settled by custom or Divine decree, and men thought of the law rather as a fixed standard by which rights and duties could in case of wrongdoing or dispute be enforced or determined.

The Great Charter therefore is not in our sense of the word a legis-lative or constitutional instrument. It is an agreed statement of what the law is, as between the king and his barons; and many of the provi-sions which seem to us to be trifling and technical indicate the points at which the king had encroached on their ancient rights. Perhaps, in their turn, the victorious barons encroached unduly on the rights of the Crown. No one at the time regarded the Charter as a final settle-ment of all outstanding issues, and its importance lay not in details but in the broad affirmation of the principle that there is a law to which the Crown itself is subject. *Rex non debet esse sub homine, sed sub Deo et lege*—the king should not be below man, but below God and the law. This at least is clear. He has his sphere of action, within which he is free from human control. If he steps outside it he must be brought back. And he will step outside it if, ignoring the ancient Council of the kingdom, and refusing to take the advice of his wise men, he tries to govern through his Household, his favourites, or his clerks.

In other words, personal government, with all its latent possibili-ties of oppression and caprice, is not to be endured. But it is not easy to prevent. The King is strong, far stronger than any great lord, and stronger than most combinations of great lords. If the Crown is to be kept within its due limits some broader basis of resistance must be found than the ancient privileges of the nobility. About this time, in the middle of the thirteenth century, we begin to have a new word, Parliament. It bears a very vague meaning, and some of those who first used it would have been startled if they could have foreseen what it would some day come to signify. But gradually the idea spreads that if it is not enough for the King to "talk things over" with his own Council; so, on the other hand, it is not enough for the barons to insist solely on their right to be considered the Council of the kingdom. Though they often claim to speak for the community of the realm, in fact they only represent themselves, and the King after all represents the whole people. Then why not call in the lesser gentry and the burgesses? They are always used in local matters. Why not use them in national concerns? Bring them up to Westminster, two gentlemen from every shire, two tradesmen from every borough. What exactly they are to do when they get there no one quite knows. Perhaps to listen while their betters speak; to let them know what the grievances of the country are; to talk things over with one another behind the scenes; to learn what the king's intentions are in Scotland and France, and to pay the more cheerfully for knowing. It is a very delicate plant, this Parliament. There is nothing inevitable about its growth, and it might have been dropped as an experiment not worth going on with. But it took root. In two or three generations a prudent statesman would no more think of governing England without a Parliament than without a king. What its actual powers are it would be very hard to say. Broadly, its consent is necessary to give legal sanction to any substantial act of authority: an important change of ancient custom can only be effected by Act of Parliament; a new tax can only be levied with the approval of the Commons. What more it can do the unfolding of time will show. But its authority is stabilised by a series of accidents. Edward III needed money for his French wars. Henry IV needed support for his seizure of the crown. And in the Wars of the Roses both the contending parties wanted some sort of public sanction for their actions, which only Parliament could provide.

Thus when in the fifteenth century the baronial structure perished in faction and civil war there remained not only the Crown, but the Crown in Parliament, now clearly shaped into its two divisions, the Lords sitting in their own right, and the Commoners as representatives of the shires and boroughs. So far nothing has changed. But the destruction of the old nobility in battle or on the morrow of battle was to tip the balance of the two Houses, and the Commons, knights and burgesses, stood for those elements in society which suffered most from anarchy and profited most by strong government. There was a natural alliance between the Crown and the Commons. The Commons had little objection to the Crown extending its prerogative at the expense of the nobility, planting Councils of the North and Councils of Wales, or in the Star Chamber exercising a remedial jurisdiction by which the small man could be defended against the great. On the other hand, the Crown was willing enough to leave local administration to the Justices of the Peace, whose interest it was to be loyal, to put down sturdy beggars, and to grow quietly and peace- fully rich. As late as 1937 the Coronation service proclaimed the ideal of Tudor government in praying that the sovereign may be blessed with "a loyal nobility, a dutiful gentry, and an honest, peaceable, and obedient commonalty." Some day perhaps that commonalty might ask whether they had no more to do with Government than to obey it.

*   *   *   *   *

Thus by the end of the fifteenth century the main characteristics and institutions of the race had taken shape. The rough German dialects of the Anglo-Saxon invaders had been modified before the Norman conquest by the passage of time and the influence of Church Latin. Vocabularies had been extended by many words of British and Danish root. This broadening and smoothing process was greatly hastened by the introduction into the islands of Norman French, and the assimilation of the two languages went on apace. Writings survive from the early thirteenth century which the ordinary man of today would recognise as a form of English, even if he could not wholly understand them. By the end of the fourteenth century, the century of Geoffrey Chaucer, it is thought that even the great magnates had ceased to use French as their principal language and commonly spoke English. Language moreover was not the only institution which had achieved a distinctively English character. Unlike the remainder of Western Europe, which still retains the imprint and tradition of Roman law and the Roman system of government, the English-speaking peoples had at the close of the period covered by this volume achieved a body of legal and what might almost be called democratic principles which survived the upheavals and onslaughts of the French and Spanish Empires. Parliament, trial by jury, local government run by local citizens, and even the beginnings of a free Press, may be discerned, at any rate in primitive form, by the time Christopher Columbus set sail for the American continent.

Every nation or group of nations has its own tale to tell. Knowledge of the trials and struggles is necessary to all who would comprehend the problems, perils, challenges, and opportunities which confront us today. It is not intended to stir a new spirit of mastery, or create a mood in the study of history which would favour national ambition at the expense of world peace. It may be indeed that an inner selective power may lead to the continuous broadening of our thought. It is in the hope that contemplation of the trials and tribulations of our forefathers may not only fortify the English-speaking peoples of today, but also play some small part in uniting the whole world, that I present this account.

W.S.C.

Chartwell

Westerham

Kent

January 15, 1956

BOOK I

THE ISLAND RACE

CHAPTER ONE

BRITANNIA

IN THE SUMMER OF THE ROMAN YEAR 699, NOW DESCRIBED AS THE year 55 before the birth of Christ, the Proconsul of Gaul, Gaius Julius Cæsar, turned his gaze upon Britain. In the midst of his wars in Germany and in Gaul he became conscious of this heavy Island which stirred his ambitions and already obstructed his designs. He knew that it was inhabited by the same type of tribesmen who confronted the Roman arms in Germany, Gaul, and Spain. The Islanders had helped the local tribes in the late campaigns along the northern coast of Gaul. They were the same Celtic stock, somewhat intensified by insular life. British volunteers had shared the defeat of the Veneti on the coasts of Brittany in the previous year. Refugees from momentarily conquered Gaul were welcomed and sheltered in Britannia. To Caesar the Island now presented itself as an integral part of his task of subjugating the Northern barbarians to the rule and system of Rome. The land not covered by forest or marsh was verdant and fertile. The climate, though far from genial, was equable and healthy. The natives, though uncouth, had a certain value as slaves for rougher work on the land, in mines, and even about the house. There was talk of a pearl fishery, and also of gold. "Even if there was not time for a campaign that season, Cæsar thought it would be of great advantage to him merely to visit the island, to see what its inhabitants were like, and to make himself acquainted with the lie of the land, the harbours, and the landing-places. Of all this the Gauls knew next to nothing."[1] Other reasons added their weight. Cæsar's colleague in the Triumvirate, Crassus, had excited the imagination of the Roman Senate and people by his spirited march towards Mesopotamia. Here, at the other end of the known world, was an enterprise equally audacious. The Romans hated and feared the sea. By a supreme effort of survival they had two hundred years before surpassed Carthage upon its own element in the Mediterranean, but the idea of Roman legions landing in the remote, unknown, fabulous Island of the vast ocean of the North would create a novel thrill and topic in all ranks of Roman society.

Moreover, Britannia was the prime centre of the Druidical religion, which, in various forms and degrees, influenced profoundly the life of Gaul and Germany. "Those who want to make a study of the subject," wrote Cæsar, "generally go to Britain for the purpose." The unnatural principle of human sacrifice was carried by the British Druids to a ruthless pitch. The mysterious priesthoods of the forests bound themselves and their votaries together by the most deadly sacrament that men can take. Here, perhaps, upon these wooden altars of a sullen island, there lay one of the secrets, awful, inflaming, unifying, of the tribes of Gaul. And whence did this sombre custom come? Was it perhaps part of the message which Carthage had given to the Western world before the Roman legions had strangled it at its source? Here then was the largest issue. Cæsar's vision pierced the centuries, and where he conquered civilisation dwelt.

Thus, in this summer fifty-five years before the birth of Christ, he withdrew his army from Germany, broke down his massive and ingenious timber bridge across the Rhine above Coblenz, and throughout July marched westward by long strides towards the Gallic shore somewhere about the modern Calais and Boulogne.

Cæsar saw the Britons as a tougher and coarser branch of the Celtic tribes whom he was subduing in Gaul. With an army of ten legions, less than fifty thousand soldiers, he was striving against a brave, warlike race which certainly comprised half a million fighting men. On his other flank were the Germans, driven westward by pressure from the East. His policy towards them was to hurl their invading yet fleeing hordes into the Rhine whenever they intruded beyond it. Although all war was then on both sides waged only with tempered iron and mastery depended upon discipline and generalship alone, Cæsar felt himself and his soldiers not unequal to these prodigies. A raid upon Britannia seemed but a minor addition to his toils and risks. But at the seashore new problems arose. There were tides unknown in the Mediterranean; storms beat more often and more fiercely on the coasts. The Roman galleys and their captains were in contact with the violence of the Northern sea. Nevertheless, only a year before they had, at remarkable odds, destroyed the fleet of the hardy, maritime Veneti. With sickles at the end of long poles they had cut the ropes and halyards of their fine sailing ships and slaughtered their crews with boarding-parties. They had gained command of the Narrow Seas which separated Britannia from the mainland. The salt water was now a path and not a barrier. Apart from the accidents of weather and the tides and currents, about which he admits he could not obtain trustworthy information, Julius Cæsar saw no difficulty in invading the Island. There was not then that far-off line of storm-beaten ships which about two thousand years later stood between the great Corsican conqueror and the dominion of the world. All that mattered was to choose a good day in the fine August weather, throw a few legions on to the nearest shore, and see what there was in this strange Island after all.

While Cæsar marched from the Rhine across Northern Gaul, perhaps through Rheims and Amiens, to the coast, he sent an officer in a warship to spy out the Island shore, and when he arrived near what is now Boulogne, or perhaps the mouth of the Somme, this captain was at hand, with other knowledgeable persons, traders, Celtic princes, and British traitors, to greet him. He had concentrated the forces which had beaten the Veneti in two ports or inlets nearest to Britannia, and now he awaited a suitable day for the descent.

*   *   *   *   *

What was, in fact, this Island which now for the first time in coherent history was to be linked with the great world? We have dug up in the present age from the gravel of Swanscombe a human skull which is certainly a quarter of a million years old. Biologists perceive important differences from the heads that hold our brains today, but there is no reason to suppose that this remote Palæolithic ancestor was not capable of all the crimes, follies, and infirmities definitely associated with mankind. Evidently, for prolonged, almost motionless, periods men and women, naked or wrapped in the skins of animals, prowled about the primeval forests and plashed through wide marshes, hunting each other and other wild beasts, cheered, as the historian Trevelyan finely says,[2] by the songs of innumerable birds. It is said that the whole of Southern Britain could in this period support upon its game no more than seven hundred families. Here indeed were the lords of creation. Seven hundred families, all this fine estate, and no work but sport and fighting. Already man had found out that a flint was better than a fist. His descendants would burrow deep in the chalk and gravel for battle-axe flints of the best size and quality, and gained survival thereby. But so far he had only learned to chip his flints into rough tools.

At the close of the Ice Age changes in climate brought about the collapse of the hunting civilisations of Old Stone Age Man, and after a very long period of time the tides of invasion brought Neolithic culture into the Western forests. The newcomers had a primitive agriculture. They scratched the soil and sowed the seeds of edible grasses. They made pits or burrows, which they gradually filled with the refuse of generations, and they clustered together for greater safety. Presently they constructed earthwork enclosures on the hilltops, into which they drove their cattle at nighttime. Windmill Hill, near Avebury, illustrates the efforts of these primitive engineers to provide for the protection of herds and men. Moreover, Neolithic man had developed a means of polishing his flints into perfect shape for killing. This betokened a great advance; but others were in prospect.

It seems that at this time "the whole of Western Europe was inhabited by a race of long-headed men, varying somewhat in appearance and especially in colouring, since they were probably always fairer in the north and darker in the south, but in most respects substantially alike. Into this area of longheaded populations there was driven a wedge of round-headed immigrants from the east, known to anthropologists as 'the Alpine race.' Most of the people that have invaded Britain have belonged to the Western European long-headed stock, and have therefore borne a general resemblance to the people already living there; and consequently, in spite of the diversities among these various newcomers, the tendency in Britain has been towards the establishment and maintenance of a tolerably uniform long-headed type."[3]

A great majority of the skulls found in Britain, of whatever age, are of the long- or medium-headed varieties. Nevertheless it is known that the Beaker people and other round-headed types penetrated here and there, and established themselves as a definite element. Cremation, almost universal in the Later Bronze Age, has destroyed all record of the blending of the long-headed and round-headed types of man, but undoubtedly both persisted, and from later traces, when in Roman times burials were resumed instead of cremation, anthropologists of the older school professed themselves able to discern a characteristic Roman-British type, although in point of fact this may have established itself long before the Roman conquest. Increasing knowledge has rendered these early categories less certain.

In early days Britain was part of the Continent. A wide plain joined England and Holland, in which the Thames and the Rhine met together and poured their waters northward. In some slight movement of the earth's surface this plain sank a few hundred feet, and admitted the ocean to the North Sea and the Baltic. Another tremor, important for our story, sundered the cliffs of Dover from those of Cape Gris Nez, and the scour of the ocean and its tides made the Straits of Dover and the English Channel. When did this tremendous severance occur? Until lately geologists would have assigned it to periods far beyond Neolithic man. But the study of striped clays, the deposits of Norwegian glaciers, shows layer by layer and year by year what the weather was like, and modern science has found other methods of counting the centuries. From these and other indications time and climate scales have been framed which cover with tolerable accuracy many thousand years of prehistoric time. These scales enable times to be fixed when through milder conditions the oak succeeded the pine in British forests, and the fossilised vegetation elaborates the tale. Trawlers bring up in their nets fragments of trees from the bottom of the North Sea, and these when fitted into the climatic scale show that oaks were growing on what is now sixty fathoms deep of stormy water less than nine thousand years ago. Britain was still little more than a promontory of Europe, or divided from it by a narrow tide race which has gradually enlarged into the Straits of Dover, when the Pyramids were a-building, and when learned Egyptians were laboriously exploring the ancient ruins of Sakkara.

While what is now our Island was still joined to the Continent another great improvement was made in human methods of destruction. Copper and tin were discovered and worried out of the earth; the one too soft and the other too brittle for the main purpose, but, blended by human genius, they opened the Age of Bronze. Other things being equal, the men with bronze could beat the men with flints. The discovery was hailed, and the Bronze Age began.

The invasion, or rather infiltration, of bronze weapons and tools from the Continent was spread over many centuries, and it is only when twenty or thirty generations have passed that any notable change can be discerned. Professor Collingwood has drawn us a picture of what is called the Late Bronze Age. "Britain," he says, "as a whole was a backward country by comparison with the Continent; primitive in its civilisation, stagnant and passive in its life, and receiving most of what progress it enjoyed through invasion and importation from overseas. Its people lived either in isolated farms or in hut-villages, situated for the most part on the gravel of river-banks, or the light upland soils such as the chalk downs or oolite plateaux, which by that time had been to a great extent cleared of their native scrub; each settlement was surrounded by small fields, tilled either with a foot-plough of the type still used not long ago by Hebridean crofters, or else at best with a light ox-drawn plough which scratched the soil without turning the sod; the dead were burnt and their ashes, preserved in urns, buried in regular cemeteries. Thus the land was inhabited by a stable and industrious peasant population, living by agriculture and the keeping of livestock, augmented no doubt by hunting and fishing. They made rude pottery without a wheel, and still used flint for such things as arrow-heads; but they were visited by itinerant bronze-founders able to make swords, spears, socketed axes, and many other types of implement and utensil, such as sickles, carpenter's tools, metal parts of wheeled vehicles, buckets, and cauldrons. Judging by the absence of towns and the scarcity of anything like true fortification, these people were little organised for warfare, and their political life was simple and undeveloped, though there was certainly a distinction between rich and poor, since many kinds of metal objects belonging to the period imply a considerable degree of wealth and luxury."

The Late Bronze Age in the southern parts of Britain, according to most authorities, began about 1000 B.C. and lasted until about 400 B.C.

At this point the march of invention brought a new factor upon the scene. Iron was dug and forged. Men armed with iron entered Britain from the Continent and killed the men of bronze. At this point we can plainly recognise across the vanished millenniums a fellow-being. A biped capable of slaying another with iron is evidently to modern eyes a man and a brother. It cannot be doubted that for smashing skulls, whether long-headed or round, iron is best.

The Iron Age overlapped the Bronze. It brought with it a keener and higher form of society, but it impinged only very gradually upon the existing population, and their customs, formed by immemorial routine, were changed only slowly and piecemeal. Certainly bronze implements remained in use, particularly in Northern Britain, until the last century before Christ.

The impact of iron upon bronze was at work in our Island before Julius Cæsar cast his eyes upon it. After about 500 B.C. successive invasions from the mainland gradually modified the whole of the southern parts of the Island. "In general," says Professor Collingwood, "settlements yielding the pottery characteristic of this culture occur all over the south-east, from Kent to the Cotswolds and the Wash. Many of these settlements indicate a mode of life not perceptibly differing from that of their late Bronze Age background; they are farms or villages, often undefended, lying among their little fields on river-gravels or light upland soils, mostly cremating their dead, storing their grain in underground pits and grinding it with primitive querns, not yet made with the upper stone revolving upon the lower; keeping oxen, sheep, goats, and pigs; still using bronze and even flint implements and possessing very little iron, but indicating their date by a change in the style of their pottery, which, however, is still made without the wheel."[4]

The Iron Age immigrations brought with them a revival of the hill-top camps, which had ceased to be constructed since the Neolithic Age. During the third and fourth centuries before Christ a large number of these were built in the inhabited parts of our Island. They consisted of a single rampart, sometimes of stone, but usually an earthwork revetted with timber and protected by a single ditch.

The size of the ramparts was generally not very great. The entrances were simply designed, though archæological excavation has in some instances revealed the remains of wooden guardrooms. These camps were not mere places of refuge. Often they were settlements containing private dwellings, and permanently inhabited. They do not seem to have served the purpose of strongholds for invaders in enemy land. On the contrary, they appear to have come into existence gradually as the iron age newcomers multiplied and developed a tribal system from which tribal wars eventually arose.

The last of the successive waves of Celtic inroad and supersession which marked the Iron Age came in the early part of the first century B.C.. "The Belgic tribes arrived in Kent and spread over Essex, Hertfordshire, and part of Oxfordshire, while other groups of the same stock ... later ... spread over Hampshire, Wiltshire, and Dorset and part of Sussex."[5] There is no doubt that the Belgæ were by far the most enlightened invaders who had hitherto penetrated the recesses of the Island. They were a people of chariots and horsemen. They were less addicted to the hill-forts in which the existing inhabitants put their trust. They built new towns in the valleys, sometimes even below the hilltop on which the old fort had stood. They introduced for the first time a coinage of silver and copper. They established themselves as a tribal aristocracy in Britain, subjugating the older stock. In the east they built Wheathampstead, Verulam (St. Albans), and Camulodunum (Colchester); in the south Calleva (Silchester) and Venta Belgarum (Winchester). They were closely akin to the inhabitants of Gaul from whom they had sprung. This active, alert, conquering, and ruling race established themselves wherever they went with ease and celerity, and might have looked forward to a long dominion. But the tramp of the legions had followed hard behind them, and they must soon defend the prize they had won against still better men and higher systems of government and war.

Meanwhile in Rome, at the centre and summit, only vague ideas prevailed about the western islands. "The earliest geographers believed that the Ocean Stream encircled the whole earth, and knew of no islands in it."[6] Herodotus about 445 B.C. had heard of the tin of mysterious islands in the far West, which he called the Cassiterides, but he cautiously treated them as being in the realms of fable. However, in the middle of the fourth century B.C. Pytheas of Marseilles—surely one of the greatest explorers in history—made two voyages in which he actually circumnavigated the British Isles. He proclaimed the existence of the "Pretanic Islands Albion and Ierne," as Aristotle had called them. Pytheas was treated as a storyteller, and his discoveries were admired only after the world he lived in had long passed away. But even in the third century B.C. the Romans had a definite conception of three large islands, Albion, Ierne, and Thule (Iceland). Here all was strange and monstrous. These were the ultimate fringes of the world. Still, there was the tin trade, in which important interests were concerned, and Polybius, writing in 140 B.C., shows that this aspect at least had been fully discussed by commercial writers.

*   *   *   *   *

We are much better informed upon these matters than was Cæsar when he set out from Boulogne. Here are some of the impressions he had collected:

> The interior of Britain is inhabited by people who claim, on the strength of an oral tradition, to be aboriginal; the coast, by Belgic immigrants who came to plunder and make war—nearly all of them retaining the names of the tribes from which they originated—and later settled down to till the soil. The population is exceedingly large, the ground thickly studded with homesteads, closely resembling those of the Gauls, and the cattle very numerous. For money they use either bronze, or gold coins, or iron ingots of fixed weights. Tin is found inland, and small quantities of iron near the coast; the

copper that they use is imported. There is timber of every kind, as in Gaul, except beech and fir. Hares, fowl, and geese they think it unlawful to eat, but rear them for pleasure and amusement. The climate is more temperate than in Gaul, the cold being less severe.

By far the most civilised inhabitants are those living in Kent (a purely maritime district), whose way of life differs little from that of the Gauls. Most of the tribes in the interior do not grow corn but live on milk and meat, and wear skins. All the Britons dye their bodies with woad, which produces a blue colour, and this gives them a more terrifying appearance in battle. They wear their hair long, and shave the whole of their bodies except the head and the upper lip. Wives are shared between groups of ten or twelve men, especially between brothers and between fathers and sons; but the offspring of these unions are counted as the children of the man with whom a particular woman cohabited first.

*   *   *   *   *

Late in August 55 B.C. Cæsar sailed with eighty transports and two legions at midnight, and with the morning light saw the white cliffs of Dover crowned with armed men. He judged the placed "quite unsuitable for landing," since it was possible to throw missiles from the cliffs on to the shore. He therefore anchored till the turn of the tide, sailed seven miles farther, and descended upon Albion on the low, shelving beach between Deal and Walmer. But the Britons, observing these movements, kept pace along the coast and were found ready to meet him. There followed a scene upon which the eye of history has rested. The Islanders, with their chariots and horsemen, advanced into the surf to meet the invader. Cæsar's transports and warships grounded in deeper water. The legionaries, uncertain of the depth, hesitated in face of the shower of javelins and stones, but the eagle-bearer of the Tenth Legion plunged into the waves with the sacred emblem, and Cæsar brought his warships with their catapults and arrow-fire upon the British flank. The Romans, thus encouraged and sustained, leaped from their ships, and, forming as best they could, waded towards the enemy. There was a short, ferocious fight amid the waves, but the Romans reached the shore, and, once arrayed, forced the Britons to flight.

Cæsar's landing however was only the first of his troubles. His cavalry, in eighteen transports, which had started three days later, arrived in sight of the camp, but, caught by a sudden gale, drifted far down the Channel, and were thankful to regain the Continent. The high tide of the full moon which Cæsar had not understood wrought grievous damage to his fleet at anchor. "A number of ships," he says, "were shattered, and the rest, having lost their cables, anchors, and the remainder of their tackle, were unusable, which naturally threw the whole army into great consternation. For they had no other vessels in which they could return, nor any materials for repairing the fleet; and, since it had been generally understood that they were to return to Gaul for the winter, they had not provided themselves with a stock of grain for wintering in Britain."

The Britons had sued for peace after the battle on the beach, but now that they saw the plight of their assailants their hopes revived and they broke off the negotiations. In great numbers they attacked the Roman foragers. But the legion concerned had not neglected precautions, and discipline and armour once again told their tale. It shows how much food there was in the Island that two legions could live for a fortnight off the cornfields close to their camp. The British submitted. Their conqueror imposed only nominal terms. Breaking up many of his ships to repair the rest, he was glad to return with some hostages and captives to the mainland. He never even pretended that his expedition had been a success. To supersede the record of it he came again the next year, this time with five legions and some cavalry conveyed in eight hundred ships. The Islanders were overawed by the size of the armada. The landing was unimpeded, but again the sea assailed him. Cæsar had marched twelve miles into the interior when he was recalled by the news that a great storm had shattered or damaged a large portion of his fleet. He was forced to spend ten days in hauling all his ships on to the shore, and in fortifying the camp of which they then formed part. This done he renewed his invasion, and, after easily destroying the forest stockades in which the British sheltered, crossed the Thames near Brentford. But the British had found a leader in the

chief Cassivellaunus, who was a master of war under the prevailing conditions. Dismissing to their homes the mass of untrained foot-soldiers
and peasantry, he kept pace with the invaders march by march with
his chariots and horsemen. Cæsar gives a detailed description of the
chariot-fighting:

> In chariot fighting the Britons begin by driving all
> over the field hurling javelins, and generally the terror
> inspired by the horses and the noise of the wheels are
> sufficient to throw their opponents' ranks into disorder.
> Then, after making their way between the squadrons of
> their own cavalry, they jump down from the chariots
> and engage on foot. In the meantime their charioteers
> retire a short distance from the battle and place the
> chariots in such a position that their masters, if hard
> pressed by numbers, have an easy means of retreat to
> their own lines. Thus they combine the mobility of cav-
> alry with the staying-power of infantry; and by daily
> training and practice they attain such proficiency that
> even on a steep incline they are able to control the
> horses at full gallop, and to check and turn them in a
> moment. They can run along the chariot pole, stand
> on the yoke, and get back into the chariot as quick
> as lightning.

Cassivellaunus, using these mobile forces and avoiding a pitched
battle with the Roman legions, escorted them on their inroad and
cut off their foraging parties. None the less Cæsar captured his first
stronghold; the tribes began to make terms for themselves; a well-
conceived plan for destroying Cæsar's base on the Kentish shore was
defeated. At this juncture Cassivellaunus, by a prudence of policy
equal to that of his tactics, negotiated a further surrender of hostages
and a promise of tribute and submission, in return for which Cæsar
was again content to quit the Island. In a dead calm, "he set sail late
in the evening and brought all the fleet safely to land at dawn." This
time he proclaimed a conquest. Cæsar had his triumph, and British
captives trod their dreary path at his tail through the streets of Rome;

but for nearly a hundred years no invading army landed upon the Island coasts.

Little is known of Cassivellaunus, and we can only hope that later defenders of the Island will be equally successful and that their measures will be as well suited to the needs of the time. The impression remains of a prudent and skilful chief, whose qualities and achievements, but for the fact that they were displayed in an outlandish theatre, might well have ranked with those of Fabius Maximus Cunctator.

CHAPTER TWO

SUBJUGATION

DURING THE HUNDRED YEARS WHICH FOLLOWED JULIUS CÆSAR'S invasion the British Islanders remained unmolested. The Belgic cities developed a life of their own, and the warrior tribes enjoyed amid their internecine feuds the comforting illusion that no one was likely to attack them again. However, their contacts with the mainland and with the civilisation of the Roman Empire grew, and trade flourished in a wide range of commodities. Roman traders established themselves in many parts, and carried back to Rome tales of the wealth and possibilities of Britannia, if only a stable Government were set up.

In the year A.D. 41 the murder of the Emperor Caligula, and a chapter of accidents, brought his uncle, the clownish scholar Claudius, to the throne of the world. No one can suppose that any coherent will to conquest resided in the new ruler, but the policy of Rome was shaped by the officials of highly competent departments. It proceeded upon broad lines, and in its various aspects attracted a growing and strong measure of support from many sections of public opinion. Eminent senators aired their views, important commercial and financial interests were conciliated, and elegant society had a new topic for gossip. Thus, in this triumphant period there were always available for a new emperor a number of desirable projects, well thought out beforehand and in harmony with the generally understood Roman system, any one of which might catch the fancy of the latest wielder of supreme power. Hence we find emperors elevated by chance whose unbridled and capricious passions were their only distinction, whose courts were debauched with lust and cruelty, who were themselves vicious or feeble-minded, who were pawns in the hands of their counsellors or favourites, decreeing great campaigns and setting their seal upon long-lasting acts of salutary legislation.

The advantages of conquering the recalcitrant island Britannia were paraded before the new monarch, and his interest was excited. He was attracted by the idea of gaining a military reputation. He gave orders that this dramatic and possibly lucrative enterprise should proceed. In the year 43, almost one hundred years after Julius Cæsar's evacuation, a powerful, well-organised Roman army of some twenty thousand men was prepared for the subjugation of Britain. "The soldiers were indignant at the thought of carrying on a campaign outside the limits of the known world." But when the Emperor's favourite freedman, Narcissus, attempted to address them they felt the insult. The spectacle of a former slave called in to stand sponsor for their commander rallied them to their duty. They taunted Narcissus with his slave origin, with the mocking shout of *"Io Saturnalia!"* (for at the festival of Saturn the slaves donned their masters' dress and held festival), but none the less they resolved to obey their chief's order.

> Their delay, however, had made their departure late in the season. They were sent over in three divisions, in order that they should not be hindered in landing—as might happen to a single force—and in their voyage across they first became discouraged because they were driven back in their course, and then plucked up courage because a flash of light rising in the east shot across to the west, the direction in which they were sailing. So they put in to the Island, and found none to oppose them. For the Britons, as the result of their inquiries, had not expected that they would come, and had therefore not assembled beforehand.[1]

The internal situation favoured the invaders. Cunobelinus (Shakespeare's Cymbeline) had established an overlordship over the south-east of the Island, with his capital at Colchester. But in his old age dissensions had begun to impair his authority, and on his death the kingdom was ruled jointly by his sons Caractacus and Togodumnus. They were not everywhere recognised, and they had no time to form a union of the tribal kingdom before Plautius and the legions arrived. The people of Kent fell back on the tactics of Cassivellaunus, and Plautius accordingly had much trouble in searching them out; but when at last he did find them he first defeated Caractacus, and then his brother somewhere in East Kent. Then, advancing along Cæsar's old line of march, he came on a river he had not heard of, the Medway. "The barbarians thought that the Romans would not be able to cross without a bridge, and consequently bivouacked in rather careless fashion on the opposite bank"; but the Roman general sent across "a detachment of Germans, who were accustomed to swim easily in full armour across the most turbulent streams. These fell unexpectedly upon the enemy, but instead of shooting at the men they disabled the horses that drew the chariots, and in the ensuing confusion not even the enemy's mounted men could save themselves."[2] Nevertheless the Britons faced them on the second day, and were only broken by a flank attack, Vespasian—some day to be Emperor himself—having discovered a ford higher up. This victory marred the stage-management of the campaign. Plautius had won his battle too soon, and in the wrong place. Something had to be done to show that the Emperor's presence was necessary to victory. So Claudius, who had been waiting on events in France, crossed the seas, bringing substantial reinforcements, including a number of elephants. A battle was procured, and the Romans won. Claudius returned to Rome to receive from the Senate the title of "Britannicus" and permission to celebrate a triumph.

But the British war continued. The Britons would not come to close quarters with the Romans, but took refuge in the swamps and the forests, hoping to wear out the invaders, so that, as in the days of Julius Cæsar, they should sail back with nothing accomplished. Caractacus escaped to the Welsh border, and, rousing its tribes, maintained an indomitable resistance for more than six years. It was not till A.D. 50 that he was finally defeated by a new general, Ostorius, an officer of energy and ability, who reduced to submission the whole of the more settled regions from the Wash to the Severn. Caractacus, escaping from the ruin of his forces in the West, sought to raise the Brigantes in the North. Their queen however handed him over to the Romans. "The fame of the British prince," writes Suetonius, "had by this time spread over the provinces of Gaul and Italy; and upon his arrival in the Roman capital the people flocked from all quarters to behold him. The ceremonial of his entrance was conducted with great solemnity. On a plain adjoining the Roman camp the Pretorian troops were drawn up in martial array. The Emperor and his court took their station in front of the lines, and behind them was ranged the whole body of the people. The procession commenced with the different trophies which had been taken from the Britons during the progress of the war. Next followed the brothers of the vanquished prince, with his wife and daughter, in chains, expressing by their supplicating looks and gestures the fears with which they were actuated. But not so Caractacus himself. With a manly gait and an undaunted countenance he marched up to the tribunal, where the Emperor was seated, and addressed him in the following terms:

> If to my high birth and distinguished rank I had added the virtues of moderation Rome had beheld me rather as a friend than a captive, and you would not have rejected an alliance with a prince descended from illustrious ancestors and governing many nations. The reverse of my fortune is glorious to you, and to me humiliating. I had arms, and men, and horses; I possessed extraordinary riches; and can it be any wonder that I was unwilling to lose them? Because Rome aspires to universal dominion must men therefore implicitly resign themselves to subjection? I opposed for a long time the progress of your arms, and had I acted otherwise would either you have had the glory of conquest or I of a brave resistance? I am now in your power. If you are determined to take revenge my fate will soon be forgotten, and you will derive no honour from the transaction. Preserve my life, and I shall remain to the latest ages a monument of your clemency.

"Immediately upon this speech Claudius granted him his liberty, as he did likewise to the other royal captives. They all returned their thanks in a manner the most grateful to the Emperor; and as soon as their chains were taken off, walking towards Agrippina, who sat upon a bench at a little distance, they repeated to her the same fervent declarations of gratitude and esteem."[3]

* * * * *

The conquest was not achieved without one frightful convulsion of revolt. "In this year A.D. 61," according to Tacitus, "a severe disaster was sustained in Britain." Suetonius, the new governor, had engaged himself deeply in the West. He transferred the operational base of the Roman army from Wroxeter to Chester. He prepared to attack "the populous island of Mona [Anglesey], which had become a refuge for fugitives, and he built a fleet of flat-bottomed vessels suitable for those shallow and shifting seas. The infantry crossed in the boats, the cavalry went over by fords: where the water was too deep the men swam alongside of their horses. The enemy lined the shore, a dense host of armed men, interspersed with women clad in black like the Furies, with their hair hanging down and holding torches in their hands. Round this were Druids uttering dire curses and stretching their hands towards heaven. These strange sights terrified the soldiers. They stayed motionless, as if paralysed, offering their bodies to the blows. At last, encouraged by the general, and exhorting each other not to quail before the rabble of female fanatics, they advanced their standards, bore down all resistance, and enveloped the enemy in their own flames."

"Suetonius imposed a garrison upon the conquered and cut down the groves devoted to their cruel superstitions; for it was part of their religion to spill the blood of captives on their altars, and to inquire of the gods by means of human entrails."

This dramatic scene on the frontiers of modern Wales was the prelude to a tragedy. The king of the East Anglian Iceni had died. Hoping to save his kingdom and family from molestation he had appointed Nero, who had succeeded Claudius as Emperor, as heir jointly with his two daughters. "But," says Tacitus, "things turned out differently. His kingdom was plundered by centurions, and his private property by slaves, as if they had been captured in war; his widow Boadicea [relished by the learned as Boudicca] was flogged, and his daughters outraged; the chiefs of the Iceni were robbed of their ancestral properties as if the Romans had received the whole country as a gift, and the king's own relatives were reduced to slavery." Thus the Roman historian.[4]

Boadicea's tribe, at once the most powerful and hitherto the most submissive, was moved to frenzy against the Roman invaders. They flew to arms. Boadicea found herself at the head of a numerous army, and nearly all the Britons within reach rallied to her standard. There followed an up-rush of hatred from the abyss, which is a measure of the cruelty of the conquest. It was a scream of rage against invincible oppression and the superior culture which seemed to lend it power. "Boadicea," said Ranke, "is rugged, earnest and terrible."[5] Her monument on the Thames Embankment opposite Big Ben reminds us of the harsh cry of liberty or death which has echoed down the ages.

In all Britain there were only four legions, at most twenty thousand men. The Fourteenth and Twentieth were with Suetonius on his Welsh campaign. The Ninth was at Lincoln, and the Second at Gloucester.

The first target of the revolt was Camulodunum (Colchester), an unwalled colony of Roman and Romanised Britons, where the recently settled veterans, supported by the soldiery, who hoped for similar licence for themselves, had been ejecting the inhabitants from their houses and driving them away from their lands. The Britons were encouraged by omens. The statue of Victory fell face foremost, as if flying from the enemy. The sea turned red. Strange cries were heard in the council chamber and the theatre. The Roman officials, business men, bankers, usurers, and the Britons who had participated in their authority and profits, found themselves with a handful of old soldiers in the midst of "a multitude of barbarians." Suetonius was a month distant. The Ninth Legion was a hundred and twenty miles away. There was neither mercy nor hope. The town was burned to ashes. The temple, whose strong walls resisted the conflagration, held out for two days. Everyone, Roman or Romanised, was massacred and everything destroyed. Meanwhile the Ninth Legion was marching to the rescue. The victorious Britons advanced from the sack of Colchester to meet it. By sheer force of numbers they overcame the Roman infantry and slaughtered them to a man, and the commander,

Petilius Cerialis, was content to escape with his cavalry. Such were the tidings which reached Suetonius in Anglesey. He realised at once that his army could not make the distance in time to prevent even greater disaster, but, says Tacitus, he, "undaunted, made his way through a hostile country to Londinium, a town which, though not dignified by the title of colony, was a busy emporium for traders." This is the first mention of London in literature. Though fragments of Gallic or Italian pottery which may or may not antedate the Roman conquest have been found there, it is certain that the place attained no prominence until the Claudian invaders brought a mass of army contractors and officials to the most convenient bridgehead on the Thames.

Suetonius reached London with only a small mounted escort. He had sent orders to the Second Legion to meet him there from Gloucester, but the commander, appalled by the defeat of the Ninth, had not complied. London was a large, undefended town, full of Roman traders and their British associates, dependants, and slaves. It contained a fortified military depot, with valuable stores and a handful of legionaries. The citizens of London implored Suetonius to protect them, but when he heard that Boadicea, having chased Cerialis towards Lincoln, had turned and was marching south he took the hard but right decision to leave them to their fate. The commander of the Second Legion had disobeyed him, and he had no force to withstand the enormous masses hastening towards him. His only course was to rejoin the Fourteenth and Twentieth Legions, who were marching with might and main from Wales to London along the line of the Roman road now known as Watling Street, and, unmoved by the entreaties of the inhabitants, he gave the signal to march, receiving within his lines all who wished to go with him.

The slaughter which fell upon London was universal. No one was spared, neither man, woman, nor child. The wrath of the revolt concentrated itself upon all of those of British blood who had lent themselves to the wiles and seductions of the invader. In recent times, with London buildings growing taller and needing deeper foundations, the power-driven excavating machines have encountered at many points the layer of ashes which marks the effacement of London at the hands of the natives of Britain.

Boadicea then turned upon Verulamium (St. Albans). Here was another trading centre, to which high civic rank had been accorded. A like total slaughter and obliteration was inflicted. "No less," according to Tacitus, "than seventy thousand citizens and allies were slain" in these three cities. "For the barbarians would have no capturing, no selling, nor any kind of traffic usual in war; they would have nothing but killing, by sword, cross, gibbet, or fire." These grim words show us an inexpiable war like that waged between Carthage and her revolted mercenaries two centuries before. Some high modern authorities think these numbers are exaggerated; but there is no reason why London should not have contained thirty or forty thousand inhabitants, and Colchester and St. Albans between them about an equal number. If the butcheries in the countryside are added the estimate of Tacitus may well stand. This is probably the most horrible episode which our Island has known. We see the crude and corrupt beginnings of a higher civilisation blotted out by the ferocious uprising of the native tribes. Still, it is the primary right of men to die and kill for the land they live in, and to punish with exceptional severity all members of their own race who have warmed their hands at the invaders' hearth.

"And now Suetonius, having with him the Fourteenth Legion, with the veterans of the Twentieth, and the auxiliaries nearest at hand, making up a force of about ten thousand fully armed men, resolved . . . for battle. Selecting a position in a defile closed in behind a wood, and having made sure that there was no enemy but in front, where there was an open flat unsuited for ambuscades, he drew up his legions in close order, with the light-armed troops on the flanks, while the cavalry was massed at the extremities of the wings." The day was bloody and decisive. The barbarian army, eighty thousand strong, attended, like the Germans and the Gauls, by their women and children in an unwieldy wagon-train, drew out their array, resolved to conquer or perish. Here was no thought of subsequent accommodation. On both sides it was all for all. At heavy adverse odds Roman discipline and tactical skill triumphed. No quarter was given, even to the women.

"It was a glorious victory, fit to rank with those of olden days. Some say that little less than eighty thousand Britons fell, our own killed being about four hundred, with a somewhat larger number wounded." These are the tales of the victors. Boadicea poisoned herself. Pœnius Postumus, camp commander of the Second Legion, who had both disobeyed his general and deprived his men of their share in the victory, on hearing of the success of the Fourteenth and Twentieth ran himself through with his sword.

Suetonius now thought only of vengeance, and indeed there was much to repay. Reinforcements of four or five thousand men were sent by Nero from Germany, and all hostile or suspect tribes were harried with fire and sword. Worst of all was the want of food; for in their confident expectation of capturing the supplies of the Romans the Britons had brought every available man into the field and left their land unsown. Yet even so their spirit was unbroken, and the extermination of the entire ancient British race might have followed but for the remonstrances of a new Procurator, supported by the Treasury officials at Rome, who saw themselves about to be possessed of a desert instead of a province. As a man of action Suetonius ranks high, and his military decisions were sound. But there was a critical faculty alive in the Roman state which cannot be discounted as arising merely through the jealousies of important people. It was held that Suetonius had been rashly ambitious of military glory and had been caught unaware by the widespread uprising of the province, that "his reverses were due to his own folly, his successes to good fortune," and that a Governor must be sent, "free from feelings of hostility or triumph, who would deal gently with our conquered enemies." The Procurator, Julius Classicianus, whose tombstone is now in the British Museum, kept writing in this sense to Rome, and pleaded vehemently for the pacification of the warrior bands, who still fought on without seeking truce or mercy, starving and perishing in the forests and the fens. In the end it was resolved to make the best of the Britons. German unrest and dangers from across the Rhine made even military circles in Rome disinclined to squander forces in remoter regions. The loss in a storm of some of Suetonius' warships was made the pretext and occasion of his supersession. The Emperor Nero sent a new Governor, who made a peace with the desperate tribesmen which enabled their blood to be perpetuated in the Island race.

*   *   *   *   *

Tacitus gives an interesting account of the new province.

> The red hair and large limbs of the inhabitants of
> Caledonia [he says] pointed quite clearly to a German
> origin, while the dark complexion of the Silures, their
> usually curly hair, and the fact that Spain lies opposite to
> them are evidence that Iberians of a former date crossed
> over and occupied these parts. Those who are nearest
> to the Gauls are also like them, either from the perma-
> nent influence of original descent, or because climate
> had produced similar qualities. . . . The religious beliefs
> of Gaul may be traced in the strongly marked British
> superstition [Druidism]. The language differs but little.
> There is the same boldness in challenging danger, and
> when it is near the same timidity in shrinking from it.
> The Britons however exhibit more spirit, being a peo-
> ple whom a long peace has not yet enervated. . . . Their
> sky is obscured by continual rain and cloud. Severity
> of old is unknown. The days exceed in length those of
> our world; the nights are bright, and in the extreme
> north so short that between sunset and dawn there is
> but little distinction. . . . With the exception of the olive
> and vine, and plants which usually grow in warmer cli-
> mates, the soil will yield all ordinary produce in plenty.
> It ripens slowly, but grows rapidly, the cause in each case
> being excessive moisture of soil and atmosphere.

In A.D. 78 Agricola, a Governor of talent and energy, was sent to
Britannia. Instead of spending his first year of office in the customary tour of ceremony, he took field against all who still disputed the
Roman authority. One large tribe which had massacred a squadron of
auxiliary cavalry was exterminated. The island of Mona, from which
Suetonius had been recalled by the rising of Boadicea, was subjugated. With military ability Agricola united a statesmanlike humanity.
According to Tacitus (who had married his daughter), he proclaimed
that "little is gained by conquest if followed by oppression." He

ROMAN BRITAIN

ANTONINE WALL

MAEATAE

HADRIAN'S WALL

BRIGANTES

Eburacum

Mona

Abus

Deva

Lindum

ORDOVICES

Ratae

ICENI

CATUVELLAUNI

Venta
Icenorum

SILURES

Camulodunum

Isca
Silurum

Glevum

Verulamium

Londinium

Sabrina

Aquae Sulis

P. Lemanis

Venta Belgarum

Regnum

Isca
Dumnoniorum

Vectis

Ictis

STATUTE MILES

0 5 10   20   30   40   50

mitigated the severity of the corn tribute. He encouraged and aided the building of temples, courts of justice, and dwelling-houses. He provided a liberal education for the sons of the chiefs, and showed "such a preference for the natural powers of the Britons over the more laboured style of the Gauls" that the well-to-do classes were concili-ated and became willing to adopt the toga and other Roman fashions. "Step by step they were led to practices which disposed to vice—the lounge, the bath, the elegant banquet. All this in their ignorance they called civilisation, when it was but part of their servitude."

Although in the Senate and governing circles in Rome it was constantly explained that the Imperial policy adhered to the prin-ciple of the great Augustus, that the frontiers should be maintained but not extended, Agricola was permitted to conduct six campaigns of expansion in Britannia. In the third he reached the Tyne, the advances of his legions being supported at every stage by a fleet of sea-borne supplies. In the fifth campaign he reached the line of the Forth and Clyde, and here on this wasp-waist of Britain he might well have dug himself in. But there was no safety or permanent peace for the British province unless he could subdue the powerful tribes and large bands of desperate warriors who had been driven northwards by his advance. Indeed, it is evident that he would never of his own will have stopped in any direction short of the ocean shore. Therefore in his sixth campaign he marched northwards again with all his forces. The position had now become formidable. Past misfortunes had taught the Britons the penalties of disunion.

Agricola's son-in-law tells us:

> Our army, elated by the glory they had won, exclaimed that they must penetrate the recesses of Caledonia and at length in an unbroken succession of battles discover the farthest limits of Britain. But the Britons, thinking them-selves baffled not so much by our valour as by our gener-al's skilful use of an opportunity, abated nothing of their arrogance, arming their youth, removing their wives and children to a place of safety, and assembling together to ratify, with sacred rites, a confederacy of all their states.

The decisive battle was fought at Mons Graupius, a place which remains unidentified, though some suggest the Pass of Killiecrankie. Tacitus describes in unconvincing detail the course of this famous struggle. The whole of Caledonia, all that was left of Britannia, a vast host of broken, hunted men, resolved on death or freedom, confronted in their superiority of four or five to one the skilfully handled Roman legions and auxiliaries, among whom no doubt many British renegades were serving. It is certain that Tacitus greatly exaggerated the dimensions of the native army in these wilds, where they could have no prepared magazines. The number, though still considerable, must have been severely limited. Apparently, as in so many ancient battles, the beaten side were the victims of misunderstanding and the fate of the day was decided against them before the bulk of the forces realised that a serious engagement had begun. Reserves descended from the hills too late to achieve victory, but in good time to be massacred in the rout. The last organised resistance of Britain to the Roman power ended at Mons Graupius. Here, according to the Roman account, "ten thousand of the enemy were slain, and on our side there were about three hundred and sixty men." Clive's victory at Plassey, which secured for the British Empire a long spell of authority in India, was gained against greater odds, with smaller forces and with smaller losses.

The way to the entire subjugation of the Island was now open, and had Agricola been encouraged or at least supported by the Imperial Government the course of history might have been altered. But Caledonia was to Rome only a sensation: the real strain was between the Rhine and the Danube. Counsels of prudence prevailed, and the remnants of the British fighting men were left to moulder in the Northern mists.

Dio Cassius, writing over a century later, describes how they were a perpetual source of expense and worry to the settled regions of the South.

> There are two very extensive tribes in Britain, the Caledonians and the Mæatæ. The Mæatæ dwell close up to the cross-wall which cuts the island in two, the

Caledonians beyond them. Both live on wild, water-
less hills or forlorn and swampy plains, without walls
or towns or husbandry, subsisting on pastoral prod-
ucts and the nuts which they gather. They have fish in
plenty, but do not eat it. They live in huts, go naked and
unshod; make no separate marriages, and rear all their
offspring. They mostly have a democratic government,
and are much addicted to robbery. . . . They can bear
hunger and cold and all manner of hardship; they will
retire into their marshes and hold out for days with only
their heads above water, and in the forest they will subsist on bark and roots.

*　　*　　*　　*　　*

In the wild North and West freedom found refuge among the mountains, but elsewhere the conquest and pacification were at length
complete and Britannia became one of the forty-five provinces of the
Roman Empire. The great Augustus had proclaimed as the Imperial
ideal the creation of a commonwealth of self-governing cantons.
Each province was organised as a separate unit, and within it municipalities received their charters and rights. The provinces were divided
between those exposed to barbarian invasion or uprising, for which
an Imperial garrison must be provided, and those which required no
such protection. The military provinces were under the direct supervision of the Emperor. The more sheltered were controlled, at least
in form, through the medium of the Senate, but in all provinces the
principle was followed of adapting the form of government to local
conditions. No prejudice of race, language, or religion obstructed
the universal character of the Roman system. The only divisions were
those of class, and these ran unchallenged throughout the ordered
world. There were Roman citizens, there was an enormous mass of
non-Roman citizens, and there were slaves, but movement to full citi-
zenship was possible to fortunate members of the servile class. On this
basis therefore the life of Britain now developed.

CHAPTER THREE

THE ROMAN PROVINCE

FOR NEARLY THREE HUNDRED YEARS BRITAIN, RECONCILED TO THE Roman system, enjoyed in many respects the happiest, most comfortable, and most enlightened times its inhabitants have ever had. Confronted with the dangers of the frontiers, the military force was moderate. The Wall was held by the auxiliaries, with a legion in support at York. Wales was pinned down by a legion at Chester and another at Caerleon-on-Usk. In all the army of occupation numbered less than forty thousand men, and after a few generations was locally recruited and almost of purely British birth. In this period, almost equal to that which separates us from the reign of Queen Elizabeth I, well-to-do persons in Britain lived better than they ever did until late Victorian times. From the year 400 till the year 1900 no one had central heating and very few had hot baths. A wealthy British-Roman citizen building a country house regarded the hypocaust which warmed it as indispensable. For fifteen hundred years his descendants lived in the cold of unheated dwellings, mitigated by occasional roastings at gigantic wasteful fires. Even now a smaller proportion of the whole population dwells in centrally heated houses than in those ancient days. As for baths, they were completely lost till the middle of the nineteenth century. In all this long, bleak intervening gap cold and dirt clung to the most fortunate and highest in the land.

In culture and learning Britain was a pale reflection of the Roman scene, not so lively as the Gallic. But there was law; there was order; there was peace; there was warmth; there was food, and a long-established custom of life. The population was free from barbarism without being sunk in sloth or luxury. Some culture spread even to the villages. Roman habits percolated; the use of Roman utensils and even of Roman speech steadily grew. The British thought themselves as good Romans as any. Indeed, it may be said that of all the provinces few assimilated the Roman system with more aptitude than the Islanders. The British legionaries and auxiliaries were rated equal or second only to the Illyrians as the finest troops in the Empire. There was a sense of pride in sharing in so noble and widespread a system. To be a citizen of Rome was to be a citizen of the world, raised upon a pedestal of unquestioned superiority above barbarians or slaves. Movement across the great Empire was as rapid as when Queen Victoria came to the throne, and no obstruction of frontiers, laws, currency, or nationalism hindered it. There is a monument at Norwich erected to his wife by a Syrian resident in Britain. Constantius Chlorus died at York. British sentinels watched along the Rhine, the Danube, and the Euphrates. Troops from Asia Minor, peering through the mists at the Scottish raiders, preserved the worship of Mithras along the Roman Wall. The cult of this Persian Sun-god spread widely throughout the Roman world, appealing especially to soldiers, merchants, and administrators. During the third century Mithraism was a powerful rival to Christianity, and, as was revealed by the impressive temple discovered at Walbrook in 1954, it could count many believers in Roman London.

The violent changes at the summit of the Empire did not affect so much as might be supposed the ordinary life of its population. Here and there were wars and risings. Rival emperors suppressed each other. Legions mutinied. Usurpers established themselves in the provinces affected on these occasions. The British took a keen interest in the politics of the Roman world and formed strong views upon the changes in the Imperial power or upon the morale of the capital. Many thrusting spirits shot forward in Britain to play a part in the deadly game of Imperial politics, with its unparalleled prizes and fatal forfeits. But all were entirely reconciled to the Roman idea. They had their law; they had their life, which flowed on broad, and, if momentarily disturbed, in the main unaltered. A poll in the fourth century would have declared for an indefinite continuance of the Roman régime.

In our own fevered, changing, and precarious age, where all is in flux and nothing is accepted, we must survey with respect a period when, with only three hundred thousand soldiers, widespread the peace in the entire known world was maintained from generation to generation, and when the first pristine impulse of Christianity lifted men's souls to the contemplation of new and larger harmonies beyond the ordered world around them.

The gift which Roman civilisation had to bestow was civic and political. Towns were planned in chessboard squares for communities dwelling under orderly government. The buildings rose in accordance with the pattern standardised throughout the Roman world. Each was complete with its forum, temples, courts of justice, gaols, baths, markets, and main drains. During the first century the builders evidently took a sanguine view of the resources and future of Britannia, and all their towns were projected to meet an increasing population. It was a period of hope.

The experts dispute the population of Roman Britain, and rival estimates vary between half a million and a million and a half. It seems certain that the army, the civil services, the townsfolk, the well-to-do, and their dependants amounted to three or four hundred thousand. To grow food for these, under the agricultural methods of the age, would have required on the land perhaps double their number. We may therefore assume a population of at least a million in the Romanised area. There may well have been more. But there are no signs that any large increase of population accompanied the Roman system. In more than two centuries of peace and order the inhabitants remained at about the same numbers as in the days of Cassivellaunus. This failure to foster and support a more numerous life spread disappointment and contraction throughout Roman Britain. The conquerors who so easily subdued and rallied the Britons to their method of social life brought with them no means, apart from stopping tribal war, of increasing the annual income derived from the productivity of the soil. The new society, with all its grace of structure, with its spice of elegance and luxury—baths, banquets, togas, schools, literature, and oratory—stood on no more sumptuous foundation than the agriculture of prehistoric times. The rude plenty in which the ancient Britons had dwelt was capable of supporting only to a moderate extent the imposing façade of Roman life. The cultivated ground was still for the most part confined to the lighter and more easily cultivated upland soils, which had for thousands of years been worked in a primitive fashion. The powerful Gallic plough on wheels was known in Britain, but it did not supplant the native implement, which could only nose along in shallow furrows. With a few exceptions, there was no large-scale attempt to clear the forests, drain the marshes, and cultivate the heavy clay soil of the valleys, in which so much fertility had been deposited. Such mining of lead and tin, such smelting, as had existed from times immemorial may have gained something from orderly administration; but there was no new science, no new thrust of power and knowledge in the material sphere. Thus the economic basis remained constant, and Britain became more genteel rather than more wealthy. The life of Britain continued upon a small scale, and in the main was stationary. The new edifice, so stately and admirable, was light and frail.

These conditions soon cast their shadows upon the boldly planned towns. The surrounding agricultural prosperity was not sufficient to support the hopes of their designers. There are several excavations which show that the original boundaries were never occupied, or that, having been at first occupied, portions of the town fell gradually into decay. There was not enough material well-being to make things go. Nevertheless men dwelt safely, and what property they had was secured by iron laws. Urban life in Britannia was a failure, not of existence, but of expansion. It ran on like the life of some cathedral city, some fading provincial town, sedate, restricted, even contracting, but not without grace and dignity.

We owe London to Rome. The military engineers of Claudius, the bureaucracy which directed the supply of the armies, the merchants who followed in their wake, brought it into a life not yet stilled. Trade followed the development of their road system. An extensive and well-planned city with mighty walls took the place of the wooden trading settlement of A.D. 61, and soon achieved a leading place in the life of the Roman province of Britain, superseding the old Belgic capital, Colchester, as the commercial centre. At the end of the third century money was coined in the London mint, and the city was the headquarters of the financial administration. In the later days of the province London seems to have been the centre of civil government, as York was of the military, although it never received the status of a *municipium*.

The efflorescence of Rome in Britain was found in its villa population all over the settled area. The villas of country gentlemen of modest station were built in the most delightful spots of a virgin countryside, amid primeval forests and the gushing of untamed streams. A very large number of comfortable dwellings, each with its lands around it, rose and thrived. At least five hundred have been explored in the southern counties. None is found farther north than Yorkshire or farther west than the Glamorgan sea-plain. The comparative unsuccess of urban life led the better-class Roman Britons to establish themselves in the country, and thus the villa system was the dominant feature of Roman Britain in its heyday. The villas retained their prosperity after the towns had already decayed. The towns were shrunken after the third century. The villas still flourished in the fourth, and in some cases lingered on into the darkening days of the fifth.

The need for strong defences at the tune when the expansion of the Empire had practically reached its limits was met by the frontier policy of the Flavian emperors. Domitian was the first to build a continuous line of fortifications. About A.D. 89 the great earth rampart was constructed on the Black Sea, and another connecting the Rhine with the Danube. By the end of the first century a standard type of frontier barrier had been evolved. The work of Agricola in Northern Britain had been left unfinished at his hasty recall. No satisfactory line of defence had been erected, and the position which he had won in Scotland had to be gradually abandoned. The legions fell back on the line of the Stanegate, a road running eastwards from Carlisle. The years which followed revealed the weakness of the British frontier. The accession of Hadrian was marked by a serious disaster. The Ninth Legion disappears from history in combating an obscure rising of the tribes in Northern Britain. The defences were disorganised and the province was in danger. Hadrian came himself to Britain in 122, and the reorganisation of the frontier began.

During the next five years a military barrier was built between the Tyne and the Solway seventy-three miles long. It consisted of a stone rampart eight to ten feet thick, sustained by seventeen forts, garrisoned each by an auxiliary cohort, about eighty castles, and double that number of signal towers. In front of the wall was a 30–foot ditch, and behind it another ditch which seems to have been designed as a customs frontier and was probably controlled and staffed by the financial administration. The works needed a supporting garrison of about fourteen thousand men, not including some five thousand who, independent of the fighting units in the forts, were engaged in patrol work along the wall. The troops were provisioned by the local population, whose taxes were paid in wheat, and each fort contained granaries capable of holding a year's supply of food.

Twenty years later, in the reign of the Emperor Antoninus Pius, the Roman troops pushed northwards again over the ground of Agricola's conquests, and a new wall was built across the Forth-Clyde isthmus thirty-seven miles in length. The object was to control the tribes of the eastern and central Lowlands; but the Roman forces in Britain were not able to man the new defences without weakening their position on Hadrian's Wall and in the West. The middle years of the second century were troubled in the military area. Somewhere about the year 186 the Antonine Wall was abandoned, and the troops were concentrated on the original line of defence. Tribal revolts and Scottish raids continually assailed the northern frontier system, and in places the Wall and its supporting camps were utterly wrecked.

It was not until the Emperor Severus came to Britain in 208 and flung his energies into the task of reorganisation that stability was achieved. So great had been the destruction, so massive were his repairs, that in later times he was thought to have built the Wall, which in fact he only reconstructed. He died at York in 211; but for a hundred years there was peace along the Roman Wall.

We can measure the Roman activity in road-building by the milestones which are discovered from time to time, recording the name of the emperor under whose decree the work was done. These long, unswerving causeways stretched in bold lines across the Island. Ordinarily the road was made with a bottoming of large stones, often embedded in sand, covered with a surface of rammed gravel, the whole on an average eighteen inches thick. In special cases, or after much repairing, the formation extended to a 3–foot thickness. Over Blackstone Edge, where the road was laid upon peat, a 16–foot road-span was made of square blocks of millstone grit, with a kerb on either side and a line of large squared stones down the middle. Upon these the wheels of ancient carts going down the steep hill, braked by skid-pans, have made their grooves.[1]

The first half-century after the Claudian invasion was very active in road-building. In the second century we find most of the work concentrated upon the frontiers of the military districts. By the third century the road system was complete, and needed only to be kept in repair. It is true that for the period of Constantine no fewer than four milestones have been unearthed, which point to some fresh exten-sion, but by 340 all new work was ended, and though repairs were carried out as long as possible no later milestones proclaim a forward movement. The same symptoms reproduced themselves in Gaul after the year 350. These pedestrian facts are one measure of the rise and decline of the Roman power.

If a native of Chester in Roman Britain could wake up today[2] he would find laws which were the direct fulfilment of many of those he had known. He would find in every village temples and priests of the new creed which in his day was winning victories everywhere. Indeed the facilities for Christian worship would appear to him to be far in excess of the number of devotees. Not without pride would he notice that his children were compelled to learn Latin if they wished to enter the most famous universities. He might encounter some serious difficulties in the pronunciation. He would find in the public libraries many of the masterpieces of ancient literature, printed on uncommonly cheap paper and in great numbers. He would find a settled government, and a sense of belonging to a worldwide empire. He could drink and bathe in the waters of Bath, or if this were too far he would find vapour baths and toilet conveniences in every city.

He would find all his own problems of currency, land tenure, public morals and decorum presented in a somewhat different aspect, but still in lively dispute. He would have the same sense of belonging to a society which was threatened, and to an imperial rule which had passed its prime. He would have the same gathering fears of some sudden onslaught by barbarian forces armed with equal weapons to those of the local legions or auxiliaries. He would still fear the people across the North Sea, and still be taught that his frontiers were upon the Rhine. The most marked changes that would confront him would be the speed of communications and the volume of printed and broadcast matter. He might find both distressing. But against these he could set chloroform, antiseptics, and a more scientific knowledge of hygiene. He would have longer history books to read, containing worse tales than those of Tacitus and Dio. Facilities would be afforded to him for seeing "regions Cæsar never knew," from which he would probably return in sorrow and wonder. He would find himself hampered in every aspect of foreign travel, except that of speed. If he wished to journey to Rome, Constantinople, or Jerusalem, otherwise than by sea, a dozen frontiers would scrutinise his entry. He would be called upon to develop a large number of tribal and racial enmities to which he had formerly been a stranger. But the more he studied the accounts of what had happened since the third century the more satisfied he would be not to have been awakened at an earlier time.

*   *   *   *   *

Carefully conserved, the resources of the Empire in men and material were probably sufficient to maintain the frontiers intact. But they were often wasted in war between rival emperors, and by the middle of the third century the Empire was politically in a state of chaos and financially ruined. Yet there was much vitality still, and from the Illyrian armies came a succession of great soldiers and administrators to restore the unity of the Empire and consolidate its defences. By the end of the century Rome seemed as powerful and stable as ever. But below the surface the foundations were cracking, and through the fissures new ideas and new institutions were thrusting themselves. The cities are everywhere in decline; trade, industry, and agriculture bend under the weight of taxation. Communications are less safe, and some provinces are infested with marauders, peasants who can no longer earn a living on the land. The Empire is gradually dissolving into units of a kind unknown to classical antiquity, which will some day be brought together in a new pattern, feudal and Christian. But before that can happen generations must pass, while the new absolutism struggles by main force to keep the roads open, the fields in cultivation, and the barbarian at bay.

Nevertheless the Roman Empire was an old system. Its sinews and arteries had borne the strain of all that the ancient world had endured. The Roman world, like an aged man, wished to dwell in peace and tranquillity and to enjoy in philosophic detachment the good gifts which life has to bestow upon the more fortunate classes. But new ideas disturbed the internal conservatism, and outside the carefully guarded frontiers vast masses of hungry, savage men surged and schemed. The essence of the Roman peace was toleration of all religions and the acceptance of a universal system of government. Every generation after the middle of the second century saw an increasing weakening of the system and a gathering movement towards a uniform religion. Christianity asked again all the questions which the Roman world deemed answered for ever, and some that it had never thought of. Although the varieties of status, with all their grievous consequences, were accepted during these centuries, even by those who suffered from them most, as part of the law of nature, the institution of slavery, by which a third of Roman society was bound, could not withstand indefinitely the new dynamic thoughts which Christianity brought with it. The alternations between fanatic profligacy and avenging puritanism which marked the succession of the emperors, the contrast between the morals at the centre of power and those practised by wide communities in many subject lands, presented problems of ever-growing unrest. At the moment when mankind seemed to have solved a very large proportion of its secular difficulties and when a supreme Government offered unlimited freedom to spiritual experiment inexorable forces both within and without drove on the forward march. No rest; no stay. "For here have we no continuing city, but we seek one to come." Strange standards of destiny were unfurled, destructive of peace and order, but thrilling the hearts of men. Before the Roman system lay troubles immeasurable—squalor, slaughter, chaos itself, and the long night which was to fall upon the world.

From outside the uncouth barbarians smote upon the barriers. Here on the mainland were savage, fighting animals, joined together in a comradeship of arms, with the best fighting men and their progeny as leaders. In the rough-and-tumble of these communities, with all their crimes and bestialities, there was a more active principle of life than in the majestic achievements of the Roman Empire. We see these forces swelling like a flood against all the threatened dykes of the Roman world, not only brimming at the lip of the dam, but percolating insidiously, now by a breach, now in a mere ooze, while all the time men become conscious of the frailty of the structure itself. Floods of new untamed life burst ceaselessly from Asia, driving westward in a succession of waves. Against these there was no easy superiority of weapons. Cold steel and discipline and the slight capital surplus necessary to move and organise armies constituted the sole defences. If the superior virtue of the legion failed all fell. Certainly from the middle of the second century all these disruptive forces were plainly manifest. However, in Roman Britain men thought for many generations that they had answered the riddle of the Sphinx. They misconceived the meaning of her smile.

CHAPTER FOUR

THE LOST ISLAND

NO ONE CAN UNDERSTAND HISTORY WITHOUT CONTINUALLY RELATING the long periods which are constantly mentioned to the experiences of our own short lives. Five years is a lot. Twenty years is the horizon to most people. Fifty years is antiquity. To understand how the impact of destiny fell upon any generation of men one must first imagine their position and then apply the time-scale of our own lives. Thus nearly all changes were far less perceptible to those who lived through them from day to day than appears when the salient features of an epoch are extracted by the chronicler. We peer at these scenes through dim telescopes of research across a gulf of nearly two thousand years. We cannot doubt that the second and to some extent the third century of the Christian era, in contrast with all that had gone before and most that was to follow, were a Golden Age for Britain. But by the early part of the fourth century shadows had fallen upon this imperfect yet none the less tolerable society. By steady, persistent steps the sense of security departed from Roman Britain. Its citizens felt by daily experience a sense that the worldwide system of which they formed a partner province was in decline. They entered a period of alarm.

The spade of the archæologist, correcting and enlarging the study of historians, the discovery and scrutiny of excavations, ruins, stones, inscriptions, coins, and skeletons, the new yields of aerial photography, are telling a tale which none can doubt. Although the main impressions of the nineteenth century are not overthrown modern knowledge has become more true, more precise, and more profound. The emphasis placed by Victorian writers upon causes and events and their chronology has been altered, especially since the First World War. Their dramas have been modified or upset. A host of solid gradations and sharp-cut refinements is being marshalled in stubborn array. We walk with shorter paces, but on firmer footholds. Famous books which their writers after a lifetime's toil believed were final are now recognised as already obsolete, and new conclusions are drawn not so much from new standpoints as from new discoveries. Nevertheless the broad story holds, for it is founded in a dominating simplicity.

From the end of the third century, when Roman civilisation in Britain and the challenge to the supreme structure were equally at their height, inroads of barbarian peoples began, both from Europe and from the forlorn Island to the westward. The Scots, whom nowadays we should call the Irish, and the Picts from Scotland began to press on Hadrian's Wall, to turn both flanks of it by sea raids on a growing scale. At the same time the Saxons rowed in long-boats across the North Sea and lay heavy all along the east coast from Newcastle to Dover. From this time forth the British countryside dwelt under the same kind of menace of cruel, bloody, and sudden inroad from the sea as do modern nations from the air. Many proofs have been drawn from the soil in recent years. All point to the same conclusion. The villa life of Britain, upon which the edifice of Roman occupation was now built, was in jeopardy. We see the signs of fear spreading through the whole country. Besides the forts along the east and south coasts, and the system of galleys based upon them, a host of new precautions becomes evident. The walls of London were furnished with bastion towers, the stones for which were taken from dwelling-houses, now no longer required by a dwindling town-population. Here and there the broad Roman gateways of townships were narrowed to half their size with masonry, a lasting proof of the increasing insecurity of the times. All over the country hoards of coins have been found, hardly any of which are later than the year A.D. 400. Over this fertile, peaceful, ordered world lay the apprehension of constant peril.

Like other systems in decay, the Roman Empire continued to function for several generations after its vitality was sapped. For nearly a hundred years our Island was one of the scenes of conflict between a dying civilisation and lusty, famishing barbarism. Up to the year 300 Hadrian's Wall, with its garrisons, barred out the Northern savages, but thereafter a new front must be added. At the side of the "Duke of the Northern Marches" there must stand the "Count of the Saxon Shore." All round the eastern and southern coasts, from the Wash to Southampton Water, a line of large fortresses was laboriously built. Eight have been examined. Of these the chief was Richborough, known to the generation of the First World War as an invaluable ferry-port for the supply of the armies in France.

There is some dispute about the strategic conceptions upon which these strongholds were called into being. Many disparaging judgments have been passed upon a policy which is accused of seeking to protect four hundred miles of coastline from these eight points. Obviously these strictures are unjust. The new line of coastal fortresses could only have had any value or reason as bases for a British-Roman fleet.

Such a fleet, the Classis Britannica, had been maintained from the first century. Tiles with an Admiralty mark show that it had permanent stations at Dover and Lympne. But the whole coast was organised for defence, and for long periods these measures proved effective. Vegetius, writing in the fourth century on the art of war, mentions a special kind of light galley attached to the British fleet. These vessels, the hulls, sails, the men's clothes, and even faces, were painted sea-green, to make them invisible, and Vegetius tells us that in naval parlance they were called "the Painted Ones." As the Imperial and British sea-power gradually became unequal to the raiders the ramparts of the fortresses grew higher and their usefulness less. Flotilla defence by oared galleys working from bases fifty to a hundred miles apart could not contend indefinitely with raiding thrusts. Even a High Sea Fleet capable of keeping the sea for months at a time off the coasts of what are now called Holland, Germany, and Denmark, though a powerful deterrent, would have been too slow to deal with oared boats in calm weather.

The Roman Britons were lively and audacious members of the Empire. They took a particularist view, yet wished to have a hand in the game themselves. As time passed the Roman garrison in Britain steadily became more British, and towards the end of the third century it assumed a strong national character. While glorying in the name of citizens and Romans, and having no desire for independence, both province and army adopted a highly critical attitude towards the Imperial Government. Emperors who disregarded British opinion, or sacrificed British interests, above all those who could be accused of neglecting the defences of the province, were the objects of active resentment. A series of mutinies and revolts aggravated the growing dangers of the times. No one can suppose that the Roman military centres at Chester, York, or Caerleon-on-Usk threw up claimants for the Imperial diadem unsupported by a strong backing in local opinion. These were not merely mutinies of discontented soldiers. They were bold bids for control of the Roman Empire by legions only a few thousand strong, but expressing the mood, sentiments, and ambitions of the society in which they lived. They left the local scene for the supreme theatre, like players who wish to quit the provinces for the capital. Unhappily they took away with them at each stage important elements of the exiguous military forces needed to man the dykes.

*　　*　　*　　*　　*

The Emperor Diocletian has gone down to history principally as the persecutor of the early Christians, and the enormous work which he achieved in restoring the frontiers of the ancient world has remained under that shadow. His policy was to construct a composite Cæsarship. There were to be two Emperors and two Caesars, he himself being the senior of the four. In due course the Emperors would retire in favour of the Cæsars, new ones would be appointed, and thus the succession would be preserved. The co-Emperor Maximian, sent to Gaul in 285, and responsible for Britannia, was deeply concerned by the raiding of the Saxon pirates. He strengthened the Channel fleet, and put at its head a sea officer from the Low Countries named Carausius. This man was tough, resolute, ambitious, and without scruple; from his base at Boulogne he encouraged the raiders to come and pillage, and then when they were laden with plunder he fell upon them with Roman-British flotillas, captured them by scores, and destroyed them without mercy. His success did not satisfy the British community; they accused him of having been in league with those he had destroyed. He explained that this was all part of his ambush; but the fact that he had retained all the spoil in his own hands told heavily against him. Maximian sought to bring him to execution, but Carausius, landing in Britain, declared himself Emperor, gained the Island garrison to his cause, and defeated Maximian in a sea battle. On this it was thought expedient to come to terms with the stubborn rebel, and in the year 287 Carausius was recognised as one of the Augusti in command of Britain and of Northern Gaul.

For six years this adventurer, possessing sea-power, reigned in our Island. He seems to have served its interests passably well. However, the Emperor Diocletian and his colleagues were only biding their time, and in the year 293 they cast away all pretence of friendship. One of the new Cæsars, Constantius Chlorus, besieged and took Boulogne, the principal Continental base of Carausius, who was soon assassinated by one of his officers. The new competitor sought to become Emperor in his stead. He did not gain the support of the British nation and the whole country fell into confusion. The Picts were not slow to seize their advantage. The Wall was pierced, and fire and sword wasted the Northern districts. Chlorus crossed the Channel as a deliverer. His colleague, with part of the force, landed near Portsmouth; he himself sailed up the Thames, and was received by London with gratitude and submission. He restored order. A gold medallion discovered at Arras in 1922 reveals him at the head of a fleet which had sailed up the Thames. He drove back the Northern invaders, and set to work to restore and improve the whole system of defence.

*　　*　　*　　*　　*

Continuous efforts were made by the Roman-British community to repel the inroads, and for two or three generations there were counter-strokes by flotillas of galleys, and hurried marchings of cohorts and of British auxiliaries towards the various thrusts of raid or invasion. But although the process of wearing down was spread over many years, and misery deepened by inches, we must recognise in the year 367 circumstances of supreme and murderous horror. In that fatal year the Picts, the Scots, and the Saxons seemed to work in combination. All fell together upon Britannia. The Imperial troops resisted manfully. The Duke of the Northern Marches and the Count of the Saxon Shore were killed in the battles. A wide-open breach was made in the defences, and murderous hordes poured in upon the fine world of country houses and homesteads. Everywhere they were blotted out. The ruins tell the tale. The splendid Mildenhall silver dinner service, now in the British Museum, is thought to have been buried at this time by its owners, when their villa was surprised by raiders. Evidently they did not live to dig it up again. The villa life of Britain only feebly recovered from the disaster. The towns were already declining. Now people took refuge in them. At least they had walls.

The pages of history reveal the repeated efforts made by the Imperial Government to protect Britannia. Again and again, in spite of revolts and ingratitude, officers and troops were sent to restore order or drive back the barbarians. After the disasters of 367 the Emperor Valentinian sent a general, Theodosius, with a considerable force to relieve the province. Theodosius achieved his task, and once again we find on the coastal fortifications the traces of a further strong reconstruction. Untaught however by continuing danger, the garrison and inhabitants of Britain in 383 yielded themselves willingly to a Spaniard, Magnus Maximus, who held the command in Britain and now declared himself Emperor. Scraping together all the troops he could find, and stripping the Wall and the fortresses of their already scanty defenders, Maximus hastened to Gaul, and defeated the Emperor Gratian near Paris. Gratian was murdered at Lyons by his troops, and Maximus became master of Gaul and Spain as well as Britain. For five years he struggled to defend his claim to these great dominions, but Theodosius, who had succeeded Gratian, at length defeated and slew him.

Meanwhile the Wall was pierced again, and Britain lay open to the raiders both from the North and from the sea. Seven years more were to pass before Theodosius could send his general, Stilicho, to the Island. This great soldier drove out the intruders and repaired the defences. The writings of Claudian, the court poet, describe in triumphant terms the liberation of Britain from its Saxon, Pictish, and

Scottish assailants in the year 400. In celebrating the first consulship of Stilicho he tells how Britain has expressed her gratitude for her deliverance from the fear of these foes. This sentiment soon fades.

Stilicho had returned to Rome, and was in chief command when in the same year Alaric and the Visigoths invaded Italy. He was forced to recall a further part of the British garrison to defend the heart of the Empire. In 402 he defeated Alaric in the great battle of Pollentia, and drove him out of Italy. No sooner was this accomplished than a new barbarian invasion swept down upon him under Radagaisus. By 405 Stilicho had completely destroyed this second vast host. Italy was scarcely clear when a confederacy of Suevi, Vandals, Avars, and Burgundians broke through the Rhine frontiers and overran Northern Gaul. The indomitable Stilicho was preparing to meet this onslaught when the British army, complaining that the province was being neglected, mutinied. They set up a rival Emperor named Marcus, and on his speedy murder elected a Briton, Gratianus, in his stead. After his assassination four months later the soldiers chose another Briton, who bore the famous name of Constantine. Constantine, instead of protecting the Island, found himself compelled to defend upon the Continent the titles he had usurped. He drained Britain of troops, and, as Magnus Maximus had done, set forth for Boulogne to try his fortune. In the supreme theatre for three years, with varying success, he contended with Stilicho, and was finally captured and executed, as Maximus had been before him. None of the troops who had accompanied him ever returned to Britain. Thus in these fatal years the civilised parts of the Island were stripped of their defenders, both in order to aid the Empire and to strike against it.

By the beginning of the fifth century all the legions had gone on one errand or another, and to frantic appeals for aid the helpless Emperor Honorius could only send his valedictory message in 410, that "the cantons should take steps to defend themselves."

*   *   *   *   *

The first glimpse we have of the British after the Roman Government had withdrawn its protection is afforded by the visit of St. Germanus in 429. The Bishop came from Auxerre in order to uproot the

Pelagian heresy, which in spite of other preoccupations our Christian Island had been able to evolve. This doctrine consisted in assigning an undue importance to free will, and cast a consequential slur upon the doctrine of original sin. It thus threatened to deprive mankind, from its very birth, of an essential part of our inheritance. The Bishop of Auxerre and another episcopal colleague arrived at St. Albans, and we are assured that they soon convinced the doubters and eradicated the evil opinions to which they had incautiously hearkened. What kind of Britain did he find? He speaks of it as a land of wealth. There is treasure; there are flocks and herds; food is abundant; institutions, civil and religious, function; the country is prosperous, but at war. An invading army from the North or the East is approaching. It was an army said to be composed of Saxons, Picts, and Scots in ill-assorted and unholy alliance.

The Bishop had been a distinguished general in his prime. He organised the local forces. He reconnoitred the surrounding districts. He noticed in the line of the enemy's advance a valley surrounded by high hills. He took command, and lay in ambush for the ferocious heathen hordes. When the enemy were entangled in the defile, suddenly "The priests shouted a triple Alleluia at their foes. . . . The cry was taken up with one mighty shout and echoed from side to side of the enclosed valley; the enemy were smitten with terror, thinking that the rocks and the very sky were falling upon them; such was their fear that they could hardly run quickly enough. They threw away their arms in their disorderly flight, glad to escape naked; a river devoured many in their headlong fear, though in their advance they had crossed it in good order. The innocent army saw itself avenged, a spectator of a victory gained without exertion. The abandoned spoils were collected, . . . and the Britons triumphed over an enemy routed without loss of blood; the victory was won by faith and not by might. . . . So the Bishop returned to Auxerre, having settled the affairs of that most wealthy Island, and overcome their foes both spiritual and carnal, that is to say, both the Pelagians and Saxons."[1]

Another twelve years passed, and a Gaulish chronicler records this sombre note in A.D. 441 or 442: "The Britons in these days by all kinds of calamities and disasters are falling into the power of the

Saxons." What had happened? Something more than the forays of the fourth century: the mass migration from North Germany had begun. Thereafter the darkness closes in.

Upon this darkness we have four windows, each obstructed by dim or coloured glass. We have the tract of Gildas the Wise, written, approximately, in A.D. 545, and therefore a hundred years after the curtain fell between Britannia and the Continent. Nearly two hundred years later the Venerable Bede, whose main theme was the history of the English Church, lets fall some precious scraps of information, outside his subject, about the settlement itself. A compilation known as the *Historia Britonum* contains some documents earlier than Bede. Finally, in the ninth century, and very likely at the direction of King Alfred, various annals preserved in different monasteries were put together as the *Anglo-Saxon Chronicle*. Checking these by each other, and by such certainties as archæology allows us to entertain, we have the following picture.

Imitating a common Roman practice, the dominant British chief about A.D. 450 sought to strengthen himself by bringing in a band of mercenaries from over the seas. They proved a trap. Once the road was open fresh fleet-loads made their way across and up the rivers, from the Humber perhaps as far round as Portsmouth. But the British resistance stiffened as the invaders got away from the coast, and their advance was brought to a standstill for nearly fifty years by a great battle won at Mount Badon. If now we draw a V-shaped line, one leg from Chester to Southampton, and the other back from Southampton to the Humber, we shall observe that the great bulk of pagan Saxon remains, and that place-names in *ing* or *ings*, usually evidence of early settlement, are to the east of this second line. Here then we have the England of about A.D. 500. The middle sector is the debatable land, and the West is still Britain.

So far this tale is confirmed, historically and geographically. Gildas could have heard the story of the mercenaries from old men whom he had known in his youth, and there is no real ground for doubting the statements of Nennius, a compiler probably of the ninth century, and Bede, who agree that the name of the deceived chief who invited these deadly foes was Vortigern. Hengist, a name frequently mentioned in

Northern story, like a medieval mercenary was ready to sell his sword and his ships to anyone who would give him land on which to support his men; and what he took was the future kingdom of Kent.

Gildas has a tale to tell of this tragedy.

> No sooner have they (the Britons) gone back to their land than the foul hosts of the Picts and Scots land promptly from their coracles. . . . These two races differ in part in their manners, but they agree in their lust for blood, and in their habit of covering their hang-dog faces with hair, instead of covering with clothing those parts of their bodies which demand it. They seize all the northern and outlying part of the country as far as to the Wall. Upon this Wall stands a timorous and unwarlike garrison. The wretched citizens are pulled down from the Wall and dashed to the ground by the hooked weapons of their naked foes. What shall I add? The citizens desert the high Wall and their towns, and take to a flight more desperate than any before. Again the enemy pursue them, and there is slaughter more cruel than ever. As lambs by butchers, so are our piteous citizens rent by their foes, till their manner of sojourning might be compared to that of wild beasts. For they maintained themselves by robbery for the sake of a little food. Thus calamities from outside were increased by native feuds; so frequent were these disasters that the country was stripped of food, save what could be procured in the chase.
>
> Therefore again did the wretched remnants send a letter to Ætius, a powerful Roman—"To Ætius, three times Consul, the groans of the Britons": "The barbarians drive us to the sea, the sea drives us to the barbarians: between these two methods of death we are either massacred or drowned." But they got no help. Meantime dire famine compelled many to surrender to their spoilers. . . . But others would in no wise surrender, but kept on sallying from the mountains, caves, passes, and thick coppices.

> And then, for the first time, trusting not in man but in
> God, they slaughtered the foes who for so many years had
> been plundering their country. . . . For a time the bold-
> ness of our enemies was checked, but not the wickedness
> of our own countrymen: the enemy left our citizens, but
> our citizens did not leave their sins.

Nennius also tells us, what Gildas omits, the name of the British soldier who won the crowning mercy of Mount Badon, and that name takes us out of the mist of dimly remembered history into the daylight of romance. There looms, large, uncertain, dim but glittering, the legend of King Arthur and the Knights of the Round Table. Somewhere in the Island a great captain gathered the forces of Roman Britain and fought the barbarian invaders to the death. Around him, around his name and his deeds, shine all that romance and poetry can bestow. Twelve battles, all located in scenes untraceable, with foes unknown, except that they were heathen, are punctiliously set forth in the Latin of Nennius. Other authorities say, "No Arthur; at least, no proof of any Arthur." It was only when Geoffrey of Monmouth six hundred years later was praising the splendours of feudalism and martial aristocracy that chivalry, honour, the Christian faith, knights in steel and ladies bewitching, are enshrined in a glorious circle lit by victory. Later this would have been retold and embellished by the genius of Mallory, Spenser, and Tennyson. True or false, they have gained an immortal hold upon the thoughts of men. It is difficult to believe it was all an invention of a Welsh writer. If it was he must have been a marvellous inventor.

Modern research has not accepted the annihilation of Arthur. Timidly but resolutely the latest and best-informed writers unite to proclaim his reality. They cannot tell when in this dark period he lived, or where he held sway and fought his battles. They are ready to believe however that there was a great British warrior, who kept the light of civilisation burning against all the storms that beat, and that behind his sword there sheltered a faithful following of which the memory did not fail. All four groups of the Celtic tribes which dwelt in the tilted uplands of Britain cheered themselves with the Arthurian legend, and each claimed their own region as the scene of his exploits. From Cornwall to Cumberland a search for Arthur's realm or sphere has been pursued.

The reserve of modern assertions is sometimes pushed to extremes, in which the fear of being contradicted leads the writer to strip himself of almost all sense and meaning. One specimen of this method will suffice.

> It is reasonably certain that a petty chieftain named Arthur did exist, probably in South Wales. It is possible that he may have held some military command uniting the tribal forces of the Celtic or highland zone or part of it against raiders and invaders (not all of them necessarily Teutonic). It is also possible that he may have engaged in all or some of the battles attributed to him; on the other hand, this attribution may belong to a later date.

This is not much to show after so much toil and learning. None the less, to have established a basis of fact for the story of Arthur is a service which should be respected. In this account we prefer to believe that the story with which Geoffrey delighted the fiction-loving Europe of the twelfth century is not all fancy.[2] If we could see exactly what happened we should find ourselves in the presence of a theme as well founded, as inspired, and as inalienable from the inheritance of mankind as the *Odyssey* or the Old Testament. It is all true, or it ought to be; and more and better besides. And wherever men are fighting against barbarism, tyranny, and massacre, for freedom, law, and honour, let them remember that the fame of their deeds, even though they themselves be exterminated, may perhaps be celebrated as long as the world rolls round. Let us then declare that King Arthur and his noble knights, guarding the Sacred Flame of Christianity and the theme of a world order, sustained by valour, physical strength, and good horses and armour, slaughtered innumerable hosts of foul barbarians and set decent folk an example for all time.

We are told he was *Dux Bellorum*. What could be more natural or more necessary than that a commander-in-chief should be accepted—a new Count of Britain, such as the Britons had appealed to Ætius to give them fifty years before? Once Arthur is recognised as the commander of a mobile field army, moving from one part of the country to another and uniting with local forces in each district, the disputes about the scenes of his actions explain themselves. Moreover the fourth century witnessed the rise of cavalry to the dominant position in the battlefield. The day of infantry had passed for a time, and the day of the legion had passed for ever. The Saxon invaders were infantry, fighting with sword and spear, and having little armour. Against such an enemy a small force of ordinary Roman cavalry might well prove invincible. If a chief like Arthur had gathered a band of mail-clad cavalry he could have moved freely about Britain, everywhere heading the local resistance to the invader and gaining repeated victories. The memory of Arthur carried with it the hope that a deliverer would return one day. The legend lived upon the increasing tribulations of the age. Arthur has been described as the last of the Romans. He understood Roman ideas, and used them for the good of the British people. "The heritage of Rome," Professor Collingwood says, "lives on in many shapes, but of the men who created that heritage Arthur was the last, and the story of Roman Britain ends with him."

Arthur's "twelfth battle," says Nennius, "was on Mount Badon, in which there fell in one day nine hundred and sixty men from the onslaught of Arthur only, and no one laid them low save he alone. And in all his battles he was victor. But they, when in all these battles they had been overthrown, sought help from Germany and increased without intermission."

All efforts to fix the battlefield of Mount Badon have failed. A hundred learned investigations have brought no results, but if, as seems most probable, it was fought in the Debatable Land to check the advance from the East, then the best claimant to the title is Liddington Camp, which looks down on Badbury, near Swindon. On the other hand, we are able to fix the date with unusual accuracy. Gildas speaks of it as having occurred forty-three years and a month from the date when he was writing, and he says that he remembers the date because it was that of his own birth. Now we know from his book that the King of North Wales, Maelgwyn, was still alive when he wrote, and the annals of Cambria tell us that he died of the plague in 547. Gildas thus wrote at the latest in this year, and the Battle of Mount Badon, forty-three years earlier, would have been fought in 503. We have also a cross-check in the Irish annals, which state that Gildas died in 569 or 570. His birth is therefore improbable before 490, and thus the date of the battle seems to be fixed between 490 and 503.

*　　*　　*　　*　　*

A broader question is keenly disputed. Did the invaders exterminate the native population, or did they superimpose themselves upon them and become to some extent blended with them? Here it is necessary to distinguish between the age of fierce forays in search of plunder and the age of settlement. Gildas is speaking of the former, and the scenes he describes were repeated in the Danish invasions three centuries later. But to the settler such raids are only occasional incidents in a life mainly occupied in subduing the soil, and in that engrossing task labour is as important as land. The evidence of place-names suggests that in Sussex extermination was the rule. Farther west there are grounds for thinking that a substantial British population survived, and the oldest West Saxon code of A.D. 694 makes careful provision for the rights of "Welshmen" of various degrees— substantial landowners, and "the King's Welshmen who ride his errands," his native gallopers in fact, who know the ancient trackways. Even where self-interest did not preserve the native villagers as labourers on Saxon farms we may cherish the hope that somewhere a maiden's cry for pity, the appeal of beauty in distress, the lustful needs of an invading force, would create some bond between victor and vanquished. Thus the blood would be preserved, thus the rigours of subjugation would fade as generations passed away. The complete obliteration of an entire race over large areas is repulsive to the human mind. There should at least have been, in default of pity, a hearing for practical advantage or the natural temptations of sex. Thus serious writers contend that the Anglo-Saxon conquest was for the bulk of the British community mainly a change of masters. The rich were slaughtered; the brave and proud fell back in large numbers upon the Western mountains. Other numerous bands escaped betimes to Brittany, whence their remote posterity were one day to return.

The Saxon was moreover a valley-settler. His notion of an economic holding was a meadow for hay near the stream, the lower slopes under the plough, the upper slopes kept for pasture. But in many places a long time must have passed before these lower grounds could be cleared and drained, and while this work was in progress what did he live on but the produce of the upland British farms? It is more natural to suppose that he would keep his natives working as serfs on the land with which they were familiar until the valley was ready for sowing. Then the old British farms would go down to grass, and the whole population would cluster in the village by the stream or the spring. But the language of the valley-settlers, living in compact groups, would be dominant over that of the hill-cultivators, scattered in small and isolated holdings. The study of modern English place-names has shown that hill, wood, and stream names are often Celtic in origin, even in regions where the village names are Anglo-Saxon. In this way, without assuming any wholesale extermination, the disappearance of the British language can be explained even in areas where we know a British population to have survived. They had to learn the language of their masters: there was no need for their masters to learn theirs. Thus it came about that both Latin and British yielded to the speech of the newcomers so completely that hardly a trace of either is to be found in our earliest records.

There was no uniformity of practice in the Island. There is good reason to think that the newcomers in Kent settled down beside the old inhabitants, whose name, Cantiaci, they adopted. In Northumbria there are strong traces of Celtic law. In Hants and Wilts a broad belt of British names, from Liss to Deverill, seems to show the natives still cultivating their old fields on the downs, while the Saxon was clearing the valleys. There was no colour bar. In physical type the two races resembled each other; and the probabilities are that in many districts a substantial British element was incorporated in the Saxon stock.

The invaders themselves were not without their yearnings for settled security. Their hard laws, the rigours they endured, were but the results of the immense pressures behind them as the hordes of avid humanity spread westward from Central Asia. The warriors returning from a six months' foray liked to sprawl in lazy repose. Evidently they were not insensible to progressive promptings, but where, asked the chiefs and elders, could safety be found? In the fifth century, as the pressure from the East grew harder and as the annual raiding parties returned from Britain with plunder and tales of wealth there was created in the ruling minds a sense of the difficulty of getting to the island, and consequently of the security which would attend its occupation by a hardy and valiant race. Here, perhaps, in this wave-lapped Island men might settle down and enjoy the good things of life without the haunting fear of subjugation by a stronger hand, and without the immense daily sacrifices inseparable from military and tribal discipline on the mainland. To these savage swords Britain seemed a refuge. In the wake of the raiders there grew steadily the plan and system of settlement. Thus, with despair behind and hope before, the migration to Britain and its occupation grew from year to year.

*   *   *   *   *

Of all the tribes of the Germanic race none was more cruel than the Saxons. Their very name, which spread to the whole confederacy of Northern tribes, was supposed to be derived from the use of a weapon, the seax, a short one-handed sword. Although tradition and the Venerable Bede assign the conquest of Britain to the Angles, Jutes, and Saxons together, and although the various settlements have tribal peculiarities, it is probable that before their general exodus from Schleswig-Holstein the Saxons had virtually incorporated the other two strains.

The history books of our childhood attempted courageously to prescribe exact dates for all the main events. In 449 Hengist and Horsa, invited by Vortigern, founded the Jutish kingdom of Kent upon the corpses of its former inhabitants. In 477 Ella and his three sons arrived to continue the inroad. In 495 Cerdic and Cynric appeared. In 501 Port, the pirate, founded Portsmouth. In 514 the West Saxons Stuf and Wihtgar descended in their turn and put the Britons to flight. In 544 Wihtgar was killed. In 547 came Ida, founder of the kingdom of Northumberland. All that can be said about these dates is that they correspond broadly to the facts, and that these successive waves of invaders, bringing behind them settlers, descended on our unhappy shores.

Other authorities draw an alternative picture. "The bulk of the homesteads within the village," J. R. Green tells us,

> were those of its freemen or ceorls; but amongst these were the larger homes of eorls, or men distinguished among their fellows by noble blood, who were held in an heredi- tary reverence, and from whom the leaders of the village were chosen in war-time or rulers in times of peace. But the choice was a purely voluntary one, and the man of noble blood enjoyed no legal privilege amongst his fellows.[3]

If this were so we might thus early have realised the democratic ideal of "the association of us all through the leadership of the best." In the tribal conceptions of the Germanic nation lie, no doubt, many of those principles which are now admired, and which have formed a recognisable part of the message which the English-speaking peoples have given to the world. But the conquerors of Roman Britain, far from practising these ideals, introduced a whole scheme of society which was fundamentally sordid and vicious. The invaders brought into Britain a principle common to all Germanic tribes, namely, the use of the money power to regulate all the legal relations of men. If there was any equality it was equality within each social grade. If there was liberty it was mainly liberty for the rich. If there were rights they were primarily the rights of property. There was no crime committed which could not be compounded by a money payment. Except failure to answer a call to join an expedition, there was no offence more heinous than that of theft.

An elaborate tariff prescribed in shillings the "wergild" or exact value or worth of every man. An ætheling, or prince, was worth 1500 shillings, a shilling being the value of a cow in Kent, or of a sheep elsewhere; an eorl, or nobleman, 300 shillings; a ceorl, now degraded to the word "churl," who was a yeoman farmer, was worth 100 shil- lings; a læt, or agricultural serf, 40–80 shillings, and a slave nothing.

All these laws were logically and mathematically pushed to their extremes. If a ceorl killed an eorl he had to pay three times as much in compensation as if the eorl were the murderer. And these laws were applied to the families of all. The life of a slaughtered man could be compounded for cash. With money all was possible; without it only retribution or loss of liberty. However, the ætheling, valued at 1500 shillings, suffered in certain respects. The penalty for slander was the tearing out of the tongue. If an ætheling were guilty of this offence his tongue was worth five times that of an eorl and fifteen times as much as that of a common læt, and he could ransom it only on these terms. Thus the abuse of a humble tongue was cheap. Wergild at least, as Alfred said long afterwards, was better than the blood feud.

The foundation of the Germanic system was blood and kin. The family was the unit, the tribe was the whole. The great transition which we witness among the emigrants is the abandonment of blood and kin as the theme of their society and its replacement by local societies and lordship based on the ownership of land. This change arose, like so many of the lessons learned by men, from the grim needs of war. Fighting for life and foothold against men as hard pressed as themselves, each pioneering band fell inevitably into the hands of the bravest, most commanding, most fortunate war-leader. This was no longer a foray of a few months, or at the outside a year. Here were settlements to be founded, new lands to be reclaimed and cultivated, land which moreover offered to the deeper plough a virgin fertility. These must be guarded, and who could guard them except the bold chieftains who had gained them over the corpses of their former owners?

Thus the settlement in England was to modify the imported structure of Germanic life. The armed farmer-colonists found themselves forced to accept a stronger state authority owing to the stresses of continued military action. In Germany they had no kings. They developed them in Britain from leaders who claimed descent from the ancient gods. The position of the king continually increased in importance, and his supporters or companions gradually formed a new class in society, which carried with it the germ of feudalism, and was in the end to dominate all other conventions. But the lord was master; he must also be protector. He must stand by his people, must back them in the courts, feed them in time of famine, and they in return must work his land and follow him in war.

The king was at first only the war-leader made permanent; but, once set up, he had his own interests, his own needs, and his own mortal dangers. To make himself secure became his paramount desire. "To be thus is nothing, but to be safely thus . . ." But how was this to be achieved? Only by the king gathering round him a band of the most successful warriors and interesting them directly in the conquest and in the settlement. He had nothing to give them except land. There must be a hierarchy. The king must be surrounded by those who had shared his deeds and his bounty. The spoils of war were soon consumed, but the land remained forever. Land there was in plenty, of varying quality and condition, but to give individual warriors a title to any particular tract was contrary to the whole tradition of the Germanic tribes. Now under the hard pressures of war and pioneering land increasingly became private property. Insensibly, at first, but with growing speed from the seventh century onwards, a landed aristocracy was created owing all they had to the king. While the resistance of the Britons was vigorously maintained, and the fortunes of the struggle swung this way and that way for nearly two hundred years, this new institution of personal leadership established in the divinely descended war-chief sank deeply into the fibre of the Anglo-Saxon invaders.

But with this movement towards a more coherent policy or structure of society there came also a welter of conflicting minor powers. Distances were usually prohibitive, and writing virtually unknown. Districts were separated from each other like islands in rough seas, and thus a host of kings and kinglets sprang into existence behind the fighting frontier of the intruding tribes. In marking the many root faults and vices which they possessed a high place must be assigned to their inability to combine. For a long time the Island presented only the spectacle of a chaos arising from the strife of small fiercely organised entities. Although from the time of the immigration the people south of the Humber were generally subject to a common overlord, they were never able to carry the evolution of kingship forward to a national throne. They remained marauders; but they had taken more pains to be sure of their booty.

Much has been written about the enervating character of Roman rule in Britain, and how the people were rendered lax and ineffectual by the modest comforts which it supplied. There is no doubt that Gildas, by his writings, imparted an impression, perhaps in this case well founded, of gross incompetence and fatuity in the society and administration which followed the decay of Roman power. But justice to this vanished epoch demands recognition of the fact that the Britons fought those who are now called the English for nearly two hundred and fifty years. For a hundred years they fought them under the ægis of Rome, with its world organisation; but for a hundred and fifty years they fought them alone. The conflict ebbed and flowed. British victories were gained, which once for a whole generation brought the conquest to a halt; and in the end the mountains which even the Romans had been unable to subdue proved an invincible citadel of the British race.

CHAPTER FIVE

ENGLAND

A RED SUNSET; A LONG NIGHT; A PALE, MISTY DAWN! BUT AS THE light grows it becomes apparent to remote posterity that everything was changed. Night had fallen on Britannia. Dawn rose on England, humble, poor, barbarous, degraded and divided, but alive. Britannia had been an active part of a world state; England was once again a barbarian island. It had been Christian, it was now heathen. Its inhabitants had rejoiced in well-planned cities, with temples, markets, academies. They had nourished craftsmen and merchants, professors of literature and rhetoric. For four hundred years there had been order and law, respect for property, and a widening culture. All had vanished. The buildings, such as they were, were of wood, not stone. The people had lost entirely the art of writing. Some miserable runic scribblings were the only means by which they could convey their thoughts or wishes to one another at a distance. Barbarism reigned in its rags, without even the stern military principles which had animated and preserved the Germanic tribes. The confusion and conflict of petty ruffians sometimes called kings racked the land. There was nothing worthy of the name of nationhood, or even of tribalism; yet this is a transition which the learned men of the nineteenth century banded themselves together to proclaim as an onward step in the march of mankind. We wake from an awful and, it might well have seemed, endless nightmare to a scene of utter prostration. Nor did the seeds of recovery spring from the savage hordes who had wrecked the Roman culture. They would certainly have continued to welter indefinitely in squalor, but for the fact that a new force was stirring beyond the seas which, moving slowly, fitfully, painfully, among the ruins of civilisation, reached at length by various paths the unhappy Island, to which, according to Procopius, the souls of the dead upon the mainland were ferried over by some uncouth Charon.

Christianity had not been established as the religion of the Empire during the first two centuries of the Roman occupation of Britain. It grew with many other cults in the large and easy tolerance of the Imperial system. There arose however a British Christian Church which sent its bishops to the early councils, and had, as we have seen, sufficient vitality to develop the Pelagian heresy from its own unaided heart-searchings. When the evil days overtook the land and the long struggle with the Saxons was fought out the British Church fell back with other survivors upon the western parts of the Island. Such was the gulf between the warring races that no attempt was made at any time by the British bishops to Christianise the invaders. Perhaps they were not given any chance of converting them. After an interval one of their leading luminaries, afterwards known as St. David, accomplished the general conversion of what is now Wales. Apart from this British Christianity languished in its refuges, and might well have become moribund but for the appearance of a remarkable and charming personality.

St. Patrick was a Roman Briton of good family dwelling probably in the Severn valley. His father was a Christian deacon, a Roman citizen, and a member of the municipal council. One day in the early fifth century there descended on the district a band of Irish raiders, burning and slaying. The young Patrick was carried off and sold into slavery in Ireland. Whether he dwelt in Connaught or in Ulster is disputed, and the evidence is contradictory. It may well be that both versions are true and that both provinces may claim the honour. For six years, wherever it was, he tended swine, and loneliness led him to seek comfort in religion. He was led by miraculous promptings to attempt escape. Although many miles separated him from the sea he made his way to a port, found a ship, and persuaded the captain to take him on board. After many wanderings we find him in one of the small islands off Marseilles, then a centre of the new monastic movement spreading westward from the Eastern Mediterranean. Later he consorted with Bishop Germanus of Auxerre. He conceived an earnest desire to return good for evil and spread the tidings he had learned among his former captors in Ireland. After fourteen years of careful training by the Bishop and self-preparation for what must have seemed a forlorn adventure Patrick sailed back in 432 to the wild regions which he had quitted. His success was speedy and undying. "He organised the Christianity already in existence; he converted kingdoms which were still pagan, especially in the West; he brought Ireland into connection with the Church of Western Europe, and made it formally part of universal Christendom." On a somewhat lower plane, although also held in perpetual memory, was the banishing of snakes and reptiles of all kinds from the Irish soil, for which from age to age his fame has been celebrated.

It was therefore in Ireland and not in Wales or England that the light of Christianity now burned and gleamed through the darkness. And it was from Ireland that the Gospel was carried to the North of Britain and for the first time cast its redeeming spell upon the Pictish invaders. Columba, born half a century after St. Patrick's death, but an offspring of his Church, and imbued with his grace and fire, proved a new champion of the faith. From the monastery which he established in the island of Iona his disciples went forth to the British kingdom of Strathclyde, to the Pictish tribes of the North, and to the Anglian kingdom of Northumbria. He is the founder of the Scottish Christian Church. Thus the message which St. Patrick had carried to Ireland came back across the stormy waters and spread through wide regions. There was however a distinction in the form of Christianity which reached England through the mission of St. Columba and that which was more generally accepted throughout the Christianised countries of Europe. It was monastic in its form, and it travelled from the East through Northern Ireland to its new home without touching at any moment the Roman centre. The Celtic churches therefore received a form of ecclesiastical government which was supported by the loosely knit communities of monks and preachers, and was not in these early decisive periods associated with the universal organisation of the Papacy.

*   *   *   *   *

In spite of the slow means of travel and scanty news, the Papacy had from an early stage followed with deep attention the results of St. Columba's labours. Its interest was excited not only by the spread of the Gospel, but also by any straying from the true path into which new Christians might be betrayed. It saw with thankfulness an ardent Christian movement afoot in these remote Northern islands, and with concern that it was from the outset independent of the Papal throne. These were the days when it was the first care of the Bishop of Rome that all Christ's sheep should be gathered into one fold. Here in the North, where so much zeal and fervour were evident, the faith seemed to be awkwardly and above all separately planted.

For various reasons, including the spreading of the Gospel, it was decided in the closing decade of the sixth century that a guide and teacher should be sent to England to diffuse and stimulate the faith, to convert the heathen, and also to bring about an effective working union between British Christians and the main body of the Church. For this high task Pope Gregory, afterwards called "the Great," and the ecclesiastical statesmen gathered in Rome selected a trusty and cultured monk named Augustine. St. Augustine, as he is known to history, began his mission in 596 under hopeful auspices. Kent had always been the part of the British Island most closely in contact with Europe, and in all its various phases the most advanced in culture. The King of Kent had married Bertha, a daughter of the Frankish king, the descendant of Clovis, now enthroned in Paris. Although her husband still worshipped Thor and Woden Queen Bertha had already begun to spread the truth through courtly circles. Her chaplain, an earnest and energetic Frank, was given full rein, and thus a powerful impulse came to the people of Kent, who were already in a receptive mood towards the dominant creed of Western Europe. St. Augustine, when he landed in Kent, was therefore aware that much had been prepared beforehand. His arrival infused a mood of action. With the aid of the Frankish princess he converted King Ethelbert, who had for reasons of policy long meditated this step. Upon the ruins of the ancient British church of St. Martin he refounded the Christian life of Canterbury, which was destined to become the centre and summit of religious England.

Ethelbert, as overlord of England, exercised an effective authority over the kingdoms of the South and West. His policy was at once skilful and ambitious; his conversion to Christianity, however sincere, was also in consonance with his secular aims. He was himself, as the only English Christian ruler, in a position where he might hold out the hand to the British princes, and, using the Christian faith as a bond of union, establish his supremacy over the whole country. This, no doubt, was also in accordance with the ideas which Augustine had carried from Rome. Thus at the opening of the seventh century Ethelbert and Augustine summoned a conference of the British Christian bishops. The place chosen in the Severn valley was on the frontier between the English and British domains, and far outside the bounds of the Kentish kingdom. Here, then, would be a chance of a general and lasting peace for both races, reconciled in the name of Christ; and of this settlement Ethelbert and his descendants could securely expect to be the heirs. We must regret that this hope, sustained by sagacious and benevolent politics, was not realised. It failed for two separate reasons: first, the sullen and jealous temper of the British bishops, and, secondly, the tactless arrogance of St. Augustine.

There were two conferences, with an interval. The discussions were ostensibly confined to interesting but uncontroversial questions. There was the date of Easter, which is still debated, and also the form of the tonsure. Augustine urged the Roman custom of shaving only the top of the head. The British bishops had perhaps imitated the Druidical method of shaving from the centre to the ears, leaving a fringe on the forehead. It was a choice of the grotesque. These were matters which might well be capable of adjustment, but which conveniently offered ample pasture upon which the conferences could browse in public, while the vital issues were settling themselves in an atmosphere of goodwill, or being definitely compacted behind the scenes.

But the British bishops were found in no mood to throw themselves into the strong embraces of Rome. Why should they, who had so long defended the Faith against horrible cruelties and oppression, now receive their guidance from a Saxon Kentish king whose conversion was brand-new, and whose political designs, however inspiring, were none the less obvious? The second conference ended in a complete rupture. When Augustine found himself in the presence of what he deemed to be unreasonable prejudice and deep-seated hostility, when he saw the few bishops who had been won over reproached by their brethren as backsliders and traitors, he fell back quite quickly upon threats. If British Christianity would not accept the fair offers now made the whole influence and prestige of Rome would be thrown against them upon the English side. The Saxon armies would be blessed and upheld by Rome and the unbroken traditions of the main Christian Church, and no sympathy would be felt for these long-faithful British Christians when they had their throats cut by the new English convert states. "If," the Saint exclaimed, "you will not have peace from your friends you shall have war from your foes." But this was no more than the British had faced for two hundred years. It was language they understood. The conference separated in enmity; the breach was irreparable. All further efforts by Rome through Ethelbert and the Kentish kingdom to establish even the slightest contact with Christian Britain were inexorably repulsed.

Augustine's mission therefore drew to a dignified but curtailed end. Except for the consecration of Mellitas as Bishop of the East Saxons in a church on the site of St. Paul's, he had made little attempt to proselytise outside Kent. From the title loosely accorded him of "Apostle of the English" he enjoyed for many centuries the credit of having re-converted the once-famous Roman province of Britannia to the Christian faith; and this halo has shone about him until comparatively recent times.

*   *   *   *   *

Almost a generation passed before envoys from Rome began to penetrate into Northern England and rally its peoples to Christianity, and then it came about in the wake of political and dynastic developments. By a series of victories Redwald, King of the East Angles, had established a wide dominion over the lands of Central England from the Dee to the Humber. With Redwald's aid the crown of

Northumbria was gained by an exiled prince, Edwin, who by his abilities won his way, step by step, to the foremost position in England. Even before the death of his ally Redwald, Edwin was recognised as overlord of all the English kingdoms except Kent, and the isles of Anglesey and Man were also reduced by his ships. He not only established his personal primacy, but the confederation founded by him foreshadowed the kingdom of all England that was later to take shape under the kings of Mercia and Wessex. Edwin married a Christian princess of Kent, whose religion he had promised to respect. Consequently, in her train from Canterbury to Edwin's capital at York there rode in 625 the first Roman missionary to Northern England, Paulinus, an envoy who had first come to Britain in the days of St. Augustine, twenty-four years before.

We have a picture agreeable and instructive of Edwin: "There was then a perfect peace in Britain wheresoever the dominion of King Edwin extended, and, as it is still proverbially said, a woman with her newborn babe might walk throughout the Island from sea to sea without receiving any harm. That King took such care for the good of his nation that in several places where he had seen clear springs near the highways he caused stakes to be fixed with proper drinking-vessels hanging on them for the refreshment of travellers, nor durst any man touch them for any other purpose than that for which they were designed, either for the great fear they had of the King or for the affection which they bore him." He revived the Roman style: "Not only were his banners borne before him in battle, but even in peace when he rode about his cities, townships, or provinces with his thanes. A standard-bearer was always wont to go before him when he walked anywhere in the streets in the Roman fashion."

Such in his heyday was the prince to whom Paulinus resorted. Paulinus converted Edwin, and the ample kingdom of Northumbria, shaped like England itself in miniature, became Christian. But this blessed event brought with it swift and dire consequences. The overlordship of Northumbria was fiercely resented by King Penda of Mercia, or, as we should now say, of the Midlands. The drama unfolded with staggering changes of fortune. In 633 Penda, the heathen, made an unnatural alliance with Cadwallon, the Christian

British King of North Wales, with the object of overthrowing the suzerainty of Edwin and breaking the Northumbrian power. Here for the first time noticed in history British and English fought side by side. Politics for once proved stronger than religion or race. In a savage battle near Doncaster Edwin was defeated and slain, and his head—not the last—was exhibited on the ramparts of captured York. It may be that York, long the home of a legion, still preserved Roman-British traditions which led them to welcome the British victors. This sudden destruction of the greatest king who had hitherto ruled in the Island brought in recoil an equally speedy vengeance. British Cadwallon had triumphed over Northumbria. Here at last was the chance, so long expected, of British vengeance upon their Saxon foes. Here was the faithful paying off of very old but very heavy debts. We might almost be seeing again the spirit of Boadicea.

But the inherent power of Northumbria was great. The name and fame of the slaughtered Edwin rang through the land. His successor, Oswald, of the house of Bernicia, which was one of the two provinces of the kingdom, had but to appear to find himself at the head of the newly Christianised and also infuriated Saxon warriors. Within a year of the death of Edwin Oswald destroyed Cadwallon and his British forces in a hard battle which fell out along the line of the Roman Wall. This was the last pitched battle between the Britons and the Saxons; and it must be admitted that the Britons fared as badly in conduct as in fortune. They had joined with the heathen Saxon Midlands to avenge their wrongs, and had exploited an English movement towards the disunity of the land. They had shattered this bright hope of the Christianity they professed, and now they were themselves overthrown and cast aside. The long story of their struggle with the invaders ended thus in no fine way; but what is important to our tale is that it had ended at last.

The destruction of Cadwallon and the clearance from Northumbria of the wild Western Britons, whose atrocities had united all the Saxon forces in the North, was the prelude to the struggle with King Penda. He was regarded by the Saxon tribes as one who had brought boundless suffering and slaughter upon them through a shameful pact with the hereditary foe. Nevertheless he prospered for a while.

He upheld the claims of Thor and Woden with all the strength of Mercia for seven years. He defeated, decapitated, and dismembered King Oswald, as he had destroyed his predecessor before him. But a younger brother of Oswald, Oswy by name, after a few years, settled the family account, and Penda fell by the sword he had drawn too often. Thus the power of Northumbria rose the stronger from the ordeal and eclipse through which its people had passed.

The failure of Ethelbert's attempt to make a Christian reunion of England and Britain left the direction of the immediate future with the Northumbrian Court. It was to York and not to Canterbury that Rome looked, and upon English, not British, armies that the hopes of organised Christendom were placed. When the disasters had overtaken Northumbria Paulinus had hastened back by sea to Canterbury. Neither he nor Augustine was the kind of man to face the brutal warfare of those times. Carefully trained as they were in the doctrines, interests, and policy of the Papacy, they were not the stuff of which martyrs or evangelists are made. This British incursion was too rough. But the lieutenant of Paulinus, one James the Deacon, stuck to his post through the whole struggle, and preached and baptised continually in the midst of rapine and carnage. Still more important than his work was that of the Celtic mission to Northumbria under St. Aidan. Much of Mercia and East Anglia, as well as Northumbria, was recovered to Christianity by the Celtic missionaries. Thus two streams of the Christian faith once more met in England, and the immediate future was to witness a struggle for supremacy between them.

With the defeat and death of Penda, and upon the surge of all the passions which had been loosed, Anglo-Saxon England was definitely rallied to the Christian faith. There was now no kingdom in which heathen practices prevailed. Indeed, apart from individuals, whose private adherence to Woden was overlooked, the whole Island was Christian. But this marvellous event, which might have brought in its train so many blessings, was marred by the new causes of division which now opened between the English and British peoples. To the ferocious British-English racial feud there was added a different view of Church government, which sundered the races almost as much as the difference between Christianity and heathenism. Henceforward the issue is no longer whether the Island shall be Christian or pagan, but whether the Roman or the Celtic view of Christianity shall prevail. These differences persisted across the centuries, much debated by the parties concerned.

The celebrated and largely successful attempt to solve them took place at the Synod of Whitby in 664. There the hinging issue was whether British Christianity should conform to the general life-plan of Christendom or whether it should be expressed by the monastic orders which had founded the Celtic Churches of the North. The issues hung in the balance, but in the end after much pious dissertation the decision was taken that the Church of Northumbria should be a definite part of the Church of Rome and of the Catholic system. Mercia soon afterwards conformed. Though the Celtic leader and his following retired in disgust to Iona, and the Irish clergy refused to submit, the importance of this event cannot be overrated. Instead of a religion controlled by the narrow views of abbots pursuing their strict rule of life in their various towns or remote resorts there was opened to every member of the English Church the broad vista of a world-state and universal communion. These events brought Northumbria to her zenith. In Britain for the first time there was achieved a unity of faith, morals, and Church government covering five-sixths of the Island. The decisive step had been taken in the spiritual sphere. The Island was now entirely Christian, and by far the greater and more powerful part was directly associated with the Papacy.

Rome had little reason to be satisfied with the mission of either Augustine or Paulinus. The Papacy realised that its efforts to guide and govern British Christianity through the kingdom of Kent had been misplaced. It now made a new plan, which illustrates the universal character of the Catholic Church. Two fresh emissaries were chosen in 668 to carry the light into the Northern mists, the first a native of Asia Minor, Theodore of Tarsus, the second an African named Hadrian from Carthage. These missionaries were of a stronger type than their precursors, and their character and integrity shone before all. When they arrived at Canterbury there were but three bishops from all England to greet them. When their work was finished the Anglican Church raised its mitred front in a majesty which has not yet been dimmed. Before he died in 690 Theodore had increased the number of bishoprics from seven to fourteen, and by his administrative skill he gave the Church a new cohesion. The Church has not canonised him as a saint. This remarkable Asiatic was the earliest of the statesmen of England, and guided her steps with fruitful wisdom.

*   *   *   *   *

There followed a long and intricate rivalry for leadership between the various Anglo-Saxon kings which occupied the seventh and eighth centuries. It was highly important to those whose span of life was cast in that period, but it left small marks on the subsequent course of history. Let a few words suffice. The primacy of Northumbria was menaced and finally ended by the inherent geographical and physical weakness of its position. It was liable to be beset from every quarter, from the north by the Picts, on the west by the British kingdom of Strathclyde, in the south by Mercia, those jealous Midlands still smarting from the suppression of Penda and the punishments inflicted upon his adherents. These antagonisms were too much for Northumbria to bear, and although great efforts were made and amid the exhausting feuds of rival kings some wise chieftains occasionally prevailed, its collapse as the leading community in the Island was inevitable.

Northumbria was fortunate however in having in this twilight scene a chronicler, to whom we have already referred, whose words have descended to us out of the long silence of the past. Bede, a monk of high ability, working unknown in the recesses of the Church, now comes forward as the most effective and almost the only audible voice from the British islands in these dim times. Unlike Gildas, Bede wrote history. The gratitude of the Middle Ages bestowed on Gildas the title of "the Wise," and the name of "the Venerable Bede" still carries with it a proud renown. He alone attempts to paint for us, and, so far as he can, explain the spectacle of Anglo-Saxon England in its first phase: a Christian England, divided by tribal, territorial, dynastic, and personal feuds into what an Elizabethan antiquary called the Heptarchy, seven kingdoms of varying strength, all professing the Gospel of Christ, and striving over each other for mastery by force and fraud. For almost exactly a hundred years, from

731 to 829, there was a period of ceaseless warfare, conducted with cruelty and rapine under a single creed.

The leadership of Saxon England passed to Mercia. For nearly eighty years two Mercian kings asserted or maintained their ascendancy over all England south of the Humber. Ethelbald and Offa reigned each for forty years. Ethelbald had been an exile before he became an autocrat. As a fugitive he consorted with monks, hermits, and holy men. On attaining power he did not discard his Christian piety, but he found himself much oppressed by the temptations of the flesh. St. Guthlac had comforted him in misfortune and poverty, but St. Boniface was constrained to rebuke him for his immorality.

The moral sense had grown so strong in matters of sex that Churchmen could now brand a king as licentious. Boniface from Germany censured Ethelbald for the "twofold sin" which he committed in nunneries by using the advantages of his royal position to gain himself favours otherwise beyond his reach. The chronicles of this sovereign are scanty. He showed charity to the poor; he preserved law and order; in the South in 733 he raided Wessex; and in 740 he laid parts of Northumbria waste while its harassed chief was struggling with the Picts. After this last victory he took to styling himself "King of the Southern English" and "King of Britain." South of the Humber these claims were made good.

*   *   *   *   *

Ethelbald, having been at length murdered by his guards, was succeeded by a greater man. Little is known of Offa, who reigned for the second forty years, but the imprint of his power is visible not only throughout England but upon the Continent. Offa was the contemporary of Charlemagne. His policy interlaced with that of Europe; he was reputed to be the first "King of the English," and he had the first quarrel since Roman times with the mainland.

Charlemagne wished one of his sons to marry one of Offa's daughters. Here we have an important proof of the esteem in which the Englishman was held. Offa stipulated that his son must simultaneously marry a daughter of Charlemagne. The founder of the Holy Roman Empire appeared at first incensed at this assumption of equality, but after a while he found it expedient to renew his friendship with Offa. It seems that "the King of the English" had placed an embargo upon Continental merchandise, and the inconvenience of this retaliation speedily overcame all points of pride and sentiment. Very soon Offa was again the Emperor's "dearest brother," and Charlemagne is seen agreeing to arrange that there should be reciprocity of royal protection in both countries for merchants, "according to the ancient custom of trading." Apparently the commodities in question were "black stones," presumably coal, from France, in return for English cloaks. There were also questions of refugees and extradition. Charlemagne was interested in repatriating a Scot who ate meat in Lent. He sent presents of an ancient sword and silken mantles. Thus we see Offa admitted to equal rank with the greatest figure in Europe. It is evident that the Island Power must have counted for a great deal in these days. Monarchs of mighty empires do not make marriage contracts for their children and beat out the details of commercial treaties with persons of no consequence.

The advantage given by these two long reigns when everything was in flux had reinstated the Island again as a recognisable factor in the world. We know that Offa styled himself not only *rex Anglorum*, but also "King of the whole land of the English" (*rex totius Anglorum patriæ*). This expression *rex Anglorum* is rightly signalised by historians as a milestone in our history. Here was an English king who ruled over the greatest part of the Island, whose trade was important, and whose daughters were fit consorts for the sons of Charles the Great. We learn about Offa almost entirely through his impact on his neighbours. It is clear from their records that he suppressed the under-kings of the Severn valley, that he defeated the West Saxons in Oxfordshire and subjugated Berkshire, that he decapitated the King of East Anglia, that he was master of London, that he extirpated the monarchy which Hengist had founded in Kent, and put down a Kentish rising with extreme severity. Henceforth he gave his own orders in Kent. He captured their mint and inscribed his name upon the coins issued by the Archbishop of Canterbury. One of these coins tells its own quaint tale. It is a gold dinar, nicely copied from an Arabic die, and is stamped with the superscription *rex Offa*. The Canterbury mint evidently regarded the Arabic as mere ornamentation, and all men would have been shocked had they known that it declared "There is no God but one and Mahomet is his Prophet." Offa established a good understanding with the Pope. The Supreme Pontiff addressed him as *rex Anglorum.* The Papal envoys in 787 were joyfully received in the hall of Offa, and were comforted by his assurances of reverence for St. Peter. These professions were implemented by a small annual tribute to the Papacy, part of it unwittingly paid in these same infidel coins which proclaimed an opposite creed.

In studying Offa we are like geologists who instead of finding a fossil find only the hollow shape in which a creature of unusual strength and size undoubtedly resided. Alcuin, one of the few recorders of this period at the Court of Charlemagne, addresses Offa in these terms: "You are a glory to Britain and a sword against its enemies." We have a tangible monument of Offa in the immense dyke which he caused to be built between converted Saxon England and the still unconquered British. The tables were now turned, and those who had never faltered in the old faith and had always maintained their independence had sunk in the estimation of men from the mere fact that they lived in barren mountainous lands, while their successful ravishers strode on in pomp and even dignity. This dyke, which runs over the hills and dales, leaving gaps for the impenetrable forests, from the mouth of the Severn to the neighbourhood of the Mersey, attests to our day the immense authority of the state over which Offa presided. When we reflect how grim was the struggle for life, and how the getting of enough food to keep body and soul together was the prime concern not only of families but of whole peoples, the fact that this extensive rampart could have been mainly the work of the lifetime and the will of a single man is startling. It conveys to us an idea of the magnitude and force of Offa's kingdom. Such works are not constructed except upon a foundation of effective political power. But "Offa's dyke" shows policy as well as man-power. In many sections it follows lines favourable to the British, and historians have concluded that it was a boundary rather than a fortification, and resulted from an agreement reached for common advantage. It was not a Roman wall, like those of Antonine and Hadrian, between savagery and civilisation, but rather the expression of a solemn treaty which for a long spell removed from Offa's problem the menace of a British incursion, and thus set him free with his back secure to parley and dispute with Europe.

*   *   *   *   *

Art and culture grew in the track of order. The English had brought with them from their Continental home a vigorous barbaric art and a primitive poetry. Once established in the Island, this art was profoundly affected by the Celtic genius for curve and colour, a genius suppressed by Roman provincialism, but breaking out again as soon as the Roman hand was removed. Christianity gave them a new range of subjects to adorn. The results are seen in such masterpieces as the Lindisfarne Gospels and the sculptured crosses of Northern England. A whole world of refinement and civilisation of which the monasteries were the home, and of which only fragments have come down to us, had come into being. Bede was universally honoured as the greatest scholar of his day. It is to his influence that the world owes the practice, adopted later, of reckoning the years from the birth of Christ. Aldhelm of Malmesbury was the most popular writer in Europe; of no author were more copies made in the monasteries of the Continent. Vernacular poetry flourished; in Wessex the first steps had been taken in the art of prose-writing. Another West Saxon, Boniface, from Crediton, near Exeter, was the Apostle of Germany. In the eighth century indeed England had claims to stand in the van of Western culture.

After the shapeless confusion of darker centuries, obscure to history and meaningless to almost all who lived through them, we now see a purpose steadily forming. England, with an independent character and personality, might scarcely yet be a part of a world civilisation as in Roman times, but there was a new England, closer than ever before to national unity, and with a native genius of her own. Henceforward an immortal spirit stood for all to see.

CHAPTER SIX

THE VIKINGS

AFTER THE FALL OF IMPERIAL ROME THE VICTORIOUS BARBARIANS were in their turn captivated and enthralled by the Gospel of Christ. Though no more successful in laying aside their sinful promptings than religious men and women are today, they had a common theme and inspiration. There was a bond which linked all the races of Europe. There was an international organisation which, standing erect in every country, was by far the most powerful, and indeed the only coherent surviving structure, and at the head of which the Bishop of Rome revived in a spiritual, or at least in an ecclesiastical form, the vanished authority of the Cæsars. The Christian Church became the sole sanctuary of learning and knowledge. It sheltered in its aisles and cloisters all the salvage of ancient days. It offered to men in their strife and error "the last solace of human woe, the last restraint of earthly power." Thus, while the light of pagan civilisation was by no means wholly extinguished, a new effulgence held, dazzled, and dominated the barbaric hordes, not only in our Island but throughout Europe. They were tamed and uplifted by the Christian revelation. Everywhere, from the Euphrates to the Boyne, old gods were forsworn, and a priest of Christ could travel far and wide, finding in every town an understanding brotherhood and a universal if sometimes austere hospitality.

Amid the turbulence and ignorance of the age of Roman decay all the intellectual elements at first found refuge in the Church, and

afterwards exercised mastery from it. Here was the school of politicians. The virtual monopoly of learning and the art of writing made
the Churchmen indispensable to the proud and violent chieftains
of the day. The clerics became the civil servants, and often the statesmen, of every Court. They fell naturally, inevitably, into the place
of the Roman magistrates whose garb they wore, and wear today.
Triumphant barbarism yielded itself insensibly to a structure, reliance
upon which was proved on numberless occasions to give success in the
unending struggle for power. After the convulsions and disorders of
the Dark Ages, when at last daylight fell again on the British Island,
she awoke to a world also profoundly changed, but devoid neither of
form nor majesty. There was even a gentler breeze in the air.

The fervour of the converted heathen brought in its train mischiefs
which opened new calamities. The Church was bound by its spirit to
inculcate mildness and mercy. It was led by zeal and by its interests
to fortify in every way the structure of its own power. The humility and
faith of the descendants of the invaders soon exposed them, in their
human frailty, to an organised exploitation which during the sixth
and seventh centuries led in many countries to an engrossment by the
Church of treasure and lands out of all proportion to its capacity to
control events. We see, then, Christendom pious but froward; spiritu-
ally united, but a prey to worldly feuds; in a state of grace, but by no
means free from ambition.

Upon this revived, convalescent, loosely-knit society there now
fell two blasting external assaults. The first came from the East. In
Arabia Mahomet unfurled the martial and sacred standards of Islam.
His celebrated escape from Mecca to Medina, called the Hejira, or
emigration, from which the Moslem era dates, took place in 622.
During the decades that followed, Mahomet and his successors, the
Caliphs, made themselves masters of all Arabia, Persia, much of
the Byzantine Empire, and the whole North African shore. At the
beginning of the next century, Islam crossed the Straits of Gibraltar
and prevailed in Spain, whence it was not finally to be dislodged
for nearly eight hundred years. At one moment France, too, seemed
about to succumb, but the Arabs were beaten back by Charles Martel,
grandfather of Charlemagne, in 732 at Poitiers. Thus, all the way

from Mecca, the power of Islam came almost to within striking distance of these islands.

For Britain, however, was reserved the second invading wave. It came from the North. In Scandinavia the Vikings fitted out their long-boats for sea. This double assault by Arab infidels and Nordic pirates distracted the weakened life of Europe for ten generations. It was not until the eleventh century that the steel-clad feudalism of medieval Christendom, itself consisting largely of the converted descendants of the Vikings, assigned limits to the Arab conquests, and established at the side of the Christian Church ample and effective military power.

*   *   *   *   *

Measure for measure, what the Saxon pirates had given to the Britons was meted out to the English after the lapse of four hundred years. In the eighth century a vehement manifestation of conquering energy appeared in Scandinavia. Norway, Sweden, and Denmark threw up bands of formidable fighting men who, in addition to all their other martial qualities, were the hardy rovers of the sea. The causes which led to this racial ebullition were the spontaneous growth of their strength and population, the thirst for adventure, and the complications of dynastic quarrels. There was here no question of the Danes or Norsemen being driven westward by new pressures from the steppes of Asia. They moved of their own accord. Their prowess was amazing. One current of marauding vigour struck southwards from Sweden, and not only reached Constantinople, but left behind it potent germs which across the centuries influenced European Russia. Another contingent sailed in their long-boats from Norway to the Mediterranean, harried all the shores of the inland sea, and were with difficulty repulsed by the Arab kingdoms of Spain and the north coast of Africa. The third far-ranging impulse carried the Scandinavian buccaneers to the British Isles, to Normandy, to Iceland, and presently across the Atlantic Ocean to the American continent.

The relations between the Danes and the Norwegians were tangled and varying. Sometimes they raided in collusion; sometimes they fought each other in desperate battles; but to Saxon England they presented themselves in the common guise of a merciless scourge. They were incredibly cruel. Though not cannibals, they were accustomed to cook their feasts of victory in cauldrons placed upon, or on spits stuck in, the bodies of their vanquished enemies. When, after a battle in Ireland between Northmen and Danes, the local Irish inhabitants—themselves none too particular—expressed horror at this disgusting habit, and, being neutral, asked them why they did it, they received the answer, "Why not? They would do it to us if they won." It was said of these Scandinavian hunters that they never wept for their sins, nor for the death of their friends. It is certain however that in many places where the raiding war-bands settled down they soon developed luxurious habits. They took baths. They wore silken robes. Their ships carried tents and beds for use on shore. Their war-chiefs in every land into which they penetrated practised polygamy, and in the East adopted quite readily the harem system. One conquering leader was credited with possessing no fewer than eight hundred concubines; but this was probably a Biblical illustration. When Limerick was captured from them in the year 936 the Irish were staggered by the beauty of the womenfolk already in the hands of the marauders, and by the mass of silks and embroideries with which they were decked. No doubt they recovered their poise before long.

*   *   *   *   *

The soul of the Vikings lay in the long-ship. They had evolved, and now, in the eighth and ninth centuries, carried to perfection, a vessel which by its shallow draught could sail far up rivers, or anchor in innumerable creeks and bays, and which by its beautiful lines and suppleness of construction could ride out the fiercest storms of the Atlantic Ocean.

We are singularly well informed about these ships. Half a dozen have been dug up almost intact. The most famous was unearthed at Gokstad, in Norway, in 1880, from a tumulus. It is almost complete, even to the cooking-pots and draught-boards of the sailors. It was remeasured with precision in 1944 in spite of other distractions. This ship was of the medium size, 76 feet 6 inches from stem to stern, 17 feet 6 inches beam, and drawing only 2 feet 9 inches amidships. She was clinker-built of sixteen strakes a side of solid oak planks, fastened with tree-nails and iron bolts, and caulked with cord of plaited animal-hair. Her planks fastened to the ribs with bast ties gave the framework great elasticity. She had a deck of loose unnailed boards, but no doubt her stores were contained in lockers which have perished. Her mast was stepped in a huge solid block, which, says Professor Collingwood (whose description I have revised to date), was so cunningly supported "that while the mast stands steady and firm there is no strain on the light elastic frame of the ship." She had sixteen oars a side, varying in length between 17 and 19 feet; the longer oars were used at the prow and stern, where the gunwale was higher above the water-line; they were all beautifully shaped, and passed through circular rowlocks cut in the main strake, which were neatly fitted with shutters that closed when the oars were shipped. Her rudder, stepped to the starboard quarter, was a large, short oar of cricket-bat shape, fitted with a movable tiller, and fastened to the ship by an ingenious contrivance which gave the blade full play. The mast, 40 feet high, had a long, heavy yard with a square sail. She could carry a smaller boat or dinghy, three of which were discovered with her. The Gokstad ship would carry a crew of fifty, and if necessary another thirty warriors or captives, in all weathers, for a month.

Such was the vessel which, in many different sizes, bore the Vikings to the plunder of the civilised world—to the assault of Constantinople, to the siege of Paris, to the foundation of Dublin, and the discovery of America. Its picture rises before us vivid and bright: the finely carved, dragon-shaped prow; the high, curving stern; the long row of shields, black and yellow alternately, ranged along the sides; the gleam of steel; the scent of murder. The long-ships in which the great ocean voyages were made were of somewhat stouter build, with a higher freeboard; but the Gokstad model was reproduced in 1892 and navigated by a Norwegian crew across the Atlantic in four weeks.

Yet this superb instrument of sea-power would have been useless without the men who handled it. All were volunteers. Parties were formed under leaders of marked ability. In the sagas we read of crews of "champions, or merry men": a ship's company picked no doubt from many applicants, "as good at the helm or oar as they were with the sword." There were strict regulations, or early "Articles of War," governing these crews once they had joined. Men were taken between the ages of sixteen and sixty, but none without a trial of his strength and activity. No feud or old quarrel must be taken up while afloat or on service. No woman was allowed on board. News was to be reported to the captain alone. All taken in war was to be brought to the pile or stake, and there sold and divided according to rule. This war booty was personal; that is to say, it was not part of the property which passed by Scandinavian law to a man's kindred. He was entitled to have it buried with him.

"With anything like equal numbers," says Oman, "the Vikings were always able to hold their own, but when the whole countryside had been raised, and the men of many shires came swarming up against the raiders, they had to beware lest they might be crushed by numbers." It was only when a fleet of very exceptional strength had come together that the Norsemen could dare to offer their opponents battle in the open field. Fighting was after all not so much their object as plunder, and when the land was rallied in overwhelming force the invaders took to their ships again and sailed off to renew their ravages in some yet intact province. They soon learned moreover to secure for themselves the power of rapid locomotion on land. When they came to shore they would sweep together all the horses of the neighbourhood and move themselves and their plunder on horseback across the land. It was with no intention of fighting as cavalry that they collected the horses, but only for swift marching. The first mention of this practice in England comes in the year 866, when "a great heathen army came to the land of the East Angles, and there was the army a-horse."[1]

When we reflect upon the brutal vices of these salt-water bandits, pirates as shameful as any whom the sea has borne, or recoil from their villainous destruction and cruel deeds, we must also remember the discipline, the fortitude, the comradeship and martial virtues which made them at this period beyond all challenge the most formidable and daring race in the world.

*   *   *   *   *

One summer's day, probably in 789, while "the innocent English people, spread through their plains, were enjoying themselves in tranquillity and yoking their oxen to the plough," news was carried to the King's officer, the Reeve of Dorchester, that three ships had arrived on the coast. The Reeve "leapt on his horse and rode with a few men to the harbour [probably Portland], thinking that they were merchants and not enemies. Giving his commands as one who had authority, he ordered them to be sent to the King's town; but they slew him on the spot and all who were with him." This was a foretaste of the murderous struggle which, with many changes of fortune, was to harry and devastate England for two hundred and fifty years. It was the beginning of the Viking Age.

In 793, on a January morning, the wealthy monastic settlement of Lindisfarne (or Holy Island), off the Northumbrian coast, was suddenly attacked by a powerful fleet from Denmark. They sacked the place, devoured the cattle, killed many of the monks, and sailed away with a rich booty in gold, jewels, and sacred emblems, and all the monks who were likely to fetch a good price in the European slave-market. This raid had been planned with care and knowledge. It was executed by complete surprise in the dead of winter before any aid from the shore could reach the island. The news of the atrocity travelled far and wide, not only in England but throughout Europe, and the loud cry of the Church sounded a general alarm. Alcuin, the Northumbrian, wrote home from the Court of Charlemagne to condole with his countrymen:

> Lo, it is almost three hundred and fifty years that we and our forefathers have dwelt in this fair land, and never has such a horror before appeared in Britain, such as we have just suffered from the heathen. It was not thought possible that they could have made such a voyage. Behold the church of St. Cuthbert sprinkled with the blood of the priests of Christ, robbed of all its ornaments. . . . In that place where, after the departure of Paulinus from York, the Christian faith had its beginning among us, there is the beginning of woe and calamity. . . . Portents of this woe came before it. . . . What signifies that rain of blood during Lent in the town of York?

When the next year the raiders returned and landed near Jarrow they were stoutly attacked while harassed by bad weather. Many were killed. Their "king" was captured and put to a cruel death, and the fugitives carried so grim a tale back to Denmark that for forty years the English coasts were unravaged. In this period the Vikings were little inclined for massed invasion or conquest, but, using their sea-power, made minor descents upon the east coast of Scotland and the Scottish islands. The monastic colonies which had hitherto found a safe retreat in these islands now found themselves as a particularly vulnerable prey. Their riches and their isolation left them the most attractive quarry of the sea-rovers. Iona was pillaged and destroyed in 802. The Irish religious establishments also presented attractive prizes to marauding greed, and from now onward their sufferings were unceasing. The vitality of the Church repaired the ruin with devoted zeal. The Vikings, having a large choice of action, allowed an interval of recovery before paying another visit. Iona was sacked thrice, and the monastery of Kildare no fewer than fourteen times.

Buccaneering had become a steady profession, and the Church was their perpetually replenished treasure-house. Charlemagne's historian, Eginhard, records that the ravages were continuous, and a new shadow of fear spread over Christendom. No effective measures were however taken, and the raiding business was so profitable that the taste for it spread throughout Scandinavia. "These merry, clean-limbed, stouthearted gentlemen of the Northlands," as one of their Scottish eulogists describes them, sailed every year in greatly increasing numbers upon their forays, and returned triumphant and enriched. And their example inspired all audacious spirits and younger sons. Other fleets ranged more widely. They broke into the Mediterranean. Charlemagne, gazing through a window in a town near Narbonne, saw these sinister ships haunting the coast and uttered an impressive warning of the wrath to come.

*   *   *   *   *

It was not till 835 that the storm broke in fury, and fleets, sometimes of three or four hundred vessels, rowed up the rivers of England, France, and Russia in predatory enterprises on the greatest scale. For thirty years Southern England was constantly attacked. Paris was more than once besieged. Constantinople was assaulted. The harbour towns in Ireland were captured and held. Dublin was founded by the

Vikings under Olaf. In many cases now the raiders settled upon the conquered territory. The Swedish element penetrated into the heart of Russia, ruling the river towns and holding the trade to ransom. The Norwegian Vikings, coming from a still more severe climate, found the Scottish islands good for settlement. They colonised the Shetlands, the Faroes, and Ireland. They reached Greenland and Stoneland (Labrador). They sailed up the St. Lawrence. They discovered America; but they set little store by the achievement.

For a long time no permanent foothold was gained in Britain or France. It was not until 865, when resistance on the Continent had temporarily stiffened, that the great Danish invasion of Northumbria and Eastern England began.

Saxon England was at this time ripe for the sickle. The invaders broke in upon the whole eastern seaboard, once guarded by the "Count of the Saxon Shore," with its Imperial fortresses in ruins, buried already under the soil of centuries. No Roman galleys plied their oars upon the patrol courses. There was no Imperial Government to send a great commander or a legion to the rescue. But on all sides were abbeys and monasteries, churches, and even cathedrals, possessed in that starveling age of treasures of gold and silver, of jewels, and also large stores of food, wine, and such luxuries as were known. The pious English had accepted far too literally the idea of the absolution of sins as the consequence of monetary payment to the Church. Their sins were many, their repentances frequent, and the Church had thrived. Here were easy prizes for sharp swords to win.

To an undue subservience to the Church the English at this time added military mismanagement. Their system of defence was adapted to keeping the survivors of the ancient Britons in their barren mountain-lands or guarding the frontier against an incursion by a Saxon neighbour. The local noble, when called upon by his chief or king, could call upon the able-bodied cultivators of the soil to serve in their own district for about forty days. This service was grudgingly given, and when it was over the army dispersed without paying any serious regard to the enemies who might be afoot or the purposes for which the campaign had been undertaken. Now they found themselves in contact with a different type of enemy. The Danes and Norsemen had not only the advantages of surprise which sea-power so long imparted, but they showed both mobility and skill on land. They adopted the habit of fortifying their camps with almost Roman thoroughness. Their stratagems also have been highly praised. Among these "feigned flight" was foremost. Again and again we read that the English put the heathen army to rout, but at the end of the day the Danes held the field. On one occasion their leader, who was besieging a town, declared himself to be dying and begged the bishop of the place to give him Christian burial. The worthy Churchman rejoiced in the conversion and acceded to the request, but when the body of the deceased Viking was brought into the town for Christian burial it suddenly appeared that the attendants were armed warriors of proved quality, disguised in mourning, who without more ado set to work on sack and slaughter. There are many informing sidelights of this kind upon the manners and customs of the Vikings. They were, in fact, the most audacious and treacherous type of pirate and shark that had ever yet appeared, and, owing to the very defective organisation of the Saxons and the conditions of the period, they achieved a fuller realisation of their desires than any of those who have emulated their proficiency—and there have been many.

*   *   *   *   *

In Viking legend at this period none was more famous than Ragnar Lodbrok, or "Hairy-breeches." He was born in Norway, but was connected with the ruling family of Denmark. He was a raider from his youth. "West over seas" was his motto. His prow had ranged from the Orkneys to the White Sea. In 845 he led a Viking fleet up the Seine and attacked Paris. The onslaught was repulsed, and plague took an unforeseeable revenge upon the buccaneers. He turned his mobile arms against Northumbria. Here again fate was adverse. According to Scandinavian story, he was captured by King Ælle of Northumbria, and cast into a snake-pit to die. Amid the coiling mass of loathsome adders he sang to the end his death-song. Ragnar had four sons, and as he lay among the venomous reptiles he uttered a potent threat: "The little pigs would grunt now if they knew how it fares with the old boar." The skalds tell us how his sons received the news. Bjorn "Ironside" gripped his spear shaft so hard that the print of his fingers remained stamped upon it. Hvitserk was playing chess, but he clenched his fingers upon a pawn so tightly that the blood started from under his nails. Sigurd "Snake-eye" was trimming his nails with a knife, and kept on paring until he cut into the bone. But the fourth son was the one who counted. Ivar, "the Boneless," demanded the precise details of his father's execution, and his face "became red, blue, and pale by turns, and his skin appeared puffed up by anger."[2]

A form of vengeance was prescribed by which sons should requite the killer of their fathers. It was known as the "Blood-red Eagle." The flesh and ribs of the killer must be cut and sawn out in an aquiline pattern, and then the dutiful son with his own hands would tear out the palpitating lungs. This was the doom which in legend overtook King Ælle. But the actual consequences to England were serious. Ivar "the Boneless" was a warrior of command and guile. He was the mastermind behind the Scandinavian invasion of England in the last quarter of the ninth century. He it was who planned the great campaigns by which East Anglia, Deira in Northumbria, and Mercia were conquered. Hitherto he had been fighting in Ireland, but he now appeared in 866 in East Anglia. In the spring of 867 his powerful army, organised on the basis of ships' companies, but now all mounted not for fighting but for locomotion, rode north along the old Roman road and was ferried across the Humber.

He laid siege to York. And now—too late—the Northumbrians, who had been divided in their loyalties between two rival kings, forgot their feuds and united in one final effort. They attacked the Danish army before York. At first they were successful; the heathens were driven back upon the city walls. The defenders sallied out, and in the confusion the Vikings defeated them all with grievous slaughter, killing both their kings and destroying completely their power of resistance. This was the end of Northumbria. The North of England never recovered its ascendancy.

As Hodgkin has put it:

The schools and monasteries dwindled into obscurity or nothingness; and the kingdom which had produced Bede and Alcuin, which had left the great stone crosses as masterpieces of Anglican art, and as evidences of Anglican poetry the poems of Cædmon and the Vision of the Rood, sank back in the generation following the defeat of the year 867 sank back into the old life of obscure barbarism. . . . A dynasty was broken, a religion was half smothered, and a culture was barbarised.[3]

Simeon of Durham, writing a hundred and fifty years after this disastrous battle at York, confirms these lamentations:

The army raided here and there and filled every place with bloodshed and sorrow. Far and wide it destroyed the churches and monasteries with fire and sword. When it departed from a place it left nothing standing but roofless walls. So great was the destruction that at the present day one can scarcely see anything left of these places, nor any sign of their former greatness.[4]

But Ivar's object was nothing less than the conquest of Mercia, which, as all men knew, had for nearly a hundred years represented the strength of England. Ivar lay before Nottingham. The King of Mercia called for help from Wessex. The old King of Wessex was dead, but his two sons, Ethelred and Alfred, answered the appeal. They marched to his aid, and offered to join him in his attack upon the besiegers' lines; but the Mercians flinched, and preferred a parley. Ivar warred with policy as well as arms. He had not harmed churches at York and Ripon. He was content to set up a vassal king, one Egbert, in Northumbria, and after ending the campaign of 868 by a treaty which left him master of Nottingham he spent the winter fortifying himself in York.

While the Danes in their formidable attempt at conquest spread out from East Anglia, subdued Mercia, and ravaged Northumbria, the King of Wessex and his brother Alfred quietly built up their strength. Their fortunes turned on balances so delicate and precarious that even the slightest addition to their burdens must have been fatal. It was therefore a deliverance when Ivar, after breaking the Treaty of Nottingham and subjecting King Edmund of East Anglia to martyrdom, suddenly quitted England for ever. The annals of Ulster explain that Olaf and Ivar, the two kings of the Northmen, came again to Dublin in 870 from Scotland, and "a very great spoil of captives, English, British, and Pictish, was carried away to Ireland." But then there is this final entry: "872. Ivar, King of the Northmen of all Ireland and Britain, ended his life." He had conquered Mercia and East Anglia. He had captured the major stronghold of the kingdom of Strathclyde, Dumbarton. Laden with loot and seemingly invincible, he settled in Dublin, and died there peacefully two years later. The pious chroniclers report that he "slept in Christ." Thus it may be that he had the best of both worlds.

*   *   *   *   *

The Danish raiders now stayed longer every year. In the summer the fleets came over to plunder and destroy, but each year the tendency was to dally in a more genial and more verdant land. At last the warrior's absence on the raids became long enough and the conditions of his conquest sure enough for him to bring over his wife and family. Thus again behind piracy and rapine there grew the process of settlement. But these settlements of the Danes differed from those of the Saxons; they were the encampment of armies, and their boundaries were the fighting fronts sustained by a series of fortified towns. Stamford, Nottingham, Lincoln, Derby, Leicester were the bases of the new invading force. Behind their frontier lines the soldiers of one decade were to become the colonists and landowners of the next. The Danish settlement in England was essentially military. They cut their way with their swords, and then planted themselves deeply in the soil. The warrior type of farmer asserted from the first a status different from the ordinary agriculturist. Without any coherent national organisation to repel from the land on which they had settled the ever-unknowable descents from the seas, the Saxons, now for four centuries entitled to be deemed the owners of the soil, very nearly succumbed completely to the Danish inroads. That they did not was due—as almost every critical turn of historic fortune has been due—to the sudden apparition in an era of confusion and decay of one of the great figures of history.

CHAPTER SEVEN

ALFRED THE GREAT

THE STORY OF ALFRED IS MADE KNOWN TO US IN SOME DETAIL in the pages of Asser, a monk of St. David's, who became Bishop of Sherborne. The Bishop dwells naturally upon the religious and moral qualities of his hero; but we must also remember that, in spite of ill-health, he was renowned as a hunter, and that his father had taken him to Rome as a boy, so that he had a lively comprehension of the great world. Alfred began as second-in-command to his elder brother, the King. There were no jealousies between them, but a marked difference of temperament. Ethelred inclined to the religious view that faith and prayer were the prime agencies by which the heathen would be overcome. Alfred, though also devout, laid the emphasis upon policy and arms.

In earlier years the overlordship of Mercia had never been popular, and her kings had made the serious mistake of quarrelling with the See of Canterbury. When, in 825, the Mercian army, invading Wessex, was overthrown by Alfred's grandfather, King Egbert, at Ellandun, near Swindon, all the South and East made haste to come to terms with the victor, and the union of Kent, the seat of the Primate, with Wessex, now the leading English kingdom, created a solid Southern block. This, which had been the aim of West Saxon policy for many generations, was achieved just in time to encounter the invasion from the North. And Wessex was strategically strong, with sharp ridges facing north, and none of those long, slow rivers up which the Danes used to steer their long-ships into the heart of Mercia. Wessex had moreover developed a local organisation which gave her exceptional resiliency under attack: the alderman at the head of the shire could act on his own account. The advantages of this system were later to be proved. Definite districts, each under an accepted commander, or governor, for civil and military purposes, constituted a great advance on the ancient tribal kingdoms, or the merely personal union of tribes under a single king. When the dynasties of Kent, Northumbria, and Mercia had disappeared all eyes turned to Wessex, where there was a royal house going back without a break to the first years of the Saxon settlement.

The Danes had occupied London, not then the English capital, but a town in the kingdom of Mercia, and their army had fortified itself at Reading. Moving forward, they met the forces of the West Saxons on the Berkshire downs, and here, in January 871, was fought the Battle of Ashdown. Both sides divided their forces into two commands. Ethelred tarried long at his devotions. The Vikings, with their brightly painted shields and banners, their finery and golden bracelets, made the West Saxons seem modest by contrast. As they slowly approached they clashed their shields and weapons and raised long, repeated, and defiant war-cries. Although archery was not much in use, missiles began to fly. The King was still at his prayers. God came first, he declared to those who warned him that the battle must soon be joined. "But Alfred," according to Bishop Asser, who had the account from "truthful eyewitnesses,"

> seeing the heathen had come quickly on to the field and were ready for battle . . . could bear the attacks of the enemy no longer, and he had to choose between withdrawing altogether or beginning the battle without waiting for his brother. At last, like a wild boar, he led the Christian forces boldly against the army of the enemy . . . in spite of the fact that the King had not yet arrived. And so, relying on God's counsel and trusting to His help, he closed the shield-wall in due order and thereupon moved his standards against the enemy.[1]

ENGLAND DURING THE DANISH INVASIONS

STRATHCLYDE

GALLOWAY

CUMBRIA

ENGLISH NORTHUMBRIA · Durham

DANISH NORTHUMBRIA · York

DANELAW

· Lincoln

Derby · Nottingham
· Leicester · Stamford
DANISH MERCIA

Brunanburh

EAST ANGLIA

GUTHRUM'S KINGDOM

ENGLISH MERCIA

WALES

GWYNEDD

POWYS

· Glastonbury

· Ashdown

· Chippenham

· Ethandun

W E S S E X

London · Maldon

Canterbury

· Wareham

CORNWALL

MILES
0   25   50   75   100

SAXON ENGLAND IN THE EIGHTH CENTURY

STRATHCLYDE

GALLOWAY

CUMBRIA

LOTHIAN

Lindisfarne

NORTHUMBRIA

DIERA

· York

MERCIA

NORTH WALES

WEST WALES

EAST ANGLIA

ESSEX

London ·

Canterbury

KENT

· Glastonbury

W E S S E X

Winchester ·

SUSSEX

MILES
0   25   50   75   100

The fight was long and hard. King Ethelred, his spiritual duty done, soon joined his brother. "The heathens," said the Bishop, "had seized the higher ground, and the Christians had to advance uphill. There was in that place a single stunted thorn tree which we have seen with our own eyes. Round about this tree, then, the opposing ranks met in conflict, with a great shouting from all men—one side bent on evil, the other side fighting for life and their loved ones and their native land." At last the Danes gave way, and, hotly pursued, fled back to Reading. They fled till nightfall; they fled through the night and the next day, and the whole breadth of Ashdown—meaning the Berkshire hills—was strewn with their corpses, among which were found the body of one of the Viking kings and five of his jarls.

The results of this victory did not break the power of the Danish army; in a fortnight they were again in the field. But the Battle of Ashdown justly takes its place among historic encounters because of the greatness of the issue. If the West Saxons had been beaten all England would have sunk into heathen anarchy. Since they were victorious the hope still burned for a civilised Christian existence in this Island. This was the first time the invaders had been beaten in the field. The last of the Saxon kingdoms had withstood the assault upon it. Alfred had made the Saxons feel confidence in themselves again. They could hold their own in open fight. The story of this conflict at Ashdown was for generations a treasured memory of the Saxon writers. It was Alfred's first battle.

All through the year 871 the two armies waged deadly war. King Ethelred soon fell sick and died. Although he had young children there was no doubt who his successor must be. At twenty-four Alfred became King, and entered upon a desperate inheritance. To and fro the fighting swayed, with varying fortunes. The Danes were strongly reinforced from overseas; "the summer army," as it was called, "innumerable," "eager to fight against the army of the West Saxons," arrived to join them. Seven or eight battles were fought, and we are told the Danes usually held the field. At Wilton, in the summer, about a month after Alfred had assumed the crown, he sustained a definite defeat in the heart of his own country. His numbers had been worn down by death and desertion, and once again in the field the Vikings' ruse of a feigned retreat was successful.

On the morrow of this misfortune Alfred thought it best to come to terms while he still had an army. We do not know the conditions, but there is no doubt that a heavy payment was among them. "The Saxons made peace with the heathen on the condition that they should depart from them, and this they did," declares the *Chronicle* laconically. But as they took three or four months before retiring upon London it seems that they waited for the Danegeld to be paid. Nevertheless Alfred and his Saxons had in all this fighting convinced the Vikings of their redoubtable force. By this inglorious treaty and stubborn campaign Alfred secured five years in which to consolidate his power.

The reasons which led the Danes to make a truce with Alfred are hard to analyse at this date. They were certainly convinced that only by prolonged and bloody fighting could they master the West Saxons. Both sides liked war, and this had been ding-dong: there was little to show but scars and corpses on either side. But Alfred had always counted upon the invaders dividing, and the stresses at work within the heathen army justified his policy.

Still maintaining their grip on London, the Danes moved back to the Midlands, which were now in complete submission. "The Mercians made peace with the army." Their king Burgred in 874 was driven overseas, and died in piety under the Papal compassion in Rome. "After his expulsion," says Asser, "the heathen subjected the whole kingdom of the Mercians to their lordship." They set up a local puppet, in a fashion which has often been imitated since, after he had given hostages and taken an oath "that he would not obstruct their wishes, and would be obedient in everything."

*   *   *   *   *

But now in the last quarter of the century a subtle, profound change came over the "Great Heathen Army." Alfred and the men of Wessex had proved too stubborn a foe for easy subjugation. Some of the Danes wished to settle on the lands they already held; the rest were for continuing the war at a suitable moment till the whole country was conquered. Perhaps these two bodies acted in concert, the former providing a sure and solid base, the latter becoming an expeditionary force. Thus, after mauling the kingdom of Strathclyde and carrying off the stock and implements of agriculture nearly half of the sea-pirates settled themselves in Northumbria and East Anglia. Henceforward they began "to till the ground for a livelihood." Here was a great change. We must remember their discipline and organisation. The ships' companies, acting together, had hitherto fought ashore as soldiers. All their organisation of settlements was military. The sailors had turned soldiers, and the soldiers had turned yeomen. They preserved that spirit of independence, regulated only by comradeship and discipline for vital purposes, which was the life of the long-ship.

The whole of the East of England thus received a class of cultivator who, except for purposes of common defence, owed allegiance to none; who had won his land with the sword, and was loyal only to the army organisation which enabled him to keep it. From Yorkshire to Norfolk this sturdy, upstanding stock took root. As time passed they forgot the sea; they forgot the army; they thought only of the land—their own land. They liked the life. Although they were sufficiently skilful agriculturists, there was nothing they could teach the older inhabitants; they brought no new implements or methods, but they were resolved to learn.

They were not dependent wholly upon their own labour. They must have exploited the former possessors and their serfs. The distribution of the land was made around a unit which could support a family. What eight oxen could plough in a certain time under prescribed conditions, much disputed by students, became the measure of the holding. They worked hard themselves, but obviously they used the local people too.

Thus the Danish differs in many ways from the Saxon settlement four hundred years earlier. There was no idea of exterminating the older population. The two languages were not very different; the way of life, the methods of cultivation, very much the same. The colonists —for such they had now become—brought their families from Scandinavia, but also it is certain that they established human and natural relations with the expropriated English. The blood-stream of these vigorous individualists, proud and successful men of the sword, mingled henceforward in the Island race. A vivifying, potent, lasting, and resurgent quality was added to the breed. As modern steel is hardened by the alloy of special metals in comparatively small quantities, this strong strain of individualism, based upon land-ownership, was afterwards to play a persistent part, not only in the blood but in the politics of England. When in the reign of Henry II, after much disorder, great laws were made and royal courts of justice were opened descendants of these hardy farmers—not only "sokemen" or independent peasants, but much smaller folk—were found in a state of high assertiveness. The tribulations of another three hundred years had not destroyed their original firmness of character nor their deep attachment to the conquered soil. All through English history this strain continues to play a gleaming part.

The reformed and placated pirate-mariners brought with them many Danish customs. They had a different notation, which they would have been alarmed to hear described as the "duodecimal system." They thought in twelves instead of tens, and in our own day in certain parts of East Anglia the expression "the long hundred" (*i.e.*, 120) is heard on market-days.

They had a different view of social justice from that entertained by the manorialised Saxons. Their customary laws as they gradually took shape were an undoubted improvement upon the Saxon theme.

> With East Anglia we enter the region within which Danish influence endured. Long before the Norman Conquest it had developed a distinctive form of rural society, which preserved many Scandinavian features, and in which the free man of peasant condition was holding his own successfully against the contemporary drift towards manorialism.[2]

Scandinavian England reared a free peasant population which the burdens of taxation and defence had made difficult in Wessex and English Mercia. And this population related itself so closely to the original invaders that students seek in the Domesday Book of the eleventh century for the means of estimating the size of the Viking armies in the ninth. We shall see presently the equitable, deferential terms which even after their final victory the Anglo-Saxon monarchs proffered to the districts settled by the Danes, known as the Danelaw. It remained only for conversion to Christianity to mingle these races inextricably in the soul and body of a nation. These considerations may aptly fill the five years' breathing-space which Alfred had gained by courageous fighting and politic Danegeld. In this interval Halfdene, the Viking king, departed like Ivar from the scene. The tortured, plundered Church requited his atrocities by declaring that God punished him in the long run by madness and a smell which made his presence unendurable to his fellows.

At Lindisfarne, in Dane-ravaged Northumbria, a pathetic tale is told. The ruined monks quitted their devastated, polluted sanctuary and carried on their shoulders the body of St. Cuthbert and the bones of St. Aidan. After seven years of pilgrimage by land and sea they established themselves in a new patrimony of St. Cuthbert as Chester-le-Street. The veneration felt throughout the North for St. Cuthbert brought such wealth to his see that in 995 its bishops began to build a new cathedral on the rock at Durham. Thither St. Cuthbert's bones were taken, and so great was his prestige that until the nineteenth century the Bishops of Durham were Prince-Bishops, exercising immense power in North-Eastern England.

*   *   *   *   *

Alfred's dear-bought truce was over. Guthrum, the new war-leader of the mobile and martial part of the heathen army, had formed a large design for the subjugation of Wessex. He operated by sea and land. The land army marched to Wareham, close to Portland Bill, where the sea army joined him in Poole harbour. In this region they fortified themselves, and proceeded to attack Alfred's kingdom by raid and storm from every quarter. The prudent King sought peace and offered an indemnity. At the same time it seems probable that he had hemmed in the land army very closely at Wareham. The Danes took the gold, and "swore upon the Holy Ring" they would depart and keep a faithful peace. With a treachery to which all adjectives are unequal they suddenly darted away and seized Exeter. Alfred, mounting his infantry, followed after, but arrived too late. "They were in the fortress, where they could not be come at." But let all heathen beware of breaking oaths! A frightful tempest smote the sea army. They sought to join their comrades by sea. They were smitten in the neighbourhood of Swanage by the elements, which in those days were believed to be personally directed by the Almighty. A hundred and twenty ships were sunk, and upwards of five thousand of these perjured marauders perished as they deserved. Thus the whole careful plan fell to pieces, and Alfred, watching and besetting Exeter, found his enemies in the summer of 877 in the mood for a new peace. They swore it with oaths of still more compliant solemnity, and they kept it for about five months.

Then in January 878 occurred the most surprising reversal of Alfred's fortunes. His headquarters and Court lay at Chippenham, in Wiltshire. It was Twelfth Night, and the Saxons, who in these days of torment refreshed and fortified themselves by celebrating the feasts of the Church, were off their guard, engaged in pious exercises, or perhaps even drunk. Down swept the ravaging foe. The whole army of Wessex, sole guarantee of England south of the Thames, was dashed into confusion. Many were killed. The most part stole away to their houses. A strong contingent fled overseas. Refugees arrived with futile appeals at the Court of France. Only a handful of officers and personal attendants hid themselves with Alfred in the marshes and forests of Somerset and the Isle of Athelney which rose from the quags. This was the darkest hour of Alfred's fortunes. It was some months before he could even start a guerrilla. He led "with thanes and vassals an unquiet life in great tribulation. . . . For he had nothing wherewith to supply his wants except what in frequent sallies he could seize either stealthily or openly, both from the heathen and from the Christians who had submitted to their rule." He lived as Robin Hood did in Sherwood Forest long afterwards.

This is the moment when those gleaming toys of history were fashioned for the children of every age. We see the warrior-king disguised as a minstrel harping in the Danish camps. We see him acting as a kitchen-boy to a Saxon housewife. The celebrated story of Alfred and the Cakes first appears in a late edition of Bishop Asser's Life. It runs: "It happened one day that the countrywoman, who was the wife of the cowherd with whom King Alfred was staying, was going to bake bread, and the King was sitting by the fireside making ready his bow and arrows and other weapons. A moment came when the woman saw that her bread was burning; she rushed up and removed it from the fire, upbraiding the undaunted King with these words (recorded, strangely, in the original in Latin hexameters): 'Alack, man, why have you not turned over the bread when you see that it is burning, especially as you so much like eating it hot.' The misguided woman little thought that she was talking to King Alfred, who had fought so vigorously against the heathens and won so many victories over them." Low were the fortunes of the once ruthless English. Pent in their mountains, the lineal descendants of the Ancient Britons, slatternly, forlorn, but unconquered, may well have grinned.

The leaders of the Danish army felt sure at this time that mastery was in their hands. To the people of Wessex it seemed that all was over. Their forces were dispersed, the country overrun; their King, if alive, was a fugitive in hiding. It is the supreme proof of Alfred's quality that he was able in such a plight to exercise his full authority and keep contact with his subjects.

Towards the end of Lent the Danes suffered an unexpected misfortune. The crews of twenty-three ships, after committing many atrocities in Wales, sailed to Devon and marched to the attack of one of Alfred's strongholds on Exmoor. The place was difficult to assail, but

> in besetting it they thought that the King's thanes would soon give way to hunger and thirst . . . since the fortress had no supply of water.
>
> The Christians, before they endured any such distress, by the inspiration of heaven judged it to be better either to suffer death or to gain the victory. Accordingly at daybreak they suddenly rushed forth against the heathen, and at the first attack they laid low most of the enemy, including their king. A few only by flight escaped to their ships.[3]

Eight hundred Danes were killed, and the spoils of the victory included an enchanted banner called the Raven, of which it was said that the three daughters of Ragnar Lodbrok had woven it in a single day, and that "in every battle in which that banner went before them the raven in the middle of the design seemed to flutter as though it were alive if they were going to have the victory." On this occasion it did not flutter, but hung listlessly in its silken folds. The event proved that it was impossible for the Danes to win under these conditions.

Alfred, cheered by this news and striving to take the field again, continued a brigand warfare against the enemy while sending his messengers to summon the "fyrd," or local militia, for the end of May. There was a general response; the King was loved and admired. The news that he was alive and active caused widespread joy. All the fighting men came back. After all, the country was in peril of subjugation, the King was a hero, and they could always go home again. The troops of Somerset, Wiltshire, and Hampshire concentrated near Selwood. A point was chosen near where the three shires met, and we can see from this the burdens which lay upon Alfred's tactics. Nevertheless here again was an army: "and when they saw the King they received him like one risen from the dead, after so great tribulations, and they were filled with great joy."

Battle must be sought before they lost interest. The Danes still lay upon their plunder at Chippenham. Alfred advanced to Ethandun, now Edington, and on the bare downs was fought the largest and culminating battle of Alfred's wars. All was staked. All hung in the scales of fate. On both sides the warriors dismounted; the horses were sent to the rear. The shield-walls were formed, the masses clashed against each other, and for hours they fought with sword and axe. But the heathen had lost the favour of God through their violated oath, and eventually from this or other causes they fled from the cruel and clanging field. This time Alfred's pursuit was fruitful. Guthrum, king of the Viking army, so lately master of the one unconquered English kingdom, found himself penned in his camp. Bishop Asser says, "the heathen, terrified by hunger, cold, and fear, and at the last full of despair, begged for peace." They offered to give without return as many hostages as Alfred should care to pick and to depart forthwith.

But Alfred had had longer ends in view. It is strange that he should have wished to convert these savage foes. Baptism as a penalty of defeat might lose its spiritual quality. The workings of the spirit are mysterious, but we must still wonder how the hearts of these hard-bitten swordsmen and pirates could be changed in a single day. Indeed these mass conversions had become almost a matter of form for defeated Viking armies. It is reported that one old veteran declared he had been through this washing twenty times, and complained that the alb with which he was supplied was by no means up to the average standard. But Alfred meant to make a lasting peace with Guthrum. He had him and his army in his power. He could have starved them into surrender and slaughtered them to a man. He wished instead to divide the land with them, and that the two races, in spite of fearful injuries given and received, should dwell together in amity. He received Guthrum with thirty prominent buccaneers in his camp. He stood godfather to Guthrum; he raised him from the font; he entertained him for twelve days; he presented him and his warriors with costly gifts; he called him his son.

This sublime power to rise above the whole force of circumstances, to remain unbiased by the extremes of victory or defeat, to persevere in the teeth of disaster, to greet returning fortune with a cool eye, to have faith in men after repeated betrayals, raises Alfred far above the turmoil of barbaric wars to his pinnacle of deathless glory.

*　　*　　*　　*　　*

Fourteen years intervened between the victory of Ethandun and any serious Danish attack. In spite of much uneasiness and disturbance, by the standards of those days there was peace. Alfred worked ceaselessly to strengthen his realm. He had been content that the Danes should settle in East Anglia, but he cultivated the best relations with the harassed kingdom of Mercia, which had become tributary to the Danes, though still largely unoccupied by them. In 886 he married his eldest daughter to the regent, Ethelred, who was striving to bear the burden abandoned to him by the fugitive king, Burhred. There had already been several inter-marriages in the Mercian and Wessex royal families, and this set the final seal upon the cooperation of the South and the Midlands.

The first result of this new unity was the recovery of London in 886. London had long been the emporium of Christian England. Ancient Rome had seen in this bridgehead of the Thames, at the convergence of all the roads and sea routes, the greatest commercial and military centre in the Island. Now the City was set on the road to becoming the national capital. We read in the *Chronicle:* "King Alfred restored London, and all the English—those of them who were free from Danish bondage—turned to him, and he then entrusted the borough to the keeping of the ealdorman Ethelred." It would seem that heavy fighting and much slaughter attended the regaining of London, but of this nothing has been recorded. We know little more than the bare fact, and that Alfred after the victory made the citizens organise an effective defence force and put their walls in the highest order.

King Alfred's main effort was to restore the defences and raise the efficiency of the West Saxon force. He reorganised the "fyrd," dividing it into two classes which practised a rotation of service. Though his armies might be smaller, Alfred's peasant soldiers were encouraged not to desert on a long campaign, because they knew that their land was being looked after by the half of the militia that had stayed at home. The modesty of his reforms shows us the enormous difficulties which he had to overcome, and proves that even in that time of mortal peril it was almost impossible to keep the English under arms. The King fortified the whole country by boroughs, running down the Channel and then across to the Severn estuary and so back by the Thames valley, assigning to each a contributory district to man the walls and keep the fortifications in repair. He saw too the vision of English sea-power. To be safe in an island it was necessary to command the sea. He made great departures in ship design, and hoped to beat the Viking numbers by fewer ships of much larger size. These conclusions have only recently become antiquated.

Then King Alfred commanded to be built against the Danish warships longships which were well-nigh twice as long as the others. Some had sixty oars, some more. They were both swifter and steadier, and also higher than the others. They were shaped neither as the Frisian nor as the Danish, but as it seemed to himself that they might be most useful.[4]

But the big ships were beyond the skill of their inexperienced seamen to handle. In an action when nine of them fought six pirate vessels several were run ashore "most awkwardly," says the *Chronicle,* and only two of the enemy fell into Alfred's hands, to afford him the limited satisfaction of hanging their crews at Winchester. Still, the beginning of the English Navy must always be linked with King Alfred.

In spite of the disorders a definite treaty was achieved after the reconquest of London in 886. Significance attaches to the terms in which the contracting parties are described. On Alfred's side there are "the counsellors of the English nation," on Guthrum's "the people who dwell in East Anglia." The organisation of the Danelaw, based entirely upon the army and the subjugated inhabitants, had not yet assumed the form of a State. The English, on the other hand, had already reached the position of "King and Witan"; and none did more to enforce the idea than Alfred himself. The treaty defined a political boundary running up the Thames, up the Lea, along the Lea to its source, then straight to Bedford, and after by the Ouse to Watling Street, beyond which no agreement was made. This line followed no natural frontiers. It recognised a war front. It was drawn in No Man's Land.

The second part of the treaty is curious and instructive. Both sides were familiar with the idea of "wergeld." In order to deal with the ceaseless murders and physical injuries which the anarchic conditions had produced, a scale for compensation or revenge must at all cost be agreed. Nothing would stop the Danes from killing and robbing the English, and *vice versa;* but if there was to be any cessation of war a tariff must be agreed. Both Danish and English independent peasants were accordingly valued at 200 silver shillings each, and men of higher rank were assigned a wergeld of 8½ marks of pure gold. In accepting this clause of the treaty Guthrum was in fact undertaking not to discriminate in wergelds between his English and his Danish subjects. Alfred had gained an important point, which is evidence of the reality of his power.

*　　*　　*　　*　　*

King Alfred's Book of Laws, or Dooms, as set out in the existing laws of Kent, Wessex, and Mercia, attempted to blend the Mosaic code with Christian principles and old Germanic customs. He inverted the Golden Rule. Instead of "Do unto others as you would that they should do unto you," he adopted the less ambitious principle, "What ye will that other men should *not* do to you, that do ye not to other men," with the comment, "By bearing this precept in mind a judge can do justice to all men; he needs no other law-books. Let him think of himself as the plaintiff, and consider what judgment would satisfy him." The King, in his preamble, explained modestly that "I have not dared to presume to set down in writing many laws of my own, for I cannot tell what will meet with the approval of our successors." The Laws of Alfred, continually amplified by his successors, grew into that body of customary law administered by the shire and hundred courts which, under the name of the Laws of St. Edward (the Confessor), the Norman kings undertook to respect, and out of which, with much manipulation by feudal lawyers, the Common Law was founded.

The King encouraged by all his means religion and learning. Above all he sought the spread of education. His rescript to the Bishop of Worcester has been preserved:

> I would have you informed that it has come into my remembrance what wise men there formerly were among the English race, both of the sacred orders and the secular; and what happy times those were throughout the English race, and how the kings who had the government of the folk in those days obeyed God and His Ministers; and they on the one hand maintained their peace and morality and their author-ity within their borders, while at the same time they enlarged their territory abroad; and how they pros-pered both in war and in wisdom, . . . how foreigners

> came to this land for wisdom and instruction. . . . So
> clean was it fallen away in the English race that there
> were very few on this side Humber who could under-
> stand their Mass-books in English, or translate a let-
> ter from Latin into English; and I ween that there
> were not many beyond the Humber.[5]

He sought to reform the monastic life, which in the general confusion had grossly degenerated.

> If anyone takes a nun from a convent without the King's
> or the bishop's leave he shall pay 120 shillings, half to
> the King, half to the bishop. . . . If she lives longer than
> he who abducted her, she shall inherit nothing of his
> property. If she bears a child it shall inherit no more of
> the property than its mother.[6]

Lastly in this survey comes Alfred's study of history. He it was
who set on foot the compiling of the *Saxon Chronicle*. The fact that
the early entries are fragmentary gives confidence that the compil-
ers did not draw on their imagination. From King Alfred's time
they are exact, often abundant, and sometimes written with historic
grasp and eloquence.

We discern across the centuries a commanding and versatile intelligence, wielding with equal force the sword of war and of justice;
using in defence arms and policy; cherishing religion, learning, and
art in the midst of adversity and danger; welding together a nation,
and seeking always across the feuds and hatreds of the age a peace
which would smile upon the land.

This King, it was said, was a wonder for wise men. "From his cradle
he was filled with the love of wisdom above all things," wrote Asser.
The Christian culture of his Court sharply contrasted with the feckless
barbarism of Viking life. The older race was to tame the warriors and
teach them the arts of peace, and show them the value of a settled
common existence. We are watching the birth of a nation. The result
of Alfred's work was the future mingling of Saxon and Dane in a
common Christian England.

In the grim time of Norman overlordship the figure of the great Alfred was a beacon-light, the bright symbol of Saxon achievement, the hero of the race. The ruler who had taught them courage and self-reliance in the eternal Danish wars, who had sustained them with his national and religious faith, who had given them laws and good governance and chronicled their heroic deeds, was celebrated in legend and song as Alfred the Great.

*   *   *   *   *

One final war awaited Alfred. It was a crisis in the Viking story. In 885 they had rowed up the Seine with hundreds of ships and an army of forty thousand men. With every device known to war they laid siege to Paris, and for more than a year battered at its walls. They were hampered by a fortified bridge which the Franks had thrown across the river. They dragged their long-ships overland to the higher reaches and laid waste the land; but they could not take Paris. Count Odo, a warrior prince, defended it against these shameless pirates, and far and wide the demand was made that the King of the Franks should come to the rescue of his capital. Charles the Great had not transmitted his qualities to his children. The nicknames which they received as their monuments sufficiently attest their degeneracy. Charles the Bald was dead, and Charles the Fat reigned in his stead. This wretched invalid was at length forced to gather a considerable army and proceed with it to the aid of Paris. His operations were ineffectual, but the city held firm under its resolute governor. The Viking attack flagged and finally collapsed. All the records are confused. We hear at this time of other battles which they fought with Germanic armies, in one of which the dyke was filled with their corpses. Evidently their thrust in all directions in Western Europe encountered resistance, which, though inefficient, was more than they could overcome. For six years they ravaged the interior of Northern France. Famine followed in their footsteps. The fairest regions had been devoured; where could they turn? Thus they began again to look to England: something might have had time to grow there in the interval. On the Continent their standards were declining, but perhaps again the Island might be their prey. "It was," says Hodgkin in his admirable account, "a hungry monster which turned to England for food as well

as plunder." A group of pagan ruffians and pirates had gained possession of an effective military and naval machine, but they faced a mass
of formidable veterans whom they had to feed and manage, and for
whom they must provide killings. Such men make plans, and certainly
their descent upon England was one of the most carefully considered
and elaborately prepared villainies of that dark time.

Guthrum died in 891, and the pact which he had sworn with
Alfred, and loosely kept, ended. Suddenly in the autumn of 892 a
hostile armada of two hundred and fifty ships appeared off Lympne,
carrying "the Great Heathen Army" that had ravaged France to the
invasion of England. They disembarked and fortified themselves at
Appledore, on the edge of the forest. They were followed by eighty
ships conveying a second force of baffled raiders from the Continent,
who sailed up the Thames and established themselves on its southern
bank at Milton, near Sittingbourne. Thus Kent was to be attacked
from both sides. This immense concerted assault confronted Alfred
with his third struggle for life. The English, as we may call them—for
the Mercians and West Saxons stood together—had secured fourteen
years of unquiet peace in which to develop their defences. Many of the
Southern towns were fortified; they were "burhs." The "fyrd" had been
improved in organisation, though its essential weaknesses had not
been removed. There had been a re-gathering of wealth and food;
there was a settled administration, and the allegiance of all was given
to King Alfred. Unlike Charlemagne, he had a valiant son. At twenty-
two Edward could lead his father's armies to the field. The Mercians
also had produced an Ethelred, who was a fit companion to the West
Saxon prince. The King, in ill-health, is not often seen in this phase at
the head of armies; we have glimpses of him, but the great episodes
of the war were centred, as they should be, upon the young leaders.

The English beat the Vikings in this third war. Owning the
command of the sea, the invaders gripped the Kentish peninsula from
the north and south. Alfred had tried to buy them off, and certainly
delayed their full attack. He persuaded Hæsten, the Viking leader,
at least to have his two young sons baptised. He gave Hæsten much
money, and oaths of peace were interchanged, only to be broken.
Meanwhile the Danes raided mercilessly, and Alfred tried to rouse

England to action. In 893 a third expedition composed of the Danish veterans who had settled in Northumbria and East Anglia sailed round the south coast, and, landing, laid siege to Exeter. But now the young leaders struck hard. Apparently they had a strong mounted force, not indeed what we should call cavalry, but possessing swiftness of movement. They fell upon a column of the raiders near the modern Aldershot, routed them, and pursued them for twenty miles till they were glad to swim the Thames and shelter behind the Colne. Unhappily, the army of the young princes was not strong enough to resume the attack, and also it had run out of provisions. The pursuit therefore had to be abandoned and the enemy escaped.

The Danes had fortified themselves at Benfleet, on the Thames below London, and it is said that their earthworks can be traced to this day. Thence, after recovering from their defeat, they sallied forth to plunder, leaving a moderate garrison in their stronghold. This the princes now assaulted. It had very rarely been possible in these wars to storm a well-fortified place; but Alfred's son and his son-in-law with a strong army from London fell upon Benfleet and "put the army to flight, stormed the fort, and took all that there was within, goods as well as women and children, and brought all to London. And all the ships they either broke in pieces or burnt or brought to London or Rochester." Such are the words of the *Saxon Chronicle.* When in the nineteenth century a railway was being made across this ground the charred fragments of the ships and numbers of skeletons were unearthed upon the site of Benfleet. In the captured stronghold the victors found Hæsten's wife and his two sons. These were precious hostages, and King Alfred was much criticised at the time, and also later, because he restored them to Hæsten. He sent back his wife on broad grounds of humanity. As for the two sons, they had been baptised; he was godfather to one of them, and Ethelred of Mercia to the other. They were therefore Christian brethren, and the King protected them from the consequences of their father's wrongful war. The ninth century found it very hard to understand this behaviour when the kingdom was fighting desperately against brutal marauders, but that is one of the reasons why in the after-time the King is called "Alfred the Great." The war went on, but so far as the records show

Hæsten never fought again. It may be that mercy and chivalry were not in vain.

In this cruel war the Vikings used their three armies: the grand army that Hæsten had brought from the Continent, the army which had landed near Lympne, and the third from the Danelaw. But in the end they were fairly beaten in full and long fight by the Christians from Mercia, Wessex, and Wales.

One other incident deserves to be noticed. The *Saxon Chronicle* says:

> Before the winter [the winter of A.D. 894–5] the Danes . . . towed their ships up the Thames and then up the Lea . . . and made a fort twenty miles above Lunden burh. . . . In the autumn [895] the King camped close to the burh while they reaped their corn, so that the Danes might not deprive them of the crop. Then one day the King rode up by the river, and looked at a place where it might be obstructed, so that they could not bring their ships out. . . . He made two forts on the two sides of the river; . . . then the army perceived that they could not bring their ships out. Therefore they left them and went across country, . . . and the men of Lunden burh fetched the ships, and all that they could not take away they broke up, and all that were worth taking they brought into Lunden burh.

In 896 the war petered out, and the Vikings, whose strength seemed at this time to be in decline, dispersed, some settling in the Danelaw, some going back to France. "By God's mercy," exclaims the *Chronicle*, in summing up the war, "the [Danish] army had not too much afflicted the English people." Alfred had well defended the Island home. He had by policy and arms preserved the Christian civilisation in England. He had built up the strength of that mighty South which has ever since sustained much of the weight of Britain, and later of her Empire. He had liberated London, and happily he left behind him descendants who, for several generations, as we shall see, carried his work forward with valour and success.

* * * * *

Alfred died in 899, but the struggle with the Vikings had yet to pass through strangely contrasted phases. Alfred's blood gave the English a series of great rulers, and while his inspiration held victory did not quit the Christian ranks. In his son Edward, who was immediately acclaimed King, the armies had already found a redoubtable leader. A quarrel arose between Edward and his cousin, Ethelwald, who fled to the Danelaw and aroused the Vikings of Northumbria and East Anglia to a renewed inroad upon his native land. In 904 Ethelwald and the Danish king crossed the upper reaches of the Thames at Cricklade and ravaged part of Wiltshire. Edward in retaliation ordered the invasion of East Anglia, with an army formed of the men of Kent and London. They devastated Middle Anglia; but the Kentish contingent, being slow to withdraw, was overtaken and brought to battle by the infuriated Danes. The Danes were victorious, and made a great slaughter; but, as fate would have it, both Eric, the Danish king, and the renegade Ethelwald perished on the field, and the new king, Guthrum II, made peace with Edward on the basis of Alfred's treaty of 886, but with additions which show that the situation had changed. It is now assumed that the Danes are Christians and will pay their tithes, while the parish priest is to be fined if he misleads his flock as to the time of a feast-day or a festival.

In 910 this treaty was broken by the Danes, and the war was renewed in Mercia. The main forces of Wessex and Kent had already been sent by Edward, who was with the fleet, to the aid of the Mercians, and in heavy fighting at Tettenhall, in Staffordshire, the Danes were decisively defeated.

This English victory was a milestone in the long conflict. The Danish armies in Northumbria never recovered from the battle, and the Danish Midlands and East Anglia thus lay open to English conquest. Up to this point Mercia and Wessex had been the defenders, often reduced to the most grievous straits. But now the tide had turned. Fear camped with the Danes.

Edward's sister had been, as we have seen, married to Earl Ethelred of Mercia. Ethelred died in 911, and his widow, Ethelfleda, succeeded and surpassed him. In those savage times the emergence of a woman

ruler was enough to betoken her possession of extraordinary qualities. Edward the Elder, as he was afterwards called, and his sister, "the
Lady of the Mercians," conducted the national war in common, and
carried its success to heights which Alfred never knew. The policy of
the two kingdoms, thus knit by blood and need, marched in perfect
harmony, and the next onslaught of the Danes was met with confident
alacrity and soon broken. The victors then set themselves deliberately
to the complete conquest of the Danelaw and its Five Boroughs. This
task occupied the next ten years, brother and sister advancing in
concert upon their respective lines, and fortifying towns they took at
every stage. In 918, when Edward stormed Tempsford, near Bedford,
and King Guthrum was killed, the whole resistance of East Anglia
collapsed, and all the Danish leaders submitted to Edward as their
protector and lord. They were granted in return their estates and the
right to live according to their Danish customs. At the same time
"the Lady of the Mercians" conquered Leicester, and received even
from York offers of submission. In this hour of success Ethelfleda
died, and Edward, hastening to Tamworth, was invited by the nobles
of Mercia to occupy the vacant throne.

Alfred's son was now undisputed King of all England south of the
Humber, and the British princes of North and South Wales hastened
to offer their perpetual allegiance. Driving northwards in the next
two years, Edward built forts at Manchester, at Thelwall in Cheshire,
and at Bakewell in the Peak Country. The Danes of Northumbria saw
their end approaching. It seemed as if a broad and lasting unity was
about to be reached. Edward the Elder reigned five years more in
triumphant peace, and when he died in 925 his authority and his gifts
passed to a third remarkable sovereign, capable in every way of carrying on the work of his father and grandfather.

→ CHAPTER EIGHT ←

THE SAXON DUSK

ATHELSTAN, THE THIRD OF THE GREAT WEST SAXON KINGS, SOUGHT at first, in accordance with the traditions of his house, peaceful relations with the unconquered parts of the Danelaw; but upon disputes arising he marched into Yorkshire in 926, and there established himself. Northumbria submitted; the Kings of the Scots and of Strathclyde acknowledged him as their "father and lord," and the Welsh princes agreed to pay tribute. There was another uneasy interlude; then in 933 came a campaign against the Scots, and in 937 a general rebellion and renewed war, organised by all the hitherto defeated characters in the drama. The whole of North Britain—Celtic, Danish, and Norwegian, pagan and Christian—together presented a hostile front under Constantine, King of the Scots, and Olaf of Dublin, with Viking reinforcements from Norway. On this occasion neither life nor time was wasted in manœuvres. The fight that followed is recorded for us in an Icelandic saga and an English poem. According to the saga-man, Athelstan challenged his foes to meet him in a pitched battle, and to this they blithely agreed. The English king even suggested the place where all should be put to the test. The armies, very large for those impoverished times, took up their stations as if for the Olympic Games, and much parleying accompanied the process. Tempers rose high as these masses of manhood flaunted their shields and blades at one another and flung their gibes across a narrow space; and there was presently a fierce clash between the

Northumbrian and the Icelandic Vikings on the one hand and a part of the English army on the other. In this, although the Northumbrian commander, fled, the English were worsted. But on the following day the real trial of strength was staged. The rival hosts paraded in all the pomp of war, and then in hearty goodwill fell on with spear, axe, and sword. All day long the battle raged.

The original victory-song on Brunanburh opens to us a view of the Anglo-Saxon mind, with its primitive imagery and war-delight. "Here Athelstan King, of earls the lord, the giver of the bracelets of the nobles, and his brother also, Edmund the Ætheling, an age-long glory won by slaughter in battle, with the edges of swords, at Brunanburh. The wall of shields they cleaved, they hewed the battle shafts with hammered weapons, the foe flinched . . . the Scottish people and the ship-fleet. . . . The field was coloured with the warriors' blood! After that the sun on high, . . . the greatest star, glided over the earth, God's candle bright! Till the noble creature hastened to her setting. There lay soldiers, many with darts struck down, Northern men over their shields shot. So were the Scotch; weary of battle, they had had their fill! They left behind them, to feast on carrion, the dusty-coated raven with horned beak, the black-coated eagle with white tail, the greedy battle-hawk, and the grey beast, the wolf in the wood."

The victory of the English was overwhelming. Constantine, "the perjured" as the victors claimed, fled back to the North, and Olaf retired with his remnants to Dublin. Thus did King Alfred's grandson, the valiant Athelstan, become one of the first sovereigns of Western Europe. He styled himself on coin and charter *Rex totius Britanniæ*.

These claims were accepted upon the Continent. His three sisters were wedded respectively to the Carolingian king, Charles the Simple, to the Capetian, Hugh the Great, and to Otto the Saxon, a future Holy Roman Emperor. He even installed a Norwegian prince, who swore allegiance and was baptised as his vassal at York. Here again one might hope that a decision in the long quarrel had been reached; yet it persisted; and when Athelstan died, two years after Brunanburh, and was succeeded by his half-brother, a youth of eighteen, the beaten forces welled up once more against him. Edmund, in the spirit of his race, held his own. He reigned only six years, but when he died in 946 he had not ceded an inch or an ell. Edmund was succeeded by his brother Edred, the youngest son of Alfred's son Edward the Elder. He too maintained the realm against all comers, and, beating them down by force of arms, seemed to have quenched for ever the rebellious fires of Northumbria.

*   *   *   *   *

Historians select the year 954 as the end of the first great episode in the Viking history of England. A hundred and twenty years had passed since the impact of the Vikings had smitten the Island. For forty years English Christian society had struggled for life. For eighty years five warrior kings—Alfred, Edward, Athelstan, Edmund, and Edred—defeated the invaders. The English rule was now restored, though in a form changed by the passage of time, over the whole country. Yet underneath it there had grown up, deeply rooted in the soil, a Danish settlement covering the great eastern plain, in which Danish blood and Danish customs survived under the authority of the English king.

In the brilliant and peaceful reign of Edgar all this long building had reached its culmination. The reconquest of England was accompanied step by step by a conscious administrative reconstruction which has governed the development of English institutions from that day to this. The shires were reorganised, each with its sheriff or reeve, a royal officer directly responsible to the Crown. The hundreds, subdivisions of the shire, were created, and the towns prepared for defence. An elaborate system of shire, hundred, and burgh courts maintained law and order and pursued criminals. Taxation was reassessed. Finally, with this military and political revival marched a great re-birth of monastic life and learning and the beginning of our native English literature. The movement was slow and English in origin, but advanced with great strides from the middle of the century as it came in contact with the religious revival on the Continent. The work of Dunstan, Archbishop of Canterbury, and his younger contemporaries, Oswald, Bishop of Worcester, and Æthelwold, Bishop of Winchester, was to revive the strict observance of religion within the monasteries, and thereby indirectly to reform the Episcopate as more and more monks were elected to bishoprics. Another and happy, if incidental, result was to promote learning and the production of splendid illuminated manuscripts which were much in demand in contemporary Europe. Many of these, designed for the religious instruction of the laity, were written in English. The Catholic Homilies of Ælfric, Abbot of Eynsham, mark, we are told, the first achievement of English as a literary language—the earliest vernacular to reach this eminence in the whole of Europe. From whatever point of view we regard it, the tenth century is a decisive step forward in the destinies of England. Despite the catastrophic decline of the monarchy which followed the death of Edgar, this organisation and English culture were so firmly rooted as to survive two foreign conquests in less than a century.

It must have seemed to contemporaries that with the magnificent coronation at Bath in 973, on which all coronation orders since have been based, the seal was set on the unity of the realm. Everywhere the courts are sitting regularly, in shire and borough and hundred; there is one coinage, and one system of weights and measures. The arts of building and decoration are reviving; learning begins to flourish again in the Church; there is a literary language, a King's English, which all educated men write. Civilisation had been restored to the Island. But now the political fabric which nurtured it was about to be overthrown. Hitherto strong men armed had kept the house. Now a child, a weakling, a vacillator, a faithless, feckless creature, succeeded to the warrior throne. Twenty-five years of peace lapped the land, and the English, so magnificent in stress and danger, so invincible under valiant leadership, relaxed under its softening influences. We have reached the days of Ethelred the Unready. But this expression, which conveys a truth, means literally Ethelred the Ill-counselled, or Ethelred the "Redeless."

In 980 serious raids began again. Chester was ravaged from Ireland. The people of Southampton were massacred by marauders from Scandinavia or Denmark. Thanet, Cornwall, and Devon all suffered butchery and pillage. We have an epic poem upon "The Battle of Maldon," fought in 991. The Danes were drawn up on Northey Island, east of Maldon, with the English facing them from the south bank of the Blackwater estuary. The battle turned upon the causeway joining Northey to the mainland, which was flooded at high

THE HOUSE
OF WESSEX

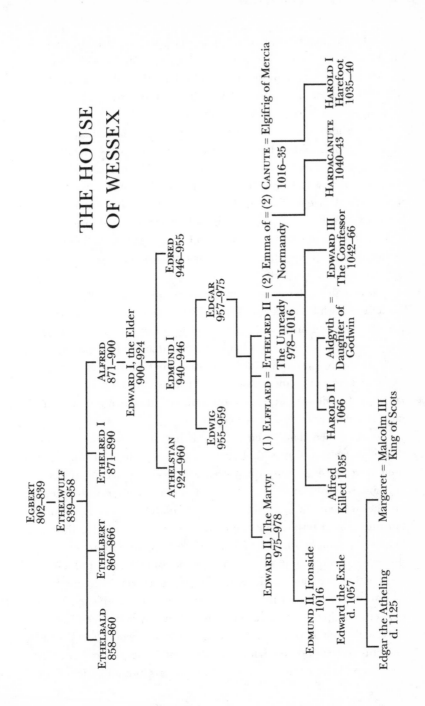

tide. The Vikings bargained in their characteristic fashion: "Send quickly rings for your safety; it is better for you to buy off with tribute this storm of spears than that we should share the bitter war. . . . We will with gold set up a truce. . . . We will go abroad with the tribute, and sail the sea, and be at peace with you."[1]

But Byrhtnoth, alderman of Essex, replied: "Hearest thou, rover, what this people saith? They will give you in tribute spears, and deadly darts, and old swords. . . . Here stands an earl not mean, with his company, who will defend this land, Æthelred's home, my prince's folk and field. The heathen shall fall in the war. Too shameful it seems to me that ye should go abroad with our tribute, unfought with, now that ye have come thus far into our land. Not so lightly shall ye come by the treasure: point and edge shall first make atonement, grim war-play, before we pay tribute."[2]

These high words were not made good by the event. As the tide was running out while these taunts were being exchanged the causeway was now exposed and the English naïvely agreed to let the Vikings cross and form on the south bank in order that the battle might be fairly drawn. No sooner had it begun than the English were worsted. Many of Byrhtnoth's men took to flight, but a group of his thanes, knowing that all was lost, fought on to the death. Then followed the most shameful period of Danegeld.

We have seen that Alfred in his day had never hesitated to use money as well as arms. Ethelred used money instead of arms. He used it in ever-increasing quantities, with ever-diminishing returns. He paid as a bribe in 991 ten thousand pounds of silver, with rations for the invaders. In 994, with sixteen thousand pounds, he gained not only a brief respite, but the baptism of the raider, Olaf, thrown in as a compliment. In 1002 he bought a further truce for twenty-four thousand pounds of silver, but on this occasion he was himself to break it. In their ruin and decay the English had taken large numbers of Danish mercenaries into their service. Ethelred suspected these dangerous helpers of a plot against his life. Panic-stricken, he planned the slaughter of all Danes in the south of England, whether in his pay or living peaceably on the land. This atrocious design was executed in 1002 on St. Brice's Day. Among the victims was Gunnhild, the wife of

Pallig, one of the chief Vikings, and sister of Sweyn, King of Denmark. Sweyn swore implacable revenge, and for two years executed it upon the wretched Islanders. Exeter, Wilton, Norwich, and Thetford all record massacres, which show how widely the retaliation was applied. The fury of the avenger was not slaked by blood. It was baffled, but only for a space, by famine. The Danish army could no longer subsist in the ruined land, and departed in 1005 to Denmark. But the annals of 1006 show that Sweyn was back again, ravaging Kent, sacking Reading and Wallingford. At last Ethelred, for thirty-six thousand pounds of silver, the equivalent of three or four years' national income, bought another short-lived truce.

A desperate effort was now made to build a fleet. In the energy of despair which had once inflamed the Carthaginians to their last effort an immense number of vessels were constructed by the poor, broken people, starving and pillaged to the bone. The new fleet was assembled at Sandwich in 1009. "But," says the *Chronicle*, "we had not the good fortune nor the worthiness that the ship-force could be of any use to this land." Its leaders quarrelled. Some ships were sunk in the fighting; others were lost in a storm, and the rest were shamefully abandoned by the naval commanders. "And then afterwards the people who were in the ships brought them to London, and they let the whole nation's toil thus lightly pass away." There is the record of a final payment to the Vikings in 1012. This tune forty-eight thousand pounds' weight of silver was exacted, and the oppressors enforced the collection by the sack of Canterbury, holding Archbishop Alphege to ransom, and finally killing him at Greenwich because he refused to coerce his flock to raise the money. The *Chronicle* states: "All these calamities fell upon us through evil counsel, because tribute was not offered to them at the right time, nor yet were they resisted; but, when they had done the most evil, then was peace made with them. And notwithstanding all this peace and tribute they went everywhere in companies, harried our wretched people, and slew them."

It is vain to recount further the catalogue of miseries. In earlier ages such horrors remain unknown because unrecorded. Just enough flickering light plays upon this infernal scene to give us the sense of its utter desolation and hopeless wretchedness and cruelty. It suffices to note that in 1013 Sweyn, accompanied by his youngest son, Canute, came again to England, subdued the Yorkshire Danes and the five boroughs in the Danelaw, was accepted as overlord of Northumbria and Danish Mercia, sacked Oxford and Winchester in a punitive foray, and, though repulsed from London, was proclaimed King of England, while Ethelred fled for refuge to the Duke of Normandy, whose sister he had married. On these triumphs Sweyn died at the beginning of 1014. There was another respite. The English turned again to Ethelred, "declaring that no lord was dearer to them than their natural lord, if he would but rule them better than he had done before."

But soon the young Danish prince, Canute, set forth to claim the English crown. At this moment the flame of Alfred's line rose again in Ethelred's son, Edmund—Edmund Ironside, as he soon was called. At twenty he was famous. Although declared a rebel by his father, and acting in complete disobedience to him, he gathered forces, and in a brilliant campaign struck a succession of heavy blows. He gained battles, he relieved London, he contended with every form of treachery; the hearts of all men went out to him. New forces sprang from the ruined land. Ethelred died, and Edmund, last hope of the English, was acclaimed King. In spite of all odds and a heavy defeat he was strong enough to make a partition of the realm, and then set himself to rally his forces for the renewal of the struggle; but in 1016, at twenty-two years of age, Edmund Ironside died, and the whole realm abandoned itself to despair.

The ecclesiastical aristocracy which played so great a part in politics dwelt long upon the prophecies of coming woe ascribed to St. Dunstan. At Southampton, even while Edmund lived, the lay and spiritual chiefs of England agreed to abandon the descendants of Ethelred forever and recognise Canute as King. All resistance, moral and military, collapsed before the Dane. The family of Ethelred was excised from the royal line, and the last sons of the house of Wessex fled into exile. The young Danish prince received this general and abject submission in a good spirit, although a number of bloody acts were required to attain and secure his position. He made good his promise to fulfill the duties of a king both in spiritual and temporal affairs to the whole country. The English magnates agreed to buy off the Danish army with a huge indemnity, and the new King, in "an oath of his soul," endorsed by his chiefs, bound himself to rule for all. Such was the compact solemnly signed by the English and Danish leaders. "The kingly house," as Ranke put it, "whose right and pre-eminence was connected with the earliest settlements, which had completed the union of the realm and delivered it from the worst distress, was at a moment of moral deterioration and disaster excluded by the spiritual and temporal chiefs, of Anglo-Saxon and Danish origin."[3]

*   *   *   *   *

There were three principles upon which sovereignty could be erected: conquest, which none could dispute; hereditary right, which was greatly respected; and election, which was a kind of compromise between the two. It was upon this last basis that Canute began his reign. It is possible that the early English ideal of kingship and just government in Alfred and Canute was affected by the example of Trajan. This emperor was a favourite of Pope Gregory, who had sent the first missionaries. There is evidence that stories of Trajan's virtue were read aloud in the English church service. Canute may also have studied, and certainly he reproduced, the poise of the Emperor Augustus. Everyone knows the lesson he administered to his flatterers when he sat on the seashore and forbade the tide to come in. He made a point of submitting himself to the laws whereby he ruled. He even in his military capacity subjected himself to the regulations of his own household troops. At the earliest moment he disbanded his great Danish army and trusted himself broadly to the loyalty of the humbled English. He married Emma of Normandy, the widow of Ethelred, and so forestalled any action by the Duke of Normandy on behalf of her descendants by Ethelred.

Canute became the ruling sovereign of the North, and was reckoned as having five or six kingdoms under him. He was already King of Denmark when he conquered England, and he made good his claim to be King of Norway. Scotland offered him its homage. The Viking power, although already undermined, still stretched across the world, ranging from Norway to North America, and through the Baltic to the East. But of all his realms Canute chose England for his home and capital. He liked, we are told, the Anglo-Saxon way of life.

He wished to be considered the "successor of Edgar," whose seventeen years of peace still shone by contrast with succeeding times. He ruled according to the laws, and he made it known that these were to be administered in austere detachment from his executive authority.

He built churches, he professed high devotion to the Christian faith and to the Papal diadem. He honoured the memory of St. Edmund and St. Alphege, whom his fellow-countrymen had murdered, and brought their relics with pious pomp to Canterbury. From Rome, as a pilgrim, in 1027, he wrote a letter to his subjects couched in exalted and generous terms, promising to administer equal justice, and laying particular emphasis upon the payment of Church dues. His daughter was married to the Emperor Conrad's eldest son, who ultimately carried his empire across Schleswig to the banks of the Eider. These remarkable achievements, under the blessing of God and the smiles of fortune, were in large measure due to his own personal qualities. Here again we see the power of a great man to bring order out of ceaseless broils and command harmony and unity to be his servants, and how the lack of such men has to be paid for by the inestimable suffering of the many.

Some early records of Canute throw a vivid light upon his character and moods. "When he entered monasteries, and was received with great honour, he proceeded humbly; keeping his eyes fixed with a wonderful reverence on the ground, and, shedding tears copiously— nay, I may say, in rivers—he devoutly sought the intervention of the Saints. But when it came to making his royal oblations, oh! How often did he fix his weeping eyes upon the earth! How often did he beat that noble breast! What sighs he gave! How often he prayed that he might not be unworthy of clemency from on high!"[4]

But this from a saga two centuries later is in a different vein:.

> When King Canute and Earl Ulf had played a while the King made a false move, at which the Earl took a knight from the King; but the King set the piece again upon the board, and told the Earl to make another move; but the Earl grew angry, threw over the chess-board, stood up, and went away. The King said, "Run away, Ulf

the Fearful." The Earl turned round at the door and said, ". . . Thou didst not call me Ulf the Fearful at Helge River, when I hastened to thy help while the Swedes were beating thee like a dog." The Earl then went out, and went to bed. . . . The morning after, while the King was putting on his clothes, he said to his foot-boy, "Go thou to Earl Ulf and kill him."

The lad went, was away a while, and then came back.

The King said, "Hast thou killed the Earl?"

"I did not kill him, for he was gone to Saint Lucius' church."

There was a man called Ivar White, a Norwegian by birth, who was the King's court-man and chamberlain. The King said to him, "Go thou and kill the Earl."

Ivar went to the church, and in at the choir, and thrust his sword through the Earl, who died on the spot. Then Ivar went to the King, with the bloody sword in his hand.

The King said, "Hast thou killed the Earl?"

"I have killed him," says he.

"Thou didst well."

After the Earl was killed the monks closed the church and locked the doors. When that was told the King he sent a message to the monks, ordering them to open the church and sing High Mass. They did as the King ordered; and when the King came to the church he bestowed on it great property, so that it had a large domain, by which that place was raised very high; and those lands have since always belonged to it.[5]

* * * * *

Meanwhile across the waters of the English Channel a new military power was growing up. The Viking settlement founded in Normandy in the early years of the tenth century had become the most vigourous military state in France. In less than a hundred years the sea-rovers had transformed themselves into a feudal society. Such records as exist are overlaid by legend. We do not even know whether Rollo, the traditional founder of the Norman state, was a Norwegian, a Dane, or a Swede. Norman history begins with the Treaty of Saint-Clairsur-Epte, made by Rollo with Charles the Simple, King of the West Franks, which affirmed the suzerainty of the King of France and defined the boundaries of the Duchy of Normandy.

In Normandy a class of knights and nobles arose who held their lands in return for military service, and sublet to inferior tenants upon the same basis. The Normans, with their craving for legality and logic, framed a general scheme of society, from which there soon emerged an excellent army. Order was strenuously enforced. No one but the Duke might build castles or fortify himself. The Court or "Curia" of the Duke consisted of his household officials, of dignitaries of the Church, and of the more important tenants, who owed him not only military service but also personal attendance at Court. Here the administration was centred. Respect for the decisions and interests of the Duke was maintained throughout Normandy by the Vicomtes, who were not merely collectors of taxes from the ducal estates, but also, in effect, prefects, in close touch with the Curia, superintending districts like English counties. The Dukes of Normany created relations with the Church which became a model for medieval Europe. They were the protectors and patrons of the monasteries in their domains. They welcomed the religious revival of the tenth century, and secured the favour and support of its leaders. But they made sure that bishops and abbots were ducal appointments.

It was from this virile and well-organised land that the future rulers of England were to come. Between the years 1028 and 1035 the Viking instincts of Duke Robert of Normandy turned him seriously to plans of invasion. His death and his failure to leave a legitimate heir suspended the project, but only for a while.

The figure of Emma, sister of Robert of Normandy, looms large in English history at this time. Ethelred had originally married her from a reasonable desire to supplement his failing armaments by a blood-tie with the most vigourous military state in Europe. Canute married her to give him a united England. Of her qualities and conduct little is known. Nevertheless few women have stood at the centre of such remarkable converging forces. In fact Emma had two husbands and two sons who were Kings of England.

In 1035 Canute died, and his empire with him. He left three sons, two by Elgiva of Northampton and one, Hardicanute, by Emma. These sons were ignorant and boorish Vikings, and many thoughts were turned to the representatives of the old West Saxon line, Alfred and Edward, sons of Ethelred and Emma, then living in exile in Normandy. The elder, Alfred, "the innocent Prince" as the chronicler calls him, hastened to England in 1036, ostensibly to visit his again-widowed mother, the ex-Queen Emma. A Wessex earl, Godwin, was the leader of the Danish party in England. He possessed great abilities and exercised the highest political influence. The venturesome Alfred was arrested and his personal attendants slaughtered. The unfortunate prince himself was blinded, and in this condition soon ended his days in the monastery at Ely. The guilt of this crime was generally ascribed to Godwin. The succession being thus simplified, Canute's sons divided the paternal inheritance. Sweyn reigned in Norway for a spell, but his two brothers who ruled England were short-lived, and within six years the throne of England was again vacant.

Godwin continued to be the leading figure in the land, and was now master of its affairs. There was still living in exile in Normandy Edward, the remaining son of Ethelred and Emma, younger brother of the ill-starred Alfred. In these days of reviving anarchy all men's minds turned to the search for some stable institution. This could only be found in monarchy, and the illustrious line of Alfred the Great possessed unequalled claims and titles. It was the Saxon monarchy which for five or six generations had provided the spearhead of resistance to the Danes. The West Saxon line was the oldest in Europe. Two generations back the house of Capet were lords of little more than Paris and the Ile de France, and the Norman dukes were Viking rovers. A sense of sanctity and awe still attached to any who could claim descent from the Great King, and beyond him to Egypt and immemorial antiquity. Godwin saw that he could consolidate his power and combine both English and Danish support by making Edward King. He bargained with the exile, threatening unless his terms were met to put a nephew of Canute on the throne. Of these the first was the restriction of Norman influence in England. Edward made no difficulty; he was welcomed home and crowned; and for the next twenty-four years, with one brief interval, England was mainly governed by Godwin and his sons. "He had been to such an extent exalted," says the *Chronicle* of Florence of Worcester, "as if he had ruled the King and all England."

Edward was a quiet, pious person without liking for war or much aptitude for administration. His Norman upbringing made him the willing though gentle agent of Norman influence, so far as Earl Godwin would allow. Norman prelates appeared in the English Church, Norman clerks in the royal household, and Norman land-owners in the English shires. To make all smooth Edward was obliged to marry Godwin's young and handsome daughter, but we are assured by contemporary writers that this union was no more than formal. According to tradition the King was a kindly, weak, chubby albino. Some later writers profess to discern a latent energy in a few of his dealings with the formidable group of Anglo-Danish warriors that surrounded him. Nevertheless his main interest in life was religious, and as he grew older his outlook was increasingly that of a monk. In these harsh times he played much the same part as Henry VI, whose nature was similar, during the Wars of the Roses. His saintliness brought him as the years passed by a reward in the veneration of his people, who forgave him his weakness for the sake of his virtues.

Meanwhile the Godwin family maintained their dictatorship under the Crown. Nepotism in those days was not merely the favouring of a man's own family; it was almost the only way in which a ruler could procure trustworthy lieutenants. The family tie, though frequently fail-ing, gave at least the assurance of a certain identity of interest. Statistics had not been collected, but there was a general impression in these primitive times that a man could trust his brother, or his wife's brother, or his son, better than a stranger. We must not therefore hasten to condemn Earl Godwin because he parcelled out the English realm among his relations; neither must we marvel that other ambitious magnates found a deep cause of complaint in this distribution of power and favour. For some years a bitter intrigue was carried on between Norman and Saxo-Danish influences at the English Court.

A crisis came in the year 1051, when the Norman party at Court succeeded in driving Godwin into exile. During Godwin's absence William of Normandy is said to have paid an official visit to the Confessor in England in quest of the succession to the Crown. Very likely King Edward promised that William should be his heir. But in the following year Godwin returned, backed by a force raised in Flanders, and with the active help of his son Harold. Together father and son obliged King Edward to take them back into power. Many of the principal Norman agents in the country were expelled, and the authority of the Godwin family was felt again throughout the land. The territories that they directly controlled stretched south of a line from the Wash to the Bristol Channel.

Seven months after his restoration Godwin died, in 1053. Since Canute first raised him to eminence he had been thirty-five years in public life. Harold, his eldest surviving son, succeeded to his father's great estates. He now filled his part to the full, and for the next thirteen adventurous years was the virtual ruler of England. In spite of the antagonism of rival Anglo-Danish earls, and the opposition of the Norman elements still attached to the Confessor's Court, the Godwins, father and son, maintained their rule under what we should now call a constitutional monarchy. A brother of Harold's became Earl of Mercia, and a third son of Godwin, Tostig, who courted the Normans, and was high in the favour of King Edward, received the Earldom of Northumbria, dispossessing the earls of those regions. But there was now no unity within the house of Godwin. Harold and Tostig soon became bitter foes. All Harold's competence, vigour, and shrewdness were needed to preserve the unity of the realm. Even so, as we shall see, the rift between the brothers left the land a prey to foreign ambitions.

*   *   *   *   *

The condition of England at the close of the reign of Edward the Confessor was one of widespread political weakness. Illuminated manuscripts, sculpture, metalwork and architecture of much artistic merit were still produced, religious life flourished, and a basis of sound law and administration remained, but the virtues and vigour of Alfred's posterity were exhausted and the Saxon monarchy itself was in decline. A strain of feeble princes, most of whom were short-lived, had died without children. Even the descendants of the prolific Ethelred the Unready died out with strange rapidity, and at this moment only a sickly boy and his sister and the aged sovereign represented the warrior dynasty which had beaten the Vikings and reconquered the Danelaw. The great earls were becoming independent in the provinces.

Though England was still the only state in Europe with a royal treasury to which sheriffs all over the country had to account, royal control over the sheriffs had grown lax. The King lived largely upon his private estates and governed as best he could through his household. The remaining powers of the monarchy were in practice severely restricted by a little group of Anglo-Danish notables. The main basis of support for the English kings had always been this select Council, never more than sixty, who in a vague manner regarded themselves as the representatives of the whole country. It was in fact a committee of courtiers, the greater thanes, and ecclesiastics. But at this time this assembly of "wise men" in no way embodied the life of the nation. It weakened the royal executive without adding any strength of its own. Its character and quality suffered in the general decay. It tended to fall into the hands of the great families. As the central power declined a host of local chieftains disputed and intrigued in every county, pursuing private and family aims and knowing no interest but their own. Feuds and disturbances were rife. The people, too, were hampered not only by the many conflicting petty authorities, but by the deep division of custom between the Saxon and the Danish districts. Absurd anomalies and contradictions obstructed the administration of justice. The system of land-tenure varied from complete manorial conditions in Wessex to the free communities of the Danelaw in the North and East. There was no defined relation between Lordship and Land. A thane owed service to the King as a personal duty, and not in respect of lands he held. The Island had come to count for little on the Continent, and had lost the thread of its own progress. The defences, both of the coast and of the towns, were neglected. To the coming conquerors the whole system, social, moral, political, and military, seemed effete.

The figure of Edward the Confessor comes down to us faint, misty, frail. The medieval legend, carefully fostered by the Church, whose devoted servant he was, surpassed the man. The lights of Saxon England were going out, and in the gathering darkness a gentle, grey-beard prophet foretold the end. When on his death-bed Edward spoke of a time of evil that was coming upon the land his inspired mutterings struck terror into the hearers. Only Archbishop Stigand, who had been Godwin's stalwart, remained unmoved, and whispered in Harold's ear that age and sickness had robbed the monarch of his wits. Thus on January 5, 1066, ended the line of the Saxon kings. The national sentiment of the English, soon to be conquered, combined in the bitter period that lay before them with the gratitude of the Church to circle the royal memory with a halo. As the years rolled by his spirit became the object of popular worship. His shrine at Westminster was a centre of pilgrimage. Canonised in 1161, he lived for centuries in the memories of the Saxon folk. The Normans also had an interest in his fame. For them he was the King by whose wisdom the crown had been left, or so they claimed, to their Duke. Hence both sides blessed his memory, and until England appropriated St. George during the Hundred Years War St. Edward the Confessor was the kingdom's patron saint. St. George proved undoubtedly more suitable to the Islanders' needs, moods, and character.

⇥ BOOK II ⇤

THE MAKING OF THE NATION

CHAPTER NINE

THE NORMAN INVASION

ENGLAND, DISTRACTED BY FACTION AND RIVALRY AT HOME, HAD FOR a long time lain under rapacious glare from overseas. The Scandinavians sought to revive the empire of Canute. The Normans claimed that their Duke held his cousin Edward's promise of the throne. William of Normandy had a virile origin and a hard career. The prize was large enough for the separate ambitions of both the hungry Powers. Their simultaneous action in the opening stages was an advantage to be shared in common.

*   *   *   *   *

One morning Duke Robert of Normandy, the fourth descendant of Rollo, was riding towards his capital town, Falaise, when he saw Arlette, daughter of a tanner, washing linen in a stream. His love was instantly fired. He carried her to his castle, and, although already married to a lady of quality, lived with her for the rest of his days. To this romantic but irregular union there was born in 1027 a son, William, afterwards famous.

Duke Robert died when William was only seven, and in those harsh times a minor's hold upon his inheritance was precarious. The great nobles who were his guardians came one by one to violent ends, and rival ambitions stirred throughout Normandy. Were they to be ruled by a bastard? Was the grandson of a tanner to be the liege lord of the many warrior families? The taint of bastardy clung, and sank deep into William's nature. It embittered and hardened him. When, many years afterwards, he besieged the town of Alençon the citizens imprudently hung out hides upon the walls, shouting, "Hides for the tanner!" William repaid this taunt by devastating the town, and mutilating or flaying alive its chief inhabitants.

It was the declared policy of King Henry of France to recognise and preserve the minor upon the ducal throne. He became his feudal guardian and overlord. But for this the boy could hardly have survived. In 1047, when he was twenty, a formidable conspiracy was organised against him, and at the outset of the revolt he narrowly missed destruction. The confederates proposed to divide the duchy among themselves, conferring on one of their number, to whom they took an oath, the nominal title of Duke. William was hunting in the heart of the disaffected country. His seizure was planned, but his fool broke in upon him with a timely warning to fly for his life. By daybreak he had ridden forty miles, and was for the moment safe in loyal Falaise. Knowing that his own strength could not suffice, he rode on ceaselessly to appeal for help to his overlord, the King of France. This was not denied. King Henry took the field. William gathered together his loyal barons and retainers. At the Battle of Val-ès-Dunes, fought entirely on both sides by cavalry, the rebels were routed, and thenceforward, for the first time, William's position as Duke of Normandy was secure.

There was room enough within the existing social system for feuds, and in some fiefs even private wars, but when the state fell into the hands of strong overlords these were kept within bounds, which did not prevent the rapid growth of a martial society, international both in its secular and military principles. The sense of affinity to the liege lord at every stage in the hierarchy, the association of the land with fighting power, the acceptance of the Papal authority in spiritual matters, united the steel-clad knights and nobles over an ever-widening area of Europe. To the full acceptance of the universal Christian Church was added the conception of a warrior aristocracy, animated by ideas of chivalry, and knit together in a system of military service based upon the holding of land. This institution was accompanied by the rise of mail-clad cavalry to a dominant position in war, and new forces were created which could not only conquer but rule.

In no part of the feudal world was the fighting quality of the new organisation carried to a higher pitch than among the Normans. William was a master of war, and thereby gave his small duchy some of the prestige which England had enjoyed thirty years before under the firm and clear-sighted government of Canute. He and his knights now looked out upon the world with fearless and adventurous eyes. Good reasons for gazing across the Channel were added to the natural ambitions of warlike men. William, like his father, was in close touch with the Saxon Court, and had watched every move on the part of the supporters of the Anglo-Danish party, headed by Godwin and his son Harold.

Fate played startlingly into the hands of the Norman Duke. On some visit of inspection, probably in 1064, Harold was driven by the winds on to the French coast. The Count of Ponthieu, who held sway there, looked upon all shipwrecked mariners and their gear as treasure-trove. He held Harold to ransom for what he was worth, which was much. The contacts between the Norman and English Courts were at this time close and friendly, and Duke William asked for the release of King Edward's thane, acting at first by civil request, and later by armed commands. The Count of Ponthieu reluctantly relinquished his windfall, and conducted Harold to the Norman Court. A friendship sprang up between William and Harold. Politics apart, they liked each other well. We see them, falcon on wrist, in sport; Harold taking the field with William against the Bretons, or rendering skilful service in hazardous broils. He was honoured and knighted by William. But the Duke looked forward to his future succession to the English crown. Here indeed was the prize to be won. Harold had one small streak of royal blood on his mother's side; but William, through his father, had a more pointed or at least less cloudy claim to the Island throne. This claim he was resolved to assert. He saw the power which Harold wielded under Edward the Confessor, and how easily he might convert it into sovereignty if he happened to be on the spot when the Confessor died. He invited Harold to make a pact with him whereby he himself should become King of England, and Harold Earl of the whole splendid province of Wessex, being assured thereof and linked to the King by marriage with William's daughter.

All this story is told with irresistible charm in the tapestry chronicle of the reign commonly attributed to William's wife, Queen Matilda, but actually designed by English artists under the guidance of his half-brother, Odo, Bishop of Bayeux. It is of course the Norman version, and was for generations proclaimed by their historians as a full justification—and already even in those days aggressors needed justifications—of William's invasion of England. The Saxons contended that this was mere Norman propaganda, and there is the usual conflict of evidence. It is probable however that Harold swore a solemn oath to William to renounce all rights or designs upon the English crown, and it is likely that if he had not done so he might never have seen either crown or England again.

The feudal significance of this oath making Harold William's man was enhanced by a trick novel to those times, yet adapted to their mentality. Under the altar or table upon which Harold swore there was concealed a sacred relic, said by some later writers to have been some of the bones of St. Edmund. An oath thus reinforced had a triple sanctity, well recognised throughout Christendom. It was a super-oath; and the obligation, although taken unbeknown, was none the less binding upon Harold. Nevertheless it cannot be said that the bargain between the two men was unreasonable, and Harold probably at the time saw good prospects in it for himself.

By this time William had consolidated his position at home. He had destroyed the revolting armies of his rivals and ambitious relations, he had stabilised his western frontier against Brittany, and in the southwest he had conquered Maine from the most powerful of the ruling houses of Northern France, the Angevins. He had forced the powers in Paris who had protected his youth to respect his manhood; and by his marriage with Matilda, daughter of the Count of Flanders, he had acquired a useful ally on his eastern flank.

Meanwhile Harold, liberated, was conducting the government of England with genuine acceptance and increasing success. At length, in January 1066, Edward the Confessor died, absolved, we trust, from such worldly sins as he had been tempted to commit. With his dying breath, in spite of his alleged promise to William, he is supposed to have commended Harold, his young, valiant counsellor and guide, as the best choice for the crown which the Witan, or Council could make. At any rate, Harold, at the beginning of the fateful year 1066, was blithely accepted by London, the Midlands, and the South, and crowned King with all solemnity in Westminster Abbey.

This event opened again the gates of war. There had been a precedent in France of a non-royal personage, Hugh Capet, becoming King; but this had been strongly resented by the nobility, whose pride, common ideas, and sentiments were increasingly giving the law to Western Europe. Every aspiring thane who heard the news of Harold's elevation was conscious of an affront, and also of the wide ranges open to ability and the sword. Moreover, the entire structure of the feudal world rested upon the sanctity of oaths. Against the breakers of oaths the censures both of chivalry and the Church were combined with blasting force. It was a further misfortune for Harold that Stigand, the Archbishop of Canterbury, had himself received the pallium from a schismatic Pope. Rome therefore could not recognise Harold as King.

At this very moment the Almighty, reaching down from His heavenly sphere, made an ambiguous gesture. The tailed comet or "hairy star" which appeared at the time of Harold's coronation is now identified by astronomers as Halley's Comet, which had previously heralded the Nativity of Our Lord; and it is evident that this example of divine economy in the movements for mundane purposes of celestial bodies might have been turned by deft interpretation to Harold's advantage. But the conquerors have told the tale, and in their eyes this portent conveyed to men the approaching downfall of a sacrilegious upstart.

Two rival projects of invasion were speedily prepared. The first was from Scandinavia. The successors of Canute in Norway determined to revive their traditions of English sovereignty. An expedition was already being organised when Tostig, Harold's exiled and revengeful half-brother, ousted from his Earldom of Northumbria, arrived with full accounts of the crisis in the Island and of the weak state of the defences. King Harold Hardrada set forth to conquer the English crown. He sailed at first to the Orkneys, gathering recruits from the Scottish isles and from the Isle of Man. With Tostig he wended towards the north-east coast of England with a large fleet and army in the late summer of 1066.

Harold of England was thus faced with a double invasion from the north-east and from the south. In September 1066 he heard that a Norwegian fleet, with Hardrada and Tostig on board, had sailed up the Humber, beaten the local levies under Earls Edwin and Morcar, and encamped near York at Stamford Bridge. He now showed the fighting qualities he possessed. The news reached him in London, where he was waiting to see which invasion would strike him first, and where. At the head of his Danish household troops he hastened northwards up the Roman road to York, calling out the local levies as he went. His rapidity of movement took the Northern invaders completely by surprise. Within five days of the defeat of Edwin and Morcar Harold reached York, and the same day marched to confront the Norwegian army ten miles from the city.

The battle began. The Englishmen charged, but at first the Norsemen, though without their armour, kept their battle array. After a while, deceived by what proved to be a feint, the common ruse of those days, they opened up their shield rampart and advanced from all sides. This was the moment for which Harold had waited. The greatest crash of weapons arose. Hardrada was hit by an arrow in the throat, and Tostig, assuming the command, took his stand by the banner "Land-ravager." In this pause Harold offered his brother peace, and also quarter to all Norsemen who were still alive; but "the Norsemen called out all of them together that they would rather fall, one across the other, than accept of quarter from the Englishmen."[1] Harold's valiant house-carls, themselves of Viking blood, charged home, and with a war shout the battle began again. At this moment a force left on board ship arrived to succour the invaders. They, unlike their comrades, were clad in proof, but, breathless and exhausted from their hurried march, they cast aside their ring-mail, threw in their lot with their hard-pressed friends, and nearly all were killed. The victorious Harold buried Hardrada in the seven feet of English earth he had scornfully promised him, but he spared his son Olaf and let him go in peace with his surviving adherents. Tostig paid for his restless malice with his life. Though the Battle of Stamford Bridge has been overshadowed by Hastings it has a claim to be regarded as one of the decisive contests of English history. Never again was a Scandinavian army able seriously to threaten the power of an English king or the unity of the realm.

At the moment of victory news reached the King from the South that "William the Bastard" had landed at Pevensey.

*   *   *   *   *

William the Conqueror's invasion of England was planned like a business enterprise. The resources of Normandy were obviously unequal to the task; but the Duke's name was famous throughout the feudal world, and the idea of seizing and dividing England commended itself to the martial nobility of many lands. The barons of Normandy at the Council of Lillebonne refused to countenance the enterprise officially. It was the Duke's venture, and not that of Normandy. But the bulk of them hastened to subscribe their quota of knights and ships. Brittany sent a large contingent. It must be remembered that some of the best stocks from Roman Britain had found refuge there, establishing a strong blood strain which had preserved a continuity with the Classic Age and with the British race. But all France was deeply interested. Mercenaries came from Flanders, and even from beyond the Alps; Normans from South Italy and Spain, nobles and knights, answered the advertisement. The shares in this enterprise were represented by knights or ships, and it was plainly engaged that the lands of the slaughtered English would be divided in proportion to the contributions, subject of course to a bonus for good work in the field. During the summer of 1066 this great gathering of audacious buccaneers, land-hungry, war-hungry, assembled in a merry company around St. Valery, at the mouth of the Somme. Ships had been built in all the French ports from the spring onwards, and by the beginning of August nearly seven hundred vessels and about seven thousand men, of whom the majority were persons of rank and quality, were ready to follow the renowned Duke and share the lands and wealth of England.

But the winds were contrary. For six whole weeks there was no day when the south wind blew. The heterogeneous army, bound by no tie of feudal allegiance, patriotism, or moral theme, began to bicker and grumble. Only William's repute as a managing director and the rich pillage to be expected held them together. At length extreme measures had to be taken with the weather. The bones of St. Edmund were brought from the church of St. Valery and carried with military and religious pomp along the seashore. This proved effective, for the very next day the wind changed, not indeed to the south, but to the south-west. William thought this sufficient, and gave the signal. The whole fleet put to sea, with all their stores, weapons, coats of mail, and great numbers of horses. Special arrangements were made to keep the fleet together, the rendezvous being at the mouth of the Somme, and the Duke by night having a lamp of special brilliancy upon his masthead. The next morning all steered towards the English coast. The Duke, who had a faster vessel, soon found himself alone in mid-Channel. He hove to and breakfasted with his staff "as if he had been in his own hall." Wine was not lacking, and after the meal he expressed himself in enthusiastic terms upon his great undertaking and the prizes and profit it would bring to all engaged therein.

On September 28 the fleet hove in sight, and all came safely to anchor in Pevensey Bay. There was no opposition to the landing. The local "fyrd" had been called out this year four times already to watch the coast, and having, in true English style, come to the conclusion that the danger was past because it had not yet arrived had gone back to their homes. William landed, as the tale goes, and fell flat on his face as he stepped out of the boat. "See," he said, turning the omen into a favourable channel, "I have taken England with both my hands." He occupied himself with organising his army, raiding for supplies in Sussex, and building some defensive works for the protection of his fleet and base. Thus a fortnight passed.

Meanwhile Harold and his house-carls, sadly depleted by the slaughter of Stamford Bridge, jingled down Watling Street on their ponies, marching night and day to London. They covered the two hundred miles in seven days. In London the King gathered all the forces he could, and most of the principal persons in Wessex and Kent hastened to join his standard, bringing their retainers and local militia with them. Remaining only five days in London, Harold marched out towards Pevensey, and in the evening of October 13 took up his position upon the slope of a hill which barred the direct march upon the capital.

The military opinion of those as of these days has criticised his staking all upon an immediate battle. The loyalty of the Northern earls, Edwin and Morcar, was doubtful. They were hastening south with a substantial reinforcement, but he could not be sure which side they would join. In the event they "withdrew themselves from the conflict." Some have suggested that he should have used the tactics which eleven hundred years before Cassivellaunus had employed against Cæsar. But these critics overlook the fact that whereas the Roman army consisted only of infantry, and the British only of charioteers and horsemen, Duke William's was essentially a cavalry force assisted by archers, while Harold had nothing but foot-soldiers who used horses only as transport. It is one thing for mounted forces to hover round and harry an infantry army, and the opposite for bands of foot-soldiers to use these tactics against cavalry. King Harold had great confidence in his redoubtable axe-men, and it was in good heart that he formed his shield-wall on the morning of October 14. There is a great dispute about the numbers engaged. Some modern authorities suppose the battle was fought by five or six thousand Norman knights and men-at-arms, with a few thousand archers, against eight to ten thousand axe- and spear-men, and the numbers on both sides may have been fewer. However it may be, at the first streak of dawn William set out from his camp at Pevensey, resolved to put all to the test; and Harold, eight miles away, awaited him in resolute array.

As the battle began Ivo Taillefer, the minstrel knight who had claimed the right to make the first attack, advanced up the hill on horseback, throwing his lance and sword into the air and catching them before the astonished English. He then charged deep into the English ranks, and was slain. The cavalry charges of William's mail-clad knights, cumbersome in manœuvre, beat in vain upon the dense, ordered masses of the English. Neither the arrow hail nor the assaults of the horsemen could prevail against them. William's left wing of cavalry was thrown into disorder, and retreated rapidly down the hill. On this the troops on Harold's right, who were mainly the local "fyrd," broke their ranks in eager pursuit. William, in the centre, turned his disciplined squadrons upon them and cut them to pieces. The Normans then re-formed their ranks and began a second series of charges upon the English masses, subjecting them in the intervals to severe archery. It has often been remarked that this part of the action resembles the afternoon at Waterloo, when Ney's cavalry exhausted themselves upon the British squares, torn by artillery in the intervals. In both cases the tortured infantry stood unbroken. Never, it was said, had the Norman knights met foot-soldiers of this stubbornness. They were utterly unable to break through the shield-walls, and they suffered serious losses from deft blows of the axe-men, or from javelins, or clubs hurled from the ranks behind. But the arrow showers took a cruel toll. So closely were the English wedged that the wounded could not be removed, and the dead scarcely found room in which to sink upon the ground.

The autumn afternoon was far spent before any result had been achieved, and it was then that William adopted the time-honoured ruse of a feigned retreat. He had seen how readily Harold's right had quitted their positions in pursuit after the first repulse of the Normans. He now organised a sham retreat in apparent disorder, while keeping a powerful force in his own hands. The house-carls around Harold preserved their discipline and kept their ranks, but the sense of relief to the less trained forces after these hours of combat was such that seeing their enemy in flight proved irresistible. They surged forward on the impulse of victory, and when half-way down the hill were savagely slaughtered by William's horsemen. There remained, as the dusk grew, only the valiant bodyguard who fought round the King and his standard. His brothers, Gyrth and Leofwine, had already been killed. William now directed his archers to shoot high into the air, so that the arrows would fall behind the shield-wall, and one of these pierced Harold in the right eye, inflicting a mortal wound. He fell at the foot of the royal standard, unconquerable except by death, which does not count in honour. The hard-fought battle was now decided. The last formed body of troops was broken, though by no means overwhelmed. They withdrew into the woods behind, and William, who had fought in the foremost ranks and had three horses killed under him, could claim the victory. Nevertheless the pursuit was heavily checked. There is a sudden deep ditch on the reverse slope of the hill of Hastings, into which large numbers of Norman horsemen fell, and in which they were butchered by the infuriated English lurking in the wood.

The dead king's naked body, wrapped only in a robe of purple, was hidden among the rocks of the bay. His mother in vain offered the weight of the body in gold for permission to bury him in holy ground. The Norman Duke's answer was that Harold would be more fittingly laid upon the Saxon shore which he had given his life to defend. The body was later transferred to Waltham Abbey, which he had founded. Although here the English once again accepted conquest and bowed in a new destiny, yet ever must the name of Harold be honoured in the Island for which he and his famous house-carls fought indomitably to the end.

CHAPTER TEN

WILLIAM THE CONQUEROR

THE INVADING ARMY HAD CAMPED UPON THE BATTLEFIELD. DUKE William knew that his work was but begun. For more than a year he had been directly planning to invade England and claim the English throne. Now he had, within a month of landing, annihilated the only organised Saxon army and killed his rival. But the internal cleavages which had riven the Island in recent years added new dangers to the task of conquest. The very disunity which had made assault successful made subjugation lengthy. Saxon lords in the North and in the West might carry on endless local struggles and cut communications with the Continent. Cautiously the advance began upon London.

William was a prime exponent of the doctrine, so well known in this civilised age as "frightfulness"[1]—of mass terrorism through the spectacle of bloody and merciless examples. Now, with a compact force of Normans, French, and Bretons, he advanced through Kent upon the capital, and at first no native came to his camp to do him homage. The people of Romney had killed a band of Norman knights. Vengeance fell upon them. The news spread through the country, and the folk flocked "like flies settling on a wound" to make their submission and avoid a similar fate. The tale of these events bit deep into the hearts of the people.

When William arrived near London he marched round the city by a circuitous route, isolating it by a belt of cruel desolation. From Southwark he moved to Wallingford, and thence through the

Chilterns to Berkhamsted, where the leading Saxon notables and clergy came meekly to his tent to offer him the crown. On Christmas Day Aldred, Archbishop of York, crowned him King of England at Westminster. He rapidly established his power over all England south of the Humber. Within two years of the conquest Duchess Matilda, who ruled Normandy in William's absence, came across the sea to her coronation at Westminster on Whit Sunday 1068, and later in the year a son, Henry, symbol and portent of dynastic stability, was born on English soil.

The North still remained under its Saxon lords, Edwin and Morcar, unsubdued and defiant. The King gathered an army and marched towards them. The track of William in the North was marked for generations upon the countryside and in the memories of the survivors and their descendants. From coast to coast the whole region was laid desolate, and hunted men took refuge in the wooded valleys of Yorkshire, to die of famine and exposure, or to sell themselves into slavery for food. For long years after tales were told of the "waste" and of the rotting bodies of the famine-stricken by the roadside. At Christmas 1069 William wintered at York, and, the feasting over, continued the man-hunt. Only one town in England had not yet been subjected to the Conqueror's will—Chester. Across England in the depth of the winter of 1070 he marched his army. The town surrendered at the summons, and submitted to the building of a castle.

England north of the Humber was now in Norman control. The great Earldom of Richmond was created, possessing broad estates in Yorkshire and in the adjacent counties as well. The Bishopric of Durham was reorganised, with wide powers of local government. It was now clear that Normandy had the force and spirit to absorb all Saxon England; but whether William would retain the whole of his conquests unchallenged from without was not settled till his closing years. The period of English subjugation was hazardous. For at least twenty years after the invasion the Normans were an army camped in a hostile country, holding the population down by the castles at key points. The Saxon resistance died hard. Legends and chroniclers have painted for us the last stand of Hereward the Wake in the broad wastes of the fens round Ely. Not until five years after Hastings, in 1071, was Hereward put down. In his cause had fallen many of the Saxon thanage, the only class from whose ranks new leaders could spring. The building of Ely Castle symbolised the end of their order.

Other internal oppositions arose. In 1075 a serious revolt of disaffected Norman knights broke out in the Midlands, East Anglia and on the Welsh border, and one surviving Saxon leader, Waltheof, who had made his peace with William, joined them. The King in Normandy must hasten back to crush the rebels. The Saxon population supported the Conqueror against chaos. The "fyrd" took the field. Vengeance was reserved for Waltheof alone, and his execution upon a hill outside Winchester is told in moving scenes by the Saxon-hearted monkish chroniclers of the time. Medieval legend ascribed the fate of William in his later years to the guilt of this execution. It marked also the final submission of England. Norman castles guarded the towns, Norman lords held the land, and Norman churches protected men's souls. All England had a master, the conquest was complete, and the work of reconstruction began.

Woe to the conquered! Here were the Normans entrenched on English soil, masters of the land and the fullness thereof. An armed warrior from Anjou or Maine or Brittany, or even from beyond the Alps and the Pyrenees, took possession of manor and county, according to his rank and prowess, and set to work to make himself secure. Everywhere castles arose. These were not at first the massive stone structures of a later century; they were simply fortified military posts consisting of an earthen rampart and a stockade, and a central keep made of logs. From these strongpoints horsemen sallied forth to rule and exploit the neighbourhood; above them all, at the summit, sat William, active and ruthless, delighting in his work, requiring punctual service from his adherents, and paying good spoil to all who did their duty.

In their early days the Normans borrowed no manners and few customs from the Islanders. The only culture was French. Surviving Saxon notables sent their sons to the monasteries of France for education. The English repeated the experience of the Ancient Britons; all who could learnt French, as formerly the contemporaries of Boadicea had learnt Latin. At first the conquerors, who despised the uncouth

English as louts and boors, ruled by the force of sharpened steel. But very soon in true Norman fashion they intermarried with the free population and identified themselves with their English past.

William's work in England is the more remarkable from the fact that all the time as Duke of Normandy he was involved in endless intrigues and conflicts with the King of France. Though England was a more valuable possession than Normandy, William and his sons were always more closely interested in their continental lands. The French kings, for their part, placed in the forefront of their policy the weakening of these Dukes of Normandy, now grown so powerful, and whose frontiers were little more than twenty miles from Paris. Hence arose a struggle that was solved only when King John lost Normandy in 1203. Meanwhile, years passed. Queen Matilda was a capable regent at Rouen, but plagued by the turbulence of her sons. The eldest, Robert, a Crusading knight, reckless and spendthrift, with his father's love of fighting and adventure but without his ruthless genius or solid practical aims, resented William's persistent hold on life and impatiently claimed his Norman inheritance. Many a time the father was called across the Channel to chastise rebellious towns and forestall the conspiracies of his son with the French Court. Robert, driven from his father's lands, found refuge in King Philip's castle of Gerberoi. William marched implacably upon him. Beneath the walls two men, visor down, met in single combat, father and son. Robert wounded his father in the hand and unhorsed him, and would indeed have killed him but for a timely rescue by an Englishman, one Tokig of Wallingford, who remounted the overthrown conqueror. Both were sobered by this chance encounter, and for a time there was reconciliation.

Matilda died, and with increasing years William became fiercer in mood. Stung to fury by the forays of the French, he crossed the frontier, spreading fire and ruin till he reached the gate of Mantes. His Normans surprised the town, and amid the horrors of the sack fire broke out. As William rode through the streets his horse stumbled among the burning ashes and he was thrown against the pommel of the saddle. He was carried in agony to the priory of St. Gervase at Rouen. There, high above the town, he lay, through the summer heat of 1087, fighting his grievous injury. When death drew near his sons

William and Henry came to him. William, whose one virtue had been filial fidelity, was named to succeed the Conqueror in England. The graceless Robert would rule in Normandy at last. For the youngest, Henry, there was nothing by five thousand pounds of silver, and the prophecy that he would one day reign over a united Anglo-Norman nation. This proved no empty blessing.

Fear fell upon the Conqueror's subjects when it was known that he was dying. What troubles would follow the end of a strong ruler? On Thursday, September 9, 1087, as the early bells of Rouen Cathedral echoed over the hills, William and his authority died. The caitiff attendants stripped the body and plundered the chamber where he lay. The clergy of Rouen bore him to the church of St. Stephen at Caen, which he had founded. Even his final journey was disturbed. In the graveyard one Ascelin cried out that his father had been deprived by the dead Duke of this plot of ground, and before all the concourse demanded justice from the startled priests. For the price of sixty shillings the Conqueror came thus humbly to his grave. But his work lived. Says the chronicler:

> He was a very stern and violent man, so that no one dared do anything contrary to his will. He had earls in his fetters, who acted against his will. He expelled bishops from their sees, and abbots from their abbacies, and put thanes in prison, and finally he did not spare his own brother, who was called Odo; he was a very powerful bishop in Normandy and was the foremost man next the king, and had an earldom in England. He [the King] put him in prison. Amongst other things the good security he made in this country is not to be forgotten—so that any honest man could travel over his kingdom without injury with his bosom full of gold: and no one dared strike another, however much wrong he had done him. And if any man had intercourse with a woman against her will, he was forthwith castrated.
>
> He ruled over England, and by his cunning it was so investigated that there was not one hide of land in

England that he did not know who owned it, and what it was worth, and then set it down in his record. Wales was in his power, and he built castles there, and he entirely controlled that race. In the same way, he also subdued Scotland to himself, because of his great strength. The land of Normandy was his by natural inheritance, and he ruled over the county called Maine: and if he could have lived two years more, he would have conquered Ireland by his prudence and without any weapons. Certainly in his time people had much oppression and very many injuries.

At this point the chronicler breaks into verse:

> He had castles built
> And poor men hard oppressed.
> The king was so very stark
> And deprived his underlings of many a mark
> Of gold and more hundreds of pounds of silver,
> That he took by weight and with great injustice
> From his people with little need for such a deed.
> Into avarice did he fall
> And loved greediness above all,
> He made great protection for the game
> And imposed laws for the same.
> That who so slew hart or hind
> Should be made blind.
>
> He preserved the harts and boars
> And loved the stags as much
> As if he were their father . . .[2]

* * * * *

The Normans introduced into England their system of land tenure based upon military service. A military caste was imposed from above. A revolution not only in warfare, but also in the upper reaches of society, had taken place. William aimed first at securing an effective and compact army, and the terms of knight-service and the quota of men due from each of his greater subjects interested him more than the social relationships prevailing on the lands they held. The Normans, a small minority, had destroyed the Saxon governing class and had thrust an alien domination upon England. But the mass of the inhabitants were only indirectly affected by the change, and the feudal superstructure was for many years as unsure as it was impressive. There were interminable controversies among the new masters of the country about the titles to their lands, and how these fitted the customs and laws of Anglo-Saxon England. The bishoprics and abbeys were especially loud in their complaints, and royal legates repeatedly summoned great assemblies of the shire courts to settle these disputes. Finally in 1086 a vast sworn inquiry was made into the whole wealth of the King's feudal vassals, from whom he derived a large part of his own income. The inquest or description, as it was called, was carried through with a degree of minuteness and regularity unique in that age and unequalled for centuries after. The history of many an English village begins with an entry in Domesday Book. The result of this famous survey showed that the underlying structure of England and its peasant life were little changed by the shock of the invasion.

But the holding of the great Domesday inquest marks a crisis. The Norman garrison in England was threatened from abroad by other claimants. The rulers of Scandinavia still yearned for the Island once the west of their empire. They had supported the rising in the North in 1069, and again in 1085, they threatened to intervene with greater vigour. A fleet was fitted out, and though it never sailed, because its leader was murdered, William took precautions. It became necessary that all feudal controversies arising out of the Conquest should be speedily settled, and it was under the shadow of this menace that Domesday Book was compiled. In 1086 William called together at Salisbury "all the land-holding men of any account throughout England whosoever men they were." The King had need of an assurance of loyalty from all his feudal tenants of substance, and this substantial body bound itself together by oath and fealty to his person.

The Norman achievement in England was not merely military in character. Although knight-service governed the holding of property and produced a new aristocracy, much was preserved of Saxon England. The Normans were administrators and lawyers rather than legislators. Their centre of government was the royal Curia, the final court of appeal and the instrument of supervision; here were preserved and developed the financial and secretarial methods of the Anglo-Saxon kingdom. The whole system of Saxon local government, also of immense usefulness for the future—the counties, the sheriffs, and the courts—survived, and through this the King maintained his widespread contacts with the country. In fact the Conqueror himself by these means collected the information for Domesday. Not only the courts, but also the dues and taxes such as Danegeld, were preserved for the sake of the Norman revenues. The local militia raised by the counties survived the Conquest, and proved serviceable to William and his successors. Thus in the future government of England both Norman and Saxon institutions were unconsciously but profoundly blended.

In some respects all this was a sudden acceleration of the drift toward the manorial system, a process which had already gone a long way in Anglo-Saxon England, and certainly in Wessex. But even in Wessex the idea still persisted that the tie of lord and man was primarily personal, so that a free man could go from one lord to another and transfer his land with him. The essence of Norman feudalism, on the other hand, was that the land remained under the lord, whatever the man might do. Thus the landed pyramid rose up tier by tier to the King, until every acre in the country could be registered as held of somebody by some form of service. But besides the services which the man owed to the lord in arms there was the service of attending the courts of the hundred and the county, which were—apart from various exemptions—courts of the King, administering old customary law. The survival of the hundred, the county court and the sheriff makes the great difference between English and Continental feudalism. In England the King is everywhere—in Northumberland as in Middlesex; a crime anywhere is a breach of his peace; if he wants to know anything he tells his officer, the sheriff, to impanel a jury and find out, or, in later days, to send some respectable persons to Westminster and tell him. But perhaps when they got to Westminster they told him that he was badly advised, and that they would not pay any taxes till he mended his ways. Far ahead we see the seventeenth-century constitutional issue. There were in Norman days no great mercantile towns in England, except London. If William had not preserved the counties and hundreds as living and active units, there would have been no body of resistance or counter-poise to the central Government, save in the great baronial families.

In the Norman settlement lay the germ of a constitutional opposition, with the effect if not the design of controlling the Government, not breaking it up. The seat of this potential opposition was found in the counties, among the smaller nobility and their untitled descendants, Justices of the Peace and knights of the shire. They were naturally for the Crown and a quiet life. Hence after centuries they rallied to the Tudor sovereigns; and in another age to the Parliament against the Crown itself. Whatever else changed they were always *there*. And the reason why they were there is that William found the old West Saxon organisation, which they alone could administer, exceedingly convenient. He did not mean to be treated as he had treated the King of France. He had seen, and profited by seeing, the mischief of a country divided into great provinces. The little provinces of England, with the King's officers at the head of each, gave him exactly the balance of power he needed for all purposes of law and finance, but were at the same time incapable of rebelling as units. The old English nobility disappeared after the Battle of Hastings. But all over Domesday Book the opinion of what we should later call the gentry of the shire is quoted as decisive. This is the class—people of some consideration in the neighbourhood, with leisure to go to the sheriff's court and thereafter to Westminster. Out of this in the process of time the Pyms and Hampdens arose.

The Conquest was the supreme achievement of the Norman race. It linked the history of England anew to Europe, and prevented for ever a drift into the narrower orbit of a Scandinavian empire. Henceforward English history marched with that of races and lands south of the Channel.

*   *   *   *   *

The effect of the Conquest on the Church was no less broad and enlivening. The bishoprics and abbeys and other high posts, were now as a matter of course given to Normans, and insular customs supplanted by the newest fashions from abroad. The age of the Conquest coincided with the many-sided reforms of the Church and advances in Papal power initiated by Hildebrand who became Pope as Gregory VII in 1073. Under its new leaders England was brought into the van of this movement. New abbeys sprang up all over the country which attested the piety of the conquerors, though few of the new houses attained to the wealth or standing of the older foundations. These monasteries and bishoprics were the chief centres of religion and learning until after a century they were gradually eclipsed by the rise of the universities. But the new Churchmen were even less disposed than the nobles to draw any deep line across history at the Norman Conquest. Slowly but surely the Frenchmen came to venerate the old English saints and English shrines, and the continuity of religious life with the age of Dunstan was maintained. Under Lanfranc and Anselm, successively Archbishops of Canterbury, the Church was ruled by two of the greatest men of the age, and through them derived incalculable benefits.

In his expedition of 1066 William had received the full support of the Pope, and his standards were blessed by orthodoxy. He was known to be a zealous ecclesiastical reformer, and the Saxon Church was thought to be insular and obstinate. Peter's Pence had not been regularly paid since the Danish invasions. Stigand, blessed only by the schismatic Benedict IX, held both Winchester and Canterbury in plurality. In face of such abuses William stood forth, the faithful son of the Church. Once the secular conquest had been made secure he turned to the religious sphere. The key appointment was the Archbishopric of Canterbury. In 1070 the Saxon Stigand was deposed and succeeded by Lanfranc. A Lombard of high administrative ability, Lanfranc had been trained in the famous North Italian schools and at the Norman Abbey of Bec, of which he became Abbot, and he rapidly infused new life into the English Church. In a series of councils such as had not been held in England since the days of

Theodore organisation and discipline were reformed. Older sees were transplanted from villages to towns—Crediton to Exeter, and Selsey to Chichester. New episcopal seats were established, and by 1087 the masons were at work on seven new cathedrals. At the same time the monastic movement, which had sprung from the Abbey of Cluny, began to spread in England. The English Church was rescued by the Conquest from the backwater in which it had languished, and came once again into contact with the wider European life of the Christian Church and its heritage of learning.

The spirit of the long-vanished Roman Empire, revived by the Catholic Church, returned once more to our Island, bringing with it three dominant ideas. First, a Europe in which nationalism or even the conception of nationality had no place, but where one general theme of conduct and law united the triumphant martial classes upon a plane far above race. Secondly, the idea of monarchy, in the sense that Kings were the expression of the class hierarchy over which they presided and the arbiters of its frequently conflicting interests. Thirdly, there stood triumphant the Catholic Church, combining in a strange fashion Roman imperialism and Christian ethics, pervaded by the social and military system of the age, jealous for its own interests and authority, but still preserving all that was left of learning and art.

→ CHAPTER ELEVEN ←

GROWTH AMID TURMOIL

THE FIRST GENERATION AFTER THE NORMAN CONQUEST FORMED A
period when the victorious army and caste were settling themselves
upon the lands they had gained, and forcing Saxon England, where
the tie between a man and his lord was mainly personal, into the
feudal pattern, where it primarily rested on landholding. Under
William the Conqueror this process had been harsh and thorough.
Under his son William, dubbed Rufus, the Red, it was not less harsh,
but also capricious. Moreover, the accession of the Conqueror's
second surviving son to the throne of England did not pass without
dispute. William I's decision to divide his English from his Norman
lands brought new troubles in its train. The greater barons possessed
property on both sides of the Channel. They therefore now owed
feudal allegiance to two soverign lords, and not unnaturally they
sought to play one against the other. Both Duke Robert and William II
were dissatisfied with the division, and their brotherly ties did not miti-
gate their covetous desires. During the thirteen years of the reign of
William the Anglo-Norman realms were vexed by fratricidal strife and
successive baronial revolts. The Saxon inhabitants of England, fearful
of a relapse into the chaos of pre-Conquest days, stood by the King
against all rebels. The "fyrd" obeyed every summons, and supported
him in the field as it had his father in 1075. Thus he was able finally to
bring Cumberland and Westmorland into the kingdom. The feckless
Robert, who had plagued the Conqueror so long, eventually departed

in a fit of gallantry on the First Crusade, leaving Normandy pawned to Rufus for the loan of 10,000 marks.

*   *   *   *   *

The Crusading spirit had for some time stirred the minds of men all over western Europe. The Christian kingdoms of Spain had led the way with their holy wars against the Arabs. Now, towards the end of the eleventh century, a new enemy of Christendom appeared fifteen hundred miles to the east. The Seljuk Turks were pressing hard upon the Byzantine Empire in Asia Minor, and harassing devout pilgrims from Europe through Syria to the Holy Land. The Byzantine Emperor appealed to the West for help, and in 1095 Pope Urban II, who had long dreamt of recovering Jerusalem for Christendom, called on the chivalry of Europe to take the Cross. The response was immediate, overwhelming, and at first disastrous. An itinerant monk named Peter the Hermit took up the cry to arms. So powerful was his preaching that in 1096 an enthusiastic but undisciplined train of twenty thousand men, most of them peasants unskilled in war, set off from Cologne for the East under his leadership. Few of them ever reached the Holy Land. After marching through Hungary and the Balkans, the majority perished by Turkish arrows amid the mountains of Asia Minor.

The so-called "People's Crusade" thus collapsed. But by now the magnates of Europe had rallied to the Cause. Four armies, each numbering perhaps ten thousand men, and led by some of the greatest nobles of the age, among them Godfrey de Bouillon, converged on Constantinople from France, Germany, Italy and the Low Countries. The Byzantine Emperor was embarrassed. He had hoped for manageable mercenaries as reinforcements from the West. Instead, he found camped around his capital four powerful and ambitious hosts.

The march of the Crusaders through his dominions into the Turkish-held lands was marred by intrigue and by grievous disputes. But there was hard fighting too. A way was hacked through Asia Minor; and Antioch, once a great bastion of the Christian faith, which the Turks had taken, was besieged and captured in 1098. The Crusaders were cheered and succoured by the arrival off the Syrian coast of a fleet manned by Englishmen and commanded by an English prince, Edgar the Atheling, great-nephew of Edward the Confessor. Thus by a strange turn of fortune the displaced heir of the Saxon royal line joined hands with Robert of Normandy, the displaced heir of William the Conqueror.

Aided by divisions among the Turkish princes and by jealousy between the Turks and the Sultans of Egypt the Crusaders pressed forward. On June 7, 1099, they reached their long-sought goal and encamped about Jerusalem, then in Egyptian hands. On July 14 the City fell to their assault. Godfrey de Bouillon, refusing to wear a crown in Christ's Holy City, was acclaimed ruler, with the title of "Defender of the Holy Sepulchre." Victory was made secure by the defeat at the Battle of Ascalon of a relieving army from Egypt. Many of the principal Crusaders thereupon went home, but for nearly a century a mixed international body of knights, all commonly called Franks, ruled over a string of Christian principalities in Palestine and along the coast of Syria. Western Christendom, so long the victim of invaders, had at last struck back and won its first great footing in the Eastern world.

*   *   *   *   *

At home Rufus's extortions and violent methods had provoked the baronage throughout his reign. In August 1100 he was mysteriously shot through the head by an arrow while hunting in the New Forest, leaving a memory of shameless exactions and infamous morals, but also a submissive realm to his successor. The main progress in his reign was financial; but the new feudal monarchy was also more firmly established, and in territory its sway was wider than at Rufus's accession. The Norman lords whom the Conqueror had settled upon the Welsh Marches had fastened a lasting grip upon Southern Wales. The Northern counties had been finally brought under Norman control, and a military frontier drawn against the Scots. While the rough hands of Rufus chafed and bruised the feudal relationship, they had also enforced the rights of a feudal king.

Prince Henry, the youngest of the royal brothers, had been a member of the fatal hunting party in the New Forest. There is no proof that he was implicated in the death of his brother, but he certainly wasted no time in mourning. He made straight for the royal treasury at Winchester, and gained possession of it after sharp argument with its custodians. Evidently he represented a strong movement of opinion among the leading classes, and he had a policy of his own. For a layman his scholarship deserved the title of Beauclerc which the custom of his day accorded him. He set the precedent, which his successor followed, of proclaiming a charter upon his accession. By this he sought to conciliate those powerful forces in Church and State which had been alienated by the rapacity and tactlessness of his predecessor. He guaranteed that the rights of the baronage and the Church should be respected. At the same time, having seen the value of Saxon loyalty in the reigns of his father and his brother, he promised the conquered race good justice and the laws of Edward the Confessor. He knew that the friction caused by the separation of Normandy from England was by no means soothed. Duke Robert was already on his way back from his Crusade with his mortgage to redeem. The barons on both sides of the Channel would profit from fraternal strife to drive hard bargains in their own interests. Henry's desire to base himself in part at least upon the Saxon population of England led him, much to the suspicion of the Norman barons, to make a marriage with Matilda, niece of the last surviving Saxon claimant to the English throne and descendant of the old English line of Kings. The barons, mollified by the charter, accepted this decisive step. The ceaseless gigantic process of intermarriage received the highest sanction.

Henry was now ready to face Robert whenever he should return. In September 1100 this event occurred. Immediately the familiar incidents of feudal rebellion were renewed in England, and for the next six years the King had to fight to make good his title under his father's will. The great house of Montgomery formed the head of the opposition in England. By a series of persevering sieges the family's strongholds fell one by one, and Henry at length destroyed their power and annexed their estates to the Crown. But the root evil lay in Normandy, and in 1105, having consolidated his position in England, Henry crossed the Channel. In September 1106 the most important battle since Hastings was fought at Tenchebrai. King Henry's victory was complete. Duke Robert was carried to his perpetual prison in England. Normandy acknowledged Henry's authority, and the control of Anglo-Norman policy passed from Rouen to London. The Saxons, who had fought heartily for Henry, regarded this battle as their military revenge for Hastings. By this new comradeship with the Crown, as well as by the royal marriage with Matilda, they felt themselves relieved from some at least of the pangs of being conquered. The shame was gone; the penalties could be endured. Through these two far-reaching factors a certain broad measure of unity was re-established in the Island.

*　　*　　*　　*　　*

There was now no challenged succession. The King of England's authority was established on both sides of the Channel. The Saxon people had proved their loyalty and the more powerful barons had been cowed. Foreign dangers having also been repelled, Henry was free for the time being to devote himself to internal government and to strengthening the power of the Crown throughout the land. He sought to invest the Anglo-Norman kingship with new and powerful attributes. There survived in medieval Europe a tradition of kingship more exalted than that of feudal overlord. The king was not merely the apex of the feudal pyramid, but the anointed Vicegerent of God upon earth. The collapse of the Roman Empire had not entirely destroyed this Roman conception of sovereignty, and Henry now set himself to inject this idea of kingship into the Anglo-Norman State; and in so doing he could not help reviving, whether consciously or not, the English conception of the King as the keeper of the peace and guardian of the people.

The centre of government, the Curia Regis, was an ill-defined body consisting of those tenants-in-chief whose feudal duty it was to attend when summoned, and those personal servants of the monarch who could be used for Government service as well as for their household duties. Henry realised that royal servants who were members of the minor baronage, if formed into a permanent nucleus, would act as a brake upon the turbulence of the greater feudatories. Here were the first beginnings, tentative, modest, but insinuating, of a civil administrative machinery, which within its limits was more efficient and persistent than anything yet known. These officials soon developed a vested interest of their own. Families like the Clintons and the Bassetts, whom the King, as the chronicler put it, had "raised from the dust to do him service," entrenched themselves in the household offices, and created what was in fact an official class.

The power of any Government depends ultimately upon its finances. It was therefore in the business of gathering and administering the revenue that this novel feature first became apparent. There was no distinction in feudal society between the private and public resources of the Crown. The King in feudal theory was only the greatest of the landowners in the State. The sheriffs of counties collected not only the taxes and fines accruing to the Crown, but also the income from the royal estates, and they were responsible, when they appeared yearly at the royal treasury, for the exact payment of what was due from each of their counties. Henry's officials created a special organ to deal with the sheriffs and the business the sheriffs transacted. This was the Exchequer, still regarded simply as the Curia meeting for financial purposes, but gradually acquiring a life of its own. It took its name from the chequered boards used for greater ease of calculation in Roman numerals, and its methods included the keeping of written records, among them the important documents called the Pipe Rolls because they were kept rolled up in the shape of a pipe. Thus the King gained a surer grip over the finances of the realm, and the earliest specialised department of royal administration was born. Its offspring still survives.

Henry took care that the sheriffs of the counties were brought under an increasingly strict control, and several commissions were appointed during the reign to revise their personnel. In troublous times the office of sheriff tended to fall into the hands of powerful barons and to become hereditary. The King saw to it that whenever possible his own men held these key positions. One of the most fertile sources of revenue arose from the fines imposed by the courts upon delinquents. The barons realised this as soon as the King, and their manorial courts provided them with important incomes, which could at once be turned into armed retainers. Within their domains they enjoyed a jurisdiction over nearly all laymen. But in the county courts and in the courts of the hundreds the Crown had at its disposal the old Saxon system of justice. These time-honoured institutions could well be used to rival the feudal courts of the baronage. Henry therefore revised and regularised the holding of the county courts, and made all men see that throughout the land there was a system of royal justice. King's officers—judges, as they became—in their occasional circuits administered this justice, and the very nature of their function brought them often into clash not only with humble suitors and malefactors, but with proud military magnates.

The King entered into a nation-wide competition with the baronage upon who could best deserve the rich spoils of the law. Through his control of the sheriffs he bound together the monarchy and the old Saxon system of local justice. The Conqueror had set the example when in the Domesday survey he combined the Continental system of getting information by means of bodies of men sworn to tell the truth with the English organisation by shire and hundred. His son for other purposes continued and intensified the process, sending officials constantly from his household through the kingdom, and convening the county courts to inquire into the claims of the royal revenue and to hear cases in which the Crown was interested. From these local inquiries by royal officials there were to spring far-reaching consequences in the reign of Henry II. The chroniclers spoke well of Henry I. "Good man he was," they declared, "and there was great awe of him. In his days no man dared to harm another." They bestowed upon him the title "Lion of Justice," and none has sought to rob him of it.

We must regard his reign as a period when the central Government, by adroit and sharp accountancy and clerking, established in a more precise form the structure and resources of the State. In the process the feudatory chiefs upon whom the local government of the land depended were angered. Thus, as the years wore on the stresses grew between the royal authority and the feudal leaders. The King's hand, though it lay heavy upon all, became increasingly a protection of the people against the injustice and caprice of the local rulers. Examples there were of admirable baronial administration, for there was a light in Norman eyes which shone above the squalid pillage and appetites of earlier ages. A country held down and exploited by feudal nobles was none the less the constant victim of local oppression. We see therefore the beginning of an attachment to the King or central Government on the part of the people, which invested the Crown with a new source of strength, sometimes forthcoming and sometimes estranged, but always to be gathered, especially after periods of weakness and disorder, by a strong and righteous ruler.

*   *   *   *   *

The Anglo-Norman State was now powerful. Henry was lord of England, Normandy, and Maine. In 1109 his only legitimate daughter, Maud, was betrothed to Henry V, Holy Roman Emperor and King of Germany. On the other hand, the reunion of England and Normandy after Tenchebrai had stirred the hostility of France. The early twelfth century saw the revival of a capital authority at Paris. With the accession of Louis VI the real strength of the French monarchy begins. It was essential for the safety of France that the unity of the Anglo-Norman State should be finally ruptured. The Duke of Normandy was technically the feudal subject of the King of France, and the existence of the son of captive Duke Robert provided the French King with innumerable pretexts for interference and offered to discontented Norman barons perennial opportunity. These Norman commitments forced Henry in the later years of his reign to intervene in the politics of Northern France. His position in Normandy was continually threatened by the claims of Robert's son, William Clito, who until his death in 1128 was backed by Louis, and also by the neighbouring state of Anjou, which disputed King Henry's rights in Maine. A wearing warfare darkened the later years of the reign. From the military point of view Henry was easily able to hold his own against any army the French could put into the field.

What may be judged malignant fortune now intervened. The King had a son, his heir apparent, successor indisputable. On this young man of seventeen many hopes and assurances were founded. In the winter of 1120 he was coming back from a visit to France in the royal yacht called the *White Ship*. Off the coast of Normandy the vessel struck a rock and all but one were drowned. The prince had indeed been embarked in a boat. He returned to rescue his sister. In this crisis the principle of equality asserted itself with such violence that at the ships's side so many leaped into the boat that it sank. Two men remained afloat, the ship's butcher and a knight. "Where is the Prince?" asked the knight above the waves. "All are drowned," replied

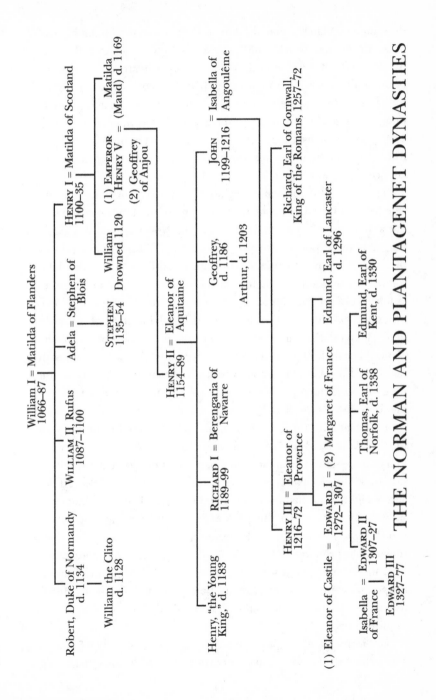

THE NORMAN AND PLANTAGENET DYNASTIES

the butcher. "Then," said the knight, "all is lost for England," and threw up his hands. The butcher came safe to shore with the tale. None dared tell it to the King. When at last he heard the tidings "he never smiled again." This was more than the agony of parental grief for an only son. It portended the breakdown of a system and prospect upon the consolidation of which the whole life's work of Henry stood. The spectre of a disputed succession glared again upon England. The forces of anarchy grew, and every noble in his castle balanced his chances upon who would succeed to the Crown.

There were two claimants, each of whom had a fair share of right. The King had a daughter, Matilda, or Maud as the English called her, but although there was no Salic Law in the Norman code this clanking, jangling aristocracy, mailed and spurred, did not take kindly to the idea of a woman's rule. Against her stood the claim of Stephen, son of the Conqueror's daughter Adela. Stephen of Blois, no inconsiderable figure on the Continent, with great estates in England added, was, after his elder brother had waived his claim, the rightful male heir. The feudal system lived entirely through the spirit of sworn allegiance. Throughout Christendom the accusation of violating an oath was almost mortal. Only great victories could atone and absolve. But here was a dilemma which every man could settle for himself according to his interests and ambitions. Split—utter, honest, total!

King Henry in the grey close of his life set himself to fill the void with his daughter Maud as female king. He spent his remaining years in trying to establish a kind of "pragmatic sanction" for a family succession which would spare his widespread domains from civil war. At the age of eight Maud had been betrothed to the Holy Roman Emperor. In 1125, five years after the *White Ship* sank, he died, and at twenty-two she was a widow and an Empress. We have many records of this remarkable princess, of whom it was said "she had the nature of a man in the frame of a woman." Fierce, proud, hard, cynical, living for politics above all other passions, however turbulent, she was fitted to bear her part in any war and be the mother of one of the greatest English kings.

Upon this daughter, after mature consideration, Henry founded all his hopes. On two separate occasions he called his murmuring barons together and solemnly swore them to stand by Maud. Subsequently, in order to enhance her unifying authority, and to protect Normandy from the claims of Anjou after his death, he married her to the Count of Anjou, thus linking the interests of the most powerful state in Northern France with the family and natural succession in England. The English mood has never in later ages barred queens, and perhaps queens have served them best. But here at this time was a deep division, and a quarrel in which all parties and all interests could take sides. The gathered political arrays awaited the death of the King. The whole interest of the baronage, supported at this juncture by the balancing weight of the Church, was to limit the power of the Crown and regain their control of their own districts. Now in a division of the royal authority they saw their chance.

After giving the Island thirty years of peace and order and largely reconciling the Saxon population to Norman rule, Henry I expired on December 1, 1135, in the confident hope that his daughter Maud would carry on his work. But she was with her husband in Anjou and Stephen was the first on the spot. Swiftly returning from Blois, he made his way to London and claimed the crown. The secular forces were divided and the decision of the Church would be decisive. Here Stephen had the advantage that his brother Henry was Bishop of Winchester, with a great voice in council. With Henry's help Stephen made terms with the Church, and, thus sustained, was crowned and anointed King. It was however part of the tacit compact that he should relax the severe central control which in the two preceding reigns had so much offended the nobility.

There was an additional complication. Henry I had a bastard son, Robert of Gloucester, a distinguished soldier and a powerful magnate in the West Country, who is usually regarded as one of the rare examples of a disinterested baron. Robert did not rate his chances sufficiently high to compete with either of the legitimate heirs. Almost from the beginning he loyally supported his half-sister Maud, and became one of Stephen's most determined opponents.

A succession established on such disputable grounds could only be maintained unchallenged by skilful sovereignty. The more we reflect upon the shortcomings of modern government the readier we shall be to make allowances for the difficulties of these times. Stephen in the early years of his reign lost the support of the three essential elements of his strength. The baronage, except those favoured by the new monarchy, were sure that this was the long-awaited moment to press their claims. The novel Civil Service, the great officials all linked together by family ties, armed with knowledge, with penmanship, trained to administration, now also began to stand aside from the new King. And many prelates were offended because Stephen violated clerical privilege by imprisoning the great administrative family of Roger, Bishop of Salisbury, whom he suspected of being about to change sides. Thus he had much of the Church against him too. There were grievous discontents among the high, the middle, and the low.

"When the traitors perceived," in the words of the *Anglo-Saxon Chronicle*, that King Stephen was "a mild man and soft and good and *did no justice*, then did they all manner of horrors. They had done homage to him and sworn oaths, but they held no faith."[1]

King David of Scotland, persuaded of the English decay, crossed the Border and laid claim to Northumbria. The Archbishop of York advanced against him, with the support of the mass of the Northern counties. He displayed the standards of St. Peter of York, St. John of Beverley, and St. Wilfred of Ripon, and in a murderous battle at Northallerton, henceforward known as the Battle of the Standard, repulsed and slaughtered the invaders. This reverse, far from discouraging the malcontents, was the prelude to civil war. In 1139 Maud, freed from entanglements that had kept her in France, entered the kingdom to claim her rights. As Stephen had done, she found her chief support in the Church. The men who had governed England under Henry II, antagonised by Stephen's weakness towards the barons, joined his enemies. In 1141 a more or less general rebellion broke out against his rule, and he himself was taken prisoner at the Battle of Lincoln. The Bishop of Winchester, Stephen's own brother and hitherto his main supporter, now went over to Maud's side. For nearly a year Maud, uncrowned, was in control of England. The Londoners after some trial liked her even less than Stephen. Rising in fury, they drove her out of the capital. She fought on indomitably. But the strain upon the system had been too great. The Island dissolved into confused civil war. During the six years that followed there was neither law nor peace in large parts of the country.

* * * * *

The civil war developed into the first successful baronial reaction against the centralising policy of the kings. Stephen, faced with powerful rivals, had failed to preserve the rights of the Crown. The royal revenues decreased, royal control of administration lapsed; much of the machinery itself passed for a time out of use. Baronial jurisdiction reasserted its control; baronial castles overawed the people. It seemed that a divided succession had wrecked the work of the Norman kings.

The sufferings of the Fen Country, where there was a particularly ferocious orgy of destruction during the anarchy, are grimly described in the *Anglo-Saxon Chronicle* by a monk of Peterborough.

> Every powerful man made his castles and held them against the King, . . . and when the castles were made they filled them with devils and evil men. Then they seized those men who they supposed had any possessions, both by night and day, men and women, and put them to prison for their gold and silver, and tortured them with unspeakable tortures. . . . Many thousands they killed with hunger. I neither can nor may tell all the horrors and all the tortures that they did to the wretched men of this land. And it lasted the nineteen winters while Stephen was King; and ever it was worse. They laid gelds [taxes] on the villages from time to time and called it "Tenserie"; when the wretched men had no more to give they robbed and burnt all the villages, so that you might go a whole day's journey and you would never find a man in a village or land being tilled. Then was corn dear, and meat and cheese and butter, because there was none in the land. Wretched men starved of hunger; some went seeking alms who at one time were rich men; others fled out of the land. . . . Wheresoever men tilled the earth bare no corn, for the land was all ruined by such deeds; and they said that Christ and his saints were asleep.

Another writer, a monk of Winchester, writes in very similar terms of the disasters that came upon his part of England: "With some men the love of country was turned to loathing and bitterness, and they preferred to migrate to distant regions. Others, in the hope of protection, built lowly huts of wattle-work round about the churches, and so passed their lives in fear and anguish. Some for want of food fed upon strange and forbidden meats—the flesh of dogs and horses; others relieved their hunger by devouring unwashed and uncooked herbs and roots. In all the shires a part of the inhabitants wasted away and died in herds from the stress of famine, while others with their wives and children went dismally into a self-inflicted exile. You might behold villages of famous names standing empty, because the country people, male and female, young and old, had left them; fields whitened with the harvest as the year [1143] verged upon autumn, but the cultivators had perished by famine and the ensuing pestilence."[2]

These horrors may not have been typical of the country as a whole. Over large parts of England fighting was sporadic and local in character. It was the central southern counties that bore the brunt of civil war. But these commotions bit deep into the consciousness of the people. It was realised how vital an institution a strong monarchy was for the security of life and property. No better reasons for monarchy could have been found than were forced upon all minds by the events of Stephen's reign. Men looked back with yearning to the efficient government of Henry I. But a greater than he was at hand.

*　　*　　*　　*　　*

In 1147 Robert of Gloucester died and the leadership of Maud's party devolved upon her son. Henry Plantagenet was born to empire. His grandfather Fulk had made of the Angevin lands, Anjou, Touraine, and Maine, a principality unsurpassed in France and in resources more than the equal of Normandy. Fulk died in 1143, King of Jerusalem, leaving two sons to succeed him on that precarious throne, and a third, Geoffrey, as heir to his French dominions. Geoffrey's marriage with Maud had united the Norman and Angevin lands, and the child of this marriage was from his birth in 1133 recognised as the "master of many peoples." To contemporaries he was best known as Henry Fitz-Empress; but he carried into English history the emblem of his house, the broom, the *Planta Genesta*, which later generations were to make the name of this great dynasty, the Plantagenets. He embodied all their ability, all their energy, and not a little of that passionate, ruthless ferocity which, it was whispered, came to the house of Anjou from no mortal source, but from a union with Satan himself.

When scarcely fifteen, in 1147, Henry had actively championed his claim to the English throne on English soil. His small band of followers was then defeated by Stephen's forces, and he took refuge in Normandy. The Empress Maud gave up her slender hopes of success in the following year and joined her son in the duchy. Nineteen years of life remained before her, but she never set foot in England again. Works of piety, natural to the times, filled many of her days. But during the years that followed Henry's triumph she played an important political part as regent in Normandy and in his hereditary Angevin dominions. During her interventions in England in quest of the crown the charge of arrogance was often levelled against her; but in her older age she proved a sagacious counsellor to her son.

Henry was involved in a further attempt against England in 1149, but the campaign projected on his behalf by the King of Scots and the Earl of Chester came to nothing. For a few years of comparative peace King Stephen was left in uneasy possession. In the meantime Henry was invested by his parents in 1150 as Duke of Normandy. The next year his father's death made him also Count of Anjou, Touraine, and Maine. In his high feudal capacity Henry repaired to Paris to render homage to his lord the King of France, of which country he already possessed, by the accepted law of the age, a large part.

Louis VII was a French Edward the Confessor; he practised with faithful simplicity the law of Christ. All his days were spent in devotion, and his nights in vigil or penance. When he left his own chapel he would delay the whole Court by waiting till the humblest person present had preceded him. These pious and exemplary habits did not endear him to his queen. Eleanor of Aquitaine was in her own right a reigning princess, with the warmth of the South in her veins. She had already complained that she had "married a monk and not a king" when this square-shouldered, ruddy youth, with his "countenance of fire," sprightly talk, and overflowing energy, suddenly presented himself before her husband as his most splendid vassal. Eleanor did not waste words in coming to a decision. The Papacy bowed to strong will in the high feudal chiefs, and Eleanor obtained a divorce from Louis VII in 1152 on the nominal grounds of consanguinity. But what staggered the French Court and opened the eyes of its prayerful King was the sudden marriage of Eleanor to Henry two months later. Thus half of France passed out of royal control into the hands of Henry. Rarely have passion and policy flowed so buoyantly together. The marriage was one of the most brilliant political strokes of the age. Henry afterwards admitted his designs, and accepted the admiration of Europe for their audacity. He was nineteen and she was probably thirty; and, uniting their immense domains, they made common cause against all comers. To Louis VII were vouchsafed the consolations of the spirit; but even these were jarred upon by the problems of government.

War in all quarters lay before the royal pair. The joining to Normandy and Anjou of Poitou, Saintonge, Périgord, the Limousin, the Angoumois, and Gascony, with claims of suzerainty over Auvergne and Toulouse, fascinated and convulsed the feudal Christian world. Everywhere men shook their heads over this concentration of power, this spectacle of so many races and states, sundered from each other by long feuds or divergent interests, now suddenly flung together by the hot blood of a love intrigue. From all sides the potentates confronted the upstart. The King of France, who certainly had every conceivable cause of complaint; King Stephen of England, who disputed Henry's title to the Norman duchy, though without force to intervene across the Channel; the Count of Champagne; the Count of Perche; and Henry's own brother, Geoffrey—all spontaneously, and with good reason, fell upon him.

A month after the marriage these foes converged upon Normandy. But the youthful Duke Henry beat them back, ruptured and broken. The Norman army proved once again its fighting quality. Before he was twenty Henry had cleared Normandy of rebels and pacified Anjou. He turned forthwith to England. It was a valiant figure that landed in January 1153, and from all over England, distracted by civil wars, hearts and eyes turned towards him. Merlin had prophesied a deliverer; had he not in his veins blood that ran back to William the Conqueror, and beyond him, through his grandmother Matilda, wife of Henry I, to Cedric and the long-vanished Anglo-Saxon line? A wild surge of hope greeted him from the tormented Islanders, and when he knelt after his landing in the first church he found "to pray for a space, in the manner of soldiers," the priest pronounced the wish of the nation in the words, "Behold there cometh the Lord, the Ruler, and the kingdom is in his hand."

There followed battles: Malmesbury, where the sleet, especially directed by Almighty God, beat upon the faces of his foes; Wallingford, where King Stephen by divine interposition fell three times from his horse before going into action. Glamour, terror, success, attended this youthful, puissant warrior, who had not only his sword, but his title-deeds. The baronage saw their interest favoured by a stalemate; they wanted neither a victorious Stephen nor a triumphant Henry. The weaker the King the stronger the nobles. A treaty was concluded at Winchester in 1153 whereby Stephen made Henry his adopted son and his appointed heir. "In the business of the kingdom," promised Stephen, "I will work by the counsel of the Duke; but in the whole realm of England, as well in the Duke's part as my own, I will exercise royal justice." On this Henry did homage and made all the formal submissions, and when a year later Stephen died he was acclaimed and crowned King of England with more general hope and rejoicing than had ever uplifted any monarch in England since the days of Alfred the Great.

CHAPTER TWELVE

HENRY PLANTAGENET

THE ACCESSION OF HENRY II BEGAN ONE OF THE MOST PREGNANT AND decisive reigns in English history. The new sovereign ruled an empire, and, as his subjects boasted, his warrant ran "from the Arctic Ocean to the Pyrenees." England to him was but one—the most solid though perhaps the least attractive—of his provinces. But he gave to England that effectual element of external control which, as in the days of William of Orange, was indispensable to the growth of national unity. He was accepted by English and Norman as the ruler of both races and the whole country. The memories of Hastings were confounded in his person, and after the hideous anarchy of civil war and robber barons all due attention was paid to his commands. Thus, though a Frenchman, with foreign speech and foreign modes, he shaped our country in a fashion of which the outline remains to the present day.

After a hundred years of being the encampment of an invading army and the battleground of its quarrelsome officers and their descendants England became finally and for all time a coherent kingdom, based upon Christianity and upon that Latin civilisation which recalled the message of ancient Rome. Henry Plantagenet first brought England, Scotland, and Ireland into a certain common relationship; he re-established the system of royal government which his grandfather, Henry I, had prematurely erected. He relaid the foundations of a central power, based upon the exchequer and the judiciary, which was ultimately to supersede the feudal system of William the

Conqueror. The King gathered up and cherished the Anglo-Saxon tradition of self-government under royal command in shire and borough; he developed and made permanent "assizes" as they survive to-day. It is to him we owe the enduring fact that the English-speaking race all over the world is governed by the English Common Law rather than by the Roman. By his Constitutions of Clarendon he sought to fix the relationship of Church and State and to force the Church in its temporal character to submit itself to the life and law of the nation. In this endeavour he had, after a deadly struggle, to retreat, and it was left to Henry VIII, though centuries later, to avenge his predecessor by destroying the shrine of St. Thomas at Canterbury.

A vivid picture is painted of this gifted and, for a while, enviable man: square, thick-set, bull-necked, with powerful arms and coarse, rough hands; his legs bandy from endless riding; a large, round head and closely cropped red hair; a freckled face; a voice harsh and cracked. Intense love of the chase; other loves, which the Church deplored and Queen Eleanor resented; frugality in food and dress; days entirely concerned with public business; travel unceasing; moods various. It was said that he was always gentle and calm in times of urgent peril, but became bad-tempered and capricious when the pressure relaxed. "He was more tender to dead soldiers than to the living, and found far more sorrow in the loss of those who were slain than comfort in the love of those who remained." He journeyed hotfoot around his many dominions, arriving unexpectedly in England when he was thought to be in the South of France. He carried with him in his tours of each province wains loaded with ponderous rolls which represented the office files of to-day. His Court and train gasped and panted behind him. Sometimes, when he had appointed an early start, he was sleeping till noon, with all the wagons and pack-horses awaiting him fully laden. Sometimes he would be off hours before the time he had fixed, leaving everyone to catch up as best they could. Everything was stirred and moulded by him in England, as also in his other much greater estates, which he patrolled with tireless attention.

But this twelfth-century monarch, with his lusts and sports, his hates and his schemes, was no materialist; he was the Lord's Anointed, he commanded, with the Archbishop of Canterbury—"those two

THE
POSSESSIONS
OF HENRY II

SCOTLAND

ULSTER
LEITRIM
MEATH
Dublin
LEINSTER
MUNSTER
PRINCIPALITY
OF WALES
THE LORDS
MARCHER.

ENGLAND

London

NORTH
SEA

THE HOLY ROMAN EMPIRE

ENGLISH CHANNEL

NORMANDY

Paris

BRITTANY

MAINE
Le Mans
ANJOU TOURAINE

FRANCE

POITOU

A·Q·U·I·T·A·I·N·E

Boundary of lands under
direct rule of Henry II

Lands owing him Suzerainty

Boundary of lands Inherited
from his father

Bordeaux

MILES

0   50   100   150   200

FRANCE

GASCONY
Toulouse

CASTILE

NAVARRE.

strong steers that drew the plough of England"—the whole allegiance of his subjects. The offices of religion, the fear of eternal damnation, the hope of even greater realms beyond the grave, accompanied him from hour to hour. At times he was smitten with remorse and engulfed in repentance. He drew all possible delights and satisfactions from this world and the next. He is portrayed to us in convulsions both of spiritual exaltation and abasement. This was no secluded monarch: the kings of those days were as accessible to all classes as a modern President of the United States. People broke in upon him at all hours with business, with tidings, with gossip, with visions, with complaints. Talk rang high in the King's presence and to His Majesty's face among the nobles and courtiers, and the jester, invaluable monitor, castigated all impartially with unstinted licence.

Few mortals have led so full a life as Henry II or have drunk so deeply of the cups of triumph and sorrow. In later life he fell out with Eleanor. When she was over fifty and he but forty-two he is said to have fallen in love with "Fair Rosamond," a damosel of high degree and transcendent beauty, and generations have enjoyed the romantic tragedy of Queen Eleanor penetrating the protecting maze at Woodstock by the clue of a silken thread and offering her hapless supplanter the hard choice between the dagger and the poisoned cup. Tiresome investigators have undermined this excellent tale, but it certainly should find its place in any history worthy of the name.

Such was the man who succeeded to the troubled and divided inheritance of Stephen. Already before his accession to the English throne Henry had fought the first of his many wars to defend his Continental inheritance. Ever since the emergence of the strong Norman power in North-West France, a hundred years before, the French monarchy had struggled ceaselessly against the encroachments of great dukedoms and countships upon the central Government. The Dukes of Normandy, of Aquitaine, and of Brittany, the Counts of Anjou, Toulouse, Flanders, and Boulogne, although in form and law vassals of the French Crown, together with a host of other feudal tenants-in-chief, aspired to independent sovereignty, and in the eclipse of the monarchy seemed at times near to achieving their ambition. The Battle of Hastings had made the greatest French subject, the Duke of Normandy, also King of England; but Henry II's accession to the Island throne in 1154 threatened France with far graver dangers. Hitherto there had always been political relief in playing off over-mighty subjects one against another. The struggle between Anjou and Normandy in the eleventh century had rejoiced the French king, who saw two of his chief enemies at grips. But when in one hour Henry II was King of England, Duke of Normandy, Lord of Aquitaine, Brittany, Poitou, Anjou, Maine, and Guienne, ruler from the Somme to the Pyrenees of more than half France, all balance of power among the feudal lords was destroyed.

Louis VII found instead of a dozen principalities, divided and jealous, one single imperial Power, whose resources far surpassed his own. He was scarcely the man to face such a combination. He had already suffered the irreparable misfortune of Eleanor's divorce, and of her joining forces and blood with his rival. By him she bore sons; by Louis only daughters. Still, some advantages remained to the French king. He managed to hold out for his lifetime against the Plantagenets; and after nearly four centuries of struggle and devastation the final victory in Europe rested with France. The Angevin Empire was indeed more impressive on the map than in reality. It was a motley, ill-knit collection of states, flung together by the chance of a single marriage, and lacked unity both of purpose and strength. The only tie between England and her Continental empire was the fact that Henry himself and some of his magnates held lands on either side of the Channel. There was no pretence of a single, central Government; no uniformity of administration or custom; no common interests or feelings of loyalty. Weak as Louis VII appeared in his struggle with the enterprising and active Henry, the tide of events flowed with the compact French monarchy, and even Louis left it more firmly established than he found it.

The main method of the French was simple. Henry had inherited vast estates; but with them also all their local and feudal discontents. Louis could no longer set the Count of Anjou against the Duke of Normandy, but he could still encourage both in Anjou and in Normandy those local feuds and petty wars which sapped the strength of the feudal potentates, in principle his vassals. Nor was the exploiting of family quarrels an unfruitful device. In the later years of his reign, the sons of Henry II, eager, turbulent, and proud, allowed themselves to be used by Louis VII and by his successor, the wily and gifted Philip Augustus, against their father.

*　　*　　*　　*　　*

How, we may ask, did all this affect the daily life of England and her history? A series of personal feudal struggles fought in distant lands, the quarrels of an alien ruling class, were little understood and less liked by the common folk. Yet these things long burdened their pilgrimage. For many generations their bravest and best were to fight and die by the marshes of the Loire or under the sun-baked hills of Southern France in pursuit of the dream of English dominion over French soil. For this two centuries later Englishmen triumphed at Crécy, Poitiers, and Agincourt, or starved in the terrible Limoges march of the Black Prince. For this they turned fertile France into a desert where even the most needed beasts died of thirst and hunger. Throughout the medieval history of England war with France is the interminable and often the dominant theme. It groped and scraped into every reach of English life, moulding and fretting the shape of English society and institutions.

No episode opens to us a wider window upon the politics of the twelfth century in England than the quarrel of Henry II with his great subject and former friend, Thomas Becket, Archbishop of Canterbury. We have to realise the gravity of this conflict. The military State in feudal Christendom bowed to the Church in things spiritual; it never accepted the idea of the transference of secular power to priestly authority. But the Church, enriched continually by the bequests of hardy barons, anxious in the death agony about their life beyond the grave, became the greatest landlord and capitalist in the community. Rome used its ghostly arts upon the superstitions of almost all the actors in the drama. The power of the State was held in constant challenge by this potent interest. Questions of doctrine might well have been resolved, but how was the government of the country to be carried on under two conflicting powers, each possessed of immense claims upon limited national resources? This conflict was not confined to England. It was the root question of the European world, as it then existed.

Under William the Conqueror schism had been avoided in England by tact and compromise. Under Lanfranc the Church worked with the Crown, and each power reinforced the other against the turbulent barons or the oppressed commonalty. But now a great personality stood at the summit of the religious hierarchy, Thomas Becket, who had been the King's friend. He had been his Chancellor, or, as Ranke first remarked, "to use a somewhat equivalent expression, his most trusted Cabinet Minister." He had in both home and foreign affairs loyally served his master. He had re-organised the imposition of scutage, a tax that allowed money to commute personal service in arms and thus eventually pierced the feudal system to its core. He had played his part in the acquisition of Brittany. The King felt sure that in Becket he had his own man—no mere servant, but a faithful comrade and colleague in the common endeavour. It was by the King's direct influence and personal effort that Becket was elected Archbishop.

From that moment all his gifts and impulses ran in another channel. Something like the transformation which carried Henry V from a rollicking prince to the august hero-King overnight was now witnessed in Becket. His private life had always been both pious and correct. He had of course been immersed in political affairs; nor was it as a sombre figure behind the throne. But whereas hitherto as a courtier and a prince he had rivalled all in magnificence and pomp, taking his part in the vivid pageant of the times, he now sought by extreme austerities to gather around himself the fame and honour of a saint. Becket pursued the same methods and ambitions in the ecclesiastical as previously he had done in the political sphere; and in both he excelled. He now championed the Church against the Crown in every aspect of their innumerable interleaving functions. He clothed this aggressive process with those universal ideas of the Catholic Church and the Papal authority which far transcended the bounds of our Island, covering Europe and reaching out into the mysterious and the sublime. After a tour upon the Continent and a conclave with the religious dignitaries of France and Italy he returned to England imbued with the resolve to establish the independence of the Church hierarchy on the State as represented by the King. Thus he opened the conflict which the wise Lanfranc had throughout his life striven to avoid. At this time the mood in England was ripe for strife upon this issue.

In a loose and undefined way Saxon England had foreshadowed the theory to which the Elizabethan reformers long afterwards returned. Both thought of the monarch as appointed by God, not only to rule the State, but to protect and guide the Church. In the eleventh century however the Papacy had been reinvigorated under Hildebrand, who became Pope Gregory VII in 1073, and his successors. Rome now began to make claims which were hardly compatible with the traditional notions of the mixed sovereignty of the King in all matters temporal and spiritual. The Gregorian movement held that the government of the Church ought to be in the hands of the clergy, under the supervision of the Pope. According to this view, the King was a mere layman whose one religious function was obedience to the hierarchy. The Church was a body apart, with its own allegiance and its own laws. By the reign of Henry II the bishop was not only a spiritual officer; he was a great landowner, the secular equal of earls; he could put forces in the field; he could excommunicate his enemies, who might be the King's friends. Who, then, was to appoint the bishop? And, when once appointed, to whom, if the Pope commanded one thing and the King another, did he owe his duty? If the King and his counsellors agreed upon a law contrary to the law of the Church, to which authority was obedience due? Thus there came about the great conflict between Empire and Papacy symbolised in the question of Investiture, of which the dispute between Henry II and Becket is the insular counterpart.

The struggle between Henry II and Becket is confused by the technical details over which it was fought. There was however good reason why the quarrel should have been engaged upon incidents of administration rather than upon the main principles which were at stake. The Crown resented the claim of the Church to interfere in the State; but in the Middle Ages no king dared to challenge the Church outright, or, much as he might hope to limit its influence, thought of a decisive breach. It was not till the sixteenth century that an English king in conflict with the Papacy dared to repudiate the authority of Rome and nakedly declare the State supreme, even in spiritual matters. In the twelfth century the only practicable course was compromise. But the Church at this time was in no mood for a bargain. In every country the secular power took up the challenge; but it was hard to meet, and in Central Europe at least the struggle ended only in the exhaustion of both Empire and Papacy.

The Church in England, like the baronage, had gained greatly in power since the days of William the Conqueror and his faithful Archbishop Lanfranc. Stephen in his straits had made sweeping concessions to the Church, whose political influence then reached its zenith. These concessions, Henry felt, compromised his royal rights. He schemed to regain what had been lost, and as the first step in 1162 appointed his trusted servant Becket to be Archbishop of Canterbury, believing he would thus secure the acquiescence of the Episcopacy. In fact he provided the Church with a leader of unequalled vigour and obstinacy. He ignored or missed the ominous signs of the change in Becket's attitude, and proceeded to his second step, the publication in 1164 of the Constitutions of Clarendon. In these Henry claimed, not without considerable truth, to be re-stating the customs of the kingdom as they had been before the anarchy of Stephen's reign. He sought to retrace thirty years and to annul the effects of Stephen's surrender. But Becket resisted. He regarded Stephen's yieldings as irrevocable gains by the Church. He refused to let them lapse. He declared that the Constitutions of Clarendon did not represent the relations between Church and Crown. When, in October 1164, he was summoned to appear before the Great Council and explain his conduct he haughtily denied the King's authority and placed himself under the protection of the Pope and God.

Thus he ruptured that unity which had hitherto been deemed vital in the English realm, and in fact declared war with ghostly weapons upon the King. Stiff in defiance, Becket took refuge on the Continent, where the same conflict was already distracting both Germany and Italy. The whole thought of the ruling classes in England was shaken by this grievous dispute. It endured for six years, during which the Archbishop of Canterbury remained in his French exile. Only in 1170 was an apparent reconciliation brought about between him and the King at Fréteval, in Touraine. Each side appeared to waive its claims in principle. The King did not mention his rights and customs. The Archbishop was not called upon to give an oath. He was promised a safe return and full possession of his see. King and Primate met for the last time in the summer of 1170 at Chaumont. "My lord," said Thomas at the end, "my heart tells me that I part from you as one whom you shall see no more in this life." "Do you hold me as a traitor?" asked the King. "That be far from thee, my lord," replied the Archbishop; but he returned to Canterbury resolved to seek from the Pope unlimited powers of excommunication wherewith to discipline his ecclesiastical forces. "The more potent and fierce the prince is," he wrote, "the stronger stick and harder chain is needed to bind him and keep him in order." "I go to England," he said, "whether to peace or to destruction I know not; but God has decreed what fate awaits me."

Meanwhile, in Becket's absence, Henry had resolved to secure the peaceful accession of his son, the young Henry, by having him crowned in his own lifetime. The ceremony had been performed by the Archbishop of York, assisted by a number of other clerics. This action was bitterly resented by Becket as an infringement of a cherished right of his see. After the Fréteval agreement Henry supposed that bygones were to be bygones. But Becket had other views.

His welcome home after the years of exile was astonishing. At Canterbury the monks received him as an angel of God. "I am come to die among you," he said in his sermon, and again, "In this church there are martyrs, and God will soon increase their number." He made a triumphal progress through London, scattering alms to the beseeching and exalted people. Then hotfoot he proceeded to renew his excommunication of the clergy who had taken part in the crowning of young Henry. These unfortunate priests and prelates traveled in a bunch to the King, who was in Normandy. They told a tale not only of an ecclesiastical challenge, but of actual revolt and usurpation. They said that the Archbishop was ready "to tear the crown from the young King's head."

Henry Plantagenet, first of all his line, with all the fire of his nature, received these tidings when surrounded by his knights and nobles. He was transported with passion. "What a pack of fools and cowards," he cried, "I have nourished in my house, that not one of them will avenge me of this turbulent priest!" Another version says "of this upstart clerk." A council was immediately summoned to devise measures for reasserting the royal authority. In the main they shared the King's anger. Second thoughts prevailed. With all the stresses that existed in that fierce and ardent society, it was not possible that the realm could support a fearful conflict between the two sides of life represented by Church and State.

But meanwhile another train of action was in process. Four knight had heard the King's bitter words spoken in the full circle. They travelled fast to the coast. They crossed the Channel. They called for horses and rode to Canterbury. There on December 29, 1170, they found the Archbishop in the cathedral. The scene and the tragedy are famous. He confronted them with Cross and mitre, fearless and resolute in warlike action, a master of the histrionic arts. After haggard parleys they fell upon him, cut him down with their swords, and left him bleeding like Julius Cæsar, with a score of wounds to cry for vengeance.

This tragedy was fatal to the King. The murder of one of the foremost of God's servants, like the breaking of a feudal oath, struck at the heart of the age. All England was filled with terror. They acclaimed the dead Archbishop as a martyr; and immediately it appeared that his relics healed incurable diseases, and robes that he had worn by their mere touch relieved minor ailments. Here indeed was a crime, vast and inexpiable. When Henry heard the appalling news he was prostrated with grief and fear. All the elaborate process of law which he had sought to set on foot against this rival power was brushed aside by a brutal, bloody act; and though he had never dreamed that such a deed would be done there were his own hot words, spoken before so many witnesses, to fasten on him, for that age at least, the guilt of murder, and, still worse, sacrilege.

The immediately following years were spent in trying to recover what he had lost by a great parade of atonement for his guilt. He made pilgrimages to the shrine of the murdered Archbishop. He subjected himself to public penances. On several anniversaries, stripped to the waist and kneeling humbly, he submitted to be scourged by the triumphant monks. We may however suppose that the corporal chastisement, which apparently from the contemporary pictures was administered with birch rods, was mainly symbolic. Under this display of contrition and submission the King laboured perseveringly to regain the rights of State. By the Compromise of Avranches in 1172 he made his peace with the Papacy on comparatively easy terms. To many deep-delving historians it seems that in fact, though not in form, he had by the end of his life re-established the main principles of the Constitutions of Clarendon, which are after all in harmony with what the English nation or any virile and rational race would mean to have as their law. Certainly the Papacy supported him in his troubles with his sons. The knights, it is affirmed, regained their salvation in the holy wars. But Becket's sombre sacrifice had not been in vain. Until the Reformation the Church retained the system of ecclesiastical courts independent of the royal authority, and the right of appeal to Rome, two of the major points upon which Becket had defied the King.

It is a proof of the quality of the age that these fierce contentions, shaking the souls of men, should have been so rigourously and yet so evenly fought out. In modern conflicts and revolutions in some great states bishops and archbishops have been sent by droves to concentration camps, or pistolled in the nape of the neck in the well-warmed, brilliantly lighted corridor of a prison. What claim have we to vaunt a superior civilisation to Henry II's times? We are sunk in a barbarism all the deeper because it is tolerated by moral lethargy and covered with a veneer of scientific conveniences.[1]

*　　*　　*　　*　　*

Eighteen years of life lay before the King after Becket's death. In a sense, they were years of glory. All Europe marvelled at the extent of Henry's domains, to which in 1171 he had added the Lordship of Ireland. Through the marriages of his daughters he was linked with the Norman King of Sicily, the King of Castile, and Henry the Lion of Saxony, who was a most powerful prince in Germany. Diplomatic agents spread his influence in the Lombard cities of northern Italy. Both Emperor and Pope invited him in the name of Christ and all Europe to lead a new Crusade and to be King of Jerusalem. Indeed, after the Holy Roman Emperor, Frederick Barbarossa, Henry stood next in Christendom. It was suspected by his contemporaries that his aim was to win for himself a kingdom in Italy and even to wear the imperial crown.

Yet Henry knew well that his splendour was personal in origin, tenuous and transient in quality; and he had also deep clouding family sorrows. During these years he was confronted with no less than four rebellions by his sons. For the three eldest he had provided glittering titles; Henry held Normandy, Maine and Anjou; Richard was given Aquitaine, and to Geoffrey went Brittany. These boys were typical sprigs of the Angevin stock. They wanted power as well as titles, and they bore their father no respect. Urged on by their mother, Queen Eleanor, who now lived in Poitiers apart from her husband, between 1173 and 1186 they rose in revolt in various combinations. On each occasion they could count on the active support of the watchful King of France. Henry treated his ungrateful children with generosity, but he had no illusions. The royal chamber at Westminster at this time was adorned with paintings done at the King's command. One represented four eaglets preying upon the parent bird, the fourth one poised at the parent's neck, ready to pick out the eyes. "The four eaglets," the King is reported to have said, "are my four sons who cease not to persecute me even unto death. The youngest of them, whom I now embrace with so much affection will sometime in the end insult me more grievously and more dangerously than any of the others."

So it was to be. John, whom he had striven to provide with an inheritance equal to that of his brothers, joined the final plot against him. In 1188 Richard, his eldest surviving son, after the death of young Henry, was making war upon him in conjunction with King Philip of France. Already desperately ill, Henry was defeated at Le Mans and recoiled to Normandy. When he saw in the list of conspirators against him the name of his son John, upon whom his affection had strangely rested, he abandoned the struggle with life. "Let things go as they will," he gasped. "Shame, shame on a conquered King." So saying, this hard, violent, brilliant and lonely man expired at Chinon on July 6, 1189. The pious were taught to regard this melancholy end as the further chastisement of God upon the murderer of Thomas Becket. Such is the bitter taste of worldly power. Such are the correctives of glory.

CHAPTER THIRTEEN

THE ENGLISH COMMON LAW

THE PLANTAGENETS WERE ROUGH MASTERS, AND THE TEMPER OF THE age was violent. It was the violence however of vigour, not of decadence. England has had greater soldier-kings and subtler diplomatists than Henry II, but no man has left a deeper mark upon our laws and institutions. His strange outbursts of frenzied energy did not exhaust themselves in politics, war, and the chase. Like his Norman predecessors and his sons, Henry II possessed an instinct for the problems of government and law, and it is here that his achievement lies. The names of his battles have vanished with their dust, but his fame will live with the English Constitution and the English Common Law.

This great King was fortunate in his moment. William I and Henry I had brought to England or preserved there all those instruments through which their successor was to work. They themselves could move but slowly and with caution. The land must settle itself to its new rules and rulers. In 1154 however Henry of Anjou had come to a country which nearly twenty years of anarchy had prepared for the acceptance of a strong hand at the centre. Himself a Frenchman, the ruler of more than half France, he brought to his task the qualities of vision, wide experience, and a strength that did not scruple to stoop to cunning. The disasters of Stephen's reign determined Henry not only to curb baronial independence and regain the ground lost by his predecessor, but to go much further. In place of a multitude of manorial courts where local magnates dispensed justice whose quality

and character varied with the customs and temper of the neighbourhood, he planned a system of royal courts which would administer a
law common to all England and all men.

The policy was not without peril. The King was wise enough to
avoid a direct assault, for he knew, as the Conqueror had known, that
to lay a finger upon the sanctity of customary rights would provoke
disaster. Faced with this barrier, Henry shrewdly opposed custom to
custom and cloaked innovation in the respected garb of conservatism.
He was careful to respect existing forms. His plan was to stretch old
principles to take on new meanings. In an unwritten Constitution
the limits of the King's traditional rights were vaguely defined. This
opened a shrewd line of advance. For centuries before the Conquest,
Church and King had been the enemies of seigneurial anarchy, but
there had been no question of swiftly extending the Crown's jurisdiction. Fastening upon the elastic Saxon concept of the King's Peace,
Henry used it to draw all criminal cases into his courts. Every man had
his own Peace, which it was a crime to break, and the more important
the man the graver the breach. The King's Peace was the most important of all, and those who broke it could be tried in the King's court.
But the King's Peace was limited, and often embraced only offences
committed in the King's presence or on the King's highway or land.
When the King died his Peace died with him and men might do as
they willed. Cautiously and quietly Henry began to claim that the
King's Peace extended over all England, and that no matter where it
was broken offenders should be tried in the King's courts. Civil cases
he attracted by straining a different principle, the old right of the
King's court to hear appeals in cases where justice had been refused
and to protect men in possession of their lands. He did not brandish
what he was about; the changes that he made were introduced gradually and without legislation, so that at first they were hardly perceived.
Rarely is it possible to state the date at which any innovation was made;
yet at the King's death a clever man might have looked back and seen
how much had been altered in the thirty-five years that Henry II had
sat on the English throne.

But if Henry was to pose as a conservative in the legal sphere he
must be consistent. Compulsion could play little part in his programme;

it had to be the first principle of his policy to attract cases to his courts rather than to compel them. A bait was needed with which to draw litigants to the royal courts; the King must offer them better justice than they could have at the hands of their lords. Henry accordingly threw open to litigants in the royal courts a startling new procedure—trial by jury. *Regale quoddam beneficium,* a contemporary called it—a royal boon; and the description illuminates both the origin of the jury and the part it played in the triumph of the Common Law. Henry did not invent the jury; he put it to a new purpose. The idea of the jury is the one great contribution of the Franks to the English legal system, for, unknown in this country before the Conquest, the germ of it lies far back in the practice of the Carolingian kings. In origin the jury was a royal instrument of administrative convenience: the King had the right to summon a body of men to bear witness under oath about the truth of any question concerning the royal interest. It was through this early form of jury that William the Conqueror had determined the Crown rights in the great Domesday survey. The genius of Henry II, perceiving new possibilities in such a procedure, turned to regular use in the courts an instrument which so far had only been used for administrative purposes.

Only the King had the right to summon a jury. Henry accordingly did not grant it to private courts, but restricted it to those who sought justice before the royal judges. It was an astute move. Until this time both civil and criminal cases had been decided through the oath, the ordeal, or the duel. The court would order one of the litigants to muster a body of men who would swear to the justice of his cause and whom it was hoped God would punish if they swore falsely; or condemn him, under the supervision of a priest, to carry a red-hot iron, or eat a morsel of bread, or be plunged in a pool of water. If the iron did not burn or the bread choke or the water reject him so that he could not sink, then Divine Providence was adjudged to have granted a visible sign that the victim was innocent. The duel, or trial by battle, was a Norman innovation based on the modern theory that the God of Battles will strengthen the arm of the righteous, and was at one time much favoured for deciding disputes about land. Monasteries and other substantial landowners took the precaution however of assisting the Almighty by retaining professional champions to protect their property and their rights. All this left small room for debate on points of law. In a more rational age men were beginning to distrust such antics, and indeed the Church refused to sanction the ordeal during the same year that Magna Carta was sealed. Thus trial by jury quickly gained favour. But the old processes were long in dying. If a defendant preferred to take his case before God man could not forbid him, and the ordeal therefore was not abolished outright. Hence a later age was to know the horrors of the *peine forte et dure*—the compulsion of the accused by slow pressure to death to agree to put himself before a jury. Time swept this away; yet so late as 1818 a litigant nonplussed the judges by an appeal to trial by battle and compelled Parliament to abolish this ancient procedure.

The jury of Henry II was not the jury that we know. There were various forms of it; but in all there was this essential difference: the jurymen were witnesses as well as judges of the facts. Good men and true were picked, not yet for their impartiality, but because they were the men most likely to know the truth. The modern jury which knows nothing about the case till it is proved in court was slow in coming. The process is obscure. A jury summoned to Westminster from distant parts might be reluctant to come. The way was long, the roads unsafe, and perhaps only three or four would arrive. The court could not wait. An adjournment would be costly. To avoid delay and expense the parties might agree to rely on a jury *de circumstantibus*, a jury of bystanders. The few jurors who knew the truth of the matter would tell their tale to the bystanders, and then the whole body would deliver their verdict. In time the jurors with local knowledge would cease to be jurors at all and become witnesses, giving their evidence in open court to a jury entirely composed of bystanders. Such, we may guess, or something like it, was what happened. Very gradually, as the laws of evidence developed, the change came. By the fifteenth century it was under way; yet the old idea lingered, and even under the Tudor kings jurymen might be tried for perjury if they gave a wrongful verdict.

The jury system has come to stand for all we mean by English justice, because so long as a case has to be scrutinised by twelve honest men, defendant and plaintiff alike have a safeguard from arbitrary

perversion of the law. It is this which distinguishes the law administered in English courts from Continental legal systems based on
Roman law. Thus amidst the great process of centralisation the old
principle was preserved, and endures to this day, that law flows from
the people. Land is not given by the King.

These methods gave good justice. Trial by jury became popular.
Professional judges removed from local prejudice, whose outlook
ranged above the interested or ignorant lord or his steward, armed
with the King's power to summon juries, secured swifter decisions,
and a strong authority to enforce them. Henry accordingly had to
build up almost from nothing a complete system of royal courts,
capable of absorbing a great rush of new work. The instrument to
which he turned was the royal Council, the organ through which
all manner of governmental business was already regularly carried
out. It was to be the common parent of Chancery and Exchequer,
of Parliament, of the Common Law courts and those Courts of
Prerogative on which the Tudors and Stuarts relied. At the outset
of Henry II's reign, it dealt almost indiscriminately with every
kind of administrative business. On the judicial side the Court of
the Exchequer, which tried cases affecting the royal revenue, was
beginning to take shape; but in the main the Council in this aspect
was scarcely more than the King's feudal court, where he did justice,
like any other lord, among his vassals. Under Henry II all this was
changed. The functions of the King's justices became more and more
specialised. During the reigns of his sons the Council began to divide
into two great courts, the King's Bench and the Common Pleas. They
did not become fully separate till a century later. Thereafter, with the
Court of the Exchequer, they formed the backbone of the Common
Law system down to the nineteenth century. In addition, travelling
justices—justices "in eyre"—were from time to time appointed to
hear all manner of business in the shires, whose courts were thus
drawn into the orbit of royal justice.

But all this was only a first step. Henry also had to provide means
whereby the litigant, eager for royal justice, could remove his case
out of the court of his lord into the King's court. The device which
Henry used was the royal writ. At all costs baronial rights must be

formally respected; but by straining the traditional rights of the Crown it was possible to claim that particular types of case fell within the King's province. Upon this principle Henry evolved a number of set formulæ, or writs, each fitted to a certain type of case; and any man who could by some fiction fit his own case to the wording of one of the royal writs might claim the King's justice. The wording of writs was rigid, but at this date new forms of writ might still be given. For about eighty years they increased in number, and with each new form a fresh blow was struck at the feudal courts. It was not until de Montfort's revolt against the third Henry in the thirteenth century that the multiplication of writs was checked and the number fixed at something under two hundred. This system then endured for six hundred years. However the times might change, society had to adapt itself to that unbending framework. Inevitably English law became weighted with archaisms and legal fictions. The whole course of a case might depend on the writ with which it was begun, forevery writ had its special procedure, mode of trial, and eventual remedy. Thus the Saxon spirit of formalism survived. Henry II had only been able to break down the primitive methods of the early courts by fastening upon the law a procedure which became no less rigid. Yet, cumbersome though it was, the writ system gave to English law a conservative spirit which guarded and preserved its continuity from that time on in an unbroken line.

*   *   *   *   *

It is a maxim of English law that legal memory begins with the accession of Richard I in 1189. The date was set for a technical reason by a statute of Edward I. It could scarcely have been more appropriately chosen however, for with the close of the reign of Henry II we are on the threshold of a new epoch in the history of English law. With the establishment of a system of royal courts, giving the same justice all over the country, the old diversity of local law was rapidly broken down, and a law common to the whole land and to all men soon took its place. A modern lawyer, transported to the England of Henry's predecessor, would find himself in strange surroundings; with the system that Henry bequeathed to his son he would feel almost at home. That is the measure of the great King's achievement. He had laid the foundations of the English Common Law, upon which succeeding generations would build. Changes in the design would arise, but its main outlines were not to be altered.

It was in these fateful and formative years that the English-speaking peoples began to devise methods of determining legal disputes which survive in substance to this day. A man can only be accused of a civil or criminal offence which is clearly defined and known to the law. The judge is an umpire. He adjudicates on such evidence as the parties choose to produce. Witnesses must testify in public and on oath. They are examined and cross-examined, not by the judge, but by the litigants themselves or their legally qualified and privately hired representatives. The truth of their testimony is weighed not by the judge by by twelve good men and true, and it is only when this jury has determined the facts that the judge is empowered to impose sentence, punishment, or penalty according to law. All might seem very obvious, even a platitude, until one contemplates the alternative system which still dominates a large portion of the world. Under Roman law, and systems derived from it, a trial in those turbulent centuries, and in some countries even to-day, is often an inquisition. The judge makes his own investigation into the civil wrong or the public crime, and such investigation is largely uncontrolled. The suspect can be interrogated in private. He must answer all questions put to him. His right to be represented by a legal adviser is restricted. The witnesses against him can testify in secret and in his absence. And only when these processes have been accomplished is the accusation or charge against him formulated and published. Thus often arises secret intimidation, enforced confessions, torture, and blackmailed pleas of guilty. These sinister dangers were extinguished from the Common Law of England more than six centuries ago. By the time Henry II's great-grandson, Edward I had died English criminal and civil procedure had settled into a mould and tradition which in the mass govern the English-speaking peoples to-day. In all claims and disputes, whether they concerned the grazing lands of the Middle West, the oilfields of California, the sheep-runs and gold-mines of Australia, or the territorial rights of the Maoris, these rules have obtained, at any rate in theory, according to the procedure and mode of trial evolved by the English Common Law.

Nor was this confined to how trials were conducted. The law that was applied to such multitudinous problems, some familiar, others novel, was in substance the Common Law of England. The law concerning murder, theft, the ownership of land, and the liberty of the individual was all transported, together with much else, to the New World, and, though often modified to suit the conditions and temper of the times, descends in unbroken line from that which governed the lives and fortunes of twelfth-century Englishmen.

Most of it was then unwritten, and in England much still remains so. The English statutes, for example, still contain no definition of the crime of murder, for this, like much other law, rested on the unwritten custom of the land as declared by the inhabitants and interpreted, developed, and applied by the judges. Lawyers could only ascertain it by studying reports and records of ancient decisions. For this they had already in this early age made their own arrangements. A century after Henry's death they began to group themselves into professional communities in London, the Inns of Court, half colleges, half law-schools, but predominantly secular, for the presence of clerics learned in the laws of Rome and the Canon Law of the Roman Church was not encouraged, and here they produced annual laws reports, or "Year Books," as they were then called, whose authority was recognised by the judges, and which continued in almost unbroken succession for nearly three centuries. In all this time however only one man attempted a general and comprehensive statement of the English Common Law. About the year 1250 a Judge of Assize named Henry of Bracton produced a book of nearly nine hundred pages entitled *A Tract on the Laws and Customs of England*. Nothing like it was achieved for several hundred years, but Bracton's method set an example, since followed throughout the English-speaking world, not so much of stating the Common Law as of explaining and commenting on it, and thus encouraging and helping later lawyers and judges to develop and expand it. Digests and codes imposed in the Roman manner by an omnipotent state on a subject people were alien to the spirit and tradition of England. The law was already there, in the customs of the land, and it was only a matter of discovering it by diligent study and comparison of recorded decisions in earlier cases, and applying it to the particular dispute before the court. In the course of time the Common Law changed. Lawyers of the reign of Henry II read into the statements of their predecessors of the tenth century meanings and principles which their authors never intended, and applied them to the novel conditions and problems of their own day. No matter. Here was a precedent. If a judge could be shown that a custom or something like it had been recognised and acted upon in an earlier and similar case he would be more ready, if it accorded with his sense of what was just and with the current feelings of the community, to follow it in the dispute before him. This slow but continuous growth of what is popularly known as "case law" ultimately achieved much the same freedoms and rights for the individual as are enshrined in other countries by written instruments such as the Declarations of the Rights of Man and the spacious and splendid provisions of the American Declaration of Independence and constitutional guarantees of civil rights. But English justice advanced very cautiously. Even the framers of Magna Carta did not attempt to lay down new law or proclaim any broad general principles. This was because both sovereign and subject were in practice bound by the Common Law, and the liberties of Englishmen rested not on any enactment of the State, but on immemorial slow-growing custom declared by juries of free men who gave their verdicts case by case in open court.

CHAPTER FOURTEEN

CŒUR DE LION

THE CHRISTIAN KINGDOM FOUNDED AT JERUSALEM AFTER THE FIRST Crusade had stood precariously for a century, guarded by the military orders of the Knights Templars and Hospitallers. Its continued existence was largely due to the disunity that prevailed among the Moslem lands surrounding it. At length the rise of a great national leader of the Turks, or Saracens, united the Moslem power. In 1169 Saladin became Vizier of Egypt. Shortly afterwards he proclaimed himself Sultan. By origin he was a Kurd, and by culture a Damascene. Soon his power was stretching out into Syria, encircling the Crusaders' principalities on the Levantine coast. He took Damascus in 1174 and Aleppo in 1183. In their anxieties at these gathering dangers the Christian community in Jerusalem, and Guy of Lusignan, the King, offered the threatened crown first to Philip of France and then to Henry II, and made the West ring with cries for help. But the quarrels of the Western princes prevented effective measures being taken in time. In 1186 Saladin in his turn proclaimed a Holy War. He promised his warlike hordes booty and adventure in this world and bliss eternal in the next, and advanced upon Jerusalem. The Christian army of occupation which took the field against him, perhaps ten thousand strong, was caught at a disadvantage in the thirsty desert and cut to pieces by greatly superior numbers at Hattin. The King, the Grand Master of the Templars, and many of the greatest nobles were taken prisoners. In October 1187 Jerusalem surrendered, and thereafter all

Palestine and Syria, except Tyre, Antioch, and Tripoli, fell again into Moslem hands.

The shock of these events resounded throughout Europe. The Pope shared the general horror of the Christian West. His legates traversed the Courts enjoining peace among Christians and war against the infidel. The sovereigns of the three greatest nations of the West responded to the call, and an intense movement stirred the chivalry of England, France, and Germany. Pictures were shown of the Holy Sepulchre defiled by the horses of the Saracen cavalry. Not only the gentle folk but to some extent all classes were swept by deep emotion. Not without sorrow, as the literature of those times shows, did many of the young Crusaders leave home and loved ones for a journey into the dangers of the distant and the unknown. The magnetism of war and adventure mingled with a deep counterpart of sacrifice and mysticism which lights the age and its efforts with the charm of true romance. In Germany the solemn Diet of Mainz "swore the expedition" to the Holy Land. The Kings of France and England agreed upon a joint Crusade, without however ceasing their immediate strife. To the religious appeal was added the spur of the tax-gatherer. The "Saladin tithe" was levied upon all who did not take the Cross. On the other hand, forgiveness of taxes and a stay in the payment of debts were granted to all Crusaders. The strongest armies ever yet sent to the East were raised. Germany marshalled a large array round the standard of Frederick Barbarossa. A Scandinavian fleet bore twelve thousand Norsemen through the Straits of Gibraltar. Thus did armoured Europe precipitate itself upon Asia. Meanwhile the first of the rescuers, Conrad of Montferrat, who, hastening from Constantinople, had saved Tyre, was already besieging Acre.

In the midst of these surgings Henry II died in sorrow and disaster. He made no attempt to prescribe the succession, and it passed naturally to Richard. The new King affected little grief at the death of a father against whom he was in arms. He knelt beside his bier no longer than would have been necessary to recite the Lord's Prayer, and turned at once to the duties of his realm. In spite of many harsh qualities, men saw in him a magnanimity which has added lustre to his military renown. At the outset of his reign he gave an outstanding example. During his rebellion against his father he had pressed hard upon Henry II's rout at Le Mans in the very forefront of the cavalry without even wearing his mail. In the rearguard of the beaten army stood Henry's faithful warrior, William the Marshal. He confronted Richard and had him at his mercy. "Spare me!" cried Richard in his disadvantage; so the Marshal turned his lance against the prince's horse and killed it, saying with scorn, "I will not slay you. The Devil may slay you." This was humiliation and insult worse than death. It was not therefore without anxiety that the Marshal and his friends awaited their treatment at the hands of the sovereign to whom their loyalties must now be transferred. But King Richard rose at once above the past. He spoke with dignity and detachment of the grim incident so fresh and smarting in his mind. He confirmed his father's true servant in all his offices and honours, and sent him to England to act in his name. He gave him in marriage the rich Crown heiress of Pembroke, and at a stroke the Marshal became one of the most powerful of English barons. Indeed it was noted that the King's favour lighted upon those who had stood loyally by his father against him, even to the detriment of those who had been his own fellow-rebels.

*   *   *   *   *

Richard, with all his characteristic virtues and faults cast in a heroic mould, is one of the most fascinating medieval figures. He has been described as the creature and embodiment of the age of chivalry. In those days the lion was much admired in heraldry, and more than one king sought to link himself with its repute. When Richard's contemporaries called him "Cœur de Lion" they paid a lasting compliment to the king of beasts. Little did the English people owe him for his services, and heavily did they pay for his adventures. He was in England only twice for a few short months in his ten years' reign; yet his memory has always stirred English hearts, and seems to present throughout the centuries the pattern of the fighting man. In all deeds of prowess as well as in large schemes of war Richard shone. He was tall and delicately shaped; strong in nerve and sinew, and most dexterous in arms. He rejoiced in personal combat, and regarded his opponents without malice as necessary agents in his fame. He loved war, not so much for the sake of glory or political ends, but as other men love science or poetry, for the excitement of the struggle and the glow of victory. By this his whole temperament was toned; and, united with the highest qualities of the military commander, love of war called forth all the powers of his mind and body.

Although a man of blood and violence, Richard was too impetuous to be either treacherous or habitually cruel. He was as ready to forgive as he was hasty to offend; he was open-handed and munificent to profusion; in war circumspect in design and skilful in execution; in politics a child, lacking in subtlety and experience. His political alliances were formed upon his likes and dislikes; his political schemes had neither unity nor clearness of purpose. The advantages gained for him by military genius were flung away through diplomatic ineptitude. When on the journey to the East Messina in Sicily was won by his arms he was easily persuaded to share with his polished, faithless ally, Philip Augustus, fruits of a victory which more wisely used might have foiled the French king's artful schemes. The rich and tenable acquisition of Cyprus was cast away even more easily than it was won. His life was one magnificent parade, which, when ended, left only an empty plain.

The King's heart was set upon the new Crusade. This task seemed made for him. It appealed to every need of his nature. To rescue the Holy Land from the pollution of the infidel, to charge as a king at the head of knightly squadrons in a cause at once glorious to man and especially acceptable to God, was a completely satisfying inspiration. The English would greatly have liked their King to look after their affairs, to give them peace and order, to nourish their growing prosperity, and to do justice throughout the land. But they understood that the Crusade was a high and sacred enterprise, and the Church taught them that in unseen ways it would bring a blessing upon them. Richard was crowned with peculiar state, by a ceremonial which, elaborating the most ancient forms and traditions of the Island monarchy, is still in all essentials observed to-day. Thereafter the King, for the sake of Christ's sepulchre, virtually put the realm up for sale. Money he must have at all costs for his campaign in far-off Palestine. He sold and re-sold every office in the State. He made new and revolutionarily heavy demands for taxation. He called for "scutage," or the commutation of military service for a money payment, and later re-introduced "carucage," a levy on every hundred acres of land. Thus he filled his chests for the Holy War.

Confiding the government to two Justiciars, William Long-champ, Bishop of Ely, and Hugh Puiset, Bishop of Durham, under the supervision of the one trustworthy member of his family, his mother, the old Queen, Eleanor of Aquitaine, he started for the wars in the summer of 1190. He had promised Philip of France to marry his sister Alice, about whom, except for her looks, the tales were none too good. Philip claimed that Richard had tried to seduce her, and there was bad feeling between the monarchs. However that may be, after Richard had marched across France and sailed to Sicily, where he rested for the winter, his mother brought out to him Berengaria, daughter of the King of Navarre, whom he had known and admired, and now resolved to marry. It was fitting that the "Lion-heart" should marry for love and not for policy, but the rejection of Alice prevented a tie between the Kings of France and England which had been deemed essential to their comradeship in the Crusade. Philip was little soothed for the affront by a compensation of ten thousand marks. The quarrels of England and France were not so lightly set aside, and jealousies and bickerings distressed the winter sojourn of the two allies in Sicily.

Meanwhile Frederick Barbarossa had led his German host from Regensburg in May 1189 through Hungary to Constantinople. As soon as the frontiers of the Byzantine Empire were reached difficulties arose. The successors of Constantine still ruled over an extensive realm in Balkan Europe and in Asia Minor. The Emperor Isaac II at this time had allied himself with Saladin, and it was only under the threat of a Crusade against these Greek schismatics that by the end of March 1190 the Germans were allowed a free passage across the Bosphorus to the Asiatic shore. Barbarossa marched through Asia Minor and reached Cilicia. Here this veteran of the Second Crusade, of forty years before, was drowned in the river Calycadnus, either through his horse slipping at the ford or through the imprudence of bathing after dining. Some of his troops turned back, many died of plague at Antioch, and of his great army, the flower of Germany, barely a thousand, under his son, reached the Crusaders' camp before Acre in October 1190. But these kept tryst. The Anglo-French armies did not quit Sicily till the spring of 1191. Philip sailed direct to Acre. Richard paused in Cyprus. He quarrelled with the local Greek ruler, declared that an insult had been offered to his betrothed, conquered the island, and there wedded Berengaria. It was not until June 8, 1191, that he arrived with powerful forces before Acre.

The glamours of chivalry illumine the tale of the Third Crusade. All the chief princes of Europe were now in line around the doomed stronghold of Saladin, rivalling each other in prowess and jealousy. The sanctity of their cause was no bar to their quarrels and intrigues. King Richard dominated the scene. Fighting always in the most dangerous places, striking down the strongest foes, he negotiated all the time with Saladin. An agreement was in fact almost reached. To save his garrison Saladin offered to surrender his Christian captives, to pay a large indemnity, and to give up the cross, captured by him in Jerusalem, on which Christ—though this after twelve hundred years was not certain—had suffered. But the negotiations failed, and Richard in his fury massacred in cold blood the two thousand Turkish hostages who had been delivered as guarantees. Within five weeks of his arrival he brought the two years' siege to a successful conclusion.

By the time Acre fell King Richard's glory as a warrior and also his skill as a general were the talk of all nations. But the quarrels of the allies paralysed the campaign. Guy of Lusignan, the exiled King of Jerusalem, was disputing with Conrad of Montferrat for the crown. Richard took the one side and Philip the other. A compromise was arranged, but immediately the French king returned home to prosecute his designs in Flanders and to intrigue with Prince John against his absent brother. Duke Leopold of Austria, whom Richard had personally insulted, also took his departure. In these circumstances the Crusading army, ably led by Richard, in spite of the victory at Arsuf, where many thousand infidels were slain, could do no more than reach an eminence which commanded a distant view of the Holy City. The King veiled his eyes, not bearing to look upon the city he could not enter. He resolved to retreat to the coast. In the next year, 1192, he captured Jaffa. Once again the distant prospect of Jerusalem alone rewarded the achievements of the Crusaders, and once again they fell back frustrated.

By now the news from England was so alarming that the King felt it imperative to return home. He renewed his negotiations with Saladin, even offering his sister Joanna in marriage to Saladin's brother as the cement of a lasting peace. In the hard fighting the Saracens had won the respect of their martial foes. A peace or truce for three years was at length effected, by which the coastal towns were divided and the Holy Sepulchre opened as a place of pilgrimage to small parties of Crusaders. It was as tourists only that they reached their goal. The hard struggle between Guy and Conrad for the Kingdom of Jerusalem settled itself, for Conrad, at the moment when his claims had at length been recognised by Richard, was murdered by the assassins belonging to a Moslem sect ruled by "the Old Man of the Mountain." Guy, despairing of regaining his inheritance, purchased Cyprus from the English king. He settled there, and founded a dynasty which, aided by the military orders of knighthood, was to maintain itself against the Turks for nearly four hundred years.

Early in 1193 the King set out for home. Wrecked in the Adriatic, he sought to make his way through Germany in disguise, but his enemy the Duke of Austria was soon upon his track. He was arrested, and held prisoner in a castle. So valuable a prize was not suffered to remain in the Duke's hands. The Emperor himself demanded the famous captive. For many months his prison was a secret of the Imperial Court, but, as a pretty legend tells us, Blondel, Richard's faithful minstrel, went from castle to castle striking the chords which the King loved best, and at last was rewarded by an answer from Richard's own harp.

*   *   *   *   *

William Longchamp, Bishop of Ely, and, with magnificent pluralism, Papal Legate, Chancellor, and Justiciar, had addressed himself with fidelity and zeal to the task of governing England, entrusted to him by Richard in 1189. Emulating the splendour of a monarch, he moved about the country with a pompous retinue, and very soon drew upon himself the envy and then the active hatred of the whole nobility. As the King's faithful servant he saw that the chief danger lay in the over-mighty position of Prince John. The indulgence of Richard had allowed his brother to form a state within a state. John held the shires of Derby, Nottingham, Somerset, Dorset, Devon, and Cornwall; the Earldom of Gloucester, with wide lands in South Wales; the honours of Lancaster, Wallingford, Eye, and Peverel. For the revenues which John drew from these lands he rendered no account to the Exchequer. Their sheriffs were responsible to him alone; their judicial business was transacted by his servants, their writs issued by his chancery and in his name. The royal officers and judges dared not enter John's shires. Bishop Longchamp determined to resist this dual system of government. His personal ostentation and arrogant airs had already multiplied his difficulties. Socially of humble origin, and by race a foreigner, he antagonised the other members of the Council, and provoked them to side with John, who knew well how to turn all this to his profit.

In the summer of 1191 there was open conflict between the two parties, and Longchamp marched against a revolt of John's adherents in the North Midlands. This was a serious crisis. Fortunately however the King, far off in the Levant, had sent home Walter de Coutances, the Archbishop of Rouen, to watch the royal interests. The Archbishop formed a third party, loyal to the King, offended by Longchamp, but unwilling to support John; and presently he succeeded to Longchamp's position when the latter fled from England in October. The return of Philip Augustus from the Crusade in this same autumn brought new opportunities to John's ambition. The French king saw in Richard's absence the chance of breaking up the Angevin power and driving the English out of France. In John he found a willing partner. It was agreed between them that Philip Augustus should attack Normandy, while John raised a revolt in England.

Early in 1193, at a moment already full of peril, the grave news reached England that the King was prisoner "somewhere in Germany." There was general and well-founded consternation among the loyal bulk of his subjects. John declared that Richard was dead, appeared in arms, and claimed the crown. That England was held for Richard in his long absence against all these powerful and subtle forces is a proof of the loyalties of the feudal age. A deep sense of his heroic character and sacred mission commanded the allegiance of a large number of resolute, independent people whose names are unknown to history. The Church never flinched; Walter de Coutances of Rouen stood firm; the Queen-Mother with septuagenarian vigour stood by her eldest son; these dominated the Council, and the Council held the country. The coasts were guarded against an impending French invasion. John's forces melted. In April the strain was relieved by the arrival of authoritative news that Richard was alive. Prince John put the best face he could upon it and stole away to France.

*   *   *   *   *

The Holy Roman Emperor demanded the prodigious ransom of 150,000 marks, twice the annual revenue of the English Crown. One hundred thousand was to be ready in London before the King was liberated. Richard approved and the English Council agreed. Meanwhile Philip and John were active on the other side. They offered the Emperor 80,000 marks to keep the English king under lock and key till Michaelmas 1194, or 1500 marks a month for each month he was kept, or 150,000 marks to deliver him into their hands. But the Emperor felt that his blackmailing honour was engaged to Richard, with whom he had, perhaps precipitately, settled the figure. Once Philip knew that the Emperor would not go back upon his bargain he sent John his notorious message: "Have a care—the Devil is unloosed."

It remained to collect the ransom. The charge staggered the kingdom. Yet nothing was more sacred than the feudal obligation to ransom the liege lord, above all when he enjoyed the sanctity of a Crusader. The Justiciar, the Archbishops, and Queen Eleanor addressed themselves to their grievous task. The Church faced its duty. It was lawful to sacrifice even the most holy ornaments of the cathedrals for the ransom of a Christian lost in the Holy War. From all the lands a new "scutage" was taken. All laymen had to give a quarter of their movables. The Church lands bore an equal burden; they gave their plate and treasure, and three of the monastic orders yielded unresistingly a year's wool crop. Prince John of course set an example in collecting these taxes throughout his shires. His agents dwelt upon the sacred duty of all to pay, and he kept the proceeds of their faith and loyalty for himself. Three separate attempts were made to gather the money, and although England and Normandy, taxed to the limit, could not scrape together the whole of the 150,000 marks required, the Emperor, satisfied that he could get no more, resolved to set his captive at liberty.

At the end of 1193 the stipulated first instalment was paid, and at the beginning of February 1194 Richard Cœur de Lion was released from bondage. He picked his way, we may be assured, with care across Europe, avoiding his French domains, and on March 16 arrived again in London among citizens impoverished but still rejoiced to see him and proud of his fame. He found John again in open rebellion, having seized castles and raised forces with French aid. The new Justiciar and the Council were already acting against the traitor prince, and Richard lent the weight of his strong right arm as well as the majesty of his name to the repression of the revolt. John fled once more to France. The King was recrowned in London with even more elaborate ceremony than before. As he was now plainly at war with Philip Augustus, his first, last, and only measures of government were to raise money and gather knights. These processes well started, he crossed the Channel to defend his French possessions. He never set foot in England again. But the Islanders owed him no grudge. All had been done as was right and due.

The mere arrival of the mighty warrior in France was enough to restore the frontiers and to throw King Philip and his forces upon an almost abject defensive. John sought pardon from the brother and liege lord he had so foully wronged. He did not sue in vain. With the full knowledge that if John had had his way he would still be a captive in a German castle, dethroned, or best of all dead—with all the long story of perfidy and unnatural malice in his mind, Cœur de Lion pardoned John, embraced him in fraternal love, and restored him to some of his estates, except certain fortresses which the barest prudence obliged him to reserve. This gesture was admired for its grandeur, though not perhaps for its wisdom, by the whole society, lay and spiritual, of Christendom.

*   *   *   *   *

The five remaining years of Richard's reign were spent in defending his French domains and raising money for that purpose from

England. Once again the country was ruled by a deputy, this time Hubert Walter, a man bred in the traditions of Henry II's official household as the right-hand man of Ranulf of Glanville; no feudal amateur, but a professional administrator by training and experience. Hubert Walter was now Archbishop of Canterbury, and Richard's Justiciar. He was to become King John's Chancellor. Thus for ten years he was the kingdom's chief Minister. He had been extremely useful to Richard on the Crusade, on which he had accompanied him, and had been prominent in the organisation of the ransom. With determination, knowledge, and deft touch he developed the system of strong centralised government devised by Henry II. Hubert Walter stands out as one of the great medieval administrators. The royal authority was reasserted in the North; commissions of inquiry dealt with unfinished judicial and financial business; other commissions, with the help of local juries, carried out exhaustive inquiries into royal rights and the administration of justice. A new machinery for keeping the peace was devised, to which the origin of the Justices of the Peace can be traced, and the office of Coroner now emerged clearly for the first time. As head of the Exchequer, Walter of Coutances, Archbishop of Rouen, attempted the revision of taxation and of the existing military system. New assessments of land were begun, weights and measures standardised, and the frauds of cloth-workers and dealers purged or curbed. New concessions, involving the precious privilege of local self-government, were granted to London and the principal towns. Throughout the length and breadth of the land the machinery of government was made to work easily and quietly. If there was discontent at the taxes few dared to voice it. One man, a demagogue, "William of the Beard," uttered sentiments which would in similar circumstances readily occur to modern politicians. He was hanged.

Although Richard was an absentee King whose causes and virtues had proved a drain and disappointment to his subjects, his realm had not suffered so much as it would have seemed. The intrigues of the nobles and the treacheries of Prince John had been restrained by an impersonal Government ruling with the force and in the name of high and also well-grounded principles. The system of administration devised by Henry II—the Civil Service as we may call it—had stood the test, and, and, undisturbed by royal interventions, consolidated itself, to the general convenience and advantage. It was proved that the King, to whom all allegiance had been rendered, was no longer the sole guarantee for law and order. There were other sureties upon which in addition the English nation could rely.

In France the war with Philip proceeded in a curious fashion. The negotiations were unceasing. Every year there was a truce, which every year was broken as the weather and general convenience permitted. Richard, studying the strategic defence of Normandy, saw in a high crag which rises at the bend of the Seine by Andelys the key to Rouen. Although inhibited by the truce from fortifying it, and regardless of an interdict launched against him by the bishop of the diocese, the King set himself during 1196 to build the most perfect fortress which his experience could devise. He called it Château Gaillard, or "Saucy Castle," and "my fair child"; and as it rose with all its outworks, bridges, and water-defences into the immense triple-walled stone structure which still scowls upon the roofs of Andelys he rejoiced that it was beyond question the strongest fortress in the world. "If its walls were iron," said Philip in his wrath, "I would take it." "If they were of butter," retorted Richard, "I would hold it." But fate was to give Philip the last word.

In 1197 the skirmishing and parleying, truce-making and truce-breaking, which had become habitual were slashed by a fierce event. Something like a battle was fought, and Richard drove the King of France and his army in headlong rout through the streets of Gisors, where the solemn oaths of the Third Crusade had been sworn barely ten years before by the Kings of France and England.

In 1199, when the difficulties of raising revenue for the endless war were at their height, good news was brought to King Richard. It was said there had been dug up near the castle of Chaluz, on the lands of one of his vassals, a treasure of wonderful quality; a group of golden images of an emperor, his wife, sons, and daughters, seated round a table, also of gold, had been unearthed. The King claimed this treasure as lord paramount. The lord of Chaluz resisted the demand, and the King laid siege to his small, weak castle. On the third day, as he rode daringly near the wall, confident in his hard-tried luck, a bolt from a crossbow struck him in the left shoulder by the neck. The wound, already deep, was aggravated by the necessary cutting out of the arrow-head. Gangrene set in, and Cœur de Lion knew that he must pay a soldier's debt. He prepared for death with fortitude and calm, and in accordance with the principles he had followed. He arranged his affairs; he divided his personal belongings among his friends or bequeathed them to charity. He sent for his mother, the redoubtable Eleanor, who was at hand. He declared John to be his heir, and made all present swear fealty to him. He ordered the archer who had shot the fatal bolt, and who was now a prisoner, to be brought before him. He pardoned him, and made him a gift of money. For seven years he had not confessed for fear of being compelled to be reconciled to Philip, but now he received the offices of the Church with sincere and exemplary piety, and died in the forty-second year of his age on April 6, 1199, worthy, by the consent of all men, to sit with King Arthur and Roland and other heroes of martial romance at some Eternal Round Table, which we trust the Creator of the Universe in His comprehension will not have forgotten to provide.

The archer was flayed alive.

CHAPTER FIFTEEN

MAGNA CARTA

THE CHARACTER OF THE PRINCE WHO NOW ASCENDED THE THRONE of England and became lord of Normandy, Anjou, Touraine, and Maine, claimant to Brittany and heir to Queen Eleanor's Aquitaine, was already well known. Richard had embodied the virtues which men admire in the lion, but there is no animal in nature that combines the contradictory qualities of John. He united the ruthlessness of a hard-ened warrior with the craft and sublety of a Machiavellian. Although from time to time he gave way to furious rages, in which "his eyes darted fire and his countenance became livid," his cruelties were conceived and executed with a cold, inhuman intelligence. Monkish chroniclers have emphasised his violence, greed, malice, treachery, and lust. But other records show that he was often judicious, always extremely capable, and on occasions even generous. He possessed an original and inquiring mind, and to the end of his life treasured his library of books. In him the restless energy of the Plantagenet race was raised to a furious pitch of instability. A French writer,[1] it is true, has tried to throw the sombre cloak of madness over his moral defor-mities, but a study of his actions shows John gifted with a deep and persistent sagacity, of patience and artifice, and with an unshakable resolve, which he fulfilled, to maintain himself upon the throne while the breath was in his body. The difficulties with which he contended, on the whole with remarkable success, deserve cool and attentive study. Moreover, when the long tally is added it will be seen that the

British nation and the English-speaking world owe far more to the vices of John than to the labours of virtuous sovereigns; for it was through the union of many forces against him that the most famous milestone of our rights and freedom was in fact set up.

Although Richard had declared John to be King there were two views upon the succession. Geoffrey, his elder brother, had left behind him a son, Arthur, Prince of Brittany. It was already possible to hold that this grandson of Henry II of an elder branch had a prior right against John, and that is now the law of primogeniture. William the Marshal put the point before the Archbishop of Canterbury, but they both decided that John had the right. Queen Eleanor stood by her son against the grandson, whose mother she had never liked. John was accepted without demur in England. In the French provinces however the opposite view prevailed. Brittany in particular adopted Arthur. The King of France and all French interests thought themselves well served by a disputed succession and the espousal of a minor's cause. Those who had supported Richard against his father, and John against Richard, found it logical to support Arthur against John. Moreover, John's irreverence on high State occasions gave offence to the Church. An evil omen sprang at the outset from his levity. When in Rouen he was handed the symbolic lance of the Dukes of Normandy he turned to make some jocular remark to his attendant courtiers and let the weapon fall to the ground.

With the accession of John there emerges plainly in the northern French provinces a sense of unity with one another and with the kingdom of France; at the same time on this side of the Channel the English baronage became ever more inclined to insular and even nationalistic ideas. Ties with the Continent were weakening through the gradual division of honours and appanages in England and Normandy between different branches of Anglo-Norman families. Moreover, the growing brilliance of the French Court and royal power in the late twelfth century was a powerful magnet which drew Continental loyalties to Paris. King John found himself compelled to fight at even greater odds than his predecessors for his possessions on the Continent. He was also opposed by an increasing resistance to taxation for that purpose in England. In his coronation sermon the

Archbishop is said to have mentioned that the English monarchy was in essence elective rather than hereditary. If, as was generally held, continuity with Edward the Confessor and the Anglo-Saxon kings was to be respected, many good precedents, Alfred the Great among them, could be cited for the doctrine. If the Archbishop preached in this sense there is no doubt he did so with John's full consent. But the principle of picking and choosing among the royal personages by no means weakened the claims of Arthur in regions where his sovereignty was desired.

From the first John feared Arthur. He had been in Brittany and at Arthur's Court when the news of Richard's death reached him. He had made good haste out of so dangerous an area. Arthur was received at Le Mans with enthusiasm. He did homage to Philip for Anjou, Maine, and Touraine. John's strength lay only in Aquitaine and in Normandy. The war and negotiations continued in the fitful style of the preceding reign, but without the prestige of Cœur de Lion on the side of the English Crown. In 1202 Philip, as John's overlord in respect of certain territories, issued a summons in due form citing John before his Court to answer charges made against him by the barons of Poitou. John replied that he was not amenable to such a process. Philip answered that he was summoned as Count of Poitou. John declared that the King of England could not submit himself to such a trial. Philip rejoined that the King of France could not lose his rights over a vassal because that vassal happened to acquire another dignity. All legal expedients being exhausted, John, who was not even promised safe-conduct for his return, refused to attend the Court, and was accordingly sentenced to be deprived of all the lands which he held in France because of his failure of service to his overlord. Thus armed with a legal right recognised by the jurists of the period, Philip invaded Normandy in the summer of 1202, capturing many towns with practically no resistance. The French king knighted Arthur, invested him with all the fiefs of which John had been deprived, except Normandy and Guienne, and betrothed him to his daughter Mary. Arthur was now sixteen.

When we reflect that the French provinces counted just as much with the Plantagenet kings as the whole realm of England it is obvious that a more virtuous man than John would be incensed at such treatment, and its consequences. His pent-up feelings roused in him an energy unexpected by his foes.

Arthur, hearing that his grandmother Eleanor was at the castle of Mirebeau in Poitou with a scanty escort, surrounded the castle, stormed the outworks, and was about to gain custody of this important and hostile old Queen. Eleanor contrived in the nick of time to send word to John, who was at Le Mans. Her son with ample forces covered the eighty miles between them in forty-eight hours, surprised Arthur and the besiegers at daybreak, and, as he declared, "by the favour of God" got the lot. Arthur and all who stood with him, Hugh Lusignan and a cluster of barons who had revolted, two hundred knights or more, fell at a stroke into John's power, and his mother was delivered from her dangerous plight.

Arthur was imprisoned at Falaise and then at Rouen. No one doubted that he lay in mortal peril. All those barons of Brittany who were still loyal to John asked that the Prince should be released, and on John's refusal went into immediate rebellion. John felt that he would never be safe so long as Arthur lived. This was certainly true. The havoc of disunity that was being wrought throughout the French provinces by the French king using Arthur as a pawn might well have weighed with a better man than John. Arthur, caught in open fight besieging his own grandmother, was a prisoner of war. The horrid crime of murder has often been committed for reasons of state upon lesser temptations than now assailed this exceptionally violent king. No one knows what happened to Arthur. An impenetrable veil descends upon the tragedy of Rouen. The officer commanding the fortress, one Hubert de Burgh, of whom more and better hereafter, gave out that upon the King's order he had delivered his prisoner at Easter 1203 to the hands of agents sent by John to castrate him, and that Arthur had died of the shock, This explanation by no means allayed the ill-feeling aroused in Brittany and elsewhere. Hubert then declared that Arthur was still alive, and John stated that he was glad his orders had been disobeyed. However, it may be, Arthur was never seen again. That he was murdered by John's orders was not disputed at the time nor afterwards, though the question whether or not he was mutilated or blinded beforehand remains unanswered.

Although high nobles and common people in large numbers were in those times frequently put to death without trial and for reasons of hate or policy, the murder by a king of an equal confirmed the bad impression which all the world had formed of John. Moreover, the odious crime did not prevent but rather hastened the loss of Normandy.

Arthur had been removed, but John failed to profit by his crime. For Arthur was no more than Philip Augustus's tool, and his disappearance left unchanged the iron purpose of the French king. Against this persistency Richard had roused men's devotion, but John's nature inspired none. Brittany and the central provinces of the Angevin Empire revolted. Philip had come to terms with each province, and at Easter 1203 he made a voyage down the Loire to Saumur. A deep wedge had already been driven between the northern and the southern halves of John's Continental possessions. Having encircled Normandy, Philip prepared to strike at the stronghold of the Angevin power. John, awake to his danger, poured in treasure and supplies to strengthen his defences. The military position was not yet desperate, and if John had not at the end of 1203 after a series of savage but ineffectual raids precipitately quitted Normandy he might, drawing supplies from England, have held the duchy indefinitely. But, as Philip took fortress after fortress in Central Normandy, John's nerve failed, and the Normans, not unwilling to find an excuse for surrender, made English indifference their justification. In March 1204 Richard's "fair child," the frowning Château Gaillard, fell, and the road to Rouen lay open. Three months later the capital itself was taken, and Normandy finally became French.

No English tears need have been shed over this loss. The Angevin Empire at its peak had no real unity. Time and geography lay on the side of the French. The separation proved as much in the interest of England as of France. It rid the Island of a dangerous, costly distraction and entanglement, turned its thought and energies to its own affairs, and above all left a ruling class of alien origin with no interest henceforth that was not English or at least insular. These consolations did not however dawn on John's contemporaries, who saw only disastrous and humiliating defeat, and blamed a King already distrusted by the people and at variance with the nobility.

*   *   *   *   *

The very success of Henry II in re-establishing order and creating an efficient central administration had left new difficulties for those who came after him. Henry II had created an instrument so powerful that it needed careful handling. He had restored order only at the cost of offending privilege. His fiscal arrangements were original, and drastic in their thoroughness. His work had infringed feudal custom at many points. All this had been accepted because of the King's tactful management and in the reaction from anarchy. Richard I, again, had left England in the hands of able administrators, and the odium of their strict government and financial ingenuity fell on them directly, and stopped short of the King, radiant in the halo of a Crusader and fortunate in his absence. John was at hand to bear the brunt in person.

John, like William Rufus, pressed to logical limits the tendencies of his father's system. There were arrears in the payment of scutage from Richard's reign, and more money was needed to fight the French King, Philip Augustus. But a division had opened in the baronage. The English barons of John's reign had become distinct from his Norman feudatories and not many families now held lands on both sides of the Channel. Even King Richard had met with refusals from his English nobles to fight abroad. Disputes about foreign service and payment of scutage lay at the root of the baronial agitation. By systematic abuse of his feudal prerogatives John drove the baronage to violent resistance. English society was steadily developing. Class interests had assumed sharper definition. Many barons regarded attendance or suit at Court as an opportunity for exerting influence rather than for rendering dutiful service. The sense of Church unity grew among the clergy, and corporate feeling in the municipalities. All these classes were needed by the new centralised Government; but John preferred to emphasise the more ruthless aspects of the royal power.

The year 1205 brought a crisis. The loss of Normandy was followed by the death of John's mother, Eleanor, to whose influence he had owed much of his position on the mainland. The death of Hubert Walter, who for the last ten years had controlled the whole machinery of administration, deprived him of the only statesman whose advice he respected and whose authority stood between the Crown and the nation. It also reopened the thorny question of who should elect the Archbishop of Canterbury.

The Papal throne at this time was occupied by Innocent III, one of the greatest of the medieval Popes, renowned for his statecraft and diplomacy, and intent on raising to its height the temporal power of the Church. The dispute between John and the monastery of Canterbury over the election to the Archbishopric offered Innocent the very chance he sought for asserting Papal authority in England. Setting aside the candidates both of the Crown and of the Canterbury clergy, he caused Stephen Langton to be selected with great pomp and solemnity at Rome in December 1206. King John, confident of sufficient influence in the Papal Court to secure the election of his own candidate, had imprudently acknowledged the validity of the Papal decision beforehand. It was with pardonable anger that he learned how neatly Innocent had introduced a third and success-ful candidate, whose qualifications were unimpeachable. Stephen Langton was an English cardinal of the highest character, and one of the most famous doctors of the Paris schools. In his wrath, and without measuring the strength of his opponents, the King proceeded to levy a bloodless war upon the Church. Innocent III and Stephen Langton were not men to be browbeaten into surrender, and they possessed in an age of faith more powerful weapons than any secular monarch. When John began to persecute the clergy and seize Church lands the Pope retaliated by laying all England under an interdict. For more than six years the bells were silent, the doors of the churches were closed against the devout; the dead must be buried in unconsecrated ground and without the last communion. Many of John's subjects were assured of damnation for themselves or their loved ones on this account alone.

When John hardened his heart to the interdict and redoubled the attacks upon Church property, the Pope, in 1209, took the supreme step of excommunication. The King's subjects were thereby absolved from their allegiance; his enemies received the blessing of the Church and were sanctified as Crusaders. But John was stubborn and unabashed. Interdict and excommunication brought no ghostly terrors to his soul. Indeed they aggravated the violence of his measures to a point which his contemporaries could only attribute to insanity. The royal administration, never more efficient, found little difficulty in coping with the fiscal and legal problems presented to it or in maintaining order. The interdict, if a menace, was also an opportunity for which John's plans were well matured. The ecclesiastical property of clerics who fled abroad was seized as forfeit by the Crown; and as more and more bishoprics and abbeys fell vacant their revenues were exploited by royal custodians. Thus the Exchequer overflowed with the spoils. But for the combination of the Church quarrel with stresses of mundane politics, the Crown might have established a position not reached till the days of Henry VIII.

After the loss of Normandy John had embarked upon a series of grandiose schemes for a Continental alliance against Philip Augustus. He found allies in the Emperor Otto IV and the Counts of Toulouse and Flanders; but his breach with the Church hastened a far more formidable league between the King of France and the Papacy, and in 1213 he had to choose between submission and a French invasion, backed by all the military and spiritual resources which Innocent III could set in motion. The King's insecurity at home forced him to bow to the threat, and Innocent rejoiced in victory upon his own terms.

John however was not at the end of his devices, and by a stroke of cunning choice enough to be called political genius he turned defeat into something very like triumph. If he could not prevail he would submit; if he submitted he would repent; if he repented there must be no limits to his contrition. At all costs he must break the closing circle of his foes. He spread before Innocent III the lure of temporal sovereignty which he knew that the Pontiff could never resist. He offered to make England a fief of the Papacy, and to do homage to the Pope as his feudal lord. Innocent leapt at this addition to his worldly dignities. He forgave the penitent King; he took him and the realm of England under his especial protection. He accepted the sovereignty of England from the hands of John, and returned it to him as his vassal with his blessing.

This turned the tables upon John's secular enemies. He was now the darling of the Church. Philip Augustus, who at heavy expense had gathered his armies to invade England as a Crusader for his own purposes, thought himself ill-used by the sudden tergiversation of his spiritual ally. He was indignant, and not at all inclined to relinquish the prey he had so long held in view. The barons also found meagre comfort in this transformation. Their grievances remained unredressed, their anger unappeased. Even in the English Church there was a keen division. The English Episcopacy saw themselves now carried into a subjection to Rome far beyond what their piety or interests required, and utterly at variance with the tradition in which they had been reared. Obedience to the Supreme Pontiff was a sacred duty, but it could be carried into excessive interpretations. Stephen Langton himself, the Pope's elect, was as good an Englishman as he was a Churchman. He foresaw the unbridled exploitation by Rome of the patronage of the English Church and the wholesale engrossment of its benefices by Italian nominees. He became almost immediately an opposing force to the Pope. King John, who had lain at Dover, quaking but calculating, may have laughed while he pulled all these strings and threw his enemies into confusion.

Both John and Innocent persevered in their new partnership, and the disaffected barons drew together under the leadership of Stephen Langton. The war with the French king was continued, and John's demands in money and service kept the barons' anger hot. In 1214 an English expedition which John had led to Poitou failed. In Northern France the army led by his nephew, Otto of Saxony, and by the Earl of Salisbury, was defeated by King Philip at Bouvines. This battle destroyed in a day the whole Continental combination on which John's hopes had been based. Here again was the opportunity of the King's domestic enemies. They formed plans to restrain the rule of a despotic and defeated King, and openly threatened revolt unless their terms were accepted. Left to themselves, they might have ruined their cause by rancourous opposition and selfish demands, but Archbishop Langton, anxious for a just peace, exercised a moderating influence upon them. Nor could John, as a Papal Vassal, openly disregard Langton's advice.

But John had still one final resource. Encouraged by the Pope, he took the vows of a Crusader and invoked sentence of excommunication upon his opponents. This was not denied him. The conditions of 1213 were now entirely reversed. The barons, who had thought to be Crusaders against an excommunicated King, were now under the ban themselves. But this agile use of the Papal thunders had robbed them of some of their virtues as a deterrent. The barons, encouraged by the King's defeat abroad, persisted in their demands in spite of the Papal Bull. A great party in the Church stood with them. In vain did John manœuvre, by the offer to grant freedom of election to the Church, to separate the clergy from the barons. Armed revolt seemed the only solution. Although in the final scene of the struggle the Archbishop showed himself unwilling to go to the extreme of civil war, it was he who persuaded the barons to base their demands upon respect for ancient custom and law, and who gave them some principle to fight for besides their own class interests. After forty years' experience of the administrative system established by Henry II the men who now confronted John had advanced beyond the magnates of King Stephen's time. They had learned to think intelligently and constructively. In place of the King's arbitrary despotism they proposed, not the withering anarchy of feudal separatism, but a system of checks and balances which would accord the monarchy its necessary strength, but would prevent its perversion by a tyrant or a fool. The leaders of the barons in 1215 groped in the dim light towards a fundamental principle. Government must henceforward mean something more than the arbitrary rule of any man, and custom and the law must stand even above the King. It was this idea, perhaps only half understood, that gave unity and force to the barons' opposition and made the Charter which they now demanded imperishable.

On a Monday morning in June, between Staines and Windsor, the barons and Churchmen began to collect on the great meadow at Runnymede. An uneasy hush fell on them from time to time. Many had failed to keep their tryst; and the bold few who had come knew that the King would never forgive this humiliation. He would hunt them down when he could, and the laymen at least were staking their lives in the cause they served. They had arranged a little throne for the

King and a tent. The handful of resolute men had drawn up, it seems, a short document on parchment. Their retainers and the groups and squadrons of horsemen in sullen steel kept at some distance and well in the background. For was not armed rebellion against the Crown the supreme feudal crime? Then events followed rapidly. A small cavalcade appeared from the direction of Windsor. Gradually men made out the faces of the King, the Papal Legate, the Archbishop of Canterbury, and several bishops. They dismounted without ceremony. Someone, probably the Archbishop, stated briefly the terms that were suggested. The King declared at once that he agreed. He said the details should be arranged immediately in his chancery. The original "Articles of the Barons" on which Magna Carta is based exist to-day in the British Museum. They were sealed in a quiet, short scene, which has become one of the most famous in our history, on June 15, 1215. Afterwards the King returned to Windsor. Four days later, probably, the Charter itself was probably engrossed. In future ages it was to be used as the foundation of principles and systems of government of which neither King John nor his nobles dreamed.

*   *   *   *   *

At the beginning of the year 1216 there had seemed to be every chance that John would still defeat the baronial opposition and wipe out the humiliation of Runnymede. Yet before the summer was out the King was dead, and the Charter survived the denunciation of the Pope and the arbitrament of war. In the next hundred years it was reissued thirty-eight times, at first with a few substantial alterations, but retaining its original characteristics. Little more was heard of the Charter until the seventeenth century. After more than two hundred years a Parliamentary Opposition struggling to check the encroachments of the Stuarts upon the liberty of the subject rediscovered it and made of it a rallying cry against oppression. Thus was created the glorious legend of the "Charter of an Englishman's liberties."

If we set aside the rhetorical praise which has been so freely lavished upon the Charter, and study the document itself, we may find it rather surprising reading. It is in a form resembling a legal contract, and consists of sixty-one clauses, each dealing either with the details of feudal administration and custom or with elaborate provisions for securing the enforcement of the promises which it embodies. It is entirely lacking in any spacious statement of the principles of democratic government or the rights of man. It is not a declaration of constitutional doctrine, but a practical document to remedy current abuses in the feudal system. In the forefront stand the questions of scutage, of feudal reliefs and of wardship. The word "freeman" was a technical feudal term, and it is doubtful whether it included even the richer merchants, far less the bondmen or humbler classes who make up the bulk of a nation. It implies on the King's part a promise of good government for the future, but the terms of the promise are restricted to the observance of the customary privileges and interests of the baronial class. The barons on their part were compelled to make some provision for their tenants, the limits forced on John being vaguely applied to the tenants-in-chief as well; but they did as little as they safely and decently could. The villeins, in so far as they were protected, received such solicitous attention as befitted valuable chattels attached to the manor and not as free citizens of the realm.

The thirteenth century was to be a great age of Parliamentary development and experiment, yet there is no mention in Magna Carta of Parliament or representation of any but the baronial class. The great watchwords of the future here find no place. The actual Charter is a redress of feudal grievances extorted from an unwilling king by a discontented ruling class insisting on its privileges, and it ignored some of the most important matters which the King and baronage had to settle, such as the terms of military service.

Magna Carta must not however be dismissed lightly, in the words of a modern writer, as "a monument of class selfishness." Even in its own day men of all ranks above the status of villeins had an interest in securing that the tenure of land should be secure from arbitrary encroachment. Moreover, the greatest magnate might hold, and often did hold, besides his estate in chief, parcels of land under the most diverse tenures, by knight service, by the privileges of "socage," or as a tenant at will. Therefore in securing themselves the barons of Runnymede were in fact establishing the rights of the whole landed class, great and small—the simple knight with two hundred acres, the farmer or small yeoman with sixty. And there is evidence that their action was so understood throughout the country. In 1218 an official endeavoured to upset by writ a judgment given in the county court of Lincolnshire. The victim was a great landowner, but the whole county rallied to his cause and to the "liberty sworn and granted," stating in their protest that they acted "with him, and for him, and for ourselves, and the community of the whole realm."

If the thirteenth-century magnates understood little and cared less for popular liberties or Parliamentary democracy, they had all the same laid hold of a principle which was to be of prime importance for the future development of English society and English institutions. Throughout the document it is implied that here is a law which is above the King and which even he must not break. This reaffirmation of a supreme law and its expression in a general charter is the great work of Magna Carta; and this alone justifies the respect in which men have held it. The reign of Henry II, according to the most respected authorities, initiates the rule of law. But the work as yet was incomplete: the Crown was still above the law; the legal system which Henry had created could become, as John showed, an instrument of oppression.

Now for the first time the King himself is bound by the law. The root principle was destined to survive across the generations and rise paramount long after the feudal background of 1215 had faded in the past. The Charter became in the process of time an enduring witness that the power of the Crown was not absolute.

The facts embodied in it and the circumstances giving rise to them were buried or misunderstood. The underlying idea of the sovereignty of law, long existent in feudal custom, was raised by it into a doctrine for the national State. And when in subsequent ages the State, swollen with its own authority, has attempted to ride roughshod over the rights or liberties of the subject it is to this doctrine that appeal has again and again been made, and never, as yet, without success.

CHAPTER SIXTEEN

ON THE ANVIL

KING JOHN DIED IN THE TOILS; BUT HE DIED AT BAY. THE MISGOVERNMENT of his reign had brought against him what seemed to be an overwhelming combination. He was at war with the English barons who had forced him to grant the Charter. They had invited Louis, son of the implacable Philip, King of France, into the country to be their liege lord, and with him came foreign troops and hardy adventurers. The insurgent barons north of the Humber had the support of Alexander, King of Scots; in the West the rebellion was sustained by Llewellyn, the powerful Prince of North Wales. The towns were mainly against the King; London was vehemently hostile. The Cinque Ports were in enemy hands. Winchester, Worcester, and Carlisle, separated by the great distances of those times, were united in opposition to the Crown.

On the other hand, the recreant King had sacrificed the status of the realm to purchase the unswerving aid of the Papacy. A strong body of mercenaries, the only regular troops in the kingdom, were in John's pay. Some of the greatest warrior-nobles, the venerable William the Marshal, and the famous, romantic Ranulf, Earl of Chester, with a strong following of the aristocracy, adhered to his cause. The mass of the people, bewildered by this new quarrel of their masters, on the whole inclined to the King against the barons, and certainly against the invading foreigners. Their part was only to suffer at the hands of both sides. Thus the forces were evenly balanced; everything threatened a long, stubborn civil war and a return to the anarchy of Stephen and Maud. John himself, after a lifetime of subtleties and double-dealing, of illegal devices and sharp, unexpected twists of religious policy, showed himself possessed, in the last months of his life, of a warlike energy and resource which astonished friend and foe. It was at this moment that he died of dysentery, aggravated by fatigue and too much food and drink. Shakespeare has limned his final agony:

> And none of you will bid the winter come
> To thrust his icy fingers in my maw. . . .
> I beg cold comfort, and you are so strait
> And so ungrateful, you deny me that.

The death of the King in this convulsion of strife changed the conditions of the conflict without ending it. The rival interests and factions that were afoot had many purposes beyond the better government of England. Louis was in the Island, and fighting. Many had plighted him their faith, already once forsworn. The rebel lords were deeply involved with their Scottish and Welsh allies; none was in the humour for peace. Yet the sole reason and justification for revolt died with John. Henry, a child of nine, was the undoubted heir to all the rights and loyalties of his grandfather's wide empire. He was the rightful King of England. Upon what grounds could the oppressions of the father be visited upon his innocent son? A page of history had been violently turned; the new parchment was blank and clear. All parties were profoundly sensible of these considerations. Nevertheless John for the moment was missed by those whose lives and fortunes were devoted to the national cause. William the Marshal acted with honesty and decision. Had he failed in his duty to the Crown the strong centralised monarchy which Henry II had created, and upon which the growing civilisation of the realm depended, might have degenerated into a heptarchy of feudal princes, or even worse. The Papal Legate, sure of the unchanging policy of Rome, aided William the Marshal. The boy King was crowned at Gloucester and began his reign of fifty-six years on October 28, 1216. He was anointed by the Legate, and in default of the diadem which John had lost in crossing the Wash a plain gold circlet was placed upon his brow. This was to prove no inadequate symbol of his rule.

William the Marshal, aged seventy, reluctantly undertook what we should now call the Regency. He joined to himself the Earl of Chester, who might well have been his rival but did not press his claims, and Hubert de Burgh, John's faithful servant. The wisdom and the weakness of the new Government were alike revealed in the reissue of the Charter, which had been too rashly quashed by the Pope in 1215. The religious character of the King's party had become predominant. The Royalists wore white crosses, the Church preached a virtual Crusade, and the chiefs of the opposing faction were excommunicated. "At a time," said Henry in after-years to Bishop Grosseteste, "when we were orphan and minor, when our subjects were not only alienated from us, but were organised against us, it was our mother, the Roman Church, which brought this realm once more under our authority, which consecrated us King, crowned us and placed us on the throne."

It was a reign of turmoil and distress and yet the forces of progress moved doggedly forward. Redhot iron was smitten on the anvil, and the hammer-blows forged a metal more tense than had yet been seen. In this period the common people, with their Anglo-Saxon tradition of ancient rights and law running back to remote antiquity, lay suffering under the armoured feet of the nobility and of the royal mercenaries, reinforced in the main by the power of the Church. But the people's masters were disunited; not only did their jealousies and ambitions and their taste for war keep them at variance, but several rending fissures were opening among them. They were divided into parties; they were cross-cut obliquely by a strong nationalism. It is an age of impulse and experiment, not controlled by any general political theory.

*   *   *   *   *

The confusion and monotony of the barons' warfare, against each other, or against the King, sometimes with the Church, more often against the Church, have repelled many readers of history. But the fact is that King Henry III survived all his troubles and left England enjoying a prosperity and peace unknown when he was a child.

The cruel war and anarchy lay only upon the surface; underneath, unformulated and largely unrealised by the hard-pressed actors, coursed all the tides which were to flow in Europe five hundred years later; and almost all the capital decisions which are demanded of the modern world were rife in this medieval society. From out of the conflict there rise the figures of heroes, both warriors and statesmen, from whose tribulations we are separated by long ages, but whose work and outlook unite them to us, as if we read their acts and words in the morning newspaper.

We must examine some of these figures at close quarters. Stephen Langton, the great Archbishop, was the indomitable, unwearying, builder of the rights of Englishmen against royal, baronial, and even ecclesiastical pretensions. He stood against King John; he stood against the Pope. Both cast upon him at times their utmost displeasure, short of taking his life. Here is a man who worked for the unity of Christendom through the Catholic Church; but also for the interests of England against the Papacy. Here is a faithful servant of the Crown, but at the same time a champion of the Charter, and all it meant, and still means. A commanding central figure, practical, resourceful, shifting from side to side as evils forced him, but quite unchanging and unchangeable in his broad, wise, brave, workaday, liberal purpose. Here was, if not an architect of our Constitution, at least a punctual and unfailing Clerk of the Works.

The second personality which emerges from the restless scene is Hubert de Burgh. Shakespeare, whose magic finger touches in succession most of the peaks of English history and lights them with the sunrise so that all can see them standing out above the mountainous disorder, has brought Hubert to our ken. Here is a soldier and a politician, armed with the practical wisdom which familiarity with courts and camps, with high authorities, ecclesiastical and armoured, may infuse into a man's conduct, and even nature. John's Justiciar, identified with the crimes and the follies of the reign, was yet known to all men as their constant resolute opponent. Under the Marshal, who was himself a star of European chivalry, Hubert was an outstanding leader of resistance to the rebellion against the monarchy. At the same time, above the warring factions, he was a solid champion of the rights of England. The

Island should not be ravaged by greedy nobles, nor pillaged by foreign adventurers, nor mutilated unduly even for the high interests of the Papacy, which so often were the interests of Christendom itself.

The rebellion of the barons was quelled by fights on land and sea. At Lincoln the King's party had gained a fantastic but none the less decisive victory. In the streets of Lincoln, during a whole day, we are told that four hundred royal knights jostled and belaboured six hundred of the baronial party. Only three were killed in the combat. Contemporary opinion declined to accord the name of battle to this brawl. It was called "the Fair of Lincoln." It is difficult to form a picture of what happened. One must suppose that the knights had upon the average at least eight or ten stalwart retainers each, and that the almost invulnerable, chain-mailed monsters waddled about in the throng, chasing away or cutting down the unarmoured folk, and welting each other when they met, hard, but perhaps not too hard. On this basis there were intricate manœuvres and stratagems, turnings of flanks, takings in rear, entry through privy ports by local treachery, odd confrontations; all kinds of devices. But in the upshot the Royalists outwitted and out-walloped the insurgents. Accidents will happen in the best regulated faction fights, and one of the leading rebel barons, Thomas, Count of Perche, had the misfortune to be killed by a sword-thrust which penetrated his visor and sank deep into his brain. But for almost all the rest of the armoured crew it was a joyous adventure. The vengeance of the victors was wreaked mainly upon their rivals' retainers and upon the civil population, who were plundered and slaughtered on a considerable scale.

"The Fair of Lincoln" gave the infant Henry III a victory on land, and de Burgh's sea-victory off Dover against French reinforcements for Louis cut the revolt from its Continental root. Negotiations proceeded continually amid the broils. They were strenuously disputed, and meanwhile each side devastated the estates of the opposing party, to the intense misery of their inhabitants. Hubert, supported by Archbishop Langton and the Papal Legate, never lost his hold upon the Charter, although this was the nominal bond of union of their opponents. There were unavoidable stresses between the devout English Royalists and the interests of the universal

Church, as interpreted by the Pope. These stresses did not however take a physical form. Compromises were reached, not only between Crown and barons, but in the ecclesiastical sphere, between England and Rome.

After a year of fighting, Louis of France was compelled to leave the country in 1217, his hopes utterly dashed. The Great Charter was now re-issued for the second time in order to show that the Government meant its word. In 1219 the old victorious Marshal died, and Hubert ruled the land for twelve years. He was a stern ruler. When Fawkes de Breauté, who had been the chief mercenary of John and William the Marshal during all these recent tumults, grew overmighty and attempted to disturb the new-found peace of the land, Hubert determined to expel him. On taking Fawkes's stronghold of Bedford Castle in 1224, after two months' siege, Hubert hanged in front of its walls the twenty-four surviving knights who had commanded the garrison. In the following year, as a sign of pacification, the Great Charter was again re-issued in what was substantially its final form. Thus it became an unchallenged part of English law and tradition. But for the turbulent years of Henry III's minority, it might have mouldered in the archives of history as a merely partisan document.

No long administration is immune from mistakes and every statesman must from time to time make concessions to wrong-headed superior powers. But Hubert throughout his tenure stood for the policy of doing the least possible to recover the King's French domains. This he carried out not only by counsel, but by paralysing action, and by organising ignominious flight before the enemy when battle seemed otherwise unavoidable. He hampered the preparation for fresh war; he stood firm against the incursions of foreign favourites and adventurers. He resisted the Papacy in its efforts to draw money at all costs out of England for its large European schemes. He maintained order, and as the King grew up he restrained the Court party which was forming about him from making inroads upon the Charter. His was entirely the English point of view.

At last in 1229 he had exhausted his goodwill and fortune and fate was upon him. The King, now twenty-two years of age, crowned and acting, arrived at Portsmouth with a large army raised by the utmost exercise of his feudal power to defend those estates in France which after the loss of Normandy still pertained to the English Crown. Hubert could not control this, but the transporting of the expedition lay apparently in his department. The King found no ships, or few, awaiting him; no supplies, no money, for his oversea venture. He flew into a rage. Although usually mild, affable, scholarly and artistic, he drew his sword and rushed upon the Justiciar, reproaching him with having betrayed his trust and being bribed by France. It certainly was a very unpleasant and awkward situation, the Army wishing to fight abroad, and the Navy and the Treasury unable or unwilling to carry them thither. The quarrel was smoothed down; the King recovered his temper; the expedition sailed in the following year and Hubert retained his place. But not for long. In 1232 he was driven from power by a small palace clique. Threatened in his life, he took sanctuary at Brentwood. He was dragged from this asylum, but the common, humble blacksmith who was ordered to put the fetters on him declared he would die any death rather than do so; and he is said to have used the words which historians have deemed to be the true monument of Hubert de Burgh: "Is he not that most faithful Hubert who so often saved England from the devastation of foreigners and restored England to England?"

*　　*　　*　　*　　*

During John's reign one of the most cruel tragedies of world history had run its course in Southern France. In the domains of Raymond VI, Count of Toulouse, there had grown up during several generations a heresy, sombre and austere in theory, but genial in practice. The Albigenses, or Cathares, "the Purified," as they were called, dismissed altogether from the human mind the resurrection of the body, Purgatory, and Hell. In their view life on earth in the flesh was the work of Satan. The material phase would soon pass and the soul, freed from its accursed encumbrance, would be resumed in eternal bliss into the Godhead. The "Perfects" of this cult practised chastity and abstinence, and professed in principle a sincere wish for death; but the mass of the population, relieved from the oppression of supernatural terror, developed, we are assured, in the delicious climate of those regions, easy morals and merry character. The thrilling sensation of being raised above the vicissitudes of this world and at the same time freed from the menaces of the next produced a great happiness in these regions, in which all classes joined, and from it sprang culture of manners and fervour of conviction.

This casting off of all spiritual chains was, naturally, unwelcome to the Papacy. The whole moral scheme of the Western world was based, albeit precariously, upon Original Sin, Redemption by Grace, and a Hell of infinite torment and duration, which could only be avoided through the ministrations of the clergy. It was some time before the Papacy realised the deadlines and the magnitude of the novel sin which was spreading in what we now call Southern France. Once the gravity of the challenge was understood it superseded even the rescue of the Holy Sepulchre from the infidel. In 1209 a Crusade for a different purpose was set on foot, and all temporal forces at the disposal of Rome were directed upon the Albigenses, under the leadership of Philip of France. At this time the burning of heretics and other undesirables, which had been practised sporadically in France, received the formal sanction of law. The process of blotting out the new heresy by the most atrocious cruelties which the human mind can conceive occupied nearly a generation. The heretics, led by the "Perfects," fought like tigers, regarding death as a final release from the curse of the body. But the work was thoroughly done. The Albigensian heresy was burned out at the stake. Only poor, hungry folk in the forests and mountains, which happily abound in these parts, still harboured those doubts about approaching damnation upon which so much of the discipline and responsibility of human beings and the authority and upkeep of the Church depended.

Of all the leaders in this Crusade none surpassed a certain Simon de Montfort, "a minor lord of the Paris region." He rose to commanding control in this war, and was acclaimed the effective leader. He was made Viscount of Béziers and Carcassonne "at the instance of the barons of God's army, the legates and the priests present." This capable, merciless man accomplished the bloody task, and when he fell at the siege of Toulouse he left behind him a son who bore his name, succeeded to his high station among the nobility of the age, and became associated with an idea which has made him for ever famous.

*   *   *   *   *

De Burgh's conduct had been far from blameless, but his fall had been deliberately engineered by men whose object was not to reform administration but to gain power. The leader of this intrigue was his former rival Peter des Roches, the Bishop of Winchester. Des Roches himself kept in the background, but at the Christmas Council of 1232 nearly every post of consequence in the administration was conferred upon his friends, most of them, like him, Poitevins. More was involved in the defeat of de Burgh than the triumph of des Roches and his party. De Burgh was the last of the great Justiciars who had wielded plenary and at times almost sovereign power. Henceforward the House-hold offices like the Wardrobe, largely dependent upon the royal will and favour, began to overshadow the great "national" offices, like the Justiciarship, filled by the baronial magnates. As they came to be occupied increasingly by foreign intruders, Poitevins, Savoyards, Provençals, the national feeling of the baronage became violently hostile. Under the leadership of Richard the Marshal, a second son of the great William, the barons began to growl against the foreigners. Des Roches retorted that the King had need of foreigners to protect him against the treachery of his natural subjects; and large numbers of Poitevin and Breton mercenaries were brought over to sustain this view. But the struggle was short. In alliance with Prince Llewellyn the young Marshal drove the King among the Welsh marches, sacked Shrewsbury, and harried des Roches's lands. In the spring of 1234 Henry was forced to accept terms, and, although the Marshal was killed in April, the new Archbishop, Edmund Rich, insisted on the fulfilment of the treaty. The Poitevin officials were dismissed, des Roches found it convenient to go on a journey to Italy, and de Burgh was honourably restored to his lands and possessions.

The Poitevins were the first of the long succession of foreign favourites whom Henry III gathered round him in the middle years of his reign. Hatred of the aliens, who dominated the King, monopo-lised the offices, and made scandalous profits out of a country to whose national interests they were completely indifferent, became the theme of baronial opposition. The King's affection was reserved for those who flattered his vanity and ministered to his caprices. He developed a love for extravagant splendour, and naturally preferred to his morose barons the brilliant adventurers of Poitou and Provence. The culture of medieval Provence, the home of the troubadours and the creed of chivalry, fascinated Henry. In 1236 he married Eleanor, the daughter of Raymond of Provence. With Eleanor came her numerous and needy kinsmen, chief among them her four uncles. A new wave of foreigners descended upon the profitable wardships, marriages, escheats, and benefices, which the disgusted baronage regarded as their own. The King delighted to shower gifts upon his charming relations, and the responsibility for all the evils of his reign was laid upon their shoulders. It is the irony of history that not the least unpopular was this same Simon de Montfort, son of the repressor of the Albigenses.

An even more copious source of discontent in England was the influence of the Papacy over the grateful and pious King. Pope Gregory IX, at desperate grips with the Holy Roman Emperor Frederick II, made ever greater demands for money, and his Legate, Otto, took an interest in English Church Reform. Otto's demand in 1240 for one-fifth of the clergy's rents and movables raised a storm. The rectors of Berkshire published a manifesto denying the right of Rome to tax the English Church, and urging that the Pope, like other bishops, should "live of his own." Nevertheless, early in 1241 Otto returned to Rome with a great treasure; and the Pope rewarded the loyalty of the Italian clergy by granting them the next three hundred vacant English benefices. The election of Innocent IV in 1243 led to renewed demands. In that year the Papal envoy forbade bishops in England to appoint to benefices until the long list of Papal nominees had been exhausted. Robert Grosseteste, scholar, scientist, and saint, a former Master of the Oxford Schools and since 1235 Bishop of Lincoln, led the English clergy in evasion or refusal of Papal demands. He became their champion. Although he still believed that the Pope was absolute, he heralded the attacks which Wyclif was more than a century later to make upon the exactions and corruption of the Roman Court.

The Church, writhing under Papal exaction, and the baronage, offended by Court encroachments, were united in hatred of foreigners. A crisis came in 1244, when a baronial commission was appointed to fix the terms of a money grant to the King. The barons insisted that the Justiciar, Chancellor, and Treasurer, besides certain judges, should be elected by the Great Council, on which they were strongly represented. Four of the King's Council were to be similarly elected, with power to summon the Great Council. The King turned in his distress to the already mulcted Church, but his appeal was rejected through the influence of Grosseteste. In 1247 the voracious Poitevins encouraged the King in despotic ideas of government. To their appetites were now added those of the King's three half-brothers, the Lusignans, the sons of John's Queen, Isabella, by her second marriage. Henry adopted a new tone. "Servants do not judge their master," he said in 1248. "Vassals do not judge their prince or bind him by conditions. They should put themselves at his disposal and be submissive to his will." Such language procured no money; and money was the pinch. Henry was forced to sell plate and jewels and give new privileges or new grants of old rights to those who would buy them. Salaries were unpaid, forced gifts extracted; the forest courts were exploited and extortion condoned. In 1252 the King, on the pretext of a Crusade, demanded a tithe of ecclesiastical rents and property for three years. On Grosseteste's advice the clergy refused this grant, because the King would not on his part confirm Magna Carta. Next year Grosseteste died, indomitable to the last against both Papal and royal exactions.

Meanwhile Henry had secretly accepted greater Continental obligations. The death of the Holy Roman Emperor Frederick in 1250 revived at Rome the old plan of uniting Sicily, over which he had ruled, to the Papal dominions. In 1254 Henry III accepted the Papal offer of the Sicilian Crown for his younger son Edmund. This was a foolish step, and the conditions attached to the gift raised it to the very height of folly. The English King was to provide an army, and he stood surety for a mass of Papal debts amounting to the vast sum in those days of about £90,000. When the King's acceptance of the Papal offer became known a storm of indignation broke over his head. Both the Great Council and the clergy refused financial aid. As if this were not enough, at the Imperial election of 1257 the King's brother, Richard of Cornwall, offered himself as Emperor, and Henry spent lavishly to secure his election. The final stroke was the King's complete failure to check the successes of Llewellyn, who in 1256 had swept the English out of Wales and intrigued to overthrow the English faction in Scotland. Despised, discredited, and frightened, without money or men, the King faced an angered and powerful opposition.

*　　*　　*　　*　　*

In the last years of Grosseteste's life he had come to hope great things of his friend, Simon de Montfort. Simon had married the King's sister and had inherited the Earldom of Leicester. He had been governor of the English lands in Gascony for four years. Strong and energetic, he had aroused the jealousy and opposition of the King's favourites; and as a result of their intrigues he had been brought to trial in 1252. The commission acquitted him; but in return for a sum of money from the King he unwillingly agreed to vacate his office. Friendship between him and the King was at an end; on the one side was contempt, on the other suspicion. In this way, from an unexpected quarter, appeared the leader whom the baronial and national opposition had long lacked.

There were many greater notables in England, and his relationship to the King was aspersed by the charge that he had seduced his bride before he married her. None the less there he stood with five resolute sons, an alien leader, who was to become the brain and driving force of the English aristocracy. Behind him gradually ranged themselves most of the great feudal chiefs, the whole strength of London as a corporate entity, all the lower clergy, and the goodwill of the nation. A letter of a Court official, written in July 1258, has been preserved. The King, so it says, had yielded to what he felt was overwhelming pressure. A commission for reform of government was set up; it was agreed that "public offices should only be occupied by the English," and that "the emissaries of Rome and the foreign merchants and bankers should be reduced to their proper station." Grants of land to foreigners, the position of the King's Household, the custody of the fortresses, were all called in question. "The barons," writes our civil servant, "have a great and difficult task which cannot be carried out easily or quickly. They are proceeding . . . *ferociter*. May the results be good!"

CHAPTER SEVENTEEN

THE MOTHER OF PARLIAMENTS

THE LATER YEARS OF HENRY III'S TROUBLED REIGN WERE MOMENTOUS in their consequences for the growth of English institutions. This may perhaps be called the seed-time of our Parliamentary system, though few participants in the sowing could have foreseen the results that were eventually to be achieved. The commission for reform set about its work seriously, and in 1258 its proposals were embodied in the Provisions of Oxford, supplemented and extended in 1259 by the Provisions of Westminster. This baronial movement represented something deeper than dislike of alien counsellors. For the two sets of Provisions, taken together, represent a considerable shift of interest from the standpoint of Magna Carta. The Great Charter was mainly concerned to define various points of law, whereas the Provisions of Oxford deal with the overriding question of by whose advice and through what officials royal government should be carried on. Many of the clauses of the Provisions of Westminster moreover mark a limitation of baronial rather than of royal jurisdiction. The fruits of Henry II's work were now to be seen; the nation was growing stronger, more self-conscious and self-confident. The notable increase in judicial activity throughout the country, the more frequent visits of the judges and officials—all of them dependent upon local co-operation—educated the country knights in political responsibility and administration. This process, which shaped the future of English institutions, had its first effects in the thirteenth century.

The staple of the barons' demand was that the King in future should govern by a Council of Fifteen, to be elected by four persons, two from the baronial party and two from the royal. It is significant that the King's proclamation accepting the arrangement in English as well as French is the first public document to be issued in both languages since the time of William the Conqueror. For a spell this Council, animated and controlled by Simon de Montfort governed the land. They held each other in proper check, sharing among themselves the greater executive offices and entrusting the actual administration to "lesser men," as was then widely thought to be desirable. The magnates, once their own class interests were guarded, and their rights—which up to a certain point were the rights of the nation—were secure, did not wish to put the levers of power in the hands of one or two of their number. This idea of a Cabinet of politicians, chosen from the patriciate, with their highly trained functionaries of no political status operating under them, had in it a long vitality and many resurrections.

It is about this time that the word "Parlement"—Parliament— began to be current. In 1086 William the Conqueror had "deep speech" with his wise men before launching the Domesday inquiry. In Latin this would have appeared as *colloquium;* and "colloquy" is the common name in the twelfth century for the consultations between the King and his magnates. The occasional colloquy "on great affairs of the Kingdom" can at this point be called a Parliament. But more often the word means the permanent Council of officials and judges which sat at Westminster to receive petitions, redress grievances, and generally regulate the course of the law. By the thirteenth century Parliament establishes itself as the name of two quite different, though united, institutions.

If we translate their functions into modern terms we may say that the first of these assemblies deals with policy, the second with legislation and administration. The debate on the Address at the beginning of a session is very like a colloquy, while the proceedings of "Parliament" have their analogue in the committee stage of a Bill. In the reign of Henry III, and even of Edward I, it was by no means a foregone conclusion that the two assemblies would be amalgamated.

Rather did it look as if the English Constitution would develop as did the French Constitution, with a King in Council as the real Government, with the magnates reduced to a mere nobility, and "Parlement" only a clearinghouse for legal business. Our history did not take this course. In the first place the magnates during the century that followed succeeded in mastering the Council and identifying their interests with it. Secondly, the English counties had a life of their own, and their representatives at Westminster were to exercise increasing influence. But without the powerful impulse of Simon de Montfort these forces might not have combined to shape a durable legislative assembly.

*   *   *   *   *

The King, the Court party, and the immense foreign interests associated therewith had no intention of submitting indefinitely to the thraldom of the Provisions. Every preparation was made to recover the lost ground. In 1259 the King returned with hopes of foreign aid from Paris, where he had been to sign a treaty of peace with the French. His son Edward was already the rising star of all who wished to see a strong monarchy. Supporters of this cause appeared among the poor and turbulent elements in London and the towns. The enthusiasm of the revolution—for it was nothing less—had not been satisfied by a baronial victory. Ideas were afoot which would not readily be put to sleep. It is the merit of Simon de Montfort that he did not rest content with a victory by the barons over the Crown. He turned at once upon the barons themselves. If the King should be curbed, so also must they in their own spheres show respect for the general interest. Upon these issues the claims of the middle classes, who had played a great part in carrying the barons to supremacy, could not be disregarded. The "apprentice" or bachelor knights, who may be taken as voicing the wishes of the country gentry, formed a virile association of their own entitled "the Community of the Bachelors of England." Simon de Montfort became their champion. Very soon he began to rebuke great lords for abuse of their privileges. He wished to extend to the baronial estates the reforms already undertaken in the royal administration. He addressed himself pointedly to Richard, Earl of Gloucester, who ruled wide estates in the South-West and in South Wales. He procured an ordinance from the Council making it plain that the great lords were under the royal authority, which was again—though this he did not stress—under the Council. Here was dictatorship in a new form. It was a dictatorship of the Commonwealth, but, as so often happens to these bold ideas, it expressed itself inevitably through a man and a leader. These developments split the baronial party from end to end; and the King and his valiant son Edward, striking in with all their own resources upon their divided opponents, felt they might put the matter to the proof.

At Easter in 1261 Henry, freed by the Pope from his oath to accept the Provisions of Oxford and Westminster, deposed the officials and Ministers appointed by the barons. There were now two Governments with conflicting titles, each interfering with the other. The barons summoned the representatives of the shires to meet them at St. Albans; the King summoned them to Windsor. Both parties competed for popular support. The barons commanded greater sympathy in the country, and only Gloucester's opposition to de Montfort held them back from sharp action. After the death of Gloucester in July 1262 the baronial party rallied to de Montfort's drastic policy. Civil war broke out, and Simon and his sons, all of whom played vigourous parts, a moiety of barons, the middle class, so far as it had emerged, and powerful allies in Wales together faced in redoubtable array the challenge of the Crown.

Simon de Montfort was a general as well as a politician. Nothing in his upbringing or circumstances would naturally have suggested to him the course he took. It is ungratefully asserted that he had no real conception of the ultimate meaning of his actions. Certainly he builded better than he knew. By September 1263 a reaction against him had become visible: he had succeeded only too well. Edward played upon the discontent among the barons, appealed to their feudal and selfish interest, fomented their jealousy of de Montfort, and so built up a strong royalist party. At the end of the year de Montfort had to agree to arbitration by Louis IX, the French king. The decision went against him. Loyal to his monarchial rank, the King of France defended the prerogative of the King of England and declared the Provisions to be illegal. As Louis was accepted as a saint in his own lifetime this was serious. Already however the rival parties had taken up arms. In the civil war that followed the feudal party more or less supported the King. The people, especially the towns, and the party of ecclesiastical reform, especially the Franciscans, rallied to de Montfort. New controls were improvised in many towns to defeat the royalist sympathies of the municipal oligarchies. In the summer of 1264 de Montfort once again came South to relieve the pressure which Henry and Edward were exerting on the Cinque Ports.

The King and Prince Edward met him in Sussex with a superior power. At Lewes a fierce battle was fought. In some ways it was a forerunner of Edgehill. Edward, like Rupert four hundred years later, conquered all before him, pursued incontinently, and returned to the battlefield only to find that all was lost. Simon had, with much craft and experience of war, laid a trap to which the peculiar conditions of the ground lent themselves, whereby when his centre had been pierced his two wings of armoured cavalry fell upon the royal main body from both flanks and crushed all resistance. He was accustomed at this time owing to a fall from his horse to be carried with the army in a sumptuous and brightly decorated litter, like the coach of an eighteenth-century general. In this he placed two or three hostages for their greater security, and set it among the Welsh in the centre, together with many banners and emblems suggesting his presence. Prince Edward, in his charge, captured this trophy, and killed the unlucky hostages from his own party who were found therein. But meanwhile the King and all his Court and principal supporters were taken prisoners by de Montfort, and the energetic prince returned only to share their plight.

Simon de Montfort was now in every respect master of England, and if he had proceeded in the brutal manner of modern times in several European countries by the wholesale slaughter of all who were in his power he might long have remained so. In those days however, for all their cruelty in individual cases, nothing was pushed to the last extreme. The influences that counted with men in contest for power at the peril of their lives were by no means only brutal. Force, though potent, was not sovereign. Simon made a treaty with the captive King and the beaten party, whereby the rights of the Crown were in theory respected, though in practice the King and his son were to be subjected to strict controls. The general balance of the realm was preserved, and it is clear from Simon's action not only that he felt the power of the opposing forces, but that he aimed at their ultimate unification. He saw himself, with the King in his hands, able to use the authority of the Crown to control the baronage and create the far broader and better political system which, whether he aimed at it or not, must have automatically followed from his success. Thus he ruled the land, with the feeble King and the proud Prince Edward prisoners in his hands. This opens the third and final stage in his career.

* * * * *

All the barons, whatever party they had chosen, saw themselves confronted with an even greater menace than that from which they had used Simon to deliver them. The combination of Simon's genius and energy with the inherent powers of a Plantagenet monarchy and the support of the middle classes, already so truculent, was a menace to their class privileges far more intimate and searching than the misgovernment of John or the foreign encumbrances of Henry III. Throughout these struggles of lasting significance the English barony never deviated from their own self-interest. At Runnymede they had served national freedom when they thought they were defending their own privilege. They had now no doubt that Simon was its enemy. He was certainly a despot, with a king in his wallet and the forces of social revolution at his back. The barons formed a hard confederacy among themselves, and with all the forces of the Court not in Simon's hands schemed night and day to overthrow him.

For the moment de Montfort was content that the necessary steps should be taken by a council of nine who controlled expenditure and appointed officials. Any long-term settlement could be left until the Parliament which he had summoned for 1265. The Earl's autocratic position was not popular, yet the country was in such a state of confusion that circumstances seemed to justify it. In the North and along the Welsh Marches the opposition was still strong and reckless; in France the Queen and the earls Hugh Bigod and Warenne intrigued for support; the Papacy backed the King. De Montfort kept command of the Narrow Seas by raising a fleet in the Cinque Ports and openly encouraging privateering. In the West however he lost the support of Gilbert de Clare, Earl of Gloucester and the son of his former rival Richard de Clare. Without openly joining the royalists Clare conspired with them and revived his father's quarrel with de Montfort. Summoned to the Parliament of 1265, he replied by accusing the Earl of appropriating for himself and his sons the revenues of the Crown and the confiscated property of the opposition nobles. There was some truth in these accusations, but Clare's main objection appears to have been that he did not share the spoils.

In January 1265 a Parliament met in London to which Simon summoned representatives both from the shires and from the towns. Its purpose was to give an appearance of legality to the revolutionary settlement, and this, under the guidance of de Montfort, it proceeded to do. Its importance lay however more in its character as a representative assembly than in its work. The constitutional significance which was once attached to it as the first representative Parliament in our history is somewhat discounted by modern opinion. The practical reason for summoning the strong popular element was de Montfort's desire to weight the Parliament with his own supporters: among the magnates only five earls and eighteen barons received writs of summons. Again he fell back upon the support of the country gentry and the burgesses against the hostility or indifference of the magnates. In this lay his message and his tactics.

The Parliament dutifully approved of de Montfort's actions and accepted his settlement embodied in the Provisions. But Clare's withdrawal to the West could only mean the renewal of war. King Henry III abode docilely in Simon's control, and was treated all the time with profound personal respect. Prince Edward enjoyed a liberty which could only have been founded upon his parole not to escape. However, as the baronial storm gathered and many divisions occurred in Simon's party, and all the difficulties of government brought inevitable unpopularity in their train, he went out hunting one day with a few friends, and forgot to return as in honour bound. He galloped away through the woodland, first after the stag and then in quest of larger game. He at once became the active organising head of the most powerful elements in English life, to all of which the destruction of Simon de Montfort and his unheard-of innovations had become the supreme object. By promising to uphold the Charters, to remedy grievances and to expel the foreigners, Edward succeeded in uniting the baronial party and in cutting away the ground from under de Montfort's feet. The Earl now appeared as no more than the leader of a personal faction, and his alliance with Llewellyn, by which he recognised the claims of the Welsh prince to territory and independence, compromised his reputation. Out-manœuvred politically by Edward, he had also placed himself at a serious military disadvantage. While Edward and the Marcher barons, as they were called, held the Severn valley de Montfort was penned in, his retreat to the east cut off, and his forces driven back into South Wales. At the beginning of August he made another attempt to cross the river and to join the forces which his son, Simon, was bringing up from the south-east. He succeeded in passing by a ford near Worcester, but his son's forces were trapped by Edward near Kenilworth and routed. Unaware of this disaster, the Earl was caught in turn at Evesham; and here on August 4 the final battle took place.

It was fought in the rain and half-darkness of a sudden storm. The Welsh broke before Edward's heavy horse, and the small group around de Montfort were left to fight desperately until sheer weight of numbers overwhelmed them. De Montfort died a hero on the field. The Marchers massacred large numbers of fugitives and prisoners and mutilated the bodies of the dead. The old King, a pathetic figure, who had been carried by the Earl in all his wanderings, was wounded by his son's followers, and only escaped death by revealing his identity with the cry, "Slay me not! I am Henry of Winchester, your King."

* * * * *

The great Earl was dead, but his movement lived widespread and deep throughout the nation. The ruthless, haphazard granting away of the confiscated lands after Evesham provoked the bitter opposition of the disinherited. In isolated centres at Kenilworth, Axholme, and Ely the followers of de Montfort held out, and pillaged the country-side in sullen despair. The Government was too weak to reduce them. The whole country suffered from confusion and unrest. The common folk did not conceal their partisanship for de Montfort's cause, and rebels and outlaws beset the roads and forests. Foreign merchants were forbidden in the King's name to come to England because their safety could not be guaranteed. A reversion to feudal independence and consequent anarchy appeared imminent. In these troubles Pope Clement IV and his Legate Ottobon enjoined moderation; and after a six-months unsuccessful siege of Kenilworth Edward realised that this was the only policy. There was strong opposition from those who had benefited from the confiscations. The Earl of Gloucester had been bitterly disillusioned by Edward's repudiation of his promises of reform. Early in 1267 he demanded the expulsion of the aliens and the re-enactment of the Provisions. To enforce his demands he entered London with general acceptance. His action and the influence of the Legate secured pardon and good terms for the disinherited on the compromise principle of "No disinheritance, but repurchase." Late in 1267 the justices were sent out through the country to apply these terms equitably. The records testify to the widespread nature of the disturbances and to the fact that locally the rebellion had been directed against the officials, that it had been supported by the lower clergy, with not a few abbots and priors, and that a considerable number of the country gentry not bound to the baronial side by feudal ties had supported de Montfort.

In the last years of his life, with de Montfort dead and Edward away on Crusade, the feeble King enjoyed comparative peace. More than half a century before, at the age of nine, he had succeeded to the troubled inheritance of his father in the midst of civil war. At times it had seemed as if he would also die in the midst of civil war. At last however the storms were over: he could turn back to the things of beauty that interested him far more than political struggles. The new Abbey of Westminster, a masterpiece of Gothic architecture, was now dedicated; its consecration had long been the dearest object of Henry III's life. And here in the last weeks of 1272 he was buried.

The quiet of these last few years should not lead us to suppose that de Montfort's struggle and the civil war had been in vain. Among the common people he was for many years worshipped as a saint, and miracles were worked at his tomb. Their support could do nothing for him at Evesham, but he had been their friend, he had inspired the hope that he could end or mend the suffering and oppression of the poor; for this they remembered him when they had forgotten his faults. Though a prince among administrators, he suffered as a politician from over-confidence and impatience. He trampled upon vested interests, broke with all traditions, did violence to all forms, and needlessly created suspicion and distrust. Yet de Montfort had lighted a fire never to be quenched in English history. Already in 1267 the Statute of Marlborough had re-enacted the chief of the Provisions of Westminster. Not less important was his influence upon his nephew, Edward, the new King, who was to draw deeply upon the ideas of the man he had slain. In this way de Montfort's purposes survived both the field of Evesham and the reaction which succeeded it, and in Edward I the great Earl found his true heir.

CHAPTER EIGHTEEN

KING EDWARD I

FEW PRINCES HAD RECEIVED SO THOROUGH AN EDUCATION IN THE ART of rulership as Edward I when at the age of thirty-three his father's death brought him to the crown. He was an experienced leader and a skilful general. He had carried his father on his shoulders; he had grappled with Simon de Montfort, and, while sharing many of his views, had destroyed him. He had learned the art of war by tasting defeat. When at any time in the closing years of King Henry III he could have taken control he had preferred a filial and constitutional patience, all the more remarkable when his own love of order and reform is contrasted with his father's indolence and incapacity and the general misgovernment of the realm.

Of elegant build and lofty stature, a head and shoulders above the height of the ordinary man, with hair always abundant, which, changing from yellow in childhood to black in manhood and snow-white in age, marked the measured progress of his life, his proud brow and regular features were marred only by the drooping left eyelid which had been characteristic of his father. If he stammered he was also eloquent. There is much talk of his limbs. His sinewy, muscular arms were those of a swordsman; his long legs gave him a grip of the saddle, and the nickname of "Longshanks." The Dominican chronicler Nicholas Trivet, by whom these traits are recorded, tells us that the King delighted in war and tournaments, and especially in hawking and hunting. When he chased the stag he did not leave his quarry to the hounds, nor even to the hunting spear; he galloped at breakneck speed to cut the unhappy beast to the ground.

All this was typical of his reign. He presents us with qualities which are a mixture of the administrative capacity of Henry II and the personal prowess and magnanimity of Cœur de Lion. No English king more fully lived up to the maxim he chose for himself: "To each his own." He was animated by a passionate regard for justice and law, as he interpreted them, and for the rights of all groups within the community. Injuries and hostility roused, even to his last breath, a passionate torrent of resistance. But submission, or a generous act, on many occasions earned a swift response and laid the foundation of future friendship.

Edward was in Sicily when his father died, but the greatest magnates in the realm, before the tomb had closed upon the corpse of Henry III, acclaimed him King, with the assent of all men. It was two years before he returned to England for his coronation. In his accession the hereditary and elective principles flowed into a common channel, none asking which was the stronger. His conflicts with Simon de Montfort and the baronage had taught him the need for the monarchy to stand on a national footing. If Simon in his distresses had called in the middle class to aid him alike against Crown and arrogant nobles, the new King of his own free will would use this force in its proper place from the outset. Proportion is the keynote of his greatest years. He saw in the proud, turbulent baronage and a rapacious Church checks upon the royal authority; but he also recognised them as oppressors of the mass of his subjects; and it was by taking into account to a larger extent than had occurred before the interests of the middle class, and the needs of the people as a whole, that he succeeded in producing a broad, well-ordered foundation upon which an active monarchy could function in the general interest. Thus inspired, he sought a national kingship, an extension of his mastery throughout the British Isles, and a preponderant influence in the councils of Europe.

His administrative reforms in England were not such as to give satisfaction to any one of the strong contending forces, but rather to do justice to the whole. If the King resented the fetters which the Charter had imposed upon his grandfather, if he desired to control the growing opulence and claims of the Church, he did not himself assume the recaptured powers, but reposed them upon a broader foundation. When in his conflicts with the recent past he took away privileges which the Church and the baronage had gained he acted always in what was acknowledged to be the interest of the whole community. Throughout all his legislation, however varied its problems, there runs a common purpose: "We must find out what is ours and due to us, and others what is theirs and due to them."

Here was a time of setting in order. The reign is memorable, not for the erection of great new landmarks, but because the beneficial tendencies of the three preceding reigns were extracted from error and confusion and organised and consolidated in a permanent structure. The framework and policies of the nation, which we have seen shaping themselves with many fluctuations, now set and hardened into a form which, surviving the tragedies of the Black Death, the Hundred Years War with France, and the Wars of the Roses, endured for the remainder of the Middle Age, and some of them for longer. In this period we see a knightly and bourgeois stage of society increasingly replacing pure feudalism. The organs of government, land tenure, the military and financial systems, the relations of Church and State, all reach definitions which last nearly till the Tudors.

*   *   *   *   *

The first eighteen years of the reign witnessed an outburst of legislative activity for which there was to be no parallel for centuries. Nearly every year was marked by an important statute. Few of these were original, most were conservative in tone, but their cumulative effect was revolutionary. Edward relied upon his Chancellor, Robert Burnell, Bishop of Bath and Wells, a man of humble birth, who had risen through the royal chancery and household to his bishopric, and until his death in 1292 remained the King's principal adviser. Burnell's whole life had been spent in the service of the Crown; all his policy was devoted to the increase of its power at the expense of feudal privilege and influence. He had not been Chancellor for more than three weeks, after Edward's return to England in 1274, before a searching inquiry into the local administration was begun. Armed with a list of forty questions, commissioners were sent throughout the land to ask what were the rights and possessions of the King, what encroachments had been made upon them, which officials were negligent or corrupt, which sheriffs "for prayer, price, or favour" concealed felonies, neglected their duties, were harsh or bribed. Similar inquests had been made before; none was so thorough or so fertile. "Masterful, but not tyrannical," the King's policy was to respect all rights and overthrow all usurpations.

The First Statute of Westminster in the Parliament of 1275 dealt with the administrative abuses exposed by the commissioners. The Statute of Gloucester in 1278 directed the justices to inquire by writs of *Quo Warranto* into the rights of feudal magnates to administer the law by their own courts and officials within their demesnes, and ordained that those rights should be strictly defined. The main usefulness of the inquiry was to remind the great feudalists that they had duties as well as rights. In 1279 the Statute of Mortmain, *De Religiosis*, forbade gifts of land to be made to the Church, though the practice was allowed to continue under royal licence. In 1285 the Statute of Winchester attacked local disorder, and in the same year was issued the Second Statute of Westminster, *De Donis Conditionalibus*, which strengthened the system of entailed estates. The Third Statute of Westminster, *Quia Emptores*, dealt with land held, not upon condition, but in fee simple. Land held on these terms might be freely alienated, but it was stipulated for the future that the buyer must hold his purchase not from the seller, but from the seller's lord, and by the same feudal services and customs as were attached to the land before the sale. It thus called a halt to the growth of sub-infeudation, and was greatly to the advantage of the Crown, as overlord, whose direct tenants now increased in number.

The purpose of this famous series of laws was essentially conservative, and for a time their enforcement was efficient. But economic pressures were wreaking great changes in the propertied life of England scarcely less deep-cutting than those which had taken place in the political sphere. Land gradually ceased to be the moral sanction upon which national society and defence were based. It became by successive steps a commodity, which could in principle, like wool or mutton, be bought and sold, and which under certain restrictions could be either transferred to new owners by gift or testament or even settled under conditions of entail on future lives which were to be the foundation of a new aristocracy.

Of course only a comparatively small proportion of the land of England came into this active if rude market; but enough of a hitherto solid element was fluid to make a deep stir. In those days, when the greatest princes were pitifully starved in cash, there was already in England one spring of credit bubbling feebly. The Jews had unseen and noiselessly lodged themselves in the social fabric of that fierce age. They were there and they were not there; and from time to time they could be most helpful to high personages in urgent need of money; and to none more than to a king who did not desire to sue Parliament for it. The spectacle of land which could be acquired on rare but definite occasions by anyone with money led the English Jews into a course of shocking imprudence. Land began to pass into the hand of Israel, either by direct sale or more often by mortgage. Enough land came into the market to make both processes advantageous. In a couple of decades the erstwhile feudal lords were conscious that they had parted permanently for fleeting lucre with a portion of the English soil large enough to be noticed.

For some time past there had been growing a wrathful reaction. Small landowners oppressed by mortgages, spendthrift nobles who had made bad bargains, were united in their complaints. Italian moneylenders were now coming into the country, who could be just as useful in times of need to the King as the Jews. Edward saw himself able to conciliate powerful elements and escape from awkward debts, by the simple and well-trodden path of anti-Semitism. The propaganda of ritual murder and other dark tales, the commonplaces of our enlightened age, were at once invoked with general acclaim. The Jews, held up to universal hatred, were pillaged, maltreated, and finally expelled the realm. Exception was made for certain physicians without whose skill persons of consequence might have lacked due attention. Once again the sorrowful, wandering race, stripped to the skin, must seek asylum and begin afresh. To Spain or North Africa the melancholy caravan, now so familiar, must move on. Not until four centuries had elapsed was Oliver Cromwell by furtive contracts with a moneyed Israelite to open again the coasts of England to the enterprise of the Jewish race. It was left to a Calvinist dictator to remove the ban which a Catholic king had imposed. The bankers of Florence and Siena, who had taken the place of the Jews, were in their turn under Edward I's grandson to taste the equities of Christendom.

*   *   *   *   *

Side by side with the large statutory achievements of the reign the King maintained a ceaseless process of administrative reform. His personal inspections were indefatigable. He travelled continually about his domain, holding at every centre strict inquiry into abuses of all kinds, and correcting the excesses of local magnates with a sharp pen and a strong hand. Legality, often pushed into pedantic interpretations, was a weapon upon which he was ever ready to lay his hands. In every direction by tireless perseverance he cleansed the domestic government of the realm, and ousted private interests from spheres which belonged not only to himself but to his people.

Edward I was remarkable among medieval kings for the seriousness with which he regarded the work of administration and good government. It was natural therefore that he should place more reliance upon expert professional help than upon what has been neatly termed "the amateurish assistance of great feudalists staggering under the weight of their own dignity." By the end of the thirteenth century three departments of specialised administration were already at work. One was the Exchequer, established at Westminster, where most of the revenue was received and the accounts kept. The second was the Chancery, a general secretariat responsible for the writing and drafting of innumerable royal charters, writs, and letters. The third was the Wardrobe, with its separate secretariat, the Privy Seal, attached to the ever-moving royal household, and combining financial and secretarial functions, which might range from financing a Continental war to buying a pennyworth of pepper for the royal cook. Burnell was a typical product of the incipient Civil Service. His place after his death was taken by an Exchequer official, Walter Langton, the Treasurer, who, like Burnell, looked upon his see of Lichfield as a reward for skilful service rather than a spiritual office.

Though the most orthodox of Churchmen, Edward I did not escape conflict with the Church. Anxious though he was to pay his dues to God, he had a far livelier sense than his father of what was due to Cæsar, and circumstances more than once forced him to protest. The leader of the Church party was John Pecham, a Franciscan friar, Archbishop of Canterbury from 1279 to 1292. With great courage and skill Pecham defended what he regarded as the just rights of the Church and its independence against the Crown. At the provincial Council held at Reading in 1279 he issued a number of pronouncements which angered the King. One was a canon against plurality of clerical offices, which struck at the principal royal method of rewarding the growing Civil Service. Another was the order that a copy of the Charter, which Edward had sworn to uphold, should be publicly posted in every cathedral and collegiate church. All who produced royal writs to stop cases in ecclesiastical courts and all who violated Magna Carta were threatened with excommunication.

Pecham bowed to Edward's anger and waited his time. In 1281, when another provincial Council was summoned to Lambeth, the King, suspecting mischief, issued writs to its members forbidding them to "hold counsel concerning matters which appertain to our crown, or touch our person, our state, or the state of our Council." Pecham was undeterred. He revived almost verbatim the principal legislation of the Reading Council, prefaced it with an explicit assertion of ecclesiastical liberty, and a month later wrote a remarkable letter to the King, defending his action. "By no human constitution," he wrote, "not even by an oath, can we be bound to ignore laws which rest undoubtedly upon divine authority." "A fine letter" was the marginal comment of an admiring clerk who copied it into the Archbishop's register.

Pecham's action might well have precipitated a crisis comparable to the quarrel between Becket and Henry II, but Edward seems to have quietly ignored the challenge. Royal writs of prohibition continued to be issued. Yet moderation was observed, and in 1286 by a famous writ Edward wisely ordered his itinerant justices to act circumspectly in matters of ecclesiastical jurisdiction, and listed the kinds of case which should be left to Church courts. The dispute thus postponed was to outlive both Archbishop and King.

* * * * *

At the beginning of the reign relations between England and France were governed by the Treaty of Paris, which the baronial party had concluded in 1259. For more than thirty years peace reigned between the two countries, though often with an undercurrent of hostility. The disputes about the execution of the terms of the treaty and the quarrels between English, Gascon, and French sailors in the Channel, culminating in a great sea-fight off Saint-Mahé in 1293, need never have led to a renewal of war, had not the presence of the English in the South of France been a standing challenge to the pride of the French and a bar to their national integrity. Even when Philip the Fair, the French king, began to seek opportunities of provocation Edward was long-suffering and patient in his attempts to reach a compromise. Finally however the Parlement of Paris declared the Duchy of Gascony forfeit. Philip asked for the token surrender of the principal Gascon fortresses, as a recognition of his legal powers as overlord. Edward complied. But once Philip was in possession he refused to give them up again. Edward now realised that he must either fight or lose his French possessions.

By 1294 the great King had changed much from his early buoyant manhood. After the long stormy years of sustaining his father he had reigned himself for nearly a quarter of a century. Meanwhile his world had changed about him; he had lost his beloved wife Eleanor of Castile, his mother, Eleanor of Provence, and his two eldest infant sons. Burnell was now dead. Wales and Scotland presented grave problems; opposition was beginning to make itself heard and felt. Alone, perplexed and ageing, the King had to face an endless succession of difficulties.

In June 1294 he explained the grounds of the quarrel with the French to what is already called "a Parliament" of magnates in London. His decision to go to war was accepted with approval, as has often been the case in more regularly constituted assemblies.

The war itself had no important features. There were campaigns in Gascony, a good deal of coastal raiding in the Channel, and a prolonged siege by the English of Bordeaux. Any enthusiasm which had been expressed at the outset wore off speedily under the inevitable increases of taxation. All wool and leather, the staple items of the English export trade, were impounded, and could only be redeemed by the payment of a customs duty of 40s. on the sack instead of the half-mark (6s. 8d.) laid down by the Parliament of 1275. In September the clergy, to their great indignation, were ordered to contribute one-half of their revenues. The Dean of St. Paul's, who attempted to voice their protests in the King's own terrifying presence, fell down in a fit and died. In November Parliament granted a heavy tax upon all movable property. As the collection proceeded a bitter and sullen discontent spread among all classes. In the winter of 1294 the Welsh revolted, and when the King had suppressed them he returned to find that Scotland had allied itself with France. From 1296 onward war with Scotland was either smouldering or flaring.

After October 1297 the French war degenerated into a series of truces which lasted until 1303. Such conditions involved expense little less than actual fighting. These were years of severe strain, both at home and abroad, and especially with Scotland. Although the King did not hesitate to recall recurrent Parliaments to Westminster and explained the whole situation to them, he did not obtain the support which he needed. Parliament was reluctant to grant the new taxes demanded of it.

The position of the clergy was made more difficult by the publication in 1296 of the Papal Bull *Clericis Laicos*, which forbade the payment of extraordinary taxation without Papal authority. At the autumn Parliament at Bury St. Edmunds the clergy, under the leadership of Robert Winchelsea, the new Primate, decided after some hesitation that they were unable to make any contribution. Edward in his anger outlawed them and declared their lay fiefs forfeit. The Archbishop retaliated by threatening with excommunication any who should disobey the Papal Bull. For a time passion ran high, but eventually a calmer mood prevailed. By the following summer the quarrel was allayed, and the Pope by a new Bull, *Etsi de Statu*, had withdrawn his extreme claims.

Edward was the more prepared to come to terms with the Church because opposition had already broken out in another quarter. He proposed to the barons at Salisbury that a number of them should serve in Gascony while he conducted a campaign in Flanders. This was ill received. Humphrey de Bohun, Earl of Hereford and Constable of England, together with the Marshal, Roger Bigod, Earl of Norfolk, declared that their hereditary offices could only be exercised in the King's company. Such excuses deceived nobody. Both the Earls had personal grudges against the King, and—much more important—they voiced the resentment felt by a large number of the barons who for the past twenty years had steadily seen the authority of the Crown increased to their own detriment. The time was ripe for a revival of the baronial opposition which a generation before had defied Edward's father.

For the moment the King ignored the challenge. He pressed forward with his preparations for war, appointed deputies in place of Hereford and Norfolk, and in August sailed for Flanders. The opposition saw in his absence their long-awaited opportunity. They demanded the confirmation of those two instruments, Magna Carta and its extension, the Charter of the Forest, which were the final version of the terms extorted from John, together with six additional articles. By these no tallage or aid was to be imposed in future except with the consent of the community of the realm; corn, wool, and the like must not be impounded against the will of their owners; the clergy and laity of the realm must recover their ancient liberties; the two Earls and their supporters were not to be penalised for their refusal to serve in Gascony; the prelates were to read the Charter aloud in their cathedrals, and to excommunicate all who neglected it. In the autumn the two Earls, backed by armed forces, appeared in London and demanded the acceptance of these proposals. The Regency, unable to resist, submitted. The articles were confirmed, and in November at Ghent the King ratified them reserving however certain financial rights of the Crown.

These were large and surprising concessions. Both King and opposition attached great importance to them, and the King was suspected, perhaps with justice, of trying to withdraw from the promises he had given. Several times the baronial party publicly drew attention to these promises before Parliament, and finally in February 1301 the King was driven by the threats and arguments of a Parliament at Lincoln to grant a new confirmation of both charters and certain further articles in solemn form.

By this crisis and its manner of resolution, two principles had been established from which important consequences flowed. One was that the King had no right to despatch the feudal host wherever he might choose. This limitation sounded the death-knell of the feudal levy, and inexorably led in the following century to the rise of indentured armies serving for pay. The second point of principle now recognised was that the King could not plead "urgent necessity" as a reason for imposing taxation without consent. Other English monarchs as late as the seventeenth century were to make the attempt. But by Edward's failure a precedent had been set up, and a long stride had been taken towards the dependence of the Crown upon Parliamentary grants.

Edward to a greater extent than any of his predecessors had shown himself prepared to govern in the national interest and with some regard for constitutional form. It was thus ironical, and to the King exasperating, that he found the principles he had emphasised applied against himself. The baronial party had not resorted to war; they had acted through the constitutional machinery the King himself had taken so much pains to create. Thereby they had shifted their ground: they spoke no longer as the representatives of the feudal aristocracy, but as the leaders of a national opposition. So the Crown was once again committed solemnly and publicly to the principles of Magna Carta, and the concession was made all the more valuable because remedies of actual recent abuses of the royal prerogative powers had been added to the original charters. Here was a real constitutional advance.

*   *   *   *   *

In their fatal preoccupation with their possessions in France the English kings had neglected the work of extending their rule within the Island of Great Britain. There had been fitful interference both in Wales and Scotland, but the task of keeping the frontiers safe had fallen mainly upon the shoulders of the local Marcher lords. As soon as the Treaty of Paris had brought a generation's respite from Continental adventures it was possible to turn to the urgent problems of internal security. Edward I was the first of the English kings to put the whole weight of the Crown's resources behind the effort of national expansion in the West and North, and to him is due the conquest of the independent areas of Wales and the securing of the Western frontier. He took the first great step towards the unification of the Island. He sought to conquer where the Romans, the Saxons, and the Normans all in their turn had failed. The mountain fastnesses of Wales nursed a hardy and unsubdued race which, under the grandson of the great Llewellyn, had in the previous reign once again made a deep dint upon the politics of England. Edward, as his father's lieutenant, had experience of the Welsh. He had encountered them in war, with questionable success. At the same time he had seen, with disapproving eye, the truculence of the barons of the Welsh Marches, the Mortimers, the Bohuns, and in the South the Clares, with the Gloucester estates, who exploited their military privileges against the interests alike of the Welsh and English people. All assertions of Welsh independence were a vexation to Edward; but scarcely less obnoxious was a system of guarding the frontiers of England by a confederacy of robber barons who had more than once presumed to challenge the authority of the Crown. He resolved, in the name of justice and progress, to subdue the unconquered refuge of petty princes and wild mountaineers in which barbaric freedom had dwelt since remote antiquity, and at the same time to curb the privileges of the Marcher lords.

Edward I, utilising all the local resources which the barons of the Welsh Marches had developed in the chronic strife of many generations, conquered Wales in several years of persistent warfare, coldly and carefully devised, by land and sea. The forces he employed were mainly Welsh levies in his pay, reinforced by regular troops from Gascony and by one of the last appearances of the feudal levy; but above all it was by the terror of winter campaigns that he broke the power of the valiant Ancient Britons. By Edward's Statute of Wales the independent principality came to an end. The land of Llewellyn's Wales was transferred entirely to the King's dominions and organised into the shires of Anglesey, Carnarvon, Merioneth, Cardigan and Camarthen. The king's son Edward, born in Carnarvon, was proclaimed the first English Prince of Wales.

The Welsh wars of Edward reveal to us the process by which the military system of England was transformed from the age-long Saxon and feudal basis of occasional service to that of paid regular troops. We have seen how Alfred the Great suffered repeatedly from the expiry of the period for which the "fyrd" could be called out. Four hundred years had passed, and Norman feudalism still conformed to this basic principle. But how were campaigns to be conducted winter and summer for fifteen months at a time by such methods? How were Continental expeditions to be launched and pursued? Thus for several reigns the principle of scutage had been agreeable alike to barons who did not wish to serve and to sovereigns who preferred a money payment with which to hire full-time soldiers. In the Welsh wars both systems are seen simultaneously at work, but the old is fading. Instead of liege service Governments now required trustworthy mercenaries, and for this purpose money was the solvent.

At the same time a counter-revolution in the balance of warfare was afoot. The mailed cavalry which from the fifth century had eclipsed the ordered ranks of the legion were wearing out their long day. A new type of infantry raised from the common people began to prove its dominating quality. This infantry operated, not by club or sword or spear, or even by hand-flung missiles, but by an archery which, after a long development, concealed from Europe, was very soon to make an astonishing entrance upon the military scene and gain a dramatic ascendancy upon the battlefields of the Continent. Here was a prize taken by the conquerors from their victims. In South Wales the practice of drawing the long-bow had already attained an astonishing efficiency, of which one of the Marcher lords has left a record. One of his knights had been hit by an arrow which pierced not only the skirts of his mailed shirt, but his mailed breeches, his thigh, and the wood of his saddle, and finally struck deep into his horse's flank. This was a new fact in the history of war, which is also a part of the history of civilisation, deserving to be mentioned with the triumph of bronze over flint, or iron over bronze. For the first time infantry possessed a weapon which could penetrate the armour of the clanking age, and which in range and rate of fire was superior to any method ever used before, or ever used again until the coming of the modern rifle. The War Office has among its records a treatise written during the peace after Waterloo by a general officer of long experience in the Napoleonic wars recommending that muskets should be discarded in favour of the long-bow on account of its superior accuracy, rapid discharge, and effective range.

Thus the Welsh war, from two separate points of departure, destroyed the physical basis of feudalism, which had already, in its moral aspect, been outsped and outclassed by the extension and refinement of administration. Even when the conquest was completed the process of holding down the subdued regions required methods which were beyond the compass of feudal barons. Castles of stone, with many elaborations, had indeed long played a conspicuous part in the armoured age. But now the extent of the towered walls must be enlarged not only to contain more numerous garrisons, but to withstand great siege engines, such as trebuchets and mangonels, which had recently been greatly improved, and to hinder attackers from approaching to the foot of the inner walls. Now, moreover, not merely troops of steel-clad warriors will ride forth, spreading random terror in the countryside, but disciplined bodies of infantry, possessing the new power of long-range action, will be led by regular commanders upon a plan prescribed by a central command.

*　　*　　*　　*　　*

The great quarrel of Edward's reign was with Scotland. For long years the two kingdoms had dwelt in amity. In the year 1286 Alexander III of Scotland, riding his horse over a cliff in the darkness, left as his heir Margaret his granddaughter, known as the Maid of Norway. The Scottish magnates had been persuaded to recognise this princess of fourteen as his successor. Now the bright project arose that the Maid of Norway should at the same moment succeed to the Scottish throne and marry Edward, the King's son. Thus would be achieved a union of royal families by which the antagonism of England and Scotland might be laid to rest. We can measure the sagacity of the age by the acceptance of this plan. Practically all the ruling forces in England and Scotland were agreed upon it. It was a dream, and it passed as a dream. The Maid of Norway embarked in 1290 upon stormy seas only to die before reaching land, and Scotland was bequeathed the problem of a disputed succession, in the decision of which the English interest must be a heavy factor. The Scottish nobility were allied at many points with the English royal family, and from a dozen claimants, some of them bastards, two men stood clearly forth, John Balliol and Robert Bruce. Bruce asserted his aged father's closeness in relationship to the common royal ancestor; Balliol, a more distant descendant, the rights of primogeniture. But partisanship was evenly balanced.

Since the days of Henry II the English monarchy had intermittently claimed an overlordship of Scotland, based on the still earlier acknowledgment of Saxon overlordship by Scottish kings. King Edward, whose legal abilities were renowned, had already arbitrated in similar circumstances between Aragon and Anjou. He now imposed himself with considerable acceptance as arbitrator in the Scottish succession. Since the alternatives were the splitting of Scotland into rival kingships or a civil war to decide the matter, the Scots were induced to seek Edward's judgment; and he, pursuing all the time a path of strict legality, consented to the task only upon the prior condition of the reaffirmation of his overlordship, betokened by the surrender of certain Scottish castles. The English King discharged his function as arbitrator with extreme propriety. He rejected the temptation presented to him by Scottish baronial intrigues of destroying the integrity of Scotland. He pronounced in 1292 in favour of John Balliol. Later judgments have in no wise impugned the correctness of his decision. But, having regard to the deep division in Scotland, and the strong elements which adhered to the Bruce claim, John Balliol inevitably became not merely his choice, but his puppet. So thought King Edward I, and plumed himself upon a just and at the same time highly profitable decision. He had confirmed his overlordship of Scotland. He had nominated its king, who stood himself in his own land upon a narrow margin. But the national feeling of Scotland was pent up behind these barriers of legal affirmation. In their distress the Scottish baronage accepted King Edward's award, but they also furnished the new King John with an authoritative council of twelve great lords to overawe him and look after the rights of Scotland. Thus King Edward saw with disgust that all his fair-seeming success left him still confronted with the integrity of Scottish nationhood, with an independent and not a subject Government, and with a hostile rather than a submissive nation.

At this very moment the same argument of overlordship was pressed upon him by the formidable French king, Philip IV. Here Edward was the vassal, proudly defending feudal interests, and the French suzerain had the lawful advantage. Moreover, if England was stronger than Scotland, France was in armed power superior to England. This double conflict imposed a strain upon the financial and military resources of the English monarchy which it could by no means meet. The rest of Edward's reign was spent in a twofold struggle North and South, for the sake of which he had to tax his subjects beyond all endurance. He journeyed energetically to and fro between Flanders and the Scottish Lowlands. He racked the land for money. Nothing else mattered; and the embryonic Parliamentary system profited vastly by the repeated concessions he made in the hope of carrying opinion with him. He confirmed the bulk of the reforms wrung from John. With some exceptions among the great lords, the nation was with him in both of his external efforts, but though time and again it complied with his demands it was not reconciled to the crushing burden. Thus we see the wise lawgiver, the thrifty scrutineer of English finances, the administrative reformer, forced to drive his people beyond their strength, and in this process to rouse oppositions which darkened his life and clouded his fame.

To resist Edward the Scots allied themselves with the French. Since Edward was at war with France he regarded this as an act of hostility. He summoned Balliol to meet him at Berwick. The Scottish nobles refused to allow their king to go, and from this moment war began. Edward struck with ruthless severity. He advanced on Berwick. The city, then the great emporium of Northern trade, was unprepared, after a hundred years of peace, to resist attack. Palisades were hurriedly raised, the citizens seized such weapons as were at hand. The English army, with hardly any loss, trampled down these improvised defences, and Berwick was delivered to a sack and slaughter which shocked even those barbaric times. Thousands were slain. The most determined resistance came from thirty Flemish merchants who held their depot, called the Red Hall, until it was burnt down. Berwick sank in a few hours from one of the active centres of European commerce to the minor seaport which exists to-day.

This act of terror quelled the resistance of the ruling classes in Scotland. Perth, Stirling, Edinburgh, yielded themselves to the King's march. Here we see how Edward I anticipated the teachings of Machiavelli; for to the frightfulness of Berwick succeeded a most gracious, forgiving spirit which welcomed and made easy submission in every form. Balliol surrendered his throne and Scotland was brought under English administration. But, as in Wales, the conqueror introduced not only an alien rule, but law and order, all of which were equally unpopular. The governing classes of Scotland had conspicuously failed, and Edward might flatter himself that all was over. It was only beginning. It has often been said that Joan of Arc first raised the standard of nationalism in the Western world. But over a century before she appeared an outlaw knight, William Wallace, arising from the recesses of South-West Scotland which had been his refuge, embodied, commanded, and led to victory the Scottish nation. Edward, warring in France with piebald fortune, was forced to listen to tales of ceaseless inroads and forays against his royal peace in Scotland, hitherto deemed so sure. Wallace had behind him the spirit of a race as stern and as resolute as any bred among men. He added military gifts of a high order. Out of an unorganised mass of valiant righting men he forged, in spite of cruel poverty and primitive administration, a stubborn, indomitable army, ready to fight at any odds and mock defeat. The structure of this army is curious. Every four men had a fifth man as leader; every nine men a tenth; every nineteen men a twentieth, and so on to every thousand; and it was agreed that the penalty for disobedience to the leader of any unit was death. Thus from the ground does freedom raise itself unconquerable.

Warenne, Earl of Surrey, was Edward's commander in the North. When the depredations of the Scottish rebels had become intolerable he advanced at the head of strong forces upon Stirling. At Stirling Bridge, near the Abbey of Cambuskenneth, in September 1297, he found himself in the presence of Wallace's army. Many Scotsmen were in the English service. One of these warned him of the dangers of trying to deploy beyond the long, narrow bridge and causeway which spanned the river. This knight pleaded calculations worthy of a modern staff officer. It would take eleven hours to move the army across the bridge, and what would happen, he asked, if the vanguard were attacked before the passage was completed? He spoke of a ford higher up, by which at least a flanking force could cross. But Earl Warenne would have none of these things. Wallace watched with measuring eye the accumulation of the English troops across the bridge, and at the right moment hurled his full force upon them, seized the bridgehead, and slaughtered the vanguard of five thousand men. Warenne evacuated the greater part of Scotland. His fortress garrisons were reduced one after the other. The English could barely hold the line of the Tweed.

It was beyond the compass of King Edward's resources to wage war with France and face the hideous struggle with Scotland at the same time. He sought at all costs to concentrate on the peril nearest home. He entered upon a long series of negotiations with the French King which were covered by truces repeatedly renewed, and reached a final Treaty of Paris in 1303. Though the formal peace was delayed for some years, it was in fact sealed in 1294 by the arrangement of a marriage between Edward and Philip's sister, the young Princess Margaret, and also by the betrothal of Edward's son and heir, Edward of Carnarvon, to Philip's daughter Isabella. This dual alliance of blood brought the French war to an effective close in 1297, although through Papal complications neither the peace nor the King's marriage were finally and formally confirmed until 1299. By these diplomatic arrangements Edward from the end of 1297 onwards was able to concentrate his strength against the Scots.

Wallace was now the ruler of Scotland, and the war was without truce or mercy. A hated English official, a tax-gatherer, had fallen at the bridge. His skin, cut into suitable strips, covered Wallace's sword-belt for the future. Edward, forced to quit his campaign in France, hastened to the scene of disaster, and with the whole feudal levy of England advanced against the Scots. The Battle of Falkirk in 1298, which he conducted in person, bears a sharp contrast to Stirling Bridge. Wallace, now at the head of stronger powers, accepted battle in a withdrawn defensive position. He had few cavalry and few archers;

but his confidence lay in the solid "schiltrons" (or circles) of spearmen, who were invincible except by actual physical destruction. The armoured cavalry of the English vanguard were hurled back with severe losses from the spear-points. But Edward, bringing up his Welsh archers in the intervals between horsemen of the second line, concentrated a hail of arrows upon particular points in the Scottish schiltrons, so that there were more dead and wounded than living men in these places. Into the gaps and over the carcasses the knighthood of England forced their way. Once the Scottish order was broken the spearmen were quickly massacred. The slaughter ended only in the depths of the woods, and Wallace and the Scottish army were once again fugitives, hunted as rebels, starving, suffering the worst of human privations, but still in arms.

The Scots were unconquerable foes. It was not until 1305 that Wallace was captured, tried with full ceremonial in Westminster Hall, and hanged, drawn, and quartered at Tyburn. But the Scottish war was one in which, as a chronicler said, "every winter undid every summer's work." Wallace was to pass the torch to Robert Bruce.

*　　*　　*　　*　　*

In the closing years of Edward's life he appears as a lonely and wrathful old man. A new generation had grown up around him with whom he had slight acquaintance and less sympathy. Queen Margaret was young enough to be his daughter, and sided often with her stepchildren against their father. Few dared to oppose the old King, but he had little love or respect in his family circle.

With Robert Bruce, grandson of the claimant of 1290, who had won his way partly by right of birth, but also by hard measures, the war in Scotland flared again. He met the chief Scotsman who represented the English interest in the solemn sanctuary of the church in the Border town of Dumfries. The two leaders were closeted together. Presently Bruce emerged alone, and said to his followers, "I doubt me I have killed the Red Comyn." Whereat his chief supporter, muttering "I'se mak' siccar!" re-entered the sacred edifice. A new champion of this grand Northern race had thus appeared in arms. King Edward was old, but his will-power was unbroken. When the news came south to Winchester, where he held his Court, that Bruce had been crowned at Scone his fury was terrible to behold. He launched a campaign in the summer of 1306 in which Bruce was defeated and driven to take refuge on Rathlin island, off the coast of Antrim. Here, according to the tale, Bruce was heartened by the persistent efforts of the most celebrated spider known to history. Next spring he returned to Scotland. Edward was now too ill to march or ride. Like the Emperor Severus a thousand years before, he was carried in a litter against this stern people, and like him he died upon the road. His last thoughts were on Scotland and on the Holy Land. He conjured his son to carry his bones in the van of the army which should finally bring Scotland to obedience, and to send his heart to Palestine with a band of a hundred knights to help recover the Sacred City. Neither wish was fulfilled by his futile and unworthy heir.

* * * * *

Edward I was the last great figure in the formative period of English law. His statutes, which settled questions of public order, assigned limits to the powers of the seigneurial courts, and restrained the sprawling and luxurious growth of judge-made law, laid down principles that remained fundamental to the law of property until the mid-nineteenth century. By these great enactments necessary bounds were fixed to the freedom of the Common Law which, without conflicting with its basic principles or breaking with the past, imparted to it its final form.

In the constitutional sphere the work of Edward I was not less durable. He had made Parliament—that is to say, certain selected magnates and representatives of the shires and boroughs—the associate of the Crown, in place of the old Court of Tenants-in-Chief. By the end of his reign this conception had been established. At first it lacked substance; only gradually did it take on flesh and blood. But between the beginning and the end of Edward's reign the decisive impulse was given. At the beginning anything or nothing might have come out of the experiments of his father's troubled time. By the end it was fairly settled in the customs and traditions of England that "sovereignty," to use a term which Edward would hardly have understood, would henceforward reside not in the Crown only, nor in the Crown and Council of the Barons, but in the Crown in Parliament.

Dark constitutional problems loomed in the future. The boundary between the powers of Parliament and those of the Crown was as yet very vaguely drawn. A statute, it was quickly accepted, was a law enacted by the King in Parliament, and could only be repealed with the consent of Parliament itself. But Parliament was still in its infancy. The initiative in the work of government still rested with the King, and necessarily he retained many powers whose limits were undefined. Did royal ordinances, made in the Privy Council on the King's sole authority, have the validity of law? Could the King in particular cases override a statute on the plea of public or royal expediency? In a clash between the powers of King and Parliament who was to say on which side right lay? Inevitably, as Parliament grew to a fuller stature, these questions would be asked; but for a final answer they were to wait until Stuart kings sat on the English throne.

Nevertheless the foundations of a strong national monarchy for a United Kingdom and of a Parliamentary Constitution had been laid. Their continuous development and success depended upon the King's immediate successor. Idle weaklings, dreamers, and adventurous boys disrupted the nascent unity of the Island. Long years of civil war, and despotism in reaction from anarchy, marred and delayed the development of its institutions. But when the traveller gazes upon the plain marble tomb at Westminster on which is inscribed, "Here lies Edward I, the Hammer of the Scots. Keep troth," he stands before the resting-place of a master-builder of British life, character, and fame.

CHAPTER NINETEEN

BANNOCKBURN

EDWARD II'S REIGN MAY FAIRLY BE REGARDED AS A MELANCHOLY appendix to his father's and the prelude to his son's. The force and fame which Edward I had gathered in his youth and prime cast their shield over the decline of his later years. We have seen him in his strength; we must see him in his weakness. Men do not live for ever, and in his final phase the bold warrior who had struck down Simon de Montfort, who had reduced the Welsh to obedience, and even discipline, who was "the Hammer of the Scots," who had laid the foundations of Parliament, who had earned the proud title of "the English Justinian" by his laws, was fighting a losing battle with a singularly narrow, embittered, and increasingly class-conscious nobility. This battle old age and death forced him to confide to his embarrassed son, who proved incapable of winning it.

A strong, capable King had with difficulty upborne the load. He was succeeded by a perverted weakling, of whom some amiable traits are recorded. Marlowe in his tragedy puts in his mouth at the moment of his death some fine lines:

> Tell Isabel the Queen I looked not thus
> When for her sake I ran at tilt in France,
> And there unhorsed the Duke of Cleremont.

Of this tribute history did not deprive the unfortunate King; but the available records say little of war or tournaments and dwell rather upon Edward's interest in thatching and ditching and other service-able arts. He was addicted to rowing, swimming, and baths. He carried his friendship for his advisers beyond dignity and decency. This was a reign which by its weakness contributed in the long run to English strength. The ruler was gone, the rod was broken, and the forces of English nationhood, already alive and conscious under the old King, resumed their march at a quicker and more vehement step. In default of a dominating Parliamentary institution, the Curia Regis, as we have seen, seemed to be the centre from which the busi-ness of government could be controlled. On the death of Edward I the barons succeeded in gaining control of this mixed body of powerful magnates and competent Household officials. They set up a committee called "the Lords Ordainers," who represented the baronial and ecclesiastical interests of the State. Scotland and France remained the external problems confronting these new masters of government, but their first anger was directed upon the favourite of the King. Piers Gaveston, a young, handsome Gascon, enjoyed his fullest confidence. His decisions made or marred. There was a temper which would submit to the rule of a King, but would not tolerate the pretensions of his personal cronies. The barons' party attacked Piers Gaveston. Edward and his favourite tried to stave off opposition by harrying the Scots. They failed, and in 1311 Gaveston was exiled to Flanders. Thence he was so imprudent as to return, in defiance of the Lords Ordainers. Compelling him to take refuge in the North, they pursued him, not so much by war as by a process of establishing their authority, occupying castles, controlling the courts, and giving to the armed forces orders which were obeyed. Besieged in the castle of Scarborough, Gaveston made terms with his foes. His life was to be spared; and on this they took him under guard. But other nobles, led by the Earl of Warwick, one of the foremost Ordainers, who had not been present at the agreement of Scarborough, violated these conditions. They overpowered the escort, seized the favourite at Deddington in Oxfordshire, and hewed off his head on Blacklow Hill, near Warwick.

In spite of these successes by the Ordainers royal power remained formidable. Edward was still in control of Government, although he was under their restraint. Troubles in France and war in Scotland confronted him. To wipe out his setbacks at home he resolved upon the conquest of the Northern kingdom. A general levy of the whole power of England was set on foot to beat the Scots. A great army crossed the Tweed in the summer of 1314. Twenty-five thousand men, hard to gather, harder still to feed in those days, with at least three thousand armoured knights and men-at-arms, moved against the Scottish host under the nominal but none the less baffling command of Edward II. The new champion of Scotland, Robert the Bruce, now faced the vengeance of England. The Scottish army, of perhaps ten thousand men, was composed, as at Falkirk, mainly of the hard, unyielding spearmen who feared nought and, once set in position, had to be killed. But Bruce had pondered deeply upon the impotence of pikemen, however faithful, if exposed to the alternations of an arrow shower and an armoured charge. He therefore, with a foresight and skill which proves his military quality, took three precautions. First, he chose a position where his flanks were secured by impenetrable woods; secondly, he dug upon his front a large number of small round holes or "pottes," afterwards to be imitated by the archers at Crécy, and covered them with branches and turfs as a trap for charging cavalry; thirdly, he kept in his own hand his small but highly trained force of mounted knights to break up any attempt at planting archers upon his flank to derange his schiltrons. These dispositions made, he awaited the English onslaught.

The English army was so large that it took three days to close up from rear to front. The ground available for deployment was little more than two thousand yards. While the host was massing itself opposite the Scottish position an incident took place. An English knight, Henry de Bohun, pushed his way forward at the head of a force of Welsh infantry to try by a surprise move to relieve Stirling Castle which was in English hands. Bruce arrived just in time to throw himself and some of his men between them and the castle walls. Bohun charged him in single combat. Bruce, though not mounted on his heavy war-horse, awaited his onset upon a well-trained hack, and, striking aside the English lance with his battle-axe, slew Bohun at a single blow before the eyes of all.

On the morning of June 24 the English advanced, and a dense wave of steel-clad horsemen descended the slope, splashed and scrambled through the Bannock Burn, and charged uphill upon the schiltrons. Though much disordered by the "pottes," they came to deadly grip with the Scottish spearmen. "And when the two hosts so came together and the great steeds of the knights dashed into the Scottish pikes as into a thick wood there rose a great and horrible crash from rending lances and dying horses, and there they stood locked together for a space." As neither side would withdraw the struggle was prolonged and covered the whole front. The strong corps of archers could not intervene. When they shot their arrows into the air, as William had done at Hastings, they hit more of their own men than of the Scottish infantry. At length a detachment of archers was brought round the Scottish left flank. But for this Bruce had made effective provision. His small cavalry force charged them with the utmost promptitude, and drove them back into the great mass waiting to engage, and now already showing signs of disorder. Continuous reinforcements streamed forward towards the English fighting line. Confusion steadily increased. At length the appearance on the hills to the English right of the camp-followers of Bruce's army, waving flags and raising loud cries, was sufficient to induce a general retreat, which the King himself, with his numerous personal guards, was not slow to head. The retreat speedily became a rout. The Scottish schiltrons hurled themselves forward down the slope, inflicting immense carnage upon the English even before they could re-cross the Bannock Burn. No more grievous slaughter of English chivalry ever took place in a single day. Even Towton in the Wars of the Roses was less destructive. The Scots claimed to have slain or captured thirty thousand men, more than the whole English army, but their feat in virtually destroying an army of cavalry and archers mainly by the agency of spearmen must nevertheless be deemed a prodigy of war.

*   *   *   *   *

In the long story of a nation we often see that capable rulers by their very virtues sow the seeds of future evil and weak or degenerate princes open the pathway of progress. At this time the unending struggle for power had entered upon new ground. We have traced the ever-growing influence, and at times authority, of the permanent officials of the royal Household. This became more noticeable, and therefore more obnoxious, when the sovereign was evidently in their hands, or not capable of overtopping them in policy or personality. The feudal baronage had striven successfully against kings. They now saw in the royal officials agents who stood in their way, yet at the same time were obviously indispensable to the widening aspects of national life. They could no more contemplate the abolition of these officials than their ancestors the destruction of the monarchy. The whole tendency of their movement was therefore in this generation to acquire control of an invaluable machine. They sought to achieve in the fourteenth century that power of choosing, or at least of supervising, the appointments to the key offices of the Household which the Whig nobility under the house of Hanover actually won.

The Lords Ordainers, as we have seen, had control of the Curia Regis; but they soon found that many of the essentials of power still eluded their grasp. In those days the King was expected to rule as well as to reign. The King's sign manual, the seal affixed to a document, a writ or warrant issued by a particular officer, were the facts upon which the courts pronounced, soldiers marched, and executioners discharged their functions. One of the main charges brought against Edward II at his deposition was that he had failed in his task of government. From early in his reign he left too much to his Household officials. To the Lords Ordainers it appeared that the high control of government had withdrawn itself from the Curia Regis, into an inner citadel described as "the King's Wardrobe." There was the King, in his Wardrobe, with his favourites and indispensable functionaries, settling a variety of matters from the purchase of the royal hose to the waging of a Continental war. Outside this select, secluded circle the rugged, arrogant, virile barons prowled morosely. The process was exasperating; like climbing a hill where always a new summit appears. Nor must we suppose that such experiences were reserved for this distant age alone. It is the nature of supreme executive power to withdraw itself into the smallest compass; and without such contraction there is no executive power. But when this exclusionary process was tainted by unnatural vice and stained by shameful defeat in the field it was clear that those who beat upon the doors had found a prosperous occasion, especially since many of the Ordainers had prudently absented themselves from the Bannockburn campaign and could thus place all the blame for its disastrous outcome upon the King.

The forces were not unequally balanced. To do violence to the sacred person of the King was an awful crime. The Church by its whole structure and tradition depended upon him. A haughty, self-interested aristocracy must remember that in most parts of the country the common people, among whom bills and bows were plentiful, had looked since the days of the Conqueror to the Crown as their protector against baronial oppression. Above all, law and custom weighed heavily with all classes, rich and poor alike, when every district had a life of its own and very few lights burned after sundown. The barons might have a blasting case against the King at Westminster, but if he appeared in Shropshire or Westmorland with his handful of guards and the royal insignia he could tell his own tale, and men, both knight and archer, would rally to him.

In this equipoise Parliament became of serious importance to the contending interests. Here at least was the only place where the case for or against the conduct of the central executive could be tried before something that resembled, however imperfectly, the nation. Thus we see in this ill-starred reign both sides operating in and through Parliament, and in this process enhancing its power. Parliament was called together no fewer than twenty-five times under King Edward II. It had no share in the initiation or control of policy. It was of course distracted by royal and baronial intrigue. Many of its knights and burgesses were but the creatures of one faction or the other. Nevertheless it could be made to throw its weight in a decisive manner from time to time. This therefore was a period highly favourable to the growth of forces in the realm which were to become inherently different in character from either the Crown or the barons.

Thomas of Lancaster, nephew to Edward I, was the forefront of the baronial opposition. Little is known to his credit. He had long been engaged in treasonable practices with the Scots. As leader of the barons he had pursued Gaveston to his death, and, although not actually responsible for the treachery which led to his execution, he bore henceforward upon his shoulders the deepest hate of which Edward II's nature was capable. Into the hands of Thomas and his fellow Ordainers Edward was now thrown by the disaster of Bannockburn, and Thomas for a while became the most important man in the land. Within a few years however the moderates among the Ordainers became so disgusted with Lancaster's incompetence and with the weakness into which the process of Government had sunk that they joined with the royalists to edge him from power. The victory of this middle party, headed by the Earl of Pembroke, did not please the King. Aiming to be more efficient than Lancaster, Pembroke and his friends tried to enforce the Ordinances more effectively, and carried out a great reform of the royal Household.

Edward, for his part, began to build up a royalist party, at the head of which were the Despensers, father and son, both named Hugh. These belonged to the nobility, and their power lay on the Welsh border. By a fortunate marriage with the noble house of Clare, and by the favour of the King, they rose precariously amid the jealousies of the English baronage to the main direction of affairs. Against both of them the hatreds grew, because of their self-seeking and the King's infatuation with the younger man. They were especially unpopular among the Marcher lords, who were disturbed by their restless ambitions in South Wales. In 1321 the Welsh Marcher lords and the Lancastrian party joined hands with intent to procure the exile of the Despensers. Edward soon recalled them, and for once showed energy and resolution. By speed of movement he defeated first the Marcher lords and then the Northern barons under Lancaster at Boroughbridge in Yorkshire in the next year. Lancaster was beheaded by the King. But by some perversity of popular sentiment miracles were reported at his grave, and his execution was adjudged by many of his contemporaries to have made him a martyr to royal oppression.

The Despensers and their King now seemed to have attained a height of power. But a tragedy with every feature of classical ruthlessness was to follow. One of the chief Marcher lords, Roger Mortimer, though captured by the King, contrived to escape to France. In 1324

Charles IV of France took advantage of a dispute in Gascony to seize the duchy, except for a coastal strip. Edward's wife, Isabella, "the she-wolf of France," who was disgusted by his passion for Hugh Despenser, suggested that she should go over to France to negotiate with her brother Charles about the restoration of Gascony. There she became the lover and confederate of the exiled Mortimer. She now hit on the stroke of having her son, Prince Edward, sent over from England to do homage for Gascony. As soon as the fourteen-year-old prince, who as heir to the throne could be used to legitimise opposition to King Edward, was in her possession she and Mortimer staged an invasion of England at the head of a large band of exiles. So unpopular and precarious was Edward's Government that Isabella's triumph was swift and complete, and she and Mortimer were emboldened to depose him. The end was a holocaust. In the furious rage which in these days led all who swayed the Government of England to a bloody fate the Despensers were seized and hanged. For the King a more terrible death was reserved. He was imprisoned in Berkeley Castle, and there by hideous methods, which left no mark upon his skin, was slaughtered. His screams as his bowels were burnt out by red-hot irons passed into his body were heard outside the prison walls, and awoke grim echoes which were long unstilled.

CHAPTER TWENTY

SCOTLAND AND IRELAND

THE FAILURES OF THE REIGN OF EDWARD II HAD PERMANENT EFFECTS on the unity of the British Isles. Bannockburn ended the possibility of uniting the English and Scottish Crowns by force. Across the Irish Sea the dream of a consolidated Anglo-Norman Ireland also proved vain. Centuries could scarcely break down the barrier that the ruthless Scottish wars had raised between North and South Britain. From Edward I's onslaught on Berwick, in 1296, the armed struggle had raged for twenty-seven years. It was not until 1323 that Robert the Bruce at last obliged Edward II to come to terms. Even then Bruce was not formally recognised as King of Scots. This title, and full independence for his country, he gained by the Treaty of Northampton signed in 1328 after Edward's murder. A year later the saviour of Scotland was dead.

One of the most famous stories of medieval chivalry tells how Sir James, the "Black" Douglas, for twenty years the faithful sword-arm of the Bruce, took his master's heart to be buried in the Holy Land, and how, touching at a Spanish port, he responded to a sudden call of chivalry and joined the hard-pressed Christians in battle with the Moors. Charging the heathen host, he threw far into the *mêlée* the silver casket containing the heart of Bruce. "Forward, brave heart, as thou wert wont. Douglas will follow thee or die!" He was killed in the moment of victory. So Froissart tells the story in prose and Aytoun in stirring verse, and so, in every generation, Scottish children have been thrilled by the story of "the Good Lord James."

While the Bruce had lived his great prestige, and the loyalty of his lieutenants, served as a substitute for the institutions and traditions that united England. His death left the throne to his son, David II, a child of six, and there ensued one of those disastrous minorities that were the curse of Scotland. The authority of the Scottish kings had often been challenged by the great magnates of the Lowlands and by the Highland chiefs. To this source of weakness were now added others. The kin of the "Red" Comyn, never forgiving his assassination by Bruce, were always ready to lend themselves to civil strife. And the barons who had supported the cause of Balliol, and lost their Scottish lands to the followers of Bruce, constantly dreamt of regaining them with English help. David II reigned for forty-two years, but no less than eighteen of them were spent outside his kingdom. For a long spell during the wars of his Regents with the Balliol factions he was a refugee in France. On his return he showed none of his father's talents. Loyalty to France led him to invade England. In 1346, the year of Crécy, he was defeated and captured at Neville's Cross in County Durham. Eleven years of imprisonment followed before he was ransomed for a sum that sorely taxed Scotland. David II was succeeded by his nephew Robert the High Steward, first king of a line destined to melancholy fame.

For many generations the Stuarts, as they came euphoniously to be called, had held the hereditary office from which they took their name. Their claim to the throne was legitimate but they failed to command the undivided loyalty of the Scots. The first two Stuarts, Robert II and Robert III, were both elderly men of no marked strength of character. The affairs of the kingdom rested largely in the hands of the magnates, whether assembled in the King's Council or dispersed about their estates. For the rest of the fourteenth century, and throughout most of the fifteenth, Scotland was too deeply divided to threaten England, or be of much help to her old ally France. A united England, free from French wars, might have taken advantage of the situation, but by the mid-fifteenth century England was herself tormented by the Wars of the Roses.

Union of the Crowns was the obvious and natural solution. But after the English attempts, spread over several reigns, had failed to impose union by force, the re-invigorated pride of Scotland offered an insurmountable obstacle. Hatred of the English was the mark of a good Scot. Though discontented nobles might accept English help and English pay, the common people were resolute in their refusal to bow to English rule in any form. The memory of Bannockburn kept a series of notable defeats at the hands of the English from breeding despair or thought of surrender.

It is convenient to pursue Scottish history further at this stage. Destiny was adverse to the House of Stuart. Dogged by calamity, they could not create enduring institutions comparable to those by whose aid the great Plantagenets tamed English feudalism. King Robert III sent his son later James I to be schooled in France. Off Flamborough Head in 1406 he was captured by the English, and taken prisoner to London. He was twelve years old. In the following month, King Robert died, and for eighteen years Scotland had no monarch. The English government was at last prepared to let King James I be ransomed and return to his country. Captivity had not daunted James. He had conceived a justfiable admiration for the English monarch's position and powers, and on his arrival in Scotland he asserted his sovereignty with vigour. During his effective reign of thirteen years he ruthlessly disciplined the Scottish baronage. It was not an experience they enjoyed. James put down his cousins of the House of Albany, whose family had been regents during his absence. He quelled the pretensions to independence of the powerful Lord of the Isles, who controlled much of the Northern mainland as well as the Hebrides. All this was accompanied by executions and widespread confiscations of great estates. At length a party of infuriated lords decided on revenge; in 1437 they found the opportunity to slay James by the sword. So died, and before his task had been accomplished, one of the most forceful of Scottish kings.

The throne once more descended to a child, James II, aged seven. After the inevitable tumults of his minority the boy grew into a popular and vigorous ruler. He had need of his gifts for the "Black" Douglases, descendants of Bruce's faithful knight, had now become over-mighty subjects and constituted a heavy menace to the Crown. Enriched by estates confiscated from Balliol supporters, they were the masters of South-West Scotland. Large territories in the East were held by their kin, the "Red" Douglases, and they also made agile use of their alliances with the clans and confederacies of the North. Moreover, they had a claim, acceptable in the eyes of some, to the throne itself.

For more than a century the Douglases had been among the foremost champions of Scotland; one of them had been the hero of the Battle of Otterburn, celebrated in the ballad of Chevy Chase. Their continual intrigues, both at home and at the English court, with which they were in touch, incensed the young and high-spirited King. In 1452, when he had not long turned twenty-one, James invited the "Black" Douglas to Stirling. Under a safe-conduct he came; and there the King himself in passion stabbed him with his own hand. The King's attendants finished his life. But to cut down the chief of the Douglases was not to stamp out the family. James found himself sorely beset by the Douglas's younger brother and by his kin. Only in 1455 did he finally succeed, by burning their castles and ravaging their lands, in driving the leading Douglases over the Border. In England they survived for many years to vex the House of Stuart with plots and conspiracies, abetted by the English Crown.

James II was now at the height of his power, but fortune seldom favoured the House of Stuart for very long. Taking advantage of the English civil wars, James in 1460 set siege to the castle of Roxburgh, a fortress that had remained in English hands. One of his special interests was cannon and fire-power. While inspecting one of his primitive siege-guns, the piece exploded, and he was killed by a flying fragment. James II was then in his thirtieth year. For the fourth time in little more than a century a minor inherited the Scottish Crown. James III was a boy of nine. As he grew up, he showed some amiable qualities; he enjoyed music and took an interest in architecture. But he failed to inherit the capacity for rule displayed by his two predecessors. His reign, which lasted into Tudor times, was much occupied by civil wars and disorders, and its most notable achievement was the rounding off of Scotland's territories by the acquisition, in lieu of a dowry, of Orkney and Shetland from the King of Denmark whose daughter James married.

*   *   *   *   *

The disunity of the kingdom, fostered by English policy and perpetuated by the tragedies that befell the Scottish sovereigns, was not the
only source of Scotland's weakness. The land was divided, in race, in
speech, and in culture. The rift between Highlands and Lowlands was
more than a geographical distinction. The Lowlands formed part of
the feudal world, and, except in the South-West, in Galloway, English
was spoken. The Highlands preserved a social order much older than
feudalism. In the Lowlands the King of Scots was a feudal magnate, in
the Highlands he was the chief of a loose federation of clans. He had,
it is true, the notable advantage of blood kinship both with the new
Anglo-Norman nobility and with the ancient Celtic kings. The Bruces
were undoubted descendants of the family of the first King of Scots
in the ninth century, Kenneth MacAlpin, as well as of Alfred the Great;
the Stuarts claimed, with some plausibility, to be the descendants of
Macbeth's contemporary, Banquo. The lustre of a divine antiquity illu-
mined princes whose pedigree ran back into the Celtic twilight of Irish
heroic legend. For all Scots, Lowland and Highland alike, the royal
house had a sanctity which commanded reverence through periods
when obedience and even loyalty were lacking; and much was excused
those in whom royal blood ran.

But reverence was not an effective instrument of government.
The Scottish Estates did not create the means of fusion of classes
that were provided by the English Parliament. In law and fact feudal
authority remained far stronger than in England. The King's justice
was excluded from a great part of Scottish life, and many of his judges
were ineffective competitors with the feudal system. There was no
equivalent of the Justice of the Peace or of the Plantagenet Justices
in Eyre.

Over much of the kingdom feudal justice itself fought a doubtful
battle with the more ancient clan law. The Highland chiefs might
formally owe their lands and power to the Crown and be classified
as feudal tenants-in-chief, but their real authority rested on the allegiance of their clansmen. Some clan chiefs, like the great house of
Gordon, in the Highlands, were also feudal magnates in the neighbouring Lowlands. In the West, the rising house of Campbell played

either rôle as it suited them. They were to exercise great influence in the years to come.

Meanwhile the Scots peasant farmer and the thrifty burgess, throughout these two hundred years of political strife, pursued their ways and built up the country's real strength, in spite of the numerous disputes among their lords and masters. The Church devoted itself to its healing mission, and many good bishops and divines adorn the annals of medieval Scotland. In the fifteenth century three Scots universities were founded, St. Andrew's, Glasgow and Aberdeen—one more than England had until the nineteenth century.

*　　*　　*　　*　　*

Historians of the English-speaking peoples have been baffled by medieval Ireland. Here in the westernmost of the British Isles dwelt one of the oldest Christian communities in Europe. It was distinguished by missionary endeavours and monkish scholarship while England was still a battlefield for heathen Germanic invaders. Until the twelfth century however Ireland had never developed the binding feudal institutions of state that were gradually evolving elsewhere. A loose federation of Gaelic-speaking rural principalities was dominated by a small group of clan patriarchs who called themselves "kings." Over all lay the shadowy authority of the High King of Tara, which was not a capital city but a sacred hill surmounted by earthworks of great antiquity. Until about the year 1000 the High King was generally a member of the powerful northern family of O'Neill. The High Kings exercised no real central authority, except as the final arbiters of genealogical disputes, and there were no towns of Irish founding from which government power could radiate.

When the long, sorrowful story began of English intervention in Ireland, the country had already endured the shock and torment of Scandinavian invasion. But although impoverished by the ravages of the Norsemen, and its accepted order of things greatly disturbed, Ireland was not remade. It was the Norsemen who built the first towns—Dublin, Waterford, Limerick and Cork. The High Kingship had been in dispute since the great Brian Boru, much lamented in song, had broken the O'Neill succession, only himself to be killed in his victory over the Danes at Clontarf in 1014. A century and a half later, one of his disputing successors, the King of Leinster, took refuge at the court of Henry II in Aquitaine. He secured permission to raise help for his cause from among Henry's Anglo-Norman knights. It was a fateful decision for Ireland. In 1169 there arrived in the country the first progenitors of the Anglo-Norman ascendancy.

Led by Richard de Clare, Earl of Pembroke and known as "Strongbow," the invaders were as much Welsh as Norman; and with their French-speaking leaders came the Welsh rank and file. Even to-day some of the commonest Irish names suggest a Welsh ancestry. Others of the leaders were of Flemish origin. But all represented the high, feudal society that ruled over Western Europe, and whose conquests already ranged from Wales to Syria. Irish military methods were no match for the newcomers, and "Strongbow," marrying the daughter of the King of Leinster, might perhaps have set up a new feudal kingdom in Ireland, as had been done by William the Conqueror in England, by Roger in Sicily, and by the Crusading chiefs in the Levant. But "Strongbow" was doubtful both of his own strength and of the attitude of his vigilant superior, Henry II. So the conquests were proffered to the King, and Henry briefly visited this fresh addition to his dominions in 1171 in order to receive the submission of his new vassals. The reviving power of the Papacy had long been offended by the traditional independence of the Irish Church. By Papal Bull in 1155 the overlordship of Ireland had been granted to the English king. The Pope at the time was Adrian IV, an Englishman and the only Englishman ever to be Pope. Here were foundations both spiritual and practical. But the Lord of England and of the greater part of France had little time for Irish problems. He left the affairs of the island to the Norman adventurers, the "Conquistadores" as they have been called. It was a pattern often to be repeated.

The century that followed Henry II's visit marked the height of Anglo-Norman expansion. More than half the country was by now directly subjected to the knightly invaders. Among them was Gerald of Windsor, ancestor of the Fitzgerald family, the branches of which, as Earls of Kildare and Lords of much else, were for long to control large tracts of southern and central Ireland. There was also William de Burgh, brother of the great English Justiciar, and ancestor of the

Earls of Ulster; and Theobald Walter, King John's butler, founder of the powerful Butler family of Ormond which took their name from his official calling. But there was no organised colonisation and settlement. English authority was accepted in the Norse towns on the Southern and Eastern coasts, and the King's writ ran over a varying area of country surrounding Dublin. This hinterland of the capital was significantly known as "The Pale," which might be defined as a defended enclosure. Immediately outside lay the big feudal lordships, and beyond these were the "wild" unconquered Irish of the west. Two races dwelt in uneasy balance, and the division between them was sharpened when a Parliament of Ireland evolved towards the end of the thirteenth century. From this body the native Irish were excluded; it was a Parliament in Ireland of the English only.

*   *   *   *   *

Within a few generations of the coming of the Anglo-Normans, however, the Irish chieftains began to recover from the shock of new methods of warfare. They hired mercenaries to help them, originally in large part recruited from the Norse-Celtic stock of the Scottish western isles. These were the terrible "galloglasses," named from the Irish words for "foreign henchmen." Supported by these ferocious axe-bearers, the clan chiefs regained for the Gaelic-speaking peoples wide regions of Ireland, and might have won more, had they not incessantly quarrelled among themselves.

Meanwhile a change of spirit had overtaken many of the Anglo-Norman Irish barons. These great feudatories were constantly tempted by the independent rôle of the Gaelic clan chief that was theirs for the taking. They could in turn be subjects of the English King or petty kings themselves, like their new allies, with whom they were frequently united by marriage. Their stock was seldom reinforced from England, except by English lords who wedded Irish heiresses, and then became absentee landlords. Gradually however a group of Anglo-Irish nobles grew up, largely assimilated to their adopted land, and as impatient as their Gaelic peasants of rule from London.

If English kings had regularly visited Ireland, or regularly appointed royal princes as resident lieutenants the ties between the two countries might have been closely and honourably woven together. As it was, when the English King was strong, English laws generally made headway; otherwise a loose Celtic anarchy prevailed. King John, in his furious fitful energy, twice went to Ireland and twice brought the quarrelsome Norman barons and Irish chiefs under his suzerainty. Although Edward I never landed in Ireland, English authority was in the ascendant. Thereafter, the Gaels revived. The shining example of Scotland was not lost upon them. The brother of the victor of Bannockburn, Edward Bruce, was called in by his relations among the Irish chiefs with an army of Scottish veterans. He was crowned King of Ireland in 1316, but after a temporary triumph and in spite of the aid of his brother was defeated and slain at Dundalk.

Thus Ireland did not break loose from the English crown and gain independence under a Scottish dynasty. But the victory of English arms did not mean a victory for English law, custom or speech. The Gaelic reaction gathered force. In Ulster the O'Neills gradually won the mastery of Tyrone. In Ulster and Connaught the feudal trappings were openly discarded when the line of the de Burgh Earls of Ulster ended in 1333 with a girl. According to feudal law, she succeeded to the whole inheritance, and was the King's ward to be married at his choice. In fact she was married to Edward III's second son, Lionel of Clarence. But in Celtic law women could not succeed to the chieftainship. The leading male members of the cadet branches of the de Burgh family accordingly "went Irish," snatched what they could of the inheritance and assumed the clan names of Burke or, after their founder, MacWilliam. They openly defied the Government in Ulster and Connaught; in the Western province both French and Irish were spoken but not English, and English authority vanished from these outer parts.

To preserve the English character of the Pale and of its surrounding Anglo-Norman lordships, a Parliament was summoned in the middle of the fourteenth century. Its purpose was to prevent the English from "going Irish" and to compel men of Irish race in the English-held parts of Ireland to conform to English ways. But its enactments had little effect. In the Pale the old Norman settlers clung to their privileged position and opposed all attempts by the representatives of the Crown to bring the "mere Irish" under the protection of English laws and institutions. Most of Ireland by now lay outside the Pale, either under native chiefs who had practically no dealings with the representatives of the English kings, or controlled by Norman dynasts such as the two branches of the Fitzgeralds, who were earls or clan chiefs, as suited them best. English authority stifled the creation of either a native or a "Norman" centre of authority, and the absentee "Lord of Ireland" in London could not provide a substitute, nor even prevent his own colonists from intermingling with the population. By Tudor times anarchic Ireland lay open to reconquest, and to the tribulations of re-imposing English royal authority was to be added from Henry VIII's Reformation onwards the fateful divisions of religious belief.

CHAPTER TWENTY-ONE

THE LONG-BOW

IT SEEMED THAT THE STRONG BLOOD OF EDWARD I HAD BUT SLUMBERED in his degenerate son, for in Edward III England once more found leadership equal to her steadily growing strength. Beneath the squalid surface of Edward II's reign there had none the less proceeded in England a marked growth of national strength and prosperity. The feuds and vengeances of the nobility, the foppish vices of a weak King, had been confined to a very limited circle. The English people stood at this time possessed of a commanding weapon, the qualities of which were utterly unsuspected abroad. The long-bow, handled by the well-trained archer class, brought into the field a yeoman type of soldier with whom there was nothing on the Continent to compare. An English army now rested itself equally upon the armoured knight-hood and the archers.

The power of the long-bow and the skill of the bowmen had developed to a point where even the finest mail was no certain protection. At two hundred and fifty yards the arrow hail produced effects never reached again by infantry missiles at such a range until the American civil war. The skilled archer was a professional soldier, earning and deserving high pay. He went to war often on a pony, but always with a considerable transport for his comfort and his arrows. He carried with him a heavy iron-pointed stake, which, planted in the ground, afforded a deadly obstacle to charging horses. Behind this shelter a company of archers in open order could deliver a discharge of arrows so rapid, continuous, and penetrating as to annihilate the cavalry attack. Moreover, in all skirmishing and patrolling the trained archer brought his man down at ranges which had never before been considered dangerous in the whole history of war. Of all this the Continent, and particularly France, our nearest neighbour, was ignorant. In France the armoured knight and his men-at-arms had long exploited their ascendancy in war. The foot-soldiers who accompanied their armies were regarded as the lowest type of auxiliary. A military caste had imposed itself upon society in virtue of physical and technical assertions which the coming of the long-bow must disprove. The protracted wars of the two Edwards in the mountains of Wales and Scotland had taught the English many hard lessons, and although European warriors had from time to time shared in them they had neither discerned nor imparted the slumbering secret of the new army. It was with a sense of unmeasured superiority that the English looked out upon Europe towards the middle of the fourteenth century.

The reign of King Edward III passed through several distinct phases. In the first he was a minor, and the land was ruled by his mother and her lover, Roger Mortimer. This Government, founded upon unnatural murder and representing only a faction in the nobility, was condemned to weakness at home and abroad. Its rule of nearly four years was marked by concession and surrender both in France and in Scotland. For this policy many plausible arguments of peace and prudence might be advanced. The guilty couple paid their way by successive abandonments of English interests. A treaty with France in March 1327 condemned England to pay a war indemnity, and restricted the English possessions to a strip of land running from Saintes in Saintonge and Bordeaux to Bayonne, and to a defenceless enclave in the interior of Gascony. In May 1328 the "Shameful Treaty of Northampton," as it was called at the time, recognised Bruce as King north of the Tweed, and implied the abandonment of all the claims of Edward I in Scotland.

The anger which these events excited was widespread. The régime might however have maintained itself for some time but for Mortimer's quarrel with the barons. After the fall of the Despensers Mortimer had taken care to put himself in the advantageous position they had occupied on the Welsh border, where he could exercise the special powers of government appropriate to the Marches. This and his exorbitant authority drew upon him the jealousies of the barons he had so lately led. His desire to make his position permanent led him to seek from a Parliament convened in October at Salisbury the title of Earl of March, in addition to the office he already held of Justice of Wales for life. Mortimer attended, backed by his armed retainers. But it then appeared that many of the leading nobles were absent, and among them Henry, Earl of Lancaster, son of the executed Thomas and cousin of the King, who held a counter-meeting in London. From Salisbury Mortimer, taking with him the young King, set forth in 1328 to ravage the lands of Lancaster, and in the disorders which followed he succeeded in checking the revolt.

It was plain that the barons themselves were too much divided to overthrow an odious but ruthless Government. But Mortimer made an overweening mistake. In 1330 the King's uncle, the Earl of Kent, was deceived into thinking that Edward II was still alive. Kent made an ineffective attempt to restore him to liberty, and was executed in March of that year. This event convinced Henry of Lancaster and other magnates that it might be their turn to suffer next at Mortimer's hands. They decided to get their blow in first by joining Edward III. All eyes were therefore turned to the young King. When seventeen in 1329 he had been married to Philippa of Hainault. In June 1330 a son was born to him; he felt himself now a grown man who must do his duty by the realm. But effective power still rested with Mortimer and the Queen-Mother. In October Parliament sat at Nottingham. Mortimer and Isabella, guarded by ample force, were lodged in the castle. It is clear that very careful thought and preparation had marked the plans by which the King should assert his rights. Were he to succeed, Parliament was at hand to acclaim him. Mortimer and Isabella did not know the secrets of the castle. An underground passage led into its heart. Through this on an October night a small band of resolute men entered, surprised Mortimer in his chamber, which as usual was next to the Queen's, and, dragging them both along the subterranean way, delivered them to the King's officers. Mortimer, conducted to London, was brought before the peers, accused of the murder in

Berkeley Castle and other crimes, and, after condemnation by the lords, hanged on November 29. Isabella was consigned by her son to perpetual captivity. Three thousand pounds a year was provided for her maintenance at Castle Rising, in Norfolk, and Edward made it his practice to pay her a periodic visit. She died nearly thirty years later.

Upon these grim preliminaries the long and famous reign began.

*　　*　　*　　*　　*

The guiding spirit of the new King was to revive the policy, assert the claims, and restore the glories of his grandfather. The quarrel with Scotland was resumed. Since Bannockburn Robert Bruce had reigned unchallenged in the North. His triumph had been followed inevitably by the ruin and expulsion of the adherents of the opposite Scottish party. Edward, the son of John Balliol, the nominee of Edward I, had become a refugee at the English Court, which extended them the same kind of patronage afterwards vouchsafed by Louis XIV to the Jacobite exiles. No schism so violent as that between Bruce and Balliol could fail to produce rankling injuries. Large elements in Scotland, after Bruce's death in 1329, looked to a reversal of fortune, and the exiles, or "disinherited," as they were termed, maintained a ceaseless intrigue in their own country and a constant pressure upon the English Government. In 1332 an endeavour was made to regain Scotland. Edward Balliol rallied his adherents and, with the secret support of Edward III, sailed from Ravenspur to Kinghorn in Fife. Advancing on Perth, he met and defeated the infant David's Regent at Dupplin Moor. Balliol received the submission of many Scottish magnates, and was crowned at Scone.

Henceforward fortune failed him. Within two months he and his supporters were driven into England. Edward III was now able to make what terms he liked with the beaten Balliol. He was recognised by Balliol as his overlord and promised the town and shire of Berwick. In 1333 therefore Edward III advanced to besiege Berwick, and routed the Scots at Halidon Hill. Here was a battle very different in character from Bannockburn. The power of the archers was allowed to play its part, the schiltrons were broken, and the exiled party re-established for a while their authority in their native land. There was a price to pay. Balliol, as we have seen, had to cede to the English King the whole of South-Eastern Scotland. In exacting this concession Edward III had overshot the mark; he had damned Balliol's cause in the eyes of all Scots. Meanwhile the descendants and followers of Robert Bruce took refuge in France. The contacts between Scotland and France, and the constant aid given by the French Court to the Scottish enemies of England, roused a deep antagonism. Thus the war in Scotland pointed the path to Flanders.

Here a new set of grievances formed a substantial basis for a conflict. The loss of all the French possessions, except Gascony, and the constant bickering on the Gascon frontiers, had been endured perforce since the days of John. Successive English kings had done homage in Paris for domains of which they had in large part long since been deprived. But in 1328 the death of Charles IV without a direct heir opened a further issue. Philip of Valois assumed the royal power and demanded homage from Edward, who made difficulties. King Edward III, in his mother's right—if indeed the female line was valid—had a remote claim to the throne of France. This claim, by and with the assent and advice of the Lords Spiritual and Temporal, and of the Commons of England, he was later to advance in support of his campaigns.

The youthful Edward was less drawn to domestic politics than to foreign adventure and the chase. He was conscious moreover from the first of the advantage to be gained by diverting the restless energies of his nobles from internal intrigues and rivalries to the unifying purpose of a foreign war. This was also in harmony with the temper of his people. The wars of John and Henry III on the mainland disclose a perpetual struggle between the King and his nobles and subjects to obtain men and money. European adventure was regarded as a matter mainly of interest to a prince concerned with his foreign possessions or claims. Now we see the picture of the Estates of the Realm becoming themselves ardently desirous of foreign conquests. Edward III did not have to wring support from his Parliament for an expedition to France. On the contrary, nobles, merchants, and citizens vied with one another in pressing the Crown to act.

The dynastic and territorial disputes were reinforced by a less sentimental but none the less powerful motive, which made its appeal to many members of the Houses of Parliament. The wool trade with the Low Countries was the staple of English exports, and almost the sole form of wealth which rose above the resources of agriculture. The Flemish towns had attained a high economic development, based upon the art of weaving cloth, which they had brought to remarkable perfection. They depended for their prosperity upon the wool of England. But the aristocracy under the Counts of Flanders nursed French sympathies which recked little of the material well-being of the burghers, regarding them as dangerous and subversive folk whose growth in wealth and power conflicted with feudal ascendancy. There was therefore for many years a complete divergence—economic, social, and political—between the Flemish towns and the nobility of the Netherlands. The former looked to England, the latter to France. Repeated obstructions were placed by the Counts of Flanders upon the wool trade, and each aroused the anger of those concerned on both sides of the narrow sea. The mercantile element in the English Parliament, already inflamed by running sea-fights with the French in the Channel, pleaded vehemently for action.

In 1336 Edward was moved to retaliate in a decisive manner. He decreed an embargo on all exports of English wool, thus producing a furious crisis in the Netherlands. The townspeople rose against the feudal aristocracy, and under Van Arteveldt, a war-like merchant of Ghent, gained control, after a struggle of much severity, over a large part of the country. The victorious burghers, threatened by aristocratic and French revenge, looked to England for aid, and their appeals met with a hearty and deeply interested response. Thus all streams of profit and ambition flowed into a common channel at a moment when the flood-waters of conscious military strength ran high, and in 1337, when Edward repudiated his grudging homage to Philip VI, the Hundred Years War began. It was never to be concluded; no general peace treaty was signed, and not until the Peace of Amiens in 1802, when France was a Republic and the French Royal heir a refugee within these isles, did the English sovereign formally renounce his claims to the throne of the Valois and the Bourbons.

*　　*　　*　　*　　*

Edward slowly assembled the expeditionary army of England. This was not a feudal levy, but a paid force of picked men. Its backbone consisted of indentured warriors, recruited where and how their captains pleased. In consequence, far less than the legal quota of unreliable militia needed to be drawn from every shire. Both knights and archers embodied the flower of the nation, and the men who gathered in the Cinque Ports formed one of the most formidable and efficient invading armies history had yet seen. These preparations were well known in France, and the whole strength of the monarchy was bent to resist them.

Philip VI looked first to the sea. For many years there had been a warfare of privateers, and bitter hatred ruled between the maritime populations on both sides of the Channel. All the resources of the French marine were strained to produce a fleet; even hired Genoese galleys appeared in the French harbours. In Normandy plans were mooted for a counter-invasion which should repeat the exploits of William the Conqueror. But Edward had not neglected his sea-power. His interest in the Navy won him from Parliament early in his reign the title of "King of the Sea." He was able to marshal a fleet equal in vessels and superior in men. A great sea battle was necessary before the transport of the English army to France and its maintenance there was feasible. In the summer of 1340 the hostile navies met off Sluys, and a struggle of nine hours ensued. "This battle," says Froissart, "was right furious and horrible, for battles by sea are more dangerous and fiercer than battles by land, for at sea there is no retreat or fleeing; there is no remedy but to fight and abide the fortune." The French admirals had been ordered, under pain of death, to prevent the invasion, and both sides fought well; but the French fleet was decisively beaten and the command of the Channel passed into the hands of the invading Power. The seas being now open, the army crossed to France. At Cadzand the landing was opposed. Large bodies of Genoese cross-bowmen and men-at-arms awaited the disembarkation. But the English archers, shooting from the ships at long range, cleared the shores and covered the invading troops.

Joined with the revolted Flemings, Edward's numbers were greatly augmented, and this combined force, which may have exceeded twenty thousand, undertook the first Anglo-Flemish siege of Tournai. The city was stubbornly defended, and as the grip of famine tightened upon the garrison the horrible spectacle was presented of the "useless mouths" being driven forth into No Man's Land to perish by inches without pity or relief. But the capture of this fortress was beyond Edward's resources in money and supplies. The power of the archers did not extend to stone walls; the first campaign of what was a great European war yielded no results, and a prolonged truce supervened.

This truce was imposed upon the combatants through lack of money, and carried with it no reconciliation. On the contrary, both sides pursued their quarrel in secondary ways. The French wreaked their vengeance on the burghers of the Netherlands, whom they crushed utterly, and Van Artevelde met his death in a popular tumult at Ghent. The English retaliated as best they could. There was a disputed succession in Brittany, which they fomented with substantial aids. The chronic warfare on the frontiers of Gascony continued. Both sides looked forward to a new trial of strength. Well-trained men, eager to fight, there were in plenty, but to maintain them in the field required funds, which to us seem pitifully small, but without which all was stopped. How could these resources be obtained? The Jews had been exploited, pillaged, and expelled in 1290. The Florentine bankers, who had found the money for the first invasion, had been ruined by royal default. The main effort, not only of the Court but of Parliament, was to secure the modest sums of ready money without which knights could not ride nor archers draw their bows. But here a fertile source was at hand. The wealthier and best-organised commercial interest in England was the wool trade, eager to profit from war. A monopoly of wool merchants was created, bound to export only through a particular town to be prescribed by the King from time to time in accordance with his needs and judgment. This system, which was called the Staple, gave the King a convenient and flexible control. By taxing the wool exports which passed through his hands at the Staple port he was assured of an important revenue independent of Parliament. Moreover, the wool merchants who held the monopoly formed a corporation interested in the war, dependent on the King, and capable of lending him money in return for considerate treatment.

This development was not welcomed by Parliament, where the smaller wool merchants were increasingly represented. They complained of the favor shown to the monopolists of the Staple, and they also pointed to the menace to Parliamentary power involved in the King's independent resources.

By the spring of 1346 Parliament had at length brought itself to the point of facing the taxation necessary to finance a new invasion. The army was reconstituted, more efficiently than before, its old elements were refreshed with carefully chosen levies. In one wave 2,400 cavalry, twelve thousand archers, and other infantry sailed, and landed unopposed at St. Vaast in Normandy on July 12, 1346. Their object this time was no less than the capture of Paris by a sudden dash. The secret was well kept; even the English army itself believed it was going to Gascony. The French could not for some time collect forces sufficient to arrest the inroad. Caen fell, and Edward advanced, burning and laying waste the country, to the very walls of Paris. But by this time the whole power of the French monarchy had gathered against him. A huge force which comprised all the chivalry of France and was probably three times as big as Edward's army assembled in the neighbourhood of St. Denis. Against such opposition, added to the walls of a fortified city, Edward's resources could not attempt to prevail. King Philip grimly invited him to choose upon which bank of the Seine he would fight a pitched battle.

The thrust had failed and retreat imposed itself upon the army. The challenger was forced to quit the lists at a pace which covered sixty miles in four days. The French army moved on a parallel line to the southward and denied the Seine valley to the retreating English. They must now make for the Somme, and hope to cross between Amiens and the sea. Our generation has become familiar with this stretch of the river, which flows through broad morasses, in those days quite undrained and passable only by lengthy causeways and bridges. All these were broken or held by the levies of Picardy. Four separate attempts to find a passage failed. The vanguard of the French main army was already at Amiens. Edward and the English host, which had tried so audacious, even foolhardy, a spring, now seemed penned in a triangle between the Somme, the seashore, and the French mass.

No means had been found to bring the fleet and its transports to any suitable harbour. To cross the Somme near the mouth was a desperate enterprise. The ford was very lengthy, and the tides, violent and treacherous, offered only a few precarious hours in any day.

Moreover, the passage was defended by strong forces popularly estimated to have been upwards of twelve thousand men. "The King of England," says Froissart, "did not sleep much that night, but, rising at midnight, ordered his trumpet to sound. Very soon everything was ready; and, the baggage being loaded, they set out about daybreak, and rode on until they came to the ford at sunrise: but the tide was at that time so full they could not cross." By the afternoon, at the ebb, the enemy's strength was manifest. But since to pause was to perish the King ordered his marshals to plunge into the water and fight their way across. The French resistance was spirited. The knighthood of Picardy rode out and encountered the English on the treacherous sands in the rising waters. "They appeared to be as fond of tilting in the water as upon dry land." By hard fighting, under conditions most deadly to men encased in mail, the passage was forced. At the landing the Genoese cross-bowmen inflicted losses and delayed the deployment until the long-bow asserted its mastery. Thus did King Edward's army escape.

Philip, at the head of a host between thirty and forty thousand strong, was hard upon the track. He had every hope of bringing the insolent Islanders to bay with their backs to the river, or catching them in transit. When he learned that they were already over he called a council of war. His generals advised that, since the tide was now in, there was no choice but to ascend to Abbeville and cross by the bridge which the French held there. To Abbeville they accordingly moved, and lay there for the night.

Edward and his army were intensely convinced of the narrowness of their deliverance. That night they rejoiced; the countryside was full of food; the King gathered his chiefs to supper and afterwards to prayer. But it was certain that they could not gain the coast without a battle. No other resolve was open than to fight at enormous odds. The King and the Prince of Wales, afterwards famous as the Black Prince, received all the offices of religion, and Edward prayed that the impending battle should at least leave him unstripped of honour.

With the daylight he marshalled about eleven thousand men in three divisions. Mounted upon a small palfrey, with a white wand in his hand, with his splendid surcoat of crimson and gold above his armour, he rode along the ranks, "encouraging and entreating the army that they would guard his honour and defend his right." "He spoke this so sweetly and with such a cheerful countenance that all who had been dispirited were directly comforted by seeing and hearing him. . . . They ate and drank at their ease . . . and seated themselves on the ground, placing their helmets and bows before them, that they might be the fresher when their enemies should arrive." Their position on the open rolling downs enjoyed few advantages, but the forest of Crécy on their flanks afforded protection and the means of a final stand.

King Philip at sunrise on this same Saturday, August 26, 1346, heard Mass in the monastery of Abbeville, and his whole army, gigantic for those times, rolled forward in their long pursuit. Four knights were sent forth to reconnoitre. About midday the King, having arrived with large masses on the farther bank of the Somme, received their reports. The English were in battle array and meant to fight. He gave the sage counsel to halt for the day, bring up the rear, form the battle-line, and attack on the morrow. These orders were carried by famous chiefs to all parts of the army. But the thought of leaving, even for a day, this hated foe, who had for so many marches fled before overwhelming forces, and was now compelled to come to grips, was unendurable to the French army. What surety had they that the morrow might not see their enemies decamped and the field bare? It became impossible to control the forward movement. All the roads and tracks from Abbeville to Crécy were black and glittering with the marching columns. King Philip's orders were obeyed by some, rejected by most. While many great bodies halted obediently, still larger masses poured forward, forcing their way through the stationary or withdrawing troops, and at about five in the afternoon came face to face with the English army lying in full view on the broad slopes of Crécy. Here they stopped.

King Philip, arriving on the scene, was carried away by the ardour of the throng around him. The sun was already low; nevertheless

290 THE BIRTH OF BRITAIN

all were determined to engage. There was a corps of six thousand Genoese cross-bowmen in the van of the army. These were ordered to make their way through the masses of horsemen, and with their missiles break up the hostile array in preparation for the cavalry attacks. The Genoese had marched eighteen miles in full battle order with their heavy weapons and store of bolts. Fatigued, they made it plain that they were in no condition to do much that day. But the Count d'Alençon, who had covered the distance on horseback, did not accept this remonstrance kindly. "This is what one gets," he exclaimed, "by employing such scoundrels, who fall off when there is anything for them to do." Forward the Genoese! At this moment, while the cross-bowmen were threading their way to the front under many scornful glances, dark clouds swept across the sun and a short, drenching storm beat upon the hosts. A large flight of crows flew cawing through the air above the French in gloomy presage. The storm, after wetting the bow-strings of the Genoese, passed as quickly as it had come, and the setting sun shone brightly in their eyes and on the backs of the English. This, like the crows, was adverse, but it was more material. The Genoese, drawing out their array, gave a loud shout, advanced a few steps, shouted again, and a third time advanced, "hooted," and discharged their bolts. Unbroken silence had wrapped the English lines, but at this the archers, six or seven thousand strong, ranged on both flanks in "portcullis" formation, who had hitherto stood motionless, advanced one step, drew their bows to the ear, and came into action. They "shot their arrows with such force and quick-ness," says Froissart, "that it seemed as if it snowed."

The effect upon the Genoese was annihilating; at a range which their own weapons could not attain they were in a few minutes killed by thousands. The ground was covered with feathered corpses. Reeling before this blast of missile destruction, the like of which had not been known in war, the survivors recoiled in rout upon the eager ranks of the French chivalry and men-at-arms, which stood just out of arrow-shot. "Kill me those scoundrels," cried King Philip in fury, "for they stop up our road without any reason." Whereupon the front line of the French cavalry rode among the retreating Genoese, cutting them down with their swords. In doing so they came within the deadly distance. The arrow snowstorm beat upon them, piercing their mail and smiting horse and man. Valiant squadrons from behind rode forward into the welter, and upon all fell the arrow hail, making the horses caper, and strewing the field with richly dressed warriors. A hideous disorder reigned. And now Welsh and Cornish light infantry, slipping through the chequered ranks of the archers, came forward with their long knives and, "falling upon earls, barons, knights, and squires, slew many, at which the King of England was afterwards exasperated." Many a fine ransom was cast away in those improvident moments.

In this slaughter fell King Philip's ally, the blind King of Bohemia, who bade his knights fasten their bridles to his in order that he might strike a blow with his own hand. Thus entwined, he charged forward in the press. Man and horse they fell, and the next day their bodies were found still linked. His son, Prince Charles of Luxembourg, who as Emperor-elect of the Holy Roman Empire signed his name as King of the Romans, was more prudent, and, seeing how matters lay, departed with his following by an unnoticed route. The main attack of the French now developed. The Count d'Alençon and the Count of Flanders led heavy cavalry charges upon the English line. Evading the archers as far as possible, they sought the men-at-arms, and French, German, and Savoyard squadrons actually reached the Prince of Wales's division. The enemy's numbers were so great that those who fought about the Prince sent to the windmill, whence King Edward directed the battle, for reinforcements. But the King would not part with his reserves, saying, "Let the boy win his spurs"—which in fact he did.

Another incident was much regarded. One of Sir John of Hainault's knights, mounted upon a black horse, the gift that day of King Philip, escaping the arrows, actually rode right through the English lines. Such was their discipline that not a man stirred to harm him, and, riding round the rear, he returned eventually to the French army. Continuous cavalry charges were launched upon the English front, until utter darkness fell upon the field. And all through the night fresh troops of brave men, resolved not to quit the field without striking their blow, struggled forward, groping their way. All these were slain, for "No quarter" was the mood of the English, though by no means the wish of their King.

When night had fallen Philip found himself with no more than sixty knights in hand. He was slightly wounded by one arrow, and his horse had been shot under him by another. Sir John Hainault, mounting him again, seized his bridle and forced him from the field upon the well-known principle which, according to Froissart, he exactly expounded, of living to fight another day. The King had but five barons with him on reaching Amiens the next morning.

"When on this Saturday night the English heard no more hooting or shouting, nor any more crying out to particular lords, or their banners, they looked upon the field as their own and their enemies as beaten. They made great fires, and lighted torches because of the obscurity of the night. King Edward who all that day had not put on his helmet, then came down from his post, and, with his whole battalion, advanced to the Prince of Wales, whom he embraced in his arms and kissed, and said, 'Sweet son, God give you good perseverance. You are my son, for most loyally have you acquitted yourself this day. You are worthy to be a sovereign.' The Prince bowed down very low, and humbled himself, giving all honour to the King his father."

On the Sunday morning fog enshrouded the battlefield, and the King sent a strong force of five hundred lancers and two thousand archers to learn what lay upon his front. These met the columns of the French rear, still marching up from Rouen to Beauvais in ignorance of the defeat, and fell upon them. After this engagement the bodies of 1,542 knights and esquires were counted on the field. Later this force met with the troops of the Archbishop of Rouen and the Grand Prior of France, who were similarly unaware of the event, and were routed with much slaughter. They also found very large numbers of stragglers and wandering knights, and "put to the sword all they met." "It has been assured to me for fact," says Froissart, "that of foot-soldiers, sent from the cities, towns, and municipalities, there were slain, this Sunday morning, four times as many as in the battle of the Saturday." This astounding victory of Crécy ranks with Blenheim, Waterloo, and the final advance in the last summer of the Great War as one of the four supreme achievements.[1]

FRANCE IN 1360,
SHOWING THE CONQUESTS
OF EDWARD III

FLANDERS

Calais
ARTOIS
PONTHIEU
Crecy
HAINAULT

Barfleur

Seine

CHAMPAGNE

NORMANDY

Paris

BRITTANY

MAINE

Loire

ANJOU

BLOIS

ORLEANS

BURGUNDY

POITOU

Poitiers

BERRY

SAINTONGE

BAY OF BISCAY

ANGOUMOIS

LIMOUSIN

PERIGORD

BOURBON

Bordeaux

GUIENNE

AGENAIS

QUERCY

ROUERGUE

DAUPHINÉ

Rhône

ARMAGNAC

COMMINGES

GASCONY

BEARN

English territories in France
on Edward III's accession.

Land ceded to England in 1360.

Edward III's march to Calais.

ENGLISH MILES

0   50   100   150

*   *   *   *   *

Edward III marched through Montreuil and Blangy to Boulogne, passed through the forest of Hardelot, and opened the siege of Calais. Calais presented itself to English eyes as the hive of that swarm of privateers who were the endless curse of the Channel. Here on the nearest point of the Continent England had long felt a festering sore. Calais was what Dunkirk was to become three centuries later. The siege lasted for nearly a year. Every new art of war was practised by land; the bombards flung cannon-balls against the ramparts with terrifying noise. By sea elaborate barriers of piles stopped the French light craft, which sought to evade the sea blockade by creeping along the coast. All reliefs by sea and land failed. But the effort of maintaining the siege strained the resources of the King to an extent we can hardly conceive. When the winter came his soldiers demanded to go home, and the fleet was on the verge of mutiny. In England everyone complained, and Parliament was morose in demeanour and reluctant in supply. The King and his army lived in their hutments, and he never recrossed the Channel to his kingdom. Machiavelli has profoundly observed that every fortress should be victualled for a year, and this precaution has covered almost every case in history.

Moreover, the siege had hardly begun when King David of Scotland, in fulfilment of the alliance with France, led his army across the Border. But the danger was foreseen, and at Neville's Cross, just west of the city of Durham, the English won a hard-fought battle. The Scottish King himself was captured, and imprisoned in the Tower. He remained there, as we have seen, for ten years until released under the Treaty of Berwick for an enormous ransom. This decisive victory removed the Scottish danger for a generation, but more than once, before and after Flodden, the French alliance was to bring disaster to this small and audacious nation.

Calais held out for eleven months, and yet this did not suffice. Famine at length left no choice to the besieged. They sued for terms. The King was so embittered that when at his demand six of the noblest citizens presented themselves in their shirts, barefoot, emaciated, he was for cutting off their heads. The warnings of his advisers that his fame would suffer in history by so cruel a deed left him obdurate.

But Queen Philippa, great with child, who had followed him to the war, fell down before him in an edifying, and perhaps prearranged, tableau of Mercy pleading with Justice. So the burghers of Calais who had devoted themselves to save their people were spared, and even kindly treated. Calais, then, was the fruit, and the sole territorial fruit so far, of the exertions, prodigious in quality, of the whole power of England in the war with France. But Crécy had a longer tale to tell.

CHAPTER TWENTY-TWO

THE BLACK DEATH

WHILE FEATS OF ARMS AND STRONG ENDEAVOURS HELD THE ENGLISH mind a far more deadly foe was marching across the continents to their doom. Christendom has no catastrophe equal to the Black Death. Vague tales are told of awful events in China and of multitudes of corpses spreading their curse afar. The plague entered Europe through the Crimea, and in the course of twenty years destroyed at least one-third of its entire population. The privations of the people, resulting from ceaseless baronial and dynastic wars, presented an easy conquest to disease. The records in England tell more by their silence than by the shocking figures which confront us wherever records were kept. We read of lawsuits where all parties died before the cases could be heard; of monasteries where half the inmates perished; of dioceses where the surviving clergy could scarcely perform the last offices for their flocks and for their brethren; of the Goldsmiths' Company, which had four Masters in a year. These are detailed indications. But far more convincing is the gap which opens in all the local annals of the nation. A whole generation is slashed through by a hideous severance.

The character of the pestilence was appalling. The disease itself, with its frightful symptoms, the swift onset, the blotches, the hardening of the glands under the armpit or in the groin, these swellings which no poultice could resolve, these tumours which, when lanced, gave no relief, the horde of virulent carbuncles which followed the dread harbingers of death, the delirium, the insanity which attended its triumph, the blank spaces which opened on all sides in human society, stunned and for a time destroyed the life and faith of the world. This affliction, added to all the severities of the Middle Ages, was more than the human spirit could endure. The Church, smitten like the rest in body, was wounded grievously in spiritual power. If a God of mercy ruled the world, what sort of rule was this? Such was the challenging thought which swept upon the survivors. Weird sects sprang into existence, and plague-haunted cities saw the gruesome procession of flagellants, each lashing his forerunner to a dismal dirge, and ghoulish practices glare at us from the broken annals. It seemed to be the death-rattle of the race.

But at length the plague abated its force. The tumours yielded to fomentations. Recoveries became more frequent; the resistant faculties of life revived. The will to live triumphed. The scourge passed, and a European population, too small for its clothes, heirs to much that had been prepared by more numerous hands, assuaging its griefs in their universality, turned with unconquerable hope to the day and to the morrow.

Philosophers might suggest that there was no need for the use of the destructive mechanism of plague to procure the changes deemed necessary among men. A more scientific reagent was at hand. Gunpowder, which we have seen used in the puny bombards which, according to some authorities, Edward had fired at Crécy and against Calais, was soon decisively to establish itself as a practical factor in war and in human affairs based on war. If cannon had not been invented the English mastery of the long-bow might have carried them even farther in their Continental domination. We know no reason why the yeoman archer should not have established a class position similar in authority to that of the armoured knights, but upon a far broader foundation.

The early fifteenth century was to see the end of the rule of the armoured men. Breastplates and backplates might long be worn as safeguards to life, but no longer as the instrument and symbol of power. If the archers faded it was not because they could not master chivalry; a more convenient agency was at hand which speedily became the common property of all nations. Amid jarring booms and billowing smoke which frequently caused more alarm to friends than foes, but none the less arrested all attention, a system which had ruled and also guided Christendom for five hundred years, which had in its day been the instrument of an immense advance in human government and stature, fell into ruins which were painfully carted away to make room for new building.

*　　*　　*　　*　　*

The calamity which fell upon mankind reduced their numbers and darkened their existence without abating their quarrels. The war between England and France continued in a broken fashion, and the Black Prince, the most renowned warrior in Europe, became a freebooter. Grave reasons of State had been adduced for Edward's invasion of France in 1338, but the character of the Black Prince's forays in Aquitaine can vaunt no such excuses. Nevertheless they produced a brilliant military episode.

In 1355 King Edward obtained from Parliament substantial grants for the renewal of active war. An ambitious strategy was adopted. The Black Prince would advance northward from the English territories of Gascony and Aquitaine towards the Loire. His younger brother, John of Gaunt, Duke of Lancaster, struck in from Brittany. The two forces were to join for a main decision. But all this miscarried, and the Black Prince found himself, with forces shrunk to about four thousand men, of whom however nearly a half were the dreaded archers, forced to retire with growing urgency before the advance of a French royal army twenty thousand strong. So grim were his straits that he proposed, as an accommodation, that he and the army should be allowed to escape to England. These terms were rejected by the Franch, who once again saw their deeply hated foe in their grasp. At Poitiers the Prince was brought to bay. Even on the morning of his victory his vanguard was already marching southwards in retreat. But King John of France was resolved to avenge Crécy and finish the war at a stroke. Forced against all reason and all odds to fight, the haggard band of English marauders who had carried pillage and arson far and wide were drawn up in array and position chosen by consummate insight. The flanks were secured by forests; the archers lined a hedgerow and commanded the only practicable passage.

Ten years had passed since Crécy, and French chivalry and high command alike had brooded upon the tyranny of that event. They had been forced to accept the fact that horses could not face the arrow storm. King Edward had won with an army entirely dismounted. The confusion wrought by English archery in a charging line of horses collapsing or driven mad through pain was, they realised, fatal to the old forms of warfare. King John was certain that all must attack on foot, and he trusted to overwhelming numbers. But the great merit of the Black Prince is that he did not rest upon the lessons of the past or prepare himself to repeat the triumphs of a former battle. He understood that the masses of mail-clad footmen who now advanced upon him in such towering numbers would not be stopped as easily as the horses. Archery alone, however good the target, would not save him. He must try the battle of manœuvre and counter-attack. He therefore did the opposite to what military convention, based upon the then known facts, would have pronounced right.

The French nobility left their horses in the rear. The Black Prince had all his knights mounted. A deadly toll was taken by the archers upon the whole front. The French chivalry, encumbered by their mail, plodded ponderously forward amid vineyards and scrub. Many fell before the arrows, but the arrows would not have been enough at the crisis. It was the English spear and axe men who charged in the old style upon ranks disordered by their fatigue of movement and the accidents of the ground. At the same time, in admirable concert, a strong detachment of mounted knights, riding round the French left flank, struck in upon the harassed and already disordered attack. The result was a slaughter as large and a victory as complete as Crécy, but with even larger gains. The whole French army was driven into ruin. King John and the flower of his nobility were captured or slain. The pillage of the field could not be gathered by the victors; they were already overburdened with the loot of four provinces. The Black Prince, whose record is dinked by many cruel acts of war, showed himself a paladin of the age when, in spite of the weariness and stresses of the desperate battle, he treated the captured monarch with all the ceremony of his rank, seated him in his own chair in the camp, and served him in person with such fare as was procurable. Thus by genius, valour, and chivalry he presents himself in a posture which history has not failed to salute.

King John was carried to London. Like King David of Scotland before him, he was placed in the Tower, and upon this personal trophy, in May 1360, the Treaty of Brétigny was signed. By this England acquired, in addition to her old possession of Gascony, the whole of Henry II's possessions in Aquitaine in full sovereignty, Edward I's inheritance of Ponthieu, and the famous port and city of Calais, which last was held for nearly two hundred years. A ransom was fixed for King John at three million gold crowns, and equivalent of £500,000 sterling. This was eight times the annual revenue of the English Crown in time of peace.

At Crécy France had been beaten on horseback; at Poitiers she was beaten on foot. These two terrible experiments against the English bit deep into French thought. A sense of hopelessness overwhelmed the French Court and army. How could these people be beaten or withstood? A similar phase of despair had swept across Europe a century earlier after the menacing battles of the Mongol invasions. But, as has been wisely observed, the trees do not grow up to the sky. For a long spell the French avoided battles; they became as careful in fighting the England of King Edward III as in the days of Marlborough they fought the England of Queen Anne. But a great French hero appeared in Bertrand du Guesclin, who, like Fabius Cunctator against Hannibal, by refusing battle and acting through sieges and surprises, rallied the factor of time to the home side. The triumph and the exhaustion of England were simultaneously complete. It was proved that the French army could not beat the English, and at the same time that England could not conquer France. The main effort of Edward III, though crowned with all the military laurels, had failed.

*　　*　　*　　*　　*

The years of the war with France are important in the history of Parliament. The need for money drove the Crown and its officials to summoning it frequently. This led to rapid and important developments. One of the main functions of the representatives of the shires and boroughs was to petition for the redress of grievances, local and national, and to draw the attention of the King and his Council to urgent matters. The stress of war forced the Government to take notice of these petitions of the Commons of England, and during the reign of Edward III the procedure of collective petition, which had started under Edward II, made progress. The fact that the Commons now petitioned as a body in a formal way, and asked, as they did in 1327, that these petitions should be transformed into Parliamentary statutes, distinguishes the lower House from the rest of Parliament. Under Edward I the Commons were not an essential element in a Parliament, but under Edward III they assumed a position distinct, vital, and permanent. They had their own clerk, who drafted their petitions and their rejoinders to the Crown's replies. The separation of the Houses now appears. The Lords had come to regard themselves not only as the natural counsellors of the Crown, but as enjoying the right of separate consultation within the framework of Parliament itself. In 1343 the prelates and magnates met in the White Chamber at Westminster, and the knights and burgesses adjourned to the Painted Chamber to discuss the business of the day. Here, in this Parliament, for the first time, the figure of a Speaker emerged. He was not on this occasion a Member of the House, and for some time to come the Commons generally spoke through an appointed deputation. But by the end of the reign the rôle of the Speaker was recognized, and the Crown became anxious to secure its own nominees for this important and prominent office.

The concessions made by Edward III to the Commons mark a decisive stage. He consented that all aids should be granted only in Parliament. He accepted the formal drafts of the Commons' collective petitions as the preliminary bases for future statutes, and by the time of his death it was recognised that the Commons had assumed a leading part in the granting of taxes and the presentation of petitions. Naturally the Commons stood in awe of the Crown. There was no long tradition of authority behind them. The assertions of the royal prerogative in the days of Edward I still echoed in their minds, and there was no suggestion that either they or Parliament as a whole had any right of control or interference in matters of administration and government. They were summoned to endorse political settlements reached often by violence, to vote money and to voice grievances. But the permanent acceptance of Parliament as an essential part of the machinery of government and of the Commons as its vital foundation is the lasting work of the fourteenth century.

Against Papal agents feeling was strong. The interventions of Rome in the days of John, the submissiveness of Henry III to the Church, the exactions of the Papal tax-collectors, the weight of clerical influence within the Household and the Council, all contributed to the growing criticism and dislike of the Church of England. The reign of Edward III brought the climax of this mood. The war with France had stimulated and embittered national sentiment, which resented the influence of an external institution whose great days were already passing. Moreover, this declining power had perforce abandoned its sacred traditional seat in Rome, and was now installed under French influence in enemy territory at Avignon. During these years Parliament passed statutes forbidding appeals to be carried to the Papal Curia for matters cognisable in the royal courts and restricting its power to make appointments in the Church of England. It is true that these statutes were only fitfully enforced, as dictated by diplomatic demands, but the drain of the war left little money for Rome, and the Papal tax-collectors gleaned the country to little avail during the greater part of the reign.

The renewal in 1369 of serious fighting in Aquitaine found England exhausted and disillusioned. The clergy claimed exemption from taxation, though not always successfully, and they could often flaunt their wealth in the teeth of poverty and economic dislocation. Churchmen were ousting the nobility from public office and anti-clerical feeling grew in Parliament. The King was old and failing, and a resurgence of baronial power was due. John of Gaunt set himself to redress the balance in favour of the Lords by a carefully planned political campaign against the Church. Ready to his hand lay an unexpected weapon. In the University of Oxford, the national centre of theological study and learning, criticism of Papal pretensions and power raised its voice. The arguments for reform set forth by a distinguished Oxford scholar named Wyclif attracted attention.

Wyclif was indignant at the corruption of the Church, and saw in its proud hierarchy and absolute claims a distortion of the true principles of Christianity. He declared that dominion over men's souls had never been delegated to mortals. The King, as the Vicar of God in things temporal, was as much bound by his office to curb the material lavishness of the clergy as the clergy to direct the spiritual life of the King. Though Pope and King was each in his sphere supreme, every Christian held not "in chief" of them, but rather of God. The final appeal was to Heaven, not to Rome.

Wyclif's doctrine could not remain the speculations of a harmless schoolman. Its application to the existing facts of Church and State opened deep rifts. It involved reducing the powers of the Church temporal in order to purify the Church spiritual. John of Gaunt was interested in the first, Wyclif in the second. The Church was opposed to both. Gaunt and Wyclif in the beginning each hoped to use the other for his special aim. In 1377 they entered into alliance. Gaunt busied himself in packing the new Parliament, and Wyclif lent moral support by "running about from church to church preaching against abuses." But counter-forces were also aroused. Wyclif's hopes of Church reform were soon involved in class and party prejudices, and Gaunt by his alliance with the revolutionary theologian consolidated the vested interest of the Episcopate against himself. Thus both suffered from their union. The bishops, recognising in Wyclif Gaunt's most dangerous supporter, arraigned him on charges of heresy at St. Paul's. Gaunt, coming to his aid, encountered the hostility of the London mob. The ill-matched partnership fell to pieces and Wyclif ceased to count in high politics.

It was at this same point that his enduring influence began. He resolved to appeal to the people. Church abuses and his own reforming doctrines had attracted many young students around him. He organised his followers into bands of poor preachers, who, like those of Wesley in a later century, spread the doctrines of poverty and holiness for the clergy throughout the countryside. He wrote English tracts, of which the most famous was *The Wicket*, which were passed from hand to hand. Finally, with his students he took the tremendous step of having the Bible translated into English.

"Cristen men and wymmen, olde and yonge, shulden studie fast in the Newe Testament, for it is of ful autorite, and opyn to undirstonding of simple men, as to the poyntis that be moost nedeful to salvacioun. . . . Each place of holy writ, both opyn and derk, techith mekenes and charite; and therfore he that kepith mekenes and charite hath the trewe undirstondyng and perfectioun of al holi writ. . . . Therefore no simple man of wit be aferd unmesurabli to studie in the text of holy writ . . . and no clerk be proude of the verrey undirstondyng of holy writ, for why undirstonding of hooly writ with outen charite that kepith Goddis [be]heestis, makith a man depper dampned . . . and pride and covetise of clerkis is cause of her blindnes and eresie, and priveth them fro verrey undirstondyng of holy writ."

The spirit of early Christianity now revived the English countryside with a keen, refreshing breeze after the weariness of sultry days. But the new vision opened to rich and poor alike profoundly disturbed the decaying society to which it was vouchsafed. The powers of Church and State were soon to realise their danger.

*   *   *   *   *

The long reign had reached its dusk. The glories of Crécy and Poitiers had faded. The warlike King, whose ruling passions were power and fame, who had been willing to barter many prerogatives for which his ancestors had striven in order to obtain money for foreign adventure, was now in old age a debtor to time and fortune. Harsh were the suits they laid against him. He saw the wide conquests which his sword and his son had made in France melt like snow at Easter. A few coastal towns alone attested the splendour of victories long to be cherished in the memories of the Island race. Queen Philippa, his loving wife, had died of plague in 1369. Even before her death the old King had fallen under the consoling thrall of Alice Perrers, a lady of indifferent extraction, but of remarkable wit and capacity, untrammelled by scruple or by prudence. The spectacle of the famous King in his sixties, infatuated by an illicit love, jarred upon the haggard yet touchy temper of the times. Here was something less romantic than the courtly love that had been symbolised in 1348 by the founding of the Order of the Garter. Nobles and people alike would not extend to the mistress of the King's old age the benefits of the commanding motto of the Order, *Honi soit qui mal y pense*. Alice not only enriched herself with the spoils of favour, and decked herself in some at least of the jewels of Queen Philippa, but played high politics with lively zest. She even took her seat with the judges on the bench trying cases in which she was concerned. The movement of the nobility and the Commons was therefore united against her.

The King, at length worn down by war, business, and pleasure, subsided into senility. He had reached the allotted span. He celebrated the jubilee of his reign. The last decade was disparaging to his repute. Apart from Alice, he concentrated his remaining hopes upon the Black Prince; but this great soldier, renowned throughout Europe, was also brought low by the fatigues of war, and was sinking fast in health. In 1376 the Black Prince expired, leaving a son not ten years old as heir apparent to the throne. King Edward III's large share of life narrowed sharply at its end. Mortally stricken, he retired to Sheen Lodge, where Alice, after the modern fashion, encouraged him to dwell on tournaments, the chase, and wide plans when he should recover. But hostile chroniclers have it that when the stupor preceding death engulfed the King she took the rings from his fingers and other movable property in the house and departed for some time to extreme privacy. We have not heard her tale, but her reappearance in somewhat buoyant situations in the new reign seems to show that she had one to tell. All accounts, alas! Confirm that King Edward died deserted by all, and that only the charity of a local priest procured him the protection and warrant of the Church in his final expedition.

The Black Prince's son was recognised as King by general assent on the very day his grandfather died, no question of election being raised, and the crown of England passed to a minor.

BOOK III

THE END OF
THE FEUDAL AGE

CHAPTER TWENTY-THREE

KING RICHARD II AND
THE SOCIAL REVOLT

JOHN OF GAUNT, DUKE OF LANCASTER, YOUNGER BROTHER OF THE
Black Prince, uncle of the King, was head of the Council of Regency
and ruled the land. Both the impact and the shadow of the Black
Death dominated the scene. A new fluidity swept English society. The
pang of almost mortal injury still throbbed, but with it crept a feeling
that there was for the moment more room in the land. A multitude
of vacant places had been filled, and many men in all classes had
the sense of unexpected promotion and enlargement about them.
A community had been profoundly deranged, reduced in collective
strength, but often individually lifted.

The belief that the English were invincible and supreme in war,
that nothing could stand before their arms, was ingrained. The
elation of Crécy and Poitiers survived the loss of all material gains in
France. The assurance of being able to meet the French or the Scots at
any time upon the battlefield overrode inquiries about the upshot of
the war. Few recognised the difference between winning battles and
making lasting conquests. Parliament in its youth was eager for war,
improvident in preparation, and resentful in paying for it. While the
war continued the Crown was expected to produce dazzlings results,
and at the same time was censured for the burden of taxation and
annoyance to the realm. A peace approached inexorably which would
in no way correspond to the sensation of overwhelming victory in

which the English indulged themselves. This ugly prospect came to Richard II as a prominent part of his inheritance.

In the economic and social sphere there arose a vast tumult. The Black Death had struck a world already in movement. Ever since the Crown had introduced the custom of employing wage-earning soldiers instead of the feudal levy the landed tie had been dissolving. Why should not the noble or knight follow the example of his liege lord? Covenants in which a small landowner undertook to serve a powerful neighbour, "except against the King," became common. The restriction would not always be observed. The old bonds of mutual loyalty were disappearing, and in their place grew private armies, the hired defenders of property, the sure precursors of anarchy.

In medieval England the lords of the manors had often based their prosperity on a serf peasantry, whose status and duties were enjoined by long custom and enforced by manorial courts. Around each manor a closely bound and self-sufficient community revolved. Although there had been more movement of labour and interchange of goods in the thirteenth and early fourteenth centuries than was formerly supposed, development had been relatively slow and the break-up of the village community gradual. The time had now come when the compartments of society and toil could no longer preserve their structure. The convulsion of the Black Death violently accelerated this deep and rending process. Nearly one-third of the population being suddenly dead, a large part of the land passed out of cultivation. The survivors turned their ploughs to the richest soils and quartered their flocks and herds on the fairest pastures. Many landowners abandoned ploughs and enclosed, often by encroachment, the best grazing. At this time, when wealth-getting seemed easier and both prices and profits ran high, the available labour was reduced by nearly a half. Small-holdings were deserted, and many manors were denuded of the peasantry who had served them from time immemorial. Ploughmen and labourers found themselves in high demand, and were competed for on all sides. They in their turn sought to better themselves, or at least to keep their living equal with the rising prices. The poet Langland gives an unsympathetic but interesting picture in *Piers Plowman:*

Labourers that have no land, to live on but their hands,
Deigned not to dine a day, on night-old wortes.
May no penny ale him pay, nor a piece of bacon,
But it be fresh flesh or fish, fried or baked,
And that chaud and plus-chaud, for chilling of their maw,
But he be highly-hired, else will he chide.

But their masters saw matters differently. They repulsed fiercely demands for increased wages; they revived ancient claims to forced or tied labour. The pedigrees of villagers were scrutinised with a care hitherto only bestowed upon persons of quality. The villeins who were declared serfs were at least free from new claims. Assertions of long-lapsed authority, however good in law, were violently resisted by the country folk. They formed unions of labourers to guard their interests. There were escapes of villeins from the estates, like those of the slaves from the Southern states of America in the 1850's. Some landlords in their embarrassment offered to commute the labour services they claimed and to procure obedience by granting leases to small-holders. On some manors the serfs were enfranchised in a body and a class of free tenants came into being. But this feature was rare. The greatest of all landlords was the Church. On the whole the Spiritual Power stood up successfully against the assault of this part of its flock. When a landlord was driven, as was the Abbot of Battle, on the manor of Hutton, to lease vacant holdings this was done on the shortest terms, which at the first tactical opportunity were reduced to a yearly basis. A similar attempt in eighteenth-century France to revive obsolete feudal claims aroused the spirit of revolution.

The turmoil through which all England passed affected the daily life of the mass of the people in a manner not seen again in our social history till the Industrial Revolution of the nineteenth century. Here was a case in which a Parliament based upon property could have a decided opinion. In England, as in France, the Crown had more than once in the past interfered with the local regulation of wages, but the Statute of Labourers (1351) was the first important attempt to fix wages and prices for the country as a whole. In the aggravated conditions following the pestilence Parliament sought to enforce these laws as fully as it dared. "Justices of labour," drawn from the rural middle classes and with fixed salaries, were appointed to try offenders. Between 1351 and 1377 nine thousand cases of breach of contract were tried before the Common Pleas. In many parts the commissioners, who were active and biased, were attacked by the inhabitants. Unrest spread wide and deep.

Still, on the morrow of the plague there was an undoubted well-being among the survivors. Revolts do not break out in countries depressed by starvation. Says Froissart, "The peasants' rebellion was caused and incited by the great ease and plenty in which the meaner folk of England lived." The people were not without the means of protesting against injustice, nor without the voice to express their discontent. Among the lower clergy the clerks with small benefices had been severely smitten by the Black Death. In East Anglia alone eight hundred priests had died. The survivors found that their stipends remained unaltered in a world of rising prices, and that the higher clergy were completely indifferent to this problem of the ecclesiastical proletarian. For this atonement was to be exacted. The episcopal manors were marked places of attack in the rising. At the fairs, on market-day, agitators, especially among the friars, collected and stirred crowds. Langland voiced the indignation of the established order against these Christian communists:

> They preach men of Plato and prove it by Seneca
> That all things under heaven ought to be in common:
> And yet he lies, as I live, that to the unlearned so preacheth.

Many vehement agitators, among whom John Ball is the best known, gave forth a stream of subversive doctrine. The country was full of broken soldiers, disbanded from the war, and all knew about the long-bow and its power to kill nobles, however exalted and well armed. The preaching of revolutionary ideas was widespread, and a popular ballad expressed the response of the masses:

> When Adam delved, and Eve span,
> Who was then a gentleman?

This was a novel question for the fourteenth century, and awkward at any time. The rigid, time-enforced framework of medieval England trembled to its foundations.

These conditions were by no means confined to the Island. Across the Channel a radical and democratic movement, with talk much akin to that of our own time, was afoot. All this rolled forward in England to the terrifying rebellion of 1381. It was a social upheaval, spontaneous and widespread, arising in various parts of the country from the same causes, and united by the same sentiments. That all this movement was the direct consequence of the Black Death is proved by the fact that the revolt was most fierce in those very districts of Kent and the East Midlands where the death-rate had been highest and the derangement of custom the most violent. It was a cry of pain and anger from a generation shaken out of submissiveness by changes in their lot, which gave rise alike to new hope and new injustice.

*　　*　　*　　*　　*

Throughout the summer of 1381 there was a general ferment. Beneath it all lay organisation. Agents moved round the villages of Central England, in touch with a "Great Society" which was said to meet in London. In May violence broke out in Essex. It was started by an attempt to make a second and more stringent collection of the poll-tax which had been levied in the previous year. The turbulent elements in London took fire, and a band under one Thomas Faringdon marched off to join the rebels. Walworth, the mayor, faced a strong municipal opposition which was in sympathy and contact with the rising. In Kent, after an attack on Lesnes Abbey, the peasants marched through Rochester and Maidstone, burning manorial and taxation records on their way. At Maidstone they released the agitator John Ball from the episcopal prison, and were joined by a military adventurer with gifts and experience of leadership, Wat Tyler.

The royal Council was bewildered and inactive. Early in June the main body of rebels from Essex and Kent moved on London. Here they found support. John Horn, fishmonger, invited them to enter; the alderman in charge of London Bridge did nothing to defend it, and Aldgate was opened treacherously to a band of Essex rioters. For three days the city was in confusion. Foreigners were murdered; two members of the Council, Simon Sudbury, the Archbishop of Canterbury and Chancellor, and Sir Robert Hales, the Treasurer, were dragged from the Tower and beheaded on Tower Hill; the Savoy palace of John of Gaunt was burnt; Lambeth and Southwark were sacked. This was the time for paying off old scores. Faringdon had drawn up proscription lists, and the extortionate financier Richard Lyons was killed. All this has a modern ring. But the loyal citizen body rallied round the mayor, and at Smithfield the King faced the rebel leaders. Among the insurgents there seems to have been a general loyalty to the sovereign. Their demands were reasonable but disconcerting. They asked for the repeal of oppressive statutes, for the abolition of villeinage, and for the division of Church property. In particular they asserted that no man ought to be a serf or do labour services to a *seigneur*, but pay fourpence an acre a year for his land and not have to serve any man against his will, but only by agreement. While the parley was going on Tyler was first wounded by Mayor Walworth and then smitten to death by one of the King's squires. As the rebel leader rolled off his horse, dead in the sight of the great assembly, the young King met the crisis by riding forward alone with the cry, "I will be your leader. You shall have from me all you seek. Only follow me to the fields outside." But the death of Tyler proved a signal for the wave of reaction. The leaderless bands wandered home and spread a vulgar lawlessness through their counties. They were pursued by reconstructed authority. Vengeance was wreaked.

The rising had spread throughout the South-West. There were riots in Bridgewater, Winchester, and Salisbury. In Hertfordshire the peasants rose against the powerful and hated Abbey of St. Albans, and marched on London under Jack Straw. There was a general revolt in Cambridgeshire, accompanied by burning of rolls and attacks on episcopal manors. The Abbey of Ramsey, in Huntingdonshire, was attacked, though the burghers of Huntingdon shut their gates against the rioters. In Norfolk and Suffolk, where the peasants were richer and more independent, the irritation against legal villeinage was stronger. The Abbey of Bury St. Edmunds was a prominent object of hatred, and the Flemish woollen-craftsmen were murdered in Lynn. Waves of revolt rippled on as far north as Yorkshire and Cheshire, and to the west in Wiltshire and Somerset.

But after Tyler's death the resistance of the ruling classes was organised. Letters were sent out from Chancery to the royal officials commanding the restoration of order, and justices under Chief Justice Tresilian gave swift judgment upon insurgents. The King, who accompanied Tresilian on the punitive circuit, pressed for the observance of legal forms in the punishment of rebels. The warlike Bishop le Despenser, of Norwich, used armed force in the Eastern Counties in defence of Church property, and a veritable battle was fought at North Walsham. Nevertheless the reaction was, according to modern examples, very restrained. Not more than a hundred and fifty executions are recorded in the rolls. There was nothing like the savagery we have seen in many parts of Europe in our own times. Law re-established ruled by law. Even in this furious class reaction no men were hanged except after trial by jury. In January 1382 a general amnesty, suggested by Parliament, was proclaimed. But the victory of property was won, and there followed the unanimous annulment of all concessions and a bold attempt to re-create intact the manorial system of the early part of the century. Yet for generations the upper classes lived in fear of a popular rising and the labourers continued to combine. Servile labour ceased to be the basis of the system. The legal aspect of serfdom became of little importance, and the development of commutation went on, speaking broadly, at an accelerated pace after 1349. Such were the more enduring legacies of the Black Death. The revolt, which to the historian is but a sudden flash of revealing light on medieval conditions among the poorer classes, struck with lasting awe the imagination of its contemporaries. It left a hard core of bitterness among the peasantry, and called forth a vigorous and watchful resistance from authority. Henceforth a fixed desire for the division of ecclesiastical property was conceived. The spread of Lollardy after the revolt drew upon it the hostility of the intimidated victors. Wyclif's "poor preachers" bore the stigma of having fomented the troubles, and their presecution was the revenge of a shaken system.

In the charged, sullen atmosphere of the England of the 1380's Wyclif's doctrines gathered wide momentum. But, faced by social revolution, English society was in no mood for Church reform. All subversive doctrines fell under censure, and although Wyclif was not directly responsible or accused of seditious preaching the result was disastrous to his cause. The landed classes gave silent assent to the ultimate suppression of the preacher by the Church. This descended swiftly and effectively. Wyclif's old opponent, Courtenay, had become Archbishop after Sudbury's murder. He found Wyclif's friends in control of Oxford. He acted with speed. The doctrines of the reformer were officially condemned. The bishops were instructed to arrest all unlicensed preachers, and the Archbishop himself rapidly became the head of a system of Church discipline; and this, with the active support of the State in Lancastrian days, eventually enabled the Church to recover from the attack of the laity. In 1382 Courtenay descended upon Oxford and held a convocation where Christ Church now stands. The chief Lollards were sharply summoned to recant. The Chancellor's protest of university privilege was brushed aside. Hard censure fell upon Wyclif's followers. They blenched and bowed. Wyclif found himself alone. His attack on Church doctrine as distinct from Church privilege had lost him the support of Gaunt. His popular preachers and the first beginnings of Bible-reading could not build a solid party against the dominant social forces.

Wyclif appealed to the conscience of his age. Baffled, though not silenced, in England, his inspiration stirred a distant and little-known land, and thence disturbed Europe. Students from Prague had come to Oxford, and carried his doctrines, and indeed the manuscripts of his writings, to Bohemia. From this sprang the movement by which the fame of John Huss eclipsed that of his English master and evoked the enduring national consciousness of the Czech people.

By his frontal attack on the Church's absolute authority over men in this world, by his implication of the supremacy of the individual conscience, and by his challenge to ecclesiastical dogma Wyclif had called down upon himself the thunderbolts of repression. But his protest had led to the first of the Oxford Movements. The cause, lost in his day, impelled the tide of the Reformation. Lollardy, as the Wyclif Movement came to be called, was driven beneath the surface. The Church, strengthening its temporal position by alliance with the State, brazenly repelled the first assault; but its spiritual authority bore henceforward and scars and enfeeblement resulting from the conflict.

Fuller, the seventeenth-century writer, wrote of Wyclif's preachers, "These men were sentinels against an army of enemies until God sent Luther to relieve them." In Oxford Wyclifite tradition lingered in Bible study until the Reformation, to be revived by Colet's lectures of 1497–98. In the country Lollardy became identified with political sedition, though this was not what Wyclif had taught. Its ecclesiastical opponents were eager to make the charge, and the passionate, sometimes ignorant, invective of the Lollard preachers, often laymen, supplied a wealth of evidence. Cruel days lay ahead. The political tradition was to be burned out in the misery of Sir John Oldcastle's rebellion under Henry V. But a vital element of resistance to the formation of a militant and triumphant Church survived in the English people. A principle had been implanted in English hearts which shaped the destiny of the race. Wyclif's failure in his own day was total, and the ray of his star faded in the light of the Reformation dawn. "Wyclif," wrote Milton in *Areopagitica*, "was a man who wanted, to render his learning consummate, nothing but his living in a happier age."

The stubborn wish for practical freedom was not broken in England, and the status and temper of the people stand in favourable contrast to the exhausted passivity of the French peasant, bludgeoned to submission by war, famine, and the brutal suppressions of the Jacquerie.

"It is cowardise and lack of hartes and corage," wrote Sir John Fortescue, the eminent jurist of Henry VI's reign, "that kepeth the Frenchmen from rysyng, and not povertye; which corage no Frenche man hath like to the English man. It hath ben often seen in Englond that iij or iv thefes, for povertie, hath sett upon vij or viij true men, and robbyd them al. But it had not been seen in Fraunce, that vij or viij thefes have ben hardy to robbe iij or iv true men. Wherefor it is right seid that few Frenchmen be hangyd for robbery, for that they have no hertys to do so terryble an acte. There be therefor mo men hangyd in Eglnd, in a yere, for robberye and manslaughter, than ther be hangid in Fraunce for such cause of crime in vij yers."

*   *   *   *   *

The King was now growing up. His keen instincts and precocious abilities were sharpened by all that he had seen and done. In the crisis of the Peasants' Revolt the brunt of many things had fallen upon him, and by his personal action he had saved the situation on a memorable occasion. It was the King's Court and the royal judges who had restored order when the feudal class had lost their nerve. Yet the King consented to a prolonged tutelage. John of Gaunt, Viceroy of Aquitaine, quitted the realm to pursue abroad interests which included claims to the kingdom of Castile. He left behind him his son, Henry, a vigorous and capable youth, to take charge of his English estates and interests.

It was not till he was twenty that Richard determined to be complete master of his Council, and in particular to escape from the control of his uncles. No King had been treated in such a way before. His grandfather had been obeyed when he was eighteen. Richard at sixteen had played decisive parts. His Household and the Court around it were deeply interested in his assumption of power. This circle comprised the brains of the Government, and the high Civil Service. Its chiefs were the Chancellor, Michael de la Pole, Chief Justice Tresilian, and Alexander Neville, Archbishop of York. Behind them Simon Burley, Richard's tutor and close intimate, was probably the guide. A group of younger nobles threw in their fortunes with the Court. Of these the head was Robert de Vere, Earl of Oxford, who now played a part resembling that of Gaveston under Edward II, and in one aspect foreshadowed that of Strafford in a future generation. The King, the fountain of honour, spread his favours among his adherents, and de Vere was soon created Duke of Ireland. This was plainly a political challenge to the magnates of the Council. Ireland was a reservoir of men and supplies, beyond the control of Parliament and the nobility, which could be used for the mastery of England.

The accumulation of Household and Government offices by the clique around the King and his effeminate favourite affronted the feudal party, and to some extent the national spirit. As so often happens, the opposition found in foreign affairs a vehicle of attack. Lack of money, fear of asking for it, and above all no military leadership, had led the Court to pacific courses. The nobility were at one with the Parliament in decrying the unmartial Chancellor Pole and the lush hedonism of the Court. "They were," they jeered, "rather knights of Venus than of Bellona." War must be waged with France; and on this theme in 1386 a coherent front was formed against the Crown. Parliament was led to appoint a commission of five Ministers and nine lords, of whom the former Councillors of Regency were the chiefs. The Court bent before the storm of Pole's impeachment. A purge of the Civil Service, supposed to be the source alike of the King's errors and of his strength, was instituted; and we may note that Geoffrey Chaucer, his equerry, but famous for other reasons, lost his two posts in the Customs.

When the commissioners presently compelled the King to dismiss his personal friends Richard in deep distress withdrew from London. In North Wales he consorted with the new Duke of Ireland, at York with Archbishop Neville, and at Nottingham with Chief Justice Tresilian. He sought to marshal his forces for civil war at the very same spot where Charles I would one day unfurl the royal standard. Irish levies, Welsh pikemen, and above all Cheshire archers from his own earldom, were gathering to form an army. Upon this basis of force Tresilian and four other royal judges pronounced that the pressure put upon him by the Lords Appellant, as they were now styled, and the Parliament was contrary to the laws and Constitution of England. This judgment, the legal soundness of which is undoubted, was followed by a bloody reprisal. The King's uncle, Gloucester, together with other heads of the baronial oligarchy, denounced the Chief Justice and those who had acted with him, including de Vere and the other royal advisers, as traitors to the realm. The King—he was but twenty—had based himself too bluntly upon his royal authority. The lords of the Council were still able to command the support of Parliament. They resorted to arms. Gloucester, with an armed power, approached

London. Richard, arriving there first, was welcomed by the people. They displayed his red and white colours, and showed attachment to his person, but they were not prepared to fight the advancing baronial army. In Westminster Hall the three principal Lords Appellant, Gloucester, Arundel, and Warwick, with an escort outside of three hundred horsemen, bullied the King into submission. He could do no more than secure the escape of his supporters.

De Vere retired to Chester and raised an armed force to secure the royal rights. With this, in December 1387, he marched towards London. But now appeared in arms the Lords Appellant, and also Gaunt's son Henry. At Radcot Bridge, in Oxfordshire, Henry and they defeated and broke de Vere. The favourite fled overseas. The King was now at the mercy of the proud faction which had usurped the rights of the monarchy. They disputed long among themselves whether or not he should be deposed and killed. The older men were for the extreme course; the younger restrained them. Richard was brutally threatened with the fate of his great-grandfather, Edward II. So severe was the discussion that only two of the Lords Appellant consented to remain with him for supper. It was Henry, the young military victor, who pleaded for moderation, possibly because his father's claim to the throne would have been overridden by the substitution of Gloucester for Richard.

The Lords Appellant, divided as they were, shrank from deposing and killing the King; but they drew the line at nothing else. They forced him to yield at every point. Cruel was the vengeance that they wreaked upon the upstart nobility of his circle and his legal adherents. The Estates of the Realm were summoned to give countenance to the new régime. On the appointed day the five Lords Appellant, in golden clothes, entered Westminster Hall arm-in-arm. "The Merciless Parliament" opened its session. The most obnoxious opponents were the royal judges, headed by Tresilian. He had promulgated at Nottingham the doctrine of the Royal Supremacy, with its courts and lawyers, over the nobles who held Parliament in their hand. To this a solemn answer was now made, which, though, as so often before, it asserted the fact of feudal power, also proclaimed the principle of Parliamentary control. The fact vanished in the turbulence of those days, but the principle echoed down into the seventeenth century.

Chief Justice Tresilian and four of the other judges responsible for the Nottingham declaration were hanged, drawn, and quartered at Tyburn. The royal tutor, Burley, was not spared. The victory of the old nobility was complete. Only the person of the King was respected, and that by the narrowest of margins. Richard, forced not only to submit but to assent to the slaughter of his friends, buried himself as low as he could in retirement.

We must suppose that this treatment produced a marked impression upon his mind. It falls to the lot of few mortals to endure such ordeals. He brooded upon his wrongs, and also upon his past mistakes. He saw in the triumphant lords men who would be tyrants not only over the King but over the people. He laid his plans for revenge and for his own rights with far more craft than before. For a year there was a sinister lull.

*   *   *   *   *

On May 3, 1389, Richard took action which none of them had foreseen. Taking his seat at the Council, he asked blandly to be told how old he was. On being answered that he was three-and-twenty he declared that he had certainly come of age, and that he would no longer submit to restrictions upon his rights which none of his subjects would endure. He would manage the realm himself; he would choose his own advisers; he would be King indeed. This stroke had no doubt been prepared with the uncanny and abnormal cleverness which marked many of Richard's schemes. It was immediately successful. Bishop Thomas, the Earl of Arundel's brother, and later Archbishop of Canterbury, surrendered the Great Seal at his demand. Bishop Gilbert quitted the Treasury, and the King's sympathisers, William of Wykeham and Thomas Brantingham, were restored to their posts as Chancellor and Treasurer. King's nominees were added to those of the Appellants on the judicial bench. Letters from the King to the sheriffs announced that he had assumed the government, and the news was accepted by the public with an unexpected measure of welcome.

Richard used his victory with prudence and mercy. In October 1389 John of Gaunt returned from Spain, and his son, Henry, now a leading personage, was reconciled to the King. The terrible combination of

1388 had dissolved. The machinery of royal government, triumphant over faction, resumed its sway, and for the next eight years Richard governed England in the guise of a constitutional and popular King.

This was an age in which the masses were totally excluded from power, and when the ruling classes, including the new middle class, even in their most deadly quarrels, always united to keep them down. Richard has been judged and his record declared by the socially powerful elements which overthrew him; but their verdict upon his character can only be accepted under reserve. That he sought to subvert and annul the constitutional rights which the rivalries of factions and of Church and baronage had unconsciously but resolutely built up cannot be denied; but whether this was for purposes of personal satisfaction or in the hope of fulfilling the pledge which he had made in the crisis of the Peasants' Revolt, "I will be your leader," is a question not to be incontinently brushed aside. It is true that to one deputation of rebels in 1381 he had testily replied, "Villeins ye are still, and villeins ye shall remain," adding that pledges made under duress went for nothing. Yet by letters patent he freed many peasants from their feudal bonds. He had solemnly promised the abolition of serfdom. He had proposed it to Parliament. He had been overruled. He had a long memory for injuries. Perhaps also it extended to his obligations.

The patience and skill with which Richard accomplished his revenge are most striking. For eight years he tolerated the presence of Arundel and Gloucester, not, as before, as the governors of the country, but still in high positions. There were moments when his passion flared. In 1394, when Arundel was late for the funeral of the Queen, Anne of Bohemia, and the whole procession was delayed, he snatched a steward's wand, struck him in the face and drew blood. The clergy raised a cry that the Church of Westminster had been polluted. Men raked up an old prophecy that God's punishment for the murder of Thomas à Becket would not be exacted from the nation until blood was shed in that sacred nave. Yet after a few weeks we see the King apparently reconciled to Arundel and all proceeding under a glittering mask.

While the lords were at variance the King sought to strengthen himself by gathering Irish resources. In 1394 he went with all the

formality of a Royal Progress to Ireland, and for this purpose created
an army dependent upon himself, which was to be useful later in
overawing opposition in England. When he returned his plans for
subduing both the baronage and the Estates to his authority were
far advanced. To free himself from the burden of war, which would
make him directly dependent upon the favours of Parliament, he
made a settlement with France. After the death of his first wife, Anne,
he had married in 1396 the child Isabelle, daughter of Charles VI of
France. Upon this a truce or pact of amity and non-aggression for
thirty years was concluded. A secret clause laid down that if Richard
were in future to be menaced by any of his subjects the King of France
would come to his aid. Although the terms of peace were the subject
of complaint the King gained immensely by his liberation from the
obligation of making a war, which he could only sustain by becoming the beggar and drudge of Parliament. So hard had the Estates
pressed the royal power, now goading it on and now complaining of
results, that we have the unique spectacle of a Plantagenet king lying
down and refusing to pull the wagon farther over such stony roads.
But this did not spring from lack of mental courage or from narrowness of outlook. It was a necessary feature in the King's far-reaching
designs. He wished beyond doubt to gain absolute power over the
nobility and Parliament. Whether he also purposed to use this dictatorship in the interests of the humble masses of his subjects is one
of the mysteries, but also the legend, long linked with his name. His
temperament, the ups and downs of his spirits, his sudden outbursts,
the almost superhuman refinements of his calculations, have all been
abundantly paraded as the causes of his ruin. But the common people
thought he was their friend. He would, they imagined, had he the
power, deliver them from the hard oppression of their masters, and
long did they cherish his memory.

*   *   *   *   *

The Irish expedition had been the first stage towards the establishment of a despotism; the alliance with France was the second. The
King next devoted himself to the construction of a compact, efficient
Court party. Both Gaunt and his son and Mowbray, Earl of Norfolk,
one of the former Appellants, were now rallied to his side, partly in

loyalty to him and partly in hostility to Arundel and Gloucester. New men were brought into the Household. Sir John Bushy and Sir Henry Greene represented local county interests and were unquestioning servants of the Crown. Drawn from the Parliamentary class, the inevitable arbiter of the feuds between Crown and aristocracy, they secured to the King the influence necessary to enable him to face the Estates of the Realm. In January 1397 the Estates were summoned to Westminster, where under deft and at the same time resolute management they showed all due submission. Thus assured, Richard decided at last to strike.

Arundel and Gloucester, though now somewhat in the shade, must have considered themselves protected by time and much friendly intercourse from the consequences of what they had done in 1388. Much had happened since then, and Chief Justice Tresilian, the tutor Burley, and other victims of that blood-bath seemed distant memories. It was with amazement that they saw the King advancing upon them in cold hatred rarely surpassed among men. Arundel and some others of his associates were declared traitors and accorded only the courtesy of decapitation. Warwick was exiled to the Isle of Man. Gloucester, arrested and taken to Calais, was there murdered by Richard's agents; and this deed, not being covered by constitutional forms, bred in its turn new retributions. A stigma rested henceforward on the King similar to that which had marked John after the murder of Arthur. But for the moment he was supreme as no King of all England had been before, and still his wrath was unassuaged.

Parliament was called only to legalise these events. It was found to be so packed and so minded that there was nothing they would not do for the King. Never has there been such a Parliament. With ardour pushed to suicidal lengths, it suspended almost every constitutional right and privilege gained in the preceding century. It raised the monarchy upon a foundation more absolute than even William the Conqueror, war-leader of his freebooting lieutenants, had claimed. All that had been won by the nation through the crimes of John and the degeneracy of Edward II, all that had been conceded or established by the two great Edwards, was relinquished. And the Parliament, having done its work with this destructive thoroughness, ended by consigning its unfinished business to the care of a committee of eighteen persons. As soon as Parliament had dispersed Richard had the record altered by inserting words that greatly enlarged the scope of the committee's work. If his object was not to do away with Parliament, it was at least to reduce it to the rôle it had played in the early days of Edward I, when it had been in fact as well as in name the "King's Parliament."

The relations between Gaunt's son, Henry, the King's cousin and contemporary, passed through drama into tragedy. Henry believed himself to have saved the King from being deposed and murdered by Gloucester, Arundel, and Warwick in the crisis of 1388. Very likely this was true. Since then he had dwelt in familiarity and friendship with Richard; he represented a different element from the old nobility who had challenged the Crown. These two young men had lived their lives in fair comradeship; the one was King, the other, as son of John of Gaunt, stood near the throne and nearer to the succession.

A quarrel arose between Henry and Thomas Mowbray, now Duke of Norfolk. Riding back from Brentford to London, Mowbray voiced his uneasiness. The King, he said, had never forgiven Radcot Bridge nor the former Appellant party, to which he and his companion had both belonged. They would be the next victims. Henry accused Mowbray of treasonable language. Conflicting reports of what had been said were laid before Parliament. Each, when challenged, gave the lie to the other. Trial by battle appeared the correct solution. The famous scene took place in September 1398. The lists were drawn; the English world assembled; the champions presented themselves; but the King, exasperating the spectators of all classes who had gathered in high expectation to see the sport, cast down his wardour, forbade the combat, and exiled Mowbray for life and Henry for a decade. Both lords obeyed the royal commands. Mowbray soon died; but Henry, astounded by what he deemed ingratitude and injustice, lived and schemed in France.

*　　*　　*　　*　　*

The year which followed was an unveiled despotism, and Richard, so patient till his vengeance was accomplished, showed restlessness and perplexity, profusion and inconsequence, in his function. Escorted by his faithful archers from Cheshire, he sped about the kingdom beguiling the weeks with feasts and tournaments, while the administration was left to minor officials at Westminster or Ministers who felt they were neither trusted nor consulted. Financial stringency followed royal extravagance, and forced loans and heavier taxes angered the merchants and country gentry.

During 1398 there were many in the nation who awoke to the fact that a servile Parliament had in a few weeks suspended many of the fundamental rights and liberties of the realm. Hitherto for some time they had had no quarrel with the King. They now saw him revealed as a despot. Not only the old nobility, who in the former crisis had been defeated, but all the gentry and merchant classes, were aghast at the triumph of absolute rule. Nor did their wrath arise from love of constitutional practices alone. They feared, perhaps with many reasons not known to us, that the King, now master, would rule over their heads, resting himself upon the submissive shoulders of the mass of the people. They felt again the terror of the social revolution which they had tasted so recently in the Peasants' Revolt. A solid amalgamation of interest, temper, and action united all the classes which had raised or found themselves above the common level. Here was a King, now absolute, who would, as they muttered, let loose the mob upon them.

In February of 1399 died old John of Gaunt, "time-honoured Lancaster." Henry, in exile, succeeded to vast domains, not only in Lancashire and the north but scattered all over England. Richard, pressed for money, could not refrain from a technical legal seizure of the Lancaster estates in spite of his promises; he declared his cousin disinherited. This challenged the position of every property-holder. And forthwith, by a fatal misjudgment of his strength and of what was stirring in the land, the King set forth in May upon a punitive expedition, which was long overdue, to assert the royal authority in Ireland. He left behind him a disordered administration, deprived of troops, and a land violently incensed against him. News of the King's departure was carried to Henry. The moment had come; the coast was clear, and the man did not tarry. In July Henry of Lancaster, as he had now become, landed in Yorkshire, declaring that he had only come to claim his lawful rights as heir to his venerated father.

He was immediately surrounded by adherents, particularly from the Lancaster estates, and the all powerful Northern Lords led by the Earl of Northumberland. The course of his revolt followed exactly that of Isabella and Mortimer against Edward II seventy-two years before. From York Henry marched across England, amid general acclamation, to Bristol, and just as Isabella had hanged Hugh Despenser upon its battlements, so now did Henry of Lancaster exact the capital forfeit from William Scrope, Earl of Wiltshire, Bushy, and Greene, King Richard's Ministers and representatives.

It took some time for the news of Henry's apparition and all that followed so swiftly from it to reach King Richard in the depths of Ireland. He hastened back, though baffled by stormy seas. Having landed in England on July 27, he made a rapid three weeks' march through North Wales in an attempt to gather forces. What he saw convinced him that all was over. The whole structure of his power, so patiently and subtly built up, had vanished as if by enchantment. The Welsh, who would have stood by him, could not face the advancing power of what was now all England. At Flint Castle he submitted to Henry, into whose hands the whole administration had now passed. He rode through London as a captive in his train. He was lodged in the Tower. His abdication was extorted; his death had become inevitable. The last of all English kings whose hereditary right was indisputable disappeared for ever beneath the portcullis of Pontefract Castle. Henry, by and with the consent of the Estates of the Realm and the Lords Spiritual and Temporal, ascended the throne as Henry IV, and thereby opened a chapter of history destined to be fatal to the medieval baronage. Although Henry's lineage afforded good grounds for his election to the Crown, and his own qualities, and still more those of his son, confirmed this decision, a higher right in blood was to descend through the house of Mortimer to the house of York, and from this after a long interval the Wars of the Roses broke out upon England.

*　　*　　*　　*　　*

The character of Richard II and his place in the regard of history remain an enigma. That he possessed qualities of a high order, both for design and action, is evident. That he was almost from childhood confronted with measureless difficulties and wrongful oppressions against which he repeatedly made head is also plain. The injuries and cruelties which he suffered at the hands of his uncle Gloucester and the high nobility may perhaps be the key to understanding him. Some historians have felt that he was prepared not only to exploit Parliamentary and legal manœuvres against the governing classes, but perhaps even that he would use social forces then and for many generations utterly submerged. At any rate, the people for their part long cherished some such notion of him. These unhappy folk, already to be numbered by the million, looked to Richard with hopes destined to be frustrated for centuries. All through the reign of Henry IV the conception they had formed of Richard was idealised. He was deemed, whether rightly or wrongly, a martyr to the causes of the weak and poor. Statutes were passed declaring it high treason even to spread the rumour that he was still alive.

We have no right in this modern age to rob him of this shaft of sunlight which rests upon his harassed, hunted life. There is however no dispute that in his nature fantastic error and true instinct succeeded each other with baffling rapidity. He was capable of more than human cunning and patience, and also of foolishness which a simpleton would have shunned. He fought four deadly duels with feudal aristocratic society. In 1386 he was overcome; in 1389 he was victorious; in 1397–98 he was supreme; in 1399 he was destroyed.

CHAPTER TWENTY-FOUR

THE USURPATION OF HENRY BOLINGBROKE

ALL POWER AND AUTHORITY FELL TO KING HENRY IV, AND ALL WHO had run risks to place him on the throne combined to secure his right, and their own lives. But the opposite theme endured with strange persistency. The Court of France deemed Henry a usurper. His right in blood was not valid while Richard lived, nor even afterwards when the lineage was scrutinised. But other rights existed. The right of conquest, on which he was inclined to base himself, was discarded by him upon good advice. But the fact that he was acclaimed by the Estates summoned in Richard's name, added to a near right by birth, afforded a broad though challenged foundation for his reign. Many agreeable qualities stand to his credit. All historians concur that he was manly, capable, and naturally merciful. The beginning of his reign was disturbed by the tolerance and lenity which he showed to the defeated party. He who had benefited most from the violent spasm and twist of fortune which had overthrown Richard was the least vindictive against Richard's adherents. He had been near the centre of all the stresses of the late reign; he had been wronged and ill-used; yet he showed a strong repugnance to harsh reprisals. In the hour of his accession he was still the bold knight, surprisingly moderate in success, averse from bloodshed, affianced to growing constitutional ideas, and always dreaming of ending his life as a Crusader. But the sullen, turbulent march of events frustrated his tolerant inclinations and eventually soured his generous nature.

From the outset Henry depended upon Parliament to make good by its weight the defects in his title, and rested on the theory of the elective, limited kingship rather than on that of absolute monarchy. He was therefore alike by mood and need a constitutional King. Great words were used at his accession. "This honourable realm of England, the most abundant angle of riches in the whole world," said Archbishop Arundel, "has been reduced to destruction by the counsels of children and widows. Now God has sent a man, knowing and discreet, for governance, who by the aid of God will be governed and counselled by the wise and ancient of his realm."

"The affairs of the kingdom lie upon us," said the Archbishop. Henry would not act by his own will nor of his own "voluntary purpose or singular opinion, but by common advice, counsel, and consent." Here we see a memorable advance in practice. Parliament itself must not however be deemed a fountain of wisdom and virtue. The instrument had no sure base. It could be packed or swayed. Many of the Parliaments of this period were dubbed with epithets: "the Good Parliament," "the Mad Parliament," "the Merciless Parliament," were fresh in memory. Moreover, the stakes in the game of power played by the great nobles were far beyond what ordinary men or magnates would risk. Who could tell that some sudden baronial exploit might not overset the whole structure upon which they stood? As each change of power had been attended by capital vengeance upon the vanquished there arose in the Commons a very solid and enduring desire to let the great lords cut each other's throats if they were so minded. Therefore the Commons, while acting with vigour, preferred to base themselves upon petition rather than resolution, thus throwing the responsibility definitely upon the most exalted ruling class.

Seeking further protection, they appealed to the King not to judge of any matter from their debates or from the part taken in them by various Members, but rather to await the collective decision of the House. They strongly pressed the doctrine of "grievances before supply," and although Henry refused to accept this claim he was kept so short of money that in practice it was largely conceded. During this time therefore Parliamentary power over finance was greatly strengthened. Not only did the Estates supply the money by voting the taxes, but they began to follow its expenditure, and to require and to receive accounts from the high officers of the State. Nothing like this had been tolerated by any of the Kings before. They had always condemned it as a presumptuous inroad upon their prerogative. These great advances in the polity of England were the characteristics of Lancastrian rule, and followed naturally from the need the house of Lancaster had to buttress its title by public opinion and constitutional authority. Thus Parliament in this early epoch appears to have gained ground never held again till the seventeenth century.

But although the spiritual and lay Estates had seemed not only to choose the sovereign but even to prescribe the succession to the Crown, and the history of these years furnished precedents which Stuart lawyers carefully studied, the actual power of Parliament at this time must not be overstated. The usurpation of Henry IV, the establishment of the rival house in the person of Edward IV, the ousting of Edward V by his uncle, were all acts of feudal violence and rebellion, covered up by declaratory statutes. Parliament was not the author, or even the powerful agent, in these changes, but only the apprehensive registrar of these results of martial and baronial struggles. Elections were not free: the pocket borough was as common in the fifteenth as in the eighteenth century, and Parliament was but the tool and seal of any successful party in the State. It had none the less been declared upon Parliamentary authority, although at Henry's instance, that the crown should pass to the King's eldest son, and to his male issue after him. Thus what had been the English usage was overridden by excluding an elder line dependent on a female link. This did not formally ban succession in the female line, but such was for a long time the practical effect.

On one issue indeed, half social, half religious, King and Parliament were heartily agreed. The Lollards' advocacy of a Church purified by being relieved of all worldly goods did not command the assent of the clergy. They resisted with wrath and vigour. Lollardy had bitten deep into the minds not only of the poorer citizens but of the minor gentry throughout the country. It was in essence a challenge first to the Church and then to the wealthy. The Lollards now sought to win the lay nobility by pointing out how readily the vast treasure of the Church might provide the money for Continental war. But this appeal fell upon deaf ears. The lords saw that their own estates stood on no better title than those of the Church. They therefore joined with the clergy in defence of their property. Very severe laws were now enacted against the Lollards. The King declared, in full agreement with the Estates, that he would destroy heresies with all his strength. In 1401 a terrible statute, *De Heretico Comburendo*, condemned relapsed heretics to be burnt alive, and left the judgment solely to the Church, requiring sheriffs to execute it without allowing an appeal to the Crown. Thus did orthodoxy and property make common cause and march together.

*　　*　　*　　*　　*

But the Estates of the Realm considered that their chief immediate safeguard lay in the blotting out of the eclipsed faction. They were the hottest against Richard and those who had been faithful to him. Henry might have been able to stem this tide of cowardly retribution but for a sinister series of events. He and most of his Court fell violently ill through something they had eaten, and poison was suspected. The Welsh, already discontented, under the leadership of Owen Glendower, presently espoused Richard's cause. The slowness of communication had enabled one set of forces to sweep the country while the opposite had hardly realized what was happening. Now they in their turn began to move. Five of the six former Lords Appellant, finding themselves in the shade, formed with friends of Richard II a plot to seize the usurping prince at Windsor. Recovered from his mysterious sickness, riding alone by dangerous roads, Henry evaded their trap. But armed risings appeared in several parts of the country. The severity with which these were quelled mounted to the summit of government. The populace in places joined with the Government forces. The townsfolk at Cirencester beheaded Lord Lumley and the Earls of Kent and Salisbury, the last a Lollard. The conspiracy received no genuine support. All the mercy of Henry's temper could not moderate the prosecutions enforced by those who shared his risks. Indeed in a year his popularity was almost destroyed by what was held to be his weakness in dealing with rebellion and attempted murder. Yet we must understand that he was a braver, stronger man than these cruel personages below him.

The unsuccessful revolt, the civil war which had begun for Richard after his fall, was fatal to the former King. A sanctity dwelt about his person, and all the ceremonial and constitutional procedure which enthroned his successor could not rob him of it. As he lay in Pontefract Castle he was the object of many sympathies both from his adherents and from the suppressed masses. And this chafed and gnawed the party in power. Richard's death was announced in February 1400. Whether he was starved, or, as the Government suggested, went on hunger strike, or whether more direct methods were used, is unknowable. The walls of Pontefract have kept their secret. But far and wide throughout England spread the tale that he had escaped, and that in concealment he awaited his hour to bring the common people of the time to the enjoyment of their own.

All this welled up against Henry of Bolingbroke. He faced continual murder plots. The trouble with the Welsh deepened into a national insurrection. Owen Glendower, who was a remarkable man, of considerable education, carried on a war which was the constant background of English affairs till 1409. The King was also forced to fight continually against the Scots. After six years of this harassment we are told that his natural magnanimity was worn out, and that he yielded himself to the temper of his supporters and of his Parliament in cruel deeds. It may well be so.

His most serious conflict was with the Percys. These lords of the Northern Marches, the old Earl of Northumberland and his fiery son Hotspur, had for nearly three years carried on the defence of England against the Scots unaided and almost entirely at their own expense. They also held important areas for the King in North Wales. They could no longer bear the burden. They demanded a settlement of the account. The Earl presented a bill for £60,000. The King, in bitter poverty, could offer but £40,000. Behind this was a longer tale. The Percys had played a great part in placing Henry on the throne. But Edmund Mortimer, Hotspur's brother-in-law, had joined Glendower in rebellion, and the family were now under suspicion. They held a great independent power, and an antagonism was perhaps inevitable. Hotspur raised the standard of revolt. But at Shrewsbury on July 21, 1403, Henry overcame and slew him in a small, fierce battle. The old

Earl, who was marching to his aid, was forced to submit, and pardon was freely extended to him. Parliament was at pains to absolve him from all charges of treason and rebellion and declared him guilty of trespass alone. This clemency was no doubt due to the necessities of the Border and to lack of any other means of defending it against the Scots. The Earl therefore addressed himself to this task, which secured his position at the head of strong forces.

But two years later, with his son's death at heart, he rebelled again, and this time the conspiracy was far-reaching. Archbishop Scrope of York and Thomas Mowbray, Earl of Nottingham, were his principal confederates. The programme of the rebellion was reform, and all personal issues were avoided. Once again Henry marched north, and once again he was successful. Northumberland was driven across the Border, where for some years he remained a menace. Scrope and Mowbray fell into the hands of the King's officers, and Henry, in spite of the appeals of the Archbishop of Canterbury, allowed them to be beheaded after a summary trial. Scrope's execution caused a profound shock throughout the land, and many compared it with the murder of Thomas Becket. At the same time the King's health failed. He was said to be smitten with leprosy, and this was attributed to the wrath of God. The diagnosis at least was incorrect. He had a disfiguring affection of the skin, and a disease of the heart, marked by fainting fits and trances. He was physically a broken man. Henceforward his reign was a struggle against death as well as life.

He still managed to triumph in the Welsh war, and Owen Glendower was forced back into his mountains. But Parliament took all advantages from the King's necessities. Henry saw safety only in surrender. He yielded himself and his burdens to the Estates with the constitutional deference of a modern sovereign. They pressed him hard, and in all the ways most intimately galling. Foreigners, not even excepting the Queen's two daughters, were to be expelled. A Council must be nominated by the King which included the Parliamentary leaders. The accounts of Government expenses were subjected to a Parliamentary audit. The King's own Household was combed and remodelled by unfriendly hands. The new Council demanded even fuller powers. The King pledged himself to govern only by their advice. By these submissions Henry became the least of kings. But he had transferred an intolerable task to others. They had the odium and the toil. They were increasingly unworthy of the trust.

*　*　*　*　*

A new figure now came upon the scene. Henry's eldest son, the Prince of Wales, showed already an extraordinary force and quality. He had led the charge against Hotspur at Shrewsbury. He had gained successes in Wales. It was only after the virtual defeat of Glendower that Prince Henry was free to turn to large political intrigue. As his father's health declined he was everywhere drawn into State business. He accepted all duties, and sought only for more. Pressed by his adherents, principally his half-uncles, the three Beaufort brothers, to take over the Government from the failing hands of an invalid, he headed a demand that the King should abdicate in his favour. But Henry of Bolingbroke, though tottering, repulsed the proposal with violent indignation. There was a stern confrontation of father and son at Westminster in 1411. The King's partisans appeared to be the more numerous or more resolute. The Prince withdrew abashed. He was removed from the presidency of the Council and his adherents were dismissed from office. He hid his head in retirement. His opponents even charged him with embezzling the pay of the Calais garrison. From this he cleared himself decisively. But there can be no doubt that the dying sovereign still gripped convulsively the reins of power. Misgovernment and decrepitude remained for a while successfully enthroned. In 1412, when the King could no longer walk and scarcely ride, he was with difficulty dissuaded by his Council from attempting to command the troops in Aquitaine. He lingered through the winter, talked of a Crusade, summoned Parliament in February, but could do no business with it. In March, when praying in Westminster Abbey, he had a prolonged fit, from which he rallied only to die in the Jerusalem Chamber on March 20, 1413.

Thus the life and reign of King Henry IV exhibit to us another instance of the vanities of ambition and the harsh guerdon which rewards its success. He had had wrongs to avenge and a cause to champion. He had hardly dared at first to aim at the crown, but he had played the final stake to gain it. He had found it less pleasing when possessed. Not only physically but morally he sank under its weight. His years of triumph were his years of care and sorrow. But none can say he had not reason and justice behind his actions, or that he was not accepted by the country at large. Upon his death a new personality, built upon a grand historic scale, long hungry for power, ascended without dispute the throne not only of England, but very soon of almost all Western Christendom.

CHAPTER TWENTY-FIVE

THE EMPIRE OF HENRY V

A GLEAM OF SPLENDOUR FALLS ACROSS THE DARK, TROUBLED STORY
of medieval England. Henry V was King at twenty-six. He felt, as his
father had never done, sure of his title. He had spent his youth in
camp and Council; he had for five or six years intermittently
conducted the government of the kingdom during his father's
decline. The romantic stories of his riotous youth and sudden
conversion to gravity and virtue when charged with the supreme
responsibility must not be pressed too far. It may well be true that
"he was in his youth a diligent follower of idle practices, much given
to instruments of music, and fired with the torches of Venus herself."
But if he had thus yielded to the vehement ebullitions of his nature
this was no more than a pastime, for always since boyhood he had
been held in the grasp of grave business.

In the surging realm, with its ailing King, bitter factions, and deep
social and moral unrest, all men had for some time looked to him;
and succeeding generations have seldom doubted that according to
the standards of his day he was all that a king should be. His face, we
are told, was oval, with a long, straight nose, ruddy complexion, dark,
smooth hair, and bright eyes, mild as a dove's when unprovoked,
but lion-like in wrath; his frame was slender, yet well-knit, strong and
active. His disposition was orthodox, chivalrous and just. He came to
the throne at a moment when England was wearied of feuds and brawl
and yearned for unity and fame. He led the nation away from internal

discord to foreign conquest; and he had the dream, and perhaps the prospect, of leading all Western Europe into the high championship of a Crusade. Council and Parliament alike showed themselves suddenly bent on war with France. As was even then usual in England, they wrapped this up in phrases of opposite import. The lords knew well, they said, "that the King will attempt nothing that is not to the glory of God, and will eschew the shedding of Christian blood; if he goes to war the cause will be the renewal of his rights, not his own wilfulness." Bishop Beaufort opened the session of 1414 with a sermon upon "Strive for the truth unto death" and the exhortation "While we have time, let us do good to all men." This was understood to mean the speedy invasion of France.

The Commons were thereupon liberal with supply. The King on his part declared that no law should be passed without their assent. A wave of reconciliation swept the land. The King declared a general pardon. He sought to assuage the past. He negotiated with the Scots for the release of Hotspur's son, and reinstated him in the Earldom of Northumberland. He brought the body, or reputed body, of Richard II to London, and re-interred it in Westminster Abbey, with pageantry and solemn ceremonial. A plot formed against him on the eve of his setting out for the wars was suppressed, by all appearance with ease and national approval, and with only a handful of executions. In particular he spared his cousin, the young Edmund Mortimer, Earl of March, who had been named as the rival King, through whose family much that was merciless was to follow later.

During the whole of 1414 Henry V was absorbed in warlike preparations by land and sea. He reorganised the Fleet. Instead of mainly taking over and arming private ships, as was the custom, he, like Alfred, built many vessels for the Royal Navy. He had at least six "great ships," with about fifteen hundred smaller consorts. The expeditionary army was picked and trained with special care. In spite of the more general resort to fighting on foot, which had been compelled by the long-bow, six thousand archers, of whom half were mounted infantry, were the bulk and staple of the army, together with two thousand five hundred noble, knightly, or otherwise substantial warriors in armour, each with his two or three attendants and aides.

In 1407 Louis, Duke of Orleans, the decisive power at the Court of the witless French King, Charles VI, had been murdered at the instigation of the Duke of Burgundy, and the strife of the two parties which divided France became violent and mortal. To this the late King of England had owed the comparative relief from foreign menace which eased the closing years of his reign. At Henry V's accession the Orleanists had gained the preponderance in France, and unfurled the Oriflamme against the Duke of Burgundy. Henry naturally allied himself with the weaker party, the Burgundians, who, in their distress, were prepared to acknowledge him as King of France. When he led the power of England across the Channel in continuation of the long revenge of history for Duke William's expedition he could count upon the support of a large part of what is now the French people. The English army of about ten thousand fighting men sailed to France on August 11, 1415, in a fleet of small ships, and landed without opposition at the mouth of the Seine. Harfleur was besieged and taken by the middle of September. The King was foremost in prowess:

Once more unto the breach, dear friends, once more;
Or close the wall up with our English dead.

In this mood he now invited the Dauphin to end the war by single combat. The challenge was declined. The attrition of the siege, and disease, which levied its unceasing toll on these medieval camps, had already wrought havoc in the English expedition. The main power of France was now in the field. The Council of War, on October 5, advised returning home by sea.

But the King, leaving a garrison in Harfleur, and sending home several thousand sick and wounded, resolved, with about a thousand knights and men-at-arms and four thousand archers, to traverse the French coast in a hundred-mile march to his fortress at Calais, where his ships were to await him. All the circumstances of this decision show that his design was to tempt the enemy to battle. This was not denied him. Marching by Fécamp and Dieppe, he had intended to cross the Somme at the tidal ford, Blanchetaque, which his great-grandfather had passed before Crécy. Falsely informed that the passage would be opposed, he moved by Abbeville; but here the bridge was broken down. He had to ascend the Somme to above Amiens by Boves and Corbie, and could only cross at the ford of Béthencourt. All these names are well known to our generation. On October 20 he camped near Péronne. He was now deeply plunged into France. It was the turn of the Dauphin to offer the grim courtesies of chivalric war. The French heralds came to the English camp and inquired, for mutual convenience, by which route His Majesty would desire to proceed. "Our path lies straight to Calais," was Henry's answer. This was not telling them much, for he had no other choice. The French army, which was already interposing itself, by a right-handed movement across his front fell back before his advance-guard behind the Canche river. Henry, moving by Albert, Frévent, and Blangy, learned that they were before him in apparently overwhelming numbers. He must now cut his way through, perish, or surrender. When one of his officers, Sir Walter Hungerford, deplored the fact "that they had not but one ten thousand of those men in England that do no work to-day," the King rebuked him and revived his spirits in a speech to which Shakespeare has given an immortal form:

> If we are marked to die, we are enough
> To do our country loss; and if to live,
> The fewer men, the greater share of honour.

"Wot you not," he actually said, "that the Lord with these few can overthrow the pride of the French?"[1] He and the "few" lay for the night at the village of Maisoncelles, maintaining utter silence and the strictest discipline. The French headquarters were at Agincourt, and it is said that they kept high revel and diced for the captives they should take.

The English victory of Crécy was gained against great odds upon the defensive. Poitiers was a counter-stroke. Agincourt ranks as the most heroic of all the land battles England has ever fought. It was a vehement assault. The French, whose numbers have been estimated at about twenty thousand, were drawn up in three lines of battle, of which a proportion remained mounted. With justifiable confidence they awaited the attack of less than a third their number, who, far from home and many marches from the sea, must win or die. Mounted upon a small grey horse, with a richly jewelled crown upon his helmet, and wearing his royal surcoat of leopards and lilies, the King drew up his array. The archers were disposed in six wedge-shaped formations, each supported by a body of men-at-arms. At the last moment Henry sought to avoid so desperate a battle. Heralds passed to and fro. He offered to yield Harfleur and all his prisoners in return for an open road to Calais. The French prince replied that he must renounce the crown of France. On this he resolved to dare the last extremity. The whole English army, even the King himself, dismounted and sent their horses to the rear; and shortly after eleven o'clock on St. Crispin's Day, October 25, he gave the order, "In the name of Almighty God and of Saint George, Avaunt Banner in the best time of the year, and Saint George this day be thine help." The archers kissed the soil in reconciliation to God, and, crying loudly, "Hurrah! Hurrah! Saint George and Merrie England!" advanced to within three hundred yards of the heavy masses in their front. They planted their stakes and loosed their arrows.

The French were once again unduly crowded upon the field. They stood in three dense lines, and neither their cross-bowmen nor their battery of cannon could fire effectively. Under the arrow storm they in their turn moved forward down the slope, plodding heavily through a ploughed field already trampled into a quagmire. Still at thirty deep they felt sure of breaking the line. But once again the long-bow destroyed all before it. Horse and foot alike went down; a long heap of armoured dead and wounded lay upon the ground, over which the reinforcements struggled bravely, but in vain. In this grand moment the archers slung their bows, and, sword in hand, fell upon the reeling squadrons and disordered masses. Then the Duke of Alençon rolled forward with the whole second line, and a stubborn hand-to-hand struggle ensued, in which the French prince struck down with his own sword Humphrey of Gloucester. The King rushed to his brother's rescue, and was smitten to the ground by a tremendous stroke; but in spite of the odds Alençon was killed, and the French second line was beaten hand to hand by the English chivalry and yeomen. It recoiled like the first, leaving large numbers of unwounded and still larger numbers of wounded prisoners in the assailants' hands.

Now occurred a terrible episode. The French third line, still intact, covered the entire front, and the English were no longer in regular array. At this moment the French camp-followers and peasantry, who had wandered round the English rear, broke pillaging into the camp and stole the King's crown, wardrobe, and Great Seal. The King, believing himself attacked from behind, while a superior force still remained unbroken on his front, issued the dread order to slaughter the prisoners. Then perished the flower of the French nobility, many of whom had yielded themselves to easy hopes of ransom. Only the most illustrious were spared. The desperate character of this act, and of the moment, supplies what defence can be found for its ferocity. It was not in fact a necessary recourse. The alarm in the rear was soon relieved; but not before the massacre was almost finished. The French third line quitted the field without attempting to renew the battle in any serious manner. Henry, who had declared at daybreak, "For me this day shall never England ransom pay,"[2] now saw his path to Calais clear before him. But far more than that: he had decisively broken in open battle at odds of more than three to one the armed chivalry of France. In two or at most three hours he had trodden underfoot at once the corpses of the slain and the will-power of the French monarchy.

After asking the name of the neighbouring castle and ordering that the battle should be called Agincourt after it, Henry made his way to Calais, short of food, but unmolested by the still superior forces which the French had set on foot. Within five months of leaving England he returned to London, having, before all Europe, shattered the French power by a feat of arms which, however it may be tested, must be held unsurpassed. He rode in triumph through the streets of London with spoils and captives displayed to the delighted people. He himself wore a plain dress, and he refused to allow his "bruised helmet and bended sword" to be shown to the admiring crowd, "lest they should forget that the glory was due to God alone." The victory of Agincourt made him the supreme figure in Europe.

When in 1416 the Holy Roman Emperor Sigismund visited London in an effort to effect a peace he recognised Henry as King of

ENGLISH POSSESSIONS
IN FRANCE IN THE
REIGN OF HENRY V

Calais
BURGUNDIAN
ARTOIS NETHERLANDS
Agincourt
LUXEM-
BURG

From
Southampton
Amiens
CHAMPAGNE
Harfleur
Seine
Paris

NORMANDY
Verneuil

BRITTANY
MAINE
Orleans
Troyes
Arc

Loire
ANJOU
TOURAINE
BERRY
BURGUNDY

Poitiers
POITOU

DAUPHINÉ

BAY OF BISCAY
LIMOUSIN
Rhône

Bordeaux
Castillon
GUIENNE

Garonne
ARMAGNAC

///// Lands held by Henry V
▶▶▶▶ First campaign of Henry V

ENGLISH MILES
0   50   100   150

France. But there followed long, costly campaigns and sieges which outran the financial resources of the Island and gradually cooled its martial ardour. A much larger expedition crossed the Channel in 1417. After a hard, long siege Caen was taken; and one by one every French stronghold in Normandy was reduced in successive years. After hideous massacres in Paris, led by the Burgundians, hot-headed supporters of the Dauphin murdered the Duke of Burgundy at Montereau in 1419, and by this deed sealed the alliance of Burgundy with England. Orleanist France was utterly defeated, not only in battle, but in the war. In May 1420, by the Treaty of Troyes, Charles VI recognised Henry as heir to the French kingdom upon his death and as Regent during his life. The English King undertook to govern with the aid of a Council of Frenchmen, and to preserve all ancient customs. Normandy was to be his in full sovereignty, but on his accession to the French throne would be reunited to France. He was accorded the title "King of England and Heir of France." To implement and consolidate these triumphs he married Charles's daughter Catherine, a comely princess, who bore him a son long to reign over impending English miseries.

"It was," says Ranke, "a very extraordinary position which Henry V now occupied. The two great kingdoms, each of which by itself has earlier or later claimed to sway the world, were (without being fused into one) to remain united for ever under him and his successors. . . . Burgundy was bound to him by ties of blood and by hostility to a common foe."[3] He induced Queen Johanna of Naples to adopt his eldest brother as her son and heir. The King of Castile and the heir of Portugal were descended from his father's sisters. Soon after his death the youngest of his brothers, Humphrey of Gloucester, married Jacqueline of Holland and Hainault, who possessed other lands as well. "The pedigrees of Southern and Western Europe alike met in the house of Lancaster, the head of which thus seemed to be the common head of all." It seemed to need only a Crusade, a high, sacred common cause against the advancing Ottoman power, to anneal the bonds which might have united, for a space at least, all Europe under an Englishman. The renewal of strife between England and France consumed powerful contingents which could have been used in defending Christendom against the Turkish menace.

This was the boldest bid the Island ever made in Europe. Henry V was no feudal sovereign of the old type with a class interest which overrode social and territorial barriers. He was entirely national in his outlook: he was the first King to use the English language in his letters and his messages home from the front; his triumphs were gained by English troops; his policy was sustained by a Parliament that could claim to speak for the English people. For it was the union of the country gentry and the rising middle class of the towns, working with the common lawyers, that gave the English Parliament thus early a character and a destiny that the States-General of France and the Cortes of Castile were not to know. Henry stood, and with him his country, at the summit of the world. He was himself endowed with the highest attributes of manhood. "No sovereign," says Stubbs, "who ever reigned has won from contemporary writers such a singular unison of praise. He was religious, pure in life, temperate, liberal, careful, and yet splendid, merciful, truthful, and honourable; 'discreet in word, provident in counsel, prudent in judgment, modest in look, magnanimous in act'; a brilliant soldier, a sound diplomatist, an able organiser and consolidator of all forces at his command; the restorer of the English Navy, the founder of our military, international, and maritime law. A true Englishman, with all the greatnesses and none of the glaring faults of his Plantagenet ancestors."

Ruthless he could also be on occasion, but the Chroniclers prefer to speak of his generosity and of how he made it a rule of his life to treat all men with consideration. He disdained in State business evasive or cryptic answers. "It is impossible" or "It shall be done" were the characteristic decisions which he gave. He was more deeply loved by his subjects of all classes than any King has been in England. Under him the English armies gained an ascendancy which for centuries was never seen again.

*   *   *   *   *

But glory was, as always, dearly bought. The imposing Empire of Henry V was hollow and false. Where Henry II had failed his successor could not win. When Henry V revived the English claims to France he opened the greatest tragedy in our medieval history. Agincourt was a glittering victory, but the wasteful and useless campaigns that followed more than outweighed its military and moral value, and the miserable, destroying century that ensued casts its black shadow upon Henry's heroic triumph.

And there is also a sad underside to the brilliant life of England in these years. If Henry V united the nation against France he set it also upon the Lollards. We can see that the Lollards were regarded not only as heretics, but as what we should now call Christian Communists. They had secured as their leader Sir John Oldcastle, a warrior of renown. They threatened nothing less than a revolution in faith and property. Upon them all domestic hatreds were turned by a devout and credulous age. It seemed frightful beyond words that they should declare that the Host lifted in the Mass was a dead thing, "less than a toad or a spider." Hostility was whetted by their policy of plundering the Church. Nor did the constancy of these martyrs to their convictions allay the public rage. As early as 1410 we have a strange, horrible scene, in which Henry, then Prince of Wales, was present at the execution of John Badby, a tailor of Worcestershire. He offered him a free pardon if he would recant. Badby refused and the faggots were lighted, but his piteous groans gave the Prince hope that he might still be converted. He ordered the fire to be extinguished, and again tempted the tortured victim with life, liberty, and a pension if he would but retract. But the tailor, with unconquerable constancy, called upon them to do their worst, and was burned to ashes, while the spectators marvelled alike at the Prince's merciful nature and the tailor's firm religious principles. Oldcastle, who, after a feeble insurrection in 1414, fled to the hills of Herefordshire, was captured at length, and suffered in his turn. These fearful obsessions weighed upon the age, and Henry, while King of the world, was but one of its slaves. This degradation lies about him and his times, and our contacts with his personal nobleness and prowess, though imperishable, are marred.

Fortune, which had bestowed upon the King all that could be dreamed of, could not afford to risk her handiwork in a long life. In the full tide of power and success he died at the end of August 1422 of a malady contracted in the field, probably dysentery, against which the medicine of those times could not make head. When he received the Sacrament and heard the penitential psalms, at the words "Build thou the walls of Jerusalem" he spoke, saying, "Good Lord, thou knowest that my intent has been and yet is, if I might live, to re-edify the walls of Jerusalem." This was his dying thought. He died with his work unfinished. He had once more committed his country to the murderous dynastic war with France. He had been the instrument of the religious and social persecution of the Lollards. Perhaps if he had lived the normal span his power might have become the servant of his virtues and produced the harmonies and tolerances which mankind so often seeks in vain. But Death drew his scythe across these prospects. The gleaming King, cut off untimely, went to his tomb amid the lamentations of his people, and the crown passed to his son, an infant nine months old.

CHAPTER TWENTY-SIX

JOAN OF ARC

A BABY WAS KING OF ENGLAND, AND TWO MONTHS LATER, ON THE death of Charles VI, was proclaimed without dispute the King of France. Bedford and Gloucester, his uncles, became Protectors, and with a Council comprising the heads of the most powerful families attempted to sustain the work of Henry V. A peculiar sanctity enshrined the hero's son, and the glory of Agincourt played radiantly around his cradle. Nurses, teachers, and presently noble guardians, carefully chosen for the boy's education and welfare, were authorised to use "reasonable chastisement" when required. But this was little needed, for the child had a mild, virtuous, honest, and merciful nature. His piety knew no bounds, and was, with hunting and a taste for literature, the stay and comfort of his long, ignominious, and terrifying pilgrimage. Through his father he inherited the physical weakness of the house of Lancaster, and through his mother the mental infirmities of Charles VI. He was feeble alike in body and mind, unwise and unstable in his judgments, profuse beyond his means to his friends, uncalculating against his enemies, so tender-hearted that it was even said he would let common thieves and murderers live, yet forced to bear the load of innumerable political executions. Flung about like a shuttlecock between the rival factions; presiding as a helpless puppet over the progressive decay of English society and power; hovering bewildered on the skirts of great battles; three times taken prisoner on the field; now paraded with all kingly pomp before Parliaments, armies, and crowds, now led in mockery through the streets, now a captive, now a homeless fugitive, hiding, hunted, hungry; afflicted from time to time by phases of total or partial idiocy, he endured in the fullest measure for nearly fifty years the extreme miseries of human existence, until the hand of murder dispatched him to a world which he was sure would be better, and could hardly have been worse than that he had known. Yet with all his shame of failure and incompetence, and the disasters these helped to bring upon his country, the English people recognised his goodness of heart and rightly ascribed to him the quality of holiness. They never lost their love for him; and in many parts of the country wherever the house of Lancaster was stubbornly defended he was venerated both as saint and martyr.

*   *   *   *   *

At the time of the great King's death the ascendancy of the English arms in France was established. In his brother, John, Duke of Bedford, who went to France as Regent and Commander-in-Chief, a successor of the highest military quality was found. The alliance with Burgundy, carrying with it the allegiance and the sympathies of Paris, persisted. The death, in October 1422, of the French king, who had signed the Treaty of Troyes, while it admitted the English infant to the kingship of France, nevertheless exposed his title to a more serious challenge. South of the Loire, except of course in Gascony, the Dauphin ruled and was now to reign. The war continued bitterly. Nothing could stand against the English archers. Many sieges and much ravaging distressed the countryside. In 1423 the Scots and French under the Earl of Buchan defeated the English at Beaugé, but three other considerable actions ended in English victories. At Cravant, in August 1423, the French found themselves aided by a strong Scottish contingent. These Scotsmen were animated by a hatred of the English which stood out above the ordinary feuds. But the English archers, with their Burgundian allies, shot most of them down. At Verneuil a year later this decision was repeated. Buchan, who had been made Constable of France after Beaugé, had induced his father-in-law, the Earl of Douglas, to bring over a new Scots army and to become Constable himself. The French, having had some success, were inclined to retire behind the Loire, but the rage of the Scots, of whom there were no fewer than five thousand under Douglas, Constable of Scotland, was uncontrollable. They forced a battle, and were nearly all destroyed by the arrow storm. Douglas, Buchan, and other Scottish chieftains fell upon the field, and so grievous was the slaughter of their followers that it was never again possible to form in these wars a separate Scottish brigade.

The English attempt to conquer all vast France with a few thousand archers led by warrior nobles, with hardly any money from home, and little food to be found in the ruined regions, reached its climax in the triumph of Verneuil. There seemed to the French to be no discoverable way to contend against these rugged, lusty, violent Islanders, with their archery, their flexible tactics, and their audacity, born of victories great and small under varying conditions and at almost any odds. Even five years later at the "Battle of the Herrings," gained in February 1429 by Sir John Falstaff, odds of six to one could not prevail. A convoy of four hundred wagons was bringing to the front the herrings indispensable to the English army during Lent. They were suddenly attacked on the road. But they formed their wagons into what we should now call a laager; the archers stood between and upon them, and at ranges greater than the muskets of Marlborough, Frederick the Great, or Napoleon could ever attain broke the whole assault. Yet the Dauphin, soon to be King Charles VII, stood for France, and everywhere, even in the subjugated provinces, a dull, deep sense of nationality, stirring not only in gentlefolk, but in all who could rise above the submerged classes, centred upon him.

At this time the loves and the acquisitiveness of the Duke of Gloucester, who in Bedford's absence in France became Protector of the English child-King, drove a wedge between England and Burgundy. Jacqueline, Princess of Hainault, Holland, and Zeeland, and heir to these provinces, a woman of remarkable spirit, at the high tide of her nature had been married for reasons of Burgundian policy to the Duke of Brabant, a sickly lout fifteen years of age. She revolted from this infliction, took refuge in England, and appealed to Gloucester for protection. This was accorded in full measure. Gloucester resolved to marry her, enjoy her company, and acquire her inheritance. Some form of divorce was obtained for Jacqueline from the Anti-Pope Benedict XIII, and the marriage took place early in 1423. This questionable romance gave deep offence to the Duke of Burgundy, whose major interests in the Low Countries were injured. Philip of Burgundy saw the world vindictively from his own standpoint. Hitherto his wrath against the treacherous murderers of his father had made him the Dauphin's relentless foe. But this English intrigue gave him a countervailing cause of personal malice, and when Gloucester in State correspondence accused him of falsehood, and in company with Jacqueline descended with a considerable force upon Hainault and Holland, his attachment to English interests became profoundly deranged. Although both Bedford in France and the English Council at home completely disclaimed Gloucester's action, and were prodigal in their efforts to repair the damage, and the Pope was moved by Philip of Burgundy to be tardy in the necessary annulments, the rift between England and Burgundy dates from this event. During these years also the Duke of Brittany detached himself from the English interest and hearkened to the appeals and offers of the French King. By the Treaty of Saumur in October 1425 he obtained the supreme direction of the war against the English. Although no results came to either side from his command the confederacy against France was weakened, and opportunity, faint, fleeting, was offered to the stricken land. The defects of the Dauphin, the exhaustion of the French monarchy, and the disorder and misery of the realm had however reached a pitch where all hung in the balance.

*　　*　　*　　*　　*

There now appeared upon the ravaged scene an Angel of Deliverance, the noblest patriot of France, the most splendid of her heroes, the most beloved of her saints, the most inspiring of all her memories, the peasant Maid, the ever-shining, ever-glorious Joan of Arc. In the poor, remote hamlet of Domrémy, on the fringe of the Vosges Forest, she served at the inn. She rode the horses of travellers, bareback, to water. She wandered on Sundays into the woods, where there were shrines, and a legend that some day from these oaks would arise one to save France. In the fields where she tended her sheep the saints of God, who grieved for France, rose before her in visions. St. Michael himself

appointed her, by right divine, to command the armies of liberation. Joan shrank at first from the awful duty, but when he returned
attended by St. Margaret and St. Catherine, patronesses of the village
church, she obeyed their command. There welled in the heart of the
Maid a pity for the realm of France, sublime, perhaps miraculous,
certainly invincible.

Like Mahomet, she found the most stubborn obstacle in her own
family. Her father was scandalised that she should wish to ride in
male attire among rough soldiers. How indeed could she procure
horses and armour? How could she gain access to the King? But
the saints no doubt felt bound to set her fair upon her course.
She convinced Baudricourt, governor of the neighbouring town,
that she was inspired. He recommended her to a Court ready to
clutch at straws. She made a perilous journey across France. She
was conducted to the King's presence in the immense stone pile of
Chinon. There, among the nobles and courtiers in the great hall,
under the flaring torches, she at once picked out the King, who had
purposely mingled with the crowd. "Most noble Lord Dauphin," she
said, "I am Joan the Maid, sent on the part of God to aid you and the
kingdom, and by His order I announce that you will be crowned in
the city of Rheims." The aspersion that he was a bastard had always
troubled Charles, and when the Maid picked him out among the
crowd he was profoundly moved. Alone with him, she spoke of State
secrets which she must either have learned from the saints or from
other high authority. She asked for an ancient sword which she had
never seen, but which she described minutely before it was found. She
fascinated the royal circle. When they set her astride on horseback
in martial guise it was seen that she could ride. As she couched her
lance the spectators were swept with delight.

Policy now, if not earlier, came to play a part. The supernatural
character of the Maid's mission was spread abroad. To make sure that
she was sent by Heaven and not from elsewhere, she was examined
by a committee of theologians, by the Parlement of Poitiers, and by
the whole Royal Council. She was declared a virgin of good intent,
inspired by God. Indeed, her answers were of such a quality that the
theory has been put forward that she had for some-time been carefully

nurtured, and trained for her mission. This at least would be a reasonable explanation of the known facts.

Orleans in 1429 lay under the extremities of siege. A few thousand English, abandoned by the Burgundians, were slowly reducing the city by an incomplete blockade. Their self-confidence and prestige hardened them to pursue the attack of a fortress deep in hostile territory, whose garrison was four times their number. They had built lines of redoubts, within which they felt themselves secure. The Maid now claimed to lead a convoy to the rescue. In armour plain and without ornament, she rode at the head of the troops. She restored their spirits; she broke the spell of English dominance. She captivated not only the rough soldiery but their hard-bitten leaders. Her plan was simple. She would march straight into Orleans between the strongest forts. But the experienced captain, Dunois, a bastard of the late Duke of Orleans, had not proposed to lead his convoy by this dangerous route. As the Maid did not know the map he embarked his supplies in boats, and brought her by other ways into the besieged town almost alone. She was received with rapture. But the convoy, beaten back by adverse winds, was forced after all to come in by the way she had prescribed; and in fact it marched for a whole day between the redoubts of the English while they gaped at it dumbfounded.

The report of a supernatural visitant sent by God to save France, which inspired the French, clouded the minds and froze the energies of the English. The sense of awe, and even of fear, robbed them of their assurance. Dunois returned to Paris, leaving the Maid in Orleans. Upon her invocation the spirit of victory changed sides, and the French began an offensive which never rested till the English invaders were driven out of France. She called for an immediate onslaught upon the besiegers, and herself led the storming parties against them. Wounded by an arrow, she plucked it out and returned to the charge. She mounted the scaling-ladders and was hurled half stunned into the ditch. Prostrate on the ground, she commanded new efforts. "Forward, fellow-countrymen!" she cried. "God has delivered them into our hands." One by one the English forts fell and their garrisons were slain. The Earl of Suffolk was captured, the siege broken, and Orleans saved. The English retired in good order, and the Maid prudently restrained the citizens from pursuing them into the open country.

Joan now was head indeed of the French army; it was dangerous even to dispute her decisions. The contingents from Orleans would obey none but her. She fought in fresh encounters; she led the assault upon Jargeau, thus opening the Loire above Orleans. In June 1429 she marched with the army that gained the victory of Patay. She told Charles he must march on Rheims to be crowned upon the throne of his ancestors. The idea seemed fantastic: Rheims lay deep in enemy country. But under her spell he obeyed, and everywhere the towns opened their gates before them and the people crowded to his aid. With all the pomp of victory and faith, with the most sacred ceremonies of ancient days, Charles was crowned at Rheims. By his side stood the Maid, resplendent, with her banner proclaiming the Will of God. If this was not a miracle it ought to be.

Joan now became conscious that her mission was exhausted; her "voices" were silent; she asked to be allowed to go home to her sheep and the horses of the inn. But all adjured her to remain. The French captains who conducted the actual operations, though restive under her military interference, were deeply conscious of her value to the cause. The Court was timid and engaged in negotiations with the Duke of Burgundy. A half-hearted attack was made upon Paris. Joan advanced to the forefront and strove to compel victory. She was severely wounded and the leaders ordered the retreat. When she recovered she again sought release. They gave her the rank and revenue of an earl.

But the attitude both of the Court and the Church was changing towards Joan. Up to this point she had championed the Orleanist cause. After her "twenty victories" the full character of her mission appeared. It became clear that she served God rather than the Church, and France rather than the Orleans party. Indeed, the whole conception of France seems to have sprung and radiated from her. Thus the powerful particularist interests which had hitherto supported her were estranged. Meanwhile she planned to regain Paris for France. When in May 1430 the town of Compiègne revolted against the decision of the King that it should yield to the English, Joan with only six hundred men attempted its succour. She had no doubt that the enterprise was desperate. It took the form of a cavalry sortie across the long causeway over the river. The enemy, at first surprised, rallied, and a panic among the French ensued. Joan, undaunted, was bridled from the field by her friends. She still fought with the rearguard across the causeway. The two sides were intermingled. The fortress itself was imperilled. Its cannon could not fire upon the confused *mêleé*. Flavy, the governor whose duty it was to save the town, felt obliged to pull up the drawbridge in her face and leave her to the Burgundians.

She was sold to the rejoicing English for a moderate sum. To Bedford and his army she was a witch, a sorceress, a harlot, a foul imp of black magic, at all costs to be destroyed. But it was not easy to frame a charge; she was a prisoner of war, and many conventions among the warring aristocrats protected her. The spiritual arm was therefore invoked. The Bishop of Beauvais, the learned doctors of Paris, pursued her for heresy. She underwent prolonged inquisition. The gravamen was that by refusing to disown her "voices" she was defying the judgment and authority of the Church. For a whole year her fate hung in the balance, while careless, ungrateful Charles lifted not a finger to save her. There is no record of any ransom being offered. Joan had recanted under endless pressure, and had been accorded all the mercy of perpetual imprisonment on bread and water. But in her cell the inexorable saints appeared to her again. Entrapping priests set her armour and man's clothes before her; with renewed exaltation she put them on. From that moment she was declared a relapsed heretic and condemned to the fire. Amid an immense concourse she was dragged to the stake in the market-place of Rouen. High upon the pyramid of faggots the flames rose towards her, and the smoke of doom wreathed and curled. She raised a cross made of firewood, and her last word was "Jesus!" History has recorded the comment of an English soldier who witnessed the scene. "We are lost," he said. "We have burnt a saint." All this proved true.

Joan was a being so uplifted from the ordinary run of mankind that she finds no equal in a thousand years. The records of her trial present us with facts alive to-day through all the mists of time. Out of her own mouth can she be judged in each generation. She embodied the natural goodness and valour of the human race in unexampled perfection. Unconquerable courage, infinite compassion, the virtue of the simple, the wisdom of the just, shone forth in her. She glorifies as she freed the soil from which she sprang. All soldiers should read her story and ponder on the words and deeds of the true warrior, who in one single year, though untaught in technical arts, reveals in every situation the key of victory.

Joan of Arc perished on May 29, 1431, and thereafter the tides of war flowed remorselessly against the English. The boy Henry was crowned in Paris in December amid chilly throngs. The whole spirit of the country was against the English claim. Burgundy became definitely hostile in 1435. Bedford died, and was succeeded by lesser captains. The opposing Captain-in-Chief, Dunois, instead of leading French chivalry to frontal attacks upon the English archer array, acted by manœuvre and surprise. The French gained a series of battles. Here they caught the English men-at-arms on one side of the river while their archers were on the other; there by a cannonade they forced a disjointed English attack. The French artillery now became the finest in the world. Seven hundred engineers, under the brothers Bureau, used a heavy battering-train of twenty-two inches calibre, firing gigantic stone balls against the numberless castles which the English still held. Places which in the days of Henry V could be reduced only by famine now fell in a few days to smashing bombardment. All Northern France, except Calais, was reconquered. Even Guienne, dowry of Eleanor of Aquitaine, for three hundred years a loyal, contented fief of the English Crown, was overran. It is remarkable however that this province almost immediately revolted against France, called upon the English to return, and had to be subdued anew. The Council of competing noble factions in England was incapable of providing effective succour. The valiant Talbot, Earl of Shrewsbury, was killed with most of his English in his foolhardy battle of Castillon in 1453. The surviving English made terms to sail home from La Rochelle. By the end of that year, through force or negotiation, the English had been driven off the Continent. Of all their conquests they held henceforward only the bridgehead of Calais, to garrison which cost nearly a third of the revenue granted by Parliament to the Crown.

CHAPTER TWENTY-SEVEN

YORK AND LANCASTER

AS HENRY VI GREW UP HIS VIRTUES AND SIMPLENESS BECAME EQUALLY apparent. He was not entirely docile. In 1431 when he was ten years old Warwick, his preceptor, reported that he was "grown in years, in stature of his person, and also in conceit and knowledge of his royal estate, the which causes him to grudge any chastising." He had spoken "of divers matters not behoveful." The Council had in his childhood made a great show of him, brought him to ceremonies, and crowned him with solemnity both in London and Paris. As time passed they became naturally inclined to keep him under stricter control. His consequence was maintained by the rivalry of the nobles, and by the unbounded hopes of the nation. A body of knights and squires had for some years been appointed to dwell with him and be his servants. As the disastrous years in France unfolded he was pressed continually to assert himself. At fifteen he was already regularly attending Council meetings. He was allowed to exercise a measure of prerogative both in pardons and rewards. When the Council differed it was agreed he should decide. He often played the part of mediator by compromise. Before he was eighteen he had absorbed himself in the foundation of his colleges at Eton and at Cambridge. He was thought by the high nobles to take a precocious and unhealthy interest in public affairs which neither his wisdom nor experience could sustain. He showed a feebleness of mind and spirit and a gentleness of nature which were little suited to the fierce rivalries of a martial age. Opinion and also interests were divided upon him. Flattering accounts of his remarkable intelligence were matched by other equally biased tales that he was an idiot almost incapable of distinguishing between right and wrong. Modern historians confirm the less complimentary view. At the hour when a strong king alone could re-create the balance between the nation and the nobility, when all demanded the restraint of faction at home and the waging of victorious war without undue expense abroad, the throne was known to be occupied by a devout simpleton suited alike by his qualities and defects to be a puppet.

These were evil days for England. The Crown was beggarly, the nobles rich. The people were unhappy and unrestful rather than unprosperous. The religious issues of an earlier century were now dominated by more practical politics. The empire so swiftly gained upon the Continent was being cast away by an incompetent and self-enriching oligarchy, and the revenues which might have sent irresistible armies to beat the French were engrossed by the Church.

The princes of the house of Lancaster disputed among themselves. After Bedford's death in 1435 the tension grew between Gloucester and the Beauforts. Cardinal Beaufort, Bishop of Winchester, and one of the legitimised sons of John of Gaunt's third union, was himself the richest man in England, and a prime master of such contributions as the Church thought it prudent to make to the State. From his private fortune, upon pledges which could only be redeemed in gold, he constantly provided the Court, and often the Council, with ready money. Leaning always to the King, meddling little with the ill-starred conduct of affairs, the Beauforts, with whom must be counted William de la Pole, Earl of Suffolk, maintained by peaceful arts and critical detachment an influence to which the martial elements were often forced to defer. The force of this faction was in 1441 turned in malice upon the Duke of Gloucester. He was now wedded, after the invalidation of his marriage with his wife Jacqueline, to the fair Eleanor Cobham, who had long been his mistress. As the weakest point in his array she was singled out for attack, and was accused with much elaboration of lending herself to the black arts. She had made, it was alleged, a wax figure of the King, and had exposed it from time to time to heat, which wasted it away.

Her object, according to her accusers, was to cause the King's life to waste away too. She was declared guilty. Barefoot, in penitential garb, she was made to walk for three days through the London streets, and then consigned to perpetual imprisonment with reasonable maintenance. Her alleged accomplices were put to death. This was of course a trial of strength between the parties and a very real pang and injury to Gloucester.

The loss of France, as it sank in year by year, provoked a deep, sullen rage throughout the land. This passion stirred not only the nobility, but the archer class with their admiring friends in every village. A strong sense of wounded national pride spread among the people. Where were the glories of Crécy and Poitiers? Where were the fruits of famous Agincourt? All were squandered, or indeed betrayed, by those who had profited from the overthrow and murder of good King Richard. There were not lacking agitators and preachers, priestly and lay, who prepared a national and social upheaval by reminding folks that the true line of succession had been changed by violence. All this was an undercurrent, but none the less potent. It was a background, shadowy but dominant. Exactly how these forces worked is unknown; but slowly, ceaselessly, there grew in the land, not only among the nobility and gentry, strong parties which presently assumed both shape and organisation.

At twenty-three it was high time that King Henry should marry. Each of the Lancastrian factions was anxious to provide him with a queen; but Cardinal Beaufort and his brothers, with their ally, Suffolk, whose ancestors, the de la Poles of Hull, had founded their fortunes upon trade, prevailed over the Duke of Gloucester, weakened as he was by maladministration and ill-success. Suffolk was sent to France to arrange a further truce, and it was implied in his mission that he should treat for a marriage between the King of England and Margaret of Anjou, niece of the King of France. This remarkable woman added to rare beauty and charm a masterly intellect and a dauntless spirit. Like Joan the Maid, though without her inspiration or her cause, she knew how to make men fight. Even from the seclusion of her family her qualities became well known. Was she not then the mate for this feeble-minded King? Would she not give him the force that he lacked? And would not those who placed her at his side secure a large and sure future for themselves?

Suffolk was well aware of the delicacy and danger of his mission. He produced from the King and the lords an assurance that if he acted to the best of his ability he should not be punished for ill consequences, and that any errors proved against him should be pardoned in advance. Thus fortified he addressed himself to his task with a zeal which proved fatal to him. The father of Margaret, René of Anjou, was not only cousin of the French King, his favourite and his Prime Minister, but in his own right King of Jerusalem and of Sicily. These magnificent titles were not sustained by practical enjoyments. Jerusalem was in the hands of the Turks, he did not own a square yard in Sicily, and half his patrimony of Anjou and Maine was for years held by the English army. Suffolk was enthralled by Margaret. He made the match; and in his eagerness, by a secret article, agreed without formal authority that Maine should be the reward of France. So strong was the basic power of Gloucester's faction, so sharp was the antagonism against France, so loud were the whispers that England had been betrayed in her wars, that the clause was guarded as a deadly secret. The marriage was solemnised in 1445 with such splendour as the age could afford. Suffolk was made a marquis, and several of his relations were ennobled. The King was radiantly happy, the Queen faithfully grateful. Both Houses of Parliament recorded their thanks to Suffolk for his public achievement. But the secret slumbered uneasily, and as the sense of defeat at the hands of France spread through ever-widening circles its inevitable disclosure boded a mortal danger.

During the six years following the condemnation of his wife Eleanor in 1441 Gloucester had been living in retirement, amusing himself with collecting books. His enemies at this grave juncture resolved upon his final overthrow. Suffolk and Edmund Beaufort, nephew of the Cardinal, supported by the Dukes of Somerset and Buckingham, with the Queen in their midst and the King in their charge, arrested Gloucester when he came to a Parliament summoned at St. Edmondsbury, where an adequate royal force had been secretly assembled. Seventeen days later Gloucester's corpse was displayed, so that all could see there was no wound upon it. But the manner of

Edward II's death was too well known for this proof to be accepted. It was generally believed, though wrongly, that Gloucester had been murdered by the express direction of Suffolk and Edmund Beaufort. It has however been suggested that his death was induced by choler and amazement at the ruin of his fortunes.

It soon appeared that immense forces of retribution were on foot. When in 1448 the secret article for the cession of Maine became public through its occupation by the French anger was expressed on all sides. England had paid a province, it was said, for a princess without a dowry; traitors had cast away much in the field, and given up the rest by intrigue. At the root of the fearful civil war soon to rend the Island there lay this national grief and wrath at the ruin of empire. All other discontents fused themselves with this. The house of Lancaster had usurped the throne, had ruined the finances, had sold the conquests, and now had stained their hands with foul murder. From these charges all men held the King absolved alike by his good heart and silly head. But henceforward the house of York increasingly becomes a rival party within the State.

Edmund Beaufort, now Duke of Somerset, became commander of the army in France. Suffolk remained at home to face a gathering vengeance. The Navy was disaffected. Bishop Moleyns, Keeper of the Privy Seal, sent to Portsmouth to pay what could be paid to the Fleet, was abused by the sailors as a traitor to the country, and murdered in a riot of the troops about to reinforce Somerset in France. The officer commanding the fortresses which were to be ceded to France had refused to deliver them. The French armies advanced and took with a strong hand all that was now denied. Suffolk was impeached. The King and Margaret strove, as in honour bound, to save him. Straining his prerogative, Henry burked the proceedings by sending him in 1450 into a five years' exile. We now see an instance of the fearful state of indiscipline into which England was drifting. When the banished Duke was crossing the Channel with his attendants and treasure in two small vessels, the *Nicholas of the Tower*, the largest warship in the Royal Navy, bore down upon him and carried him on board. He was received by the captain with the ominous words "Welcome, traitor," and two days later he was lowered into a boat and beheaded by six strokes of a rusty sword. It is a revealing sign of the times that a royal ship should seize and execute a royal Minister who was travelling under the King's special protection.

In June and July a rising took place in Kent, which the Lancastrians claimed to bear the marks of Yorkist support. Jack Cade, a soldier of capacity and bad character, home from the wars, gathered several thousand men, all summoned in due form by the constables of the districts, and marched on London. He was admitted to the city, but on his executing Lord Say, the Treasurer, in Cheapside, after a mob trial, the magistrates and citizens turned against him, his followers dispersed under terms of pardon, and he himself was pursued and killed. This success restored for the moment the authority of the Government, and Henry enjoyed a brief interlude in which he devoted himself anew to his colleges at Eton and Cambridge, and to Margaret, who had gained his love and obedience.

As the process of expelling the English from France continued fortresses fell, towns and districts were lost, and their garrisons for the most part came home. The speed of this disaster contributed powerfully to shock English opinion and to shake not only the position of individual Ministers but the very foundations of the Lancastrian dynasty. With incredible folly and bad faith the English broke the truce at Fougères in March 1449. By August 1450 the whole of Normandy was lost. By August 1451 the whole of Gascony, English for three centuries, had been lost as well, and of all the conquests of Henry V which had taken England eleven years of toil and blood to win only Calais remained. Edmund Beaufort, the King's commander, friend, and Lancastrian cousin, bore the blame for unbroken defeat, and this reacted on the King himself. England became full of what we should call "ex-Service men," who did not know why they had been beaten, but were sure they had been mishandled and had fought in vain. The nobles, in the increasing disorder, were glad to gather these hardened fighters to their local defence. All the great houses kept bands of armed retainers, sometimes almost amounting to private armies. They gave them pay or land, or both, and uniforms or liveries bearing the family crest. The Earl of Warwick, perhaps the greatest landowner, who aspired to a leading part in politics, had thousands of dependants who ate what was called "his bread," and of these a large proportion were organised troops proud to display the badge of the Bear and the Ragged Staff. Other magnates emulated this example according to their means. Cash and ambition ruled and the land sank rapidly towards anarchy. The King was a helpless creature, respected, even beloved, but no prop for any man. Parliament, both Lords and Commons, was little more than a clearing-house for the rivalries of nobles.

A statute of 1429 had fixed the county franchise at the forty-shilling freeholder. It is hard to realise that this arbitrarily contracted franchise ruled in England for four hundred years, and that all the wars and quarrels, the decision of the greatest causes, the grandest events at home and abroad, proceeded upon this basis until the Reform Bill of 1832. In the preamble to this Act it was alleged that the participation in elections of too great a number of people "of little substance or worth" had led to homicides, riots, assaults, and feuds. So was a backward but enduring step taken in Parliamentary representation. Yet never for centuries had the privilege of Parliament stood so high. Never for centuries was it more blatantly exploited.

The force of law was appropriated by intrigue. Baronial violence used or defied legal forms with growing impunity. The Constitution was turned against the public. No man was safe in life or lands, or even in his humblest right, except through the protection of his local chief. The celebrated Paston Letters show that England, enormously advanced as it was in comprehension, character, and civilisation, was relapsing from peace and security into barbaric confusion. The roads were insecure. The King's writ was denied or perverted. The royal judges were flouted or bribed. The rights of sovereignty were stated in the highest terms, but the King was a weak and handled fool. The powers of Parliament could be turned this way and that according as the factions gripped it. Yet the suffering, toiling, unconquerable community had moved far from the days of Stephen and Maud, of Henry II and Thomas à Becket, and of King John and the barons. There was a highly complex society, still growing in spite of evils in many regions. The poverty of the Executive, the difficulties of communication, and the popular strength in bills and bows all helped to hold it in balance. There was a public opinion. There was a collective moral sense. There were venerated customs. Above all there was a national spirit.

*   *   *   *   *

It was upon this community that the agonies of the Wars of the Roses were now to fall. We must not underrate either the great issues which led to the struggle or the conscious, intense, prolonged efforts made to avert it. The need of all men and their active desire was for a strong and capable Government. Some thought this could only be obtained by aiding the lawful, established régime. Others had been for a long time secretly contending that a usurpation had been imposed upon them which had now become incompetent. The claims and hopes of the opposition to the house of Lancaster were embodied in Richard, Duke of York. According to established usage he had a prior right to the crown. York was the son of Richard, Earl of Cambridge, and grandson of Edmund, Duke of York, a younger brother of John of Gaunt. As the great-grandson of Edward III he was the only other person besides Henry VI with an unbroken male descent from Edward III, but in the female line he had also a superior claim through his descent from Gaunt's elder brother, Lionel of Clarence. By the Act of 1407 the Beauforts—Gaunt's legitimised bastards—had been barred from the succession. If Henry VI should succeed in annulling the Act of 1407 then Edmund Beaufort (Somerset) would have a better good male claim with York. It was this that York feared. York had taken Gloucester's place as first Prince of the Blood. After Gloucester's death there survived no male of the legitimate house of Lancaster save Henry VI. Around York and beneath him there gathered an immense party of discontent, which drove him hesitantly to demand a place in the Government, and eventually, through Queen Margaret's increasing hostility, the throne itself.

A Yorkist network grew up in all parts of the country, but mainly in the South and West of England, in Kent, in London, and in Wales. It was significant that Jack Cade, at the head of the Kentish insurgents, had pretended to the name of Mortimer. It was widely believed that the Yorkists, as they began to style themselves, had procured the murder of Bishop Moleyns at Portsmouth, and of Suffolk on the high seas. Blood had thus already flowed between the houses of Lancaster and York.

In these conditions the character of Richard of York deserves close study. He was a virtuous, law-respecting, slow-moving, and highly competent prince. Every office entrusted to him by the Lancastrian régime had been ably and faithfully discharged. He had given good service. He would have been content with the government of Calais and what was left of France, but being deprived of this for the sake of Somerset he accepted the government of Ireland. Not only did he subdue part of that island, but in the very process he won the good-will of the Irish people. Thus we see on the one side a weak King with a defective title in the hands of personages discredited by national disaster, and now with blood-guilt upon them, and on the other an upright and wise administrator supported by a nation-wide party and with some superior title to the crown.

Anyone who studies the argument which now tore the realm will see how easily honest men could convince themselves of either cause. When King Henry VI realised that his right to the throne was impugned he was mildly astonished. "Since my cradle, for forty years," he said, "I have been King. My father was King; his father was King. You have all sworn fealty to me on many occasions, as your fathers swore it to my father." But the other side declared that oaths not based on truth were void, that wrong must be righted, that successful usurpation gained no sanctity by time, that the foundation of the monarchy could only rest upon law and justice, that to recognise a dynasty of interlopers was to invite rebellion whenever occasion served, and thus dissolve the very frame of English society; and, finally, that if expediency were to rule, who could compare the wretched half-wit King, under whom all was going to ruin, with a prince who had proved himself a soldier and a statesman of the highest temper and quality?

All England was divided between these two conceptions. Although the Yorkists predominated in the rich South, and the Lancastrians were supreme in the warlike North, there were many interlacements and overlaps. While the townsfolk and the mass of the people, upon the whole, abstained from active warfare in this struggle of the upper classes and their armed retainers, and some thought "the fewer nobles

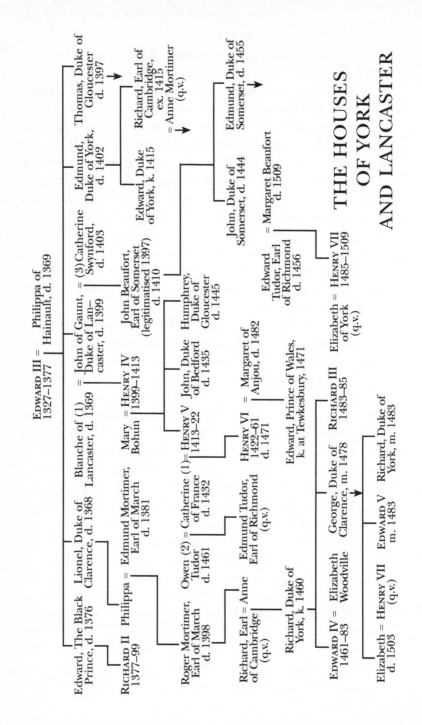

THE HOUSES
OF YORK
AND LANCASTER

the better," their own opinion was also profoundly divided. They venerated the piety and goodness of the King; they also admired the virtues and moderation of the Duke of York. The attitude and feeling of the public, in all parts and at all times, weighed heavily with both contending factions. Thus Europe witnessed the amazing spectacle of nearly thirty years of ferocious war, conducted with hardly the sack of a single town, and with the mass of the common people little affected and the functions of local government very largely maintained.

*　　*　　*　　*　　*

In 1450 the ferment of discontent and rivalries drew the Duke of York into his first overt act. He quitted his government in Ireland and landed unbidden in Wales. During the Parliamentary session of the following year a member of the Commons, one Young, boldly proposed that the Duke of York should be declared heir to the throne. This demand was formidable, not only for its backing, but for its good sense. The King had now been married for six years and had no child. The repute in which he stood made it seem unlikely that he would have any. Ought he not, men asked at this time, to designate his successor? If not York, whom then? It could only be Somerset or another representative of the Beaufort line. One can see how shrewdly this thrust was made. But the King, animated certainly by Margaret, repulsed it with unwonted vigour. He refused to abandon his hope of progeny, and, as soon as the Parliament had dispersed, sent the presumptuous Member to the Tower. At this time, also, he broke with the Duke of York, who retired to his castle at Ludlow, on the borders of Wales.

Disgusted by the Government's failure to restore order and justice at home, and to prevent military disasters in France, York became more and more convinced that the Beaufort party, which dominated the weak-willed King, must be driven from power. Prayers and protests had failed; there remained the resort to arms. Accordingly, on February 3, 1452, York sent an address to the citizens of Shrewsbury, accusing Somerset of the disgrace in France and of "labouring continually about the King's Highness for my undoing, and to corrupt my blood and to disinherit me and my heirs and such persons as be about me . . . Seeing that the said Duke ever prevaileth and ruleth about the King's person, and advises him so ill that the land is likely to be destroyed, I may full conclude to proceed in all haste against him with the help of my kinsmen and friends." On this he marched from Shrewsbury towards London, with an army of several thousand men, including artillery. He moved into Kent, plainly expecting that those who had marched with Jack Cade would rally to his cause. The response was disappointing. London closed its gates against his emissaries. The King was carried by Margaret, Somerset, and the Lancastrian interests to Blackheath, with a superior force. Civil war seemed about to begin.

But York felt himself the weaker. He was constitutionally averse from violence. Norfolk was on his side, and other great nobles, but the Earl of Warwick, twenty-four years old, was with the King. Every effort was made to prevent bloodshed. Parleys were unending. In the event York dispersed his forces and presented himself unarmed and bareheaded before King Henry, protesting his loyalty, but demanding redress. His life hung by a thread. Few about the King's person would have scrupled to slay him. But all knew the consequences. York stood for a cause; he was supported by the Commons; half the nation was behind him; his youthful son, the Earl of March, had a second army on foot on the Welsh border. York declared himself "the King's liegeman and servant." Since he was supported by the Commons and evidently at the head of a great party, the King promised that "a sad and substantial Council" should be formed of which he should be a member. The Court had still to choose between Somerset and York. The Queen, always working with Somerset, decided the issue in his favour. He was appointed Constable of Calais, garrisoned by the only regular troops in the pay of the Crown, and was in fact for more than a year at the head of affairs both in France and at home.

Then in quick succession a series of grave events occurred. The disasters culminated in France. Talbot's attempt to reconquer Gascony failed; he was defeated at Castillon in July 1453, and Bordeaux fell in October. Somerset, the chief commander, bore the burden of defeat. In this situation the King went mad. He had gone down to Wiltshire to spend July and August. Suddenly his memory failed. He recognised no one, not even the Queen. He could eat and drink, but his speech was childish or incoherent. He could not walk. For another fifteen months he remained entirely without comprehension. Afterwards, when he recovered, he declared he remembered nothing. The pious Henry had been withdrawn from the worry of existence to an island of merciful oblivion. His body gaped and drivelled over the bristling realm.

When these terrible facts became known Queen Margaret aspired to be Protector. But the adverse forces were too strong for the Lancastrian party to make the challenge. Moreover, she had another preoccupation. On October 13 she gave birth to a son. How far this event was expected is not clear, but, as long afterwards with James II, it inevitably hardened the hearts of all men. It seemed to shut out for ever the Yorkist claim. Hitherto neither side had been inclined to go to extremes. If Lancaster ruled during the life of Henry, York would succeed at his death, and both sides could accommodate themselves to this natural and lawful process. Now it seemed there would be a Lancastrian ascendancy for ever.

The insanity of the King defeated Somerset: he could no longer withstand York. Norfolk, one of York's supporters, presented a petition against him to the Council, and in December 1453 he was committed to the Tower. The strength of York's position bore him to the Protectorate. He moved by Parliamentary means and with great moderation, but he was not to be withstood. He obtained full control of the Executive, and enjoyed the support of both Houses of Parliament. He had not long to show his qualities, but an immediate improvement in the administration was recognised. He set to work with cool vigour to suppress livery and maintenance and to restore order on the roads and throughout the land. He did not hesitate to imprison several of his own most prominent adherents, among them the Earl of Devonshire, for levying a private war. If he refrained from bringing Somerset, who was still imprisoned, to trial, this was only from mercy. His party were astounded at his tolerance. When the Government was in his hands, when his future was marred by the new heir, to the Crown, when his power or his life might be destroyed at any moment by the King's recovery, he kept absolute faith with right and justice. Here then is his monument and justification. He stands before history as a patriot ready to risk his life to protect good government, but unwilling to raise his hand against the State in any personal interest.

Surprises continued. When it was generally believed that Henry's line was extinct he had produced an heir. When he seemed to have sunk into permanent imbecility he suddenly recovered. At Christmas 1454 he regained all his faculties. He inquired whether he had been asleep and what had happened meanwhile. Margaret showed him his son, and told him she had named him Edward. Hitherto he had looked with dull eyes upon the infant. Every effort to rouse him had been in vain. Now he was as good as he had ever been. He held up his hands and thanked God, and, according to the Paston Letters, he said he "never knew till that time, nor wist not what was said to him, nor wist where he had been while he had been sick, till now." He sent his almoner to Canterbury with a thank-offering, and declared himself "in charity with all the world," remarking that he "only wished the lords were too."

CHAPTER TWENTY-EIGHT

THE WARS OF THE ROSES

IN THE SPRING OF 1455 THE RED ROSE OF LANCASTER BLOOMED AGAIN. York ceased legally to be Protector from the moment that the King's mental recovery was known; he made no effort to retain the power. Queen Margaret took the helm. Somerset was not only released but restored to his key position. York's government of Calais, which had been conferred upon him for seven years, was handed back to his rival. He was no longer invited to the King's Council board; and when a Great Council of peers was convened at Leicester he feared that he was summoned only to be tried. He retired to Sandal, in Yorkshire, and, being joined by the Earls of Warwick and Salisbury, together with a large company of nobles, strongly attended, he denounced Somerset as the man who, having lost Normandy and Guienne, was now about to ruin the whole kingdom. York's lords agreed upon a resort to arms. With three thousand men they marched south. At the same time the Duke of Norfolk appeared at the head of several thousand men, and Shrewsbury and Sir Thomas Stanley of a few thousands more. All these forces moved towards London, with St. Albans as their point of concentration. The King, the Queen, Somerset, and the Court and Lancastrian party, with their power, which numbered less than three thousand men, moved to Watford to meet them.

St. Albans was an open town. The ancient, powerful monastery there had prevented the citizens from "girding themselves about with a great wall," lest they should become presumptuous. For this reason it was a convenient rendezvous. The King's army got there first, and the royal standard was unfurled in St. Peter's Street and Hollowell Street. York, Salisbury, and Warwick did not wait for the heavy reinforcements that were approaching them. They saw that their forces had the advantage and that hours counted. This time there was a fight. It was a collision rather than a battle; but it was none the less decisive. Lord Clifford held for the King the barrier across the street, which York attacked with archery and cannon; but Warwick, circling the town, came in upon him from behind, slew him, and put the royal troops to flight. Somerset was killed "fighting for a cause which was more his own than the King's." The Duke of Buckingham and his son were wounded by arrows; Somerset's son, the Earl of Dorset, was captured sorely wounded and carried home in a cart. The King himself was slightly wounded by an arrow. He did not fly, but took refuge in a tradesman's house in the main street. There presently the Duke of York came to him, and, falling upon his knees, assured him of his fealty and devotion. Not more than three hundred men perished in this clash at St. Albans, but these included an extraordinary proportion of the nobles on the King's side. The rank and file were encouraged to spare one another; the leaders fought to the death. The bodies of Somerset and Clifford lay naked in the street for many hours, none daring to bury them. The Yorkist triumph was complete. They had now got the King in their hands. Somerset was dead. Margaret and her child had taken sanctuary. The victors declared their devotion to the royal person and rejoiced that he was rid of evil counsellors. Upon this Parliament was immediately summoned in the King's name.

Historians have shrunk from the Wars of the Roses, and most of those who have catalogued their events have left us only a melancholy and disjointed picture. We are however in the presence of the most ferocious and implacable quarrel of which there is factual record. The individual actors were bred by generations of privilege and war, into which the feudal theme had brought its peculiar sense of honour, and to which the Papacy contributed such spiritual sanction as emerged from its rivalries and intrigues. It was a conflict in which personal hatreds reached their maximum, and from which mass effects were happily excluded. There must have been many similar convulsions in the human story. None however has been preserved with characters at once so worldly and so expensively chiselled.

Needless causes of confusion may be avoided. Towns must not be confused with titles. The mortal struggle of York and Lancaster did not imply any antagonism between the two well-known English counties. York was in fact the stronghold of the Lancastrians, and the Yorkists founded their strength upon the Midlands and the south of England. The ups and downs of fortune were so numerous and startling, the family feuds so complicated, the impact of national feeling in moments of crisis so difficult to measure, that it has been the fashion to disparage this period. Only Shakespeare, basing himself largely upon Hall's *Chronicle,* has portrayed its savage yet heroic lineaments. He does not attempt to draw conclusions, and for dramatic purposes telescopes events and campaigns. Let us now set forth the facts as they occurred.

*   *   *   *   *

St. Albans was the first shedding of blood in strife. The Yorkists gained possession of the King. But soon we see the inherent power of Lancaster. They had the majority of the nobles on their side, and the majesty of the Crown. In a few months they were as strong as ever. Continual trials of strength were made. There were risings in the country and grim assemblies of Parliament. Legality, constitutionalism, and reverence for the Crown were countered, but not yet overthrown, by turbulent and bloody episodes. The four years from 1456 to 1459 were a period of uneasy truce. All seemed conscious of the peril to themselves and to their order. But Fate lay heavy upon them. There were intense efforts at reconciliation. The spectacle was displayed to the Londoners of the King being escorted to Westminster by a procession in which the Duke of York and Queen Margaret walked side by side, followed by the Yorkist and Lancastrian lords, the most opposed in pairs. Solemn pledges of amity were exchanged; the Sacrament was taken in common by all the leaders; all sought peace where there was no peace. Even when a kind of settlement was reached in London it was upset by violence in the North. In 1459 fighting broke out again. A gathering near Worcester of armed Yorkists in arms dispersed in the presence of the royal army and their chiefs scattered. York returned to Ireland, and Warwick to his captaincy of Calais, in which he had succeeded Somerset.

War began in earnest in July 1460. York was still in Ireland; but the Yorkist lords under Warwick, holding bases in Wales and at Calais, with all their connections and partisans, supported by the Papal Legate and some of the bishops, and, on the whole, by the Commons, confronted the Lancastrians and the Crown at Northampton. Henry VI stood entrenched, and new cannon guarded his line. But when the Yorkists attacked, Lord Grey of Ruthven, who commanded a wing, deserted him and helped the Yorkists over the breastworks. The royal forces fled in panic. King Henry VI remained in his tent, "sitting alone and solitary." The victors presented themselves to him, bowing to the ground. As after St. Albans, they carried him again to London, and, having him in their power once more, ruled in his name. The so-called compromise in which all the Estates of the Realm concurred was then attempted. "The Duke of York," says Gregory's *Chronicle* "kept King Harry at Westminster by force and strength, till at last the King, for fear of death, granted him the Crown, for a man that hath but little wit will soon be afeared of death." Henry was to be King for life; York was to conduct the government and succeed him at his death. All who sought a quiet life for the nation hailed this arrangement. But the settlement defied the fact that Queen Margaret, with her son, the Prince of Wales, was at liberty at Harlech Castle, in Wales. The King in bondage had disinherited his own son. The Queen fought on.

With her army of the North and of North Wales Margaret advanced to assert the birthright of her son. The Duke of York, disdaining to remain in the security of Sandal Castle until his whole strength was gathered, marched against her. At Wakefield on December 30, 1460, the first considerable battle of the war was fought. The Lancastrians, with superior forces, caught the Yorkists by surprise, when many were foraging, and a frightful rout and massacre ensued. Here there was no question of sparing the common men; many hundreds were slaughtered; but the brunt fell upon the chiefs. No quarter was given. The Duke of York was killed; his son, the Earl of Rutland, eighteen years old, was flying, but the new Lord Clifford remembering St. Albans, slaughtered him with joy, exclaiming, "By God's blood, thy father slew

ENGLAND AND WALES
DURING THE
WARS OF THE ROSES

Battlefields marked ✕

mine; and so will I do thee, and all thy kin." Henceforward this was the rule of the war. The old Earl of Salisbury, caught during the night, was beheaded immediately by Lord Exeter, a natural son of the Duke of Buckingham. Margaret's hand has been discerned in this severity. The heads of the three Yorkist nobles were exposed over the gates and walls of York. The great Duke's head, with a paper crown, grinned upon the landscape, summoning the avengers.

Hitherto the struggle had been between mature, comfortable magnates, deeply involved in State affairs and trying hard to preserve some limits. Now a new generation took charge. There was a new Lord Clifford, a new Duke of Somerset, above all a new Duke of York, all in the twenties, sword in hand, with fathers to avenge and England as the prize. When York's son, hitherto Earl of March, learned that his father's cause had devolved upon him he did not shrink. He fell upon the Earl of Wiltshire and the Welsh Lancastrians, and on February 2, 1461, at the Battle of Mortimer's Cross, near Hereford, he beat and broke them up. He made haste to repay the cruelties of Wakefield. "No quarter" was again the word. Among those executed after the battle was Owen Tudor, a harmless notable, who, with the axe and block before him, hardly believed that he would be beheaded until the collar of his red doublet was ripped off. His son Jasper lived, as will be seen, to carry on the quarrel.

The victorious Yorkists under their young Duke now marched to help the Earl of Warwick, who had returned from Calais and was being hard pressed in London; but Queen Margaret forestalled him, and on February 17, at the second Battle of St. Albans, she inflicted upon Warwick a bloody defeat. Warwick, who was at this time the real leader of the Yorkist party, with many troops raised abroad and with the latest firearms and his own feudal forces, had carried the captive King with him and claimed to be acting in his name. But Margaret's onset took him by surprise. "Their prickers [scouts] came not home to bring tidings how nigh the Queen was, save one came and said that she was nine mile off." Warwick and Norfolk escaped; half their army was slaughtered. King Henry had been carted to the scene. There, beneath a large tree, he watched what happened with legitimate and presently unconcealed satisfaction. Two knights of high renown in the French war, one the redoubtable Sir Thomas Kyriel, had been appointed as his warders and guardians. Above all they were to make sure no harm came to him. They therefore remained with him under his tree, and all were surrounded by the victorious army. Among the many captains of consequence whom Margaret put to death in cold blood the next morning these two cases needed special consideration. King Henry said he had asked them to bide with him and that they had done so for his own safety. Queen Margaret produced her son Edward, now seven years old, to whose disinheritance the King had perforce consented, and asked this child, already precociously fierce, to pronounce. "Fair son, with what death shall these two knights die whom you see there?" "Their heads should be cut off" was the ready answer. As Kyriel was being led away to his doom he exclaimed, "May the wrath of God fall on those who have taught a child to speak such words." Thus was pity banished from all hearts, and death or vengeance was the cry.

*   *   *   *   *

Margaret now had her husband safe back in her hands, and with him the full authority of the Crown. The road to London was open, but she did not choose to advance upon it. The fierce hordes she had brought from the North had already disgraced themselves by their ravages far and wide along their line of march. They had roused against them the fury of the countryside. The King's friends said, "They deemed that the Northern men would have been too cruel in robbing if they had come to London." The city was, upon the whole, steadfast in the Yorkist cause, but it was also said, "If the King and Queen had come with their army to London they would have had all things as they wished." We cannot judge the circumstances fully. Edward of York was marching with the triumphant army of Mortimer's Cross night and day to reach London. Warwick had joined him in Oxfordshire with the survivors of St. Albans. Perhaps King Henry pleaded that the capital should not become a battlefield, but at any rate Margaret and her advisers did not dare to make it so. Flushed with victory, laden with spoil, reunited with the King, the Lancastrians retired through Dunstable to the North, and thus disguised the fact that their Scottish mercenaries were already joggling home with all that they could carry. According to Holinshed, "The Queen, having little trust in Essex, less in Kent, and least of all in London, . . . departed from St. Albans into the North Country, where the foundation of her strength and refuge only rested."

This was the turning-point in the struggle. Nine days after the second Battle of St. Albans Edward of York entered London. The citizens, who might have submitted to Margaret and the King, now hailed the Yorkists with enthusiasm. They thanked God and said, "Let us walk in a new vineyard, and let us make a gay garden in the month of March, with this fair white rose and herb, the Earl of March."[1] It was a vineyard amid thorns. The pretence of acting in the King's name could serve no longer. The Yorkists had become without disguise traitors and rebels against the Crown. But the mood of the youthful warrior who had triumphed and butchered at Mortimer's Cross recked little of this charge. As he saw it, his father had been ruined and killed through respect for the majesty of Henry VI. He and his friends would palter no longer with such conceptions. Forthwith he claimed the crown; and such was the feeling of London and the strength of his army, now upon the spot, that he was able to make good show of public authority for his act. He declared himself King, and on March 4, 1461, was proclaimed at Westminster with such formalities as were possible. Henceforward he declared that the other side were guilty of treason, and that he would enforce upon them every penalty.

These assertions must now be made good, and King Edward IV marched north to settle once and for all with King Henry VI. Near York the Queen, with the whole power of Lancaster, confronted him not far from Tadcaster, by the villages of Saxton and Towton. Some accounts declare that a hundred thousand men were on the field, the Yorkists having forty and the Lancastrians sixty thousand; but later authorities greatly reduce these figures.

On March 28 the Yorkist advance-guard was beaten back at Ferry Bridge by the young Lord Clifford, and Warwick himself was wounded; but as heavier forces arrived the bridge was carried, Clifford was slain, and the Yorkist army passed over. The next day one of the most ruthless battles on English soil was fought. The Lancastrians held a good position on rising ground, their right flank being protected by

the flooded stream of the Cock, in many places unfordable. Although
Edward's army was not complete and the Duke of Norfolk's wing was
still approaching, he resolved to attack. The battle began in a blind-
ing snowstorm, which drove in the faces of the Lancastrians. Under
this cover clumps of Yorkist spearmen moved up the slope. The wind
gave superior range to the archery of the attack and the Lancastrian
shafts fell short, while they themselves suffered heavily. Under this
pressure the decision was taken to advance downhill upon the foe. For
six hours the two sides grappled furiously, with varying success. At the
height of the battle Warwick is said to have dismounted and slain his
horse to prove to his men he would not quit them alive. But all hung
in the balance until late in the afternoon, when the arrival of the Duke
of Norfolk's corps upon the exposed flank of the Lancastrians drove
the whole mass into retreat, which soon became a rout.

Now the Cock beck, hitherto a friend, became an enemy. The
bridge towards Tadcaster was block with fugitives. Many thousands of
men, heavily armoured, plunged into the swollen stream, and were
drowned in such numbers that hideous bridges were formed of the
corpses and some escaped thereby. The pursuit was carried on far into
the night. Margaret and her son escaped to York, where King Henry
had been observing the rites of Palm Sunday. Gathering him up, the
imperious Queen set out with her child and a cluster of spears for
the Northern border. The bodies of several thousand Englishmen lay
upon the field. Edward, writing to his mother, conceals his own losses,
but claims that twenty-eight thousand Lancastrian dead had been
counted. It is certain that the flower of the Lancastrian nobility and
knighthood fell upon the field. For all prisoners there was but death.
The Earl of Devonshire and "the bastard of Exeter" alone were spared,
and only for a day. When Edward reached the town of York his first
task was to remove the heads of his father and others of Margaret's
victims and to replace them with those of his noblest captives. Three
months later, on June 28, he was crowned King at Westminster, and
the Yorkist triumph seemed complete. It was followed by wholesale
proscriptions and confiscations. Parliament in November 1461 passed
an Act of Attainder which, surpassing all previous severities, lapped
a hundred and thirty-three notable persons in its withering sweep.

Not only the throne but one-third of the estates in England changed hands. It was measure for measure.

*   *   *   *   *

After Towton the Lancastrian cause was sustained by the unconquerable will of Queen Margaret. Never has her tenacity and rarely have her vicissitudes been surpassed in any woman. Apart from the sullen power of Lancaster in the North, she had the friendly regard of two countries, Scotland and France. Both had felt the heavy arm of England in former reigns; both rejoiced at its present division and weakness. The hatred of the Scots for the English still excited by its bitterness the wonder of foreigners. When Louis XI succeeded his father, Charles VII, in 1461, the year of Towton, he found his country almost a desert, horrible to see. The fields were untilled; the villages were clusters of ruined hovels. Amid the ruins, the weeds and brushwood—to use a term which recurs—of what were formerly cultivated and fertile fields there dwelt a race of peasants reduced to the conditions and roused to the ferocity of wolves. All this was the result of the English invasion. Therefore it was a prime aim of Scottish and French policy, always moving hand-in-hand, to foster the internal strife of England and to sustain the weaker party there.

Margaret, as Queen of England and Princess of France, was an outstanding personage in the West of Europe. Her qualities of courage and combativeness, her commanding, persuasive personality, her fury against those who had driven her and her husband from the throne, produced from this one woman's will-power a long series of desperate, forlorn struggles after the main event had been decided, and after the lapse of years for one brief spell reversed it. English national interests did not enter her mind. She had paid her way with Scotland by the surrender of Berwick. She clinched her bargain with Louis XI by mortgaging Calais to him for 20,000 gold livres.

In 1462 Margaret, after much personal appeal to the Courts of France, Burgundy, and Scotland, found herself able to land with a power, and whether by treachery or weakness the three strongest Northern castles, Bamburgh, Alnwick, and Dunstanburgh, opened their gates to her. Louis XI had lent her the services of a fine soldier, Pierre de Brézé, who under her spell spent his large fortune in her cause. In the winter of 1462 therefore King Edward gathered his Yorkist powers, and, carrying his new train of artillery by sea to Newcastle, began the sieges of these lost strongholds. The King himself lay stricken with measles at Durham, and Lord Warwick conducted the operations. The heavy cannon, each with its pet name, played havoc with the masonry of the castles. So vigorously were the sieges conducted that even Christmas leave was forbidden. Margaret, from Berwick, in vain attempted the relief of Alnwick. All three fortresses fell in a month.

The behaviour of Edward at this moment constitutes a solid defence for his character. This voluptuous young King, sure of his position, now showed a clemency unheard of in the Wars of the Roses. Not only did he pardon the Lancastrian nobles who were caught in the fortresses, but he made solemn pacts with them and took them into his full confidence. The Duke of Somerset and Sir Ralph Percy, on swearing allegiance, were not merely allowed to go free, but restored to their estates. Percy was even given the guardianship of two of the castles. Somerset, son of the great Minister slaughtered in the first Battle of St. Albans, was admitted to even higher favour. Having made his peace, he was given a high command and a place in the inner councils of the royal army. In this new position at first he gave shrewd military advice, and was granted special pensions by the King.

Edward's magnanimity and forgiveness were ill repaid. When Margaret returned with fresh succours from France and Scotland in 1463 Percy opened the gates of Bamburgh to the Scots, and Alnwick was betrayed about the same time by a soured Yorkist officer, Sir Ralph Grey. Meanwhile Queen Margaret, with King Henry in her hands, herself besieged the castle of Norham, on the Tweed, near Berwick. Once again Edward and the Yorkists took the field, and the redoubtable new artillery, at that time esteemed as much among the leading nations as atomic weapons are to-day, was carried to the North. The great guns blew chunks off the castles. Margaret fled to France, while Henry buried himself amid the valleys and the pious foundations of Cumberland. This was the final parting of King Henry VI and his Queen—Queen she was. Margaret took the Prince with her on her travels. These were remarkable. With the Duke of Exeter, six knights, and her faithful Pierre de Brézé she landed at Sluys, and appealed to the renowned chivalry of the house of Burgundy. She came "without royal habit or estate"; she and her seven waiting-women had only the clothes they were wearing. Brézé paid for their food. Nevertheless she was treated even in this adverse Court with royal honours. Philip, Duke of Burgundy, was aged; his son Charles was surnamed "the Bold." The ambassadors of England were active. Margaret got nothing from Burgundy except the gifts and courtesies which old-time hospitality would afford to "a dame in distress." It is however from these contacts that our knowledge of Margaret's adventures is derived.

Chastellain, the Burgundian chronicler, recorded her tales. Thus only has history heard how she, King Henry, and her son had lived for five days without bread, upon a herring each day between them. At Mass once the Queen found herself without even a penny for the offertory. She asked a Scottish archer near by to lend her something. "Somewhat stiffly and regretfully" he drew a groat from his purse. At the latest disaster at Norham, recounted the Queen, she had been captured by plundering Yorkist soldiers, robbed, and brought before the captain to be beheaded. Only a quarrel of her captors over the spoil delayed her execution. But there stood a Yorkist squire, and to him she turned, "speaking pitifully." "Madam," he said, "mount behind me, and Monseigneur the Prince in front, and I will save you or die, seeing that death is more likely to come to me than not." Three-a-back they plunged into the forest, Margaret in terror for her son's life, on which her cause depended. The Yorkist squire now rode off. The forest was a known haunt of bandits, and mother and son crouched in its recesses. Soon there appeared a man of hideous and horrible aspect, with obvious intention to kill and rob. But once more Margaret, by her personal force, prevailed. She said who she was, and confided her son, the heir to the throne, to the brigand's honour. The robber was faithful to his charge. The Queen and the Prince at last both reached the shelter of the fugitive King.

*　　*　　*　　*　　*

Edward's clemency had been betrayed by Percy, but he did not withdraw his confidence from Somerset. The King was a man capable of the most bloody deeds when compelled, as he thought, by necessity, and at the same time eager to practise not only magnanimity, but open-hearted confidence. The confidence he showed to Somerset must have led him into deadly perils. This third Duke was during the beginning of 1463 high in the King's favour. "And the King made full much of him, in so much he lodged with the King in his own bed many nights, and sometimes rode a-hunting behind the King, the King having about him not passing six horse at the most, and yet three were of the Duke's men of Somerset."

When in the autumn of 1463 he went to the North Somerset and two hundred of his own men were his bodyguard. At Northampton, where bitter memories of the battle lingered, the townsfolk were first astounded and then infuriated to see this bearer of an accursed name in company with their Yorkist sovereign. Only King Edward's personal exertions saved his new-found follower from being torn to pieces. After this he found it necessary to provide other employment for Somerset and his escort. Somerset was sent to Holt Castle, in Denbighshire. The brawl at Northampton we must suppose convinced him that even the King could not protect him from his Yorkist foes. At Christmas 1463 Somerset deserted Edward and returned to the Lancastrian side. The names of these great nobles were magnets in their own territories. The unstable Duke had hoped to gain possession of Newcastle, and many of his adherents on the report that he was in the neighbourhood came out to him; but he was driven away, and they were caught and beheaded.

Again the banner of Lancaster was raised. Somerset joined King Henry. Alnwick and Bamburgh still held out. Norham and Skipton had been captured, but now Warwick's brother Montagu with a substantial army was in the field. On April 25, 1464, at Hedgeley Moor, near Alnwick, he broke and destroyed the Lancastrian revolt. The leaders perished on the field, or afterwards on the block. Sir Ralph Percy fought to the death, and used the expression, remarkable for one who had accepted pardon and even office from King Edward, "I have saved the bird in my bosom." What was this "bird?" It was the cause of Lancaster, which might be dissembled or even betrayed under duress, but still remained, when occasion served, the lodestar of its adherents. There were many who had this bird in their bosoms, but could never have coined Percy's grand phrase or stooped to his baseness.

Edward's experiment of mercy in this quarrel was now at an end, and the former rigours were renewed in their extreme degree. Somerset, defeated with a small following at Hexham on May 15, 1464, was beheaded the next morning. Before the month was out in every Yorkish camp Lancastrian nobles and knights by dozens and half-dozens were put to death. There was nothing for it but to still these unquiet spirits. John Tiptoft, Earl of Worcester, Constable of England, versed in the civil war, and with Italian experience, presided over drumhead courts-martial, and by adding needless cruelties to his severities justified a vengeance one day to be exacted.

Meanwhile the diplomacy of the English Crown had effected a fifteen years' truce with the King of Scotland, and was potent both at the Courts of France and Burgundy. Margaret remained help- less at *Bar-le-Duc*. Poor King Henry was at length tracked down near Clitheroe, in Lancashire, and conveyed to London. This time there was no ceremonial entry. With his feet tied by leather thongs to the stirrups, and with a straw hat on his head, the futile but saintly figure around whom such storms had beaten was led three times round the pillory, and finally hustled to the Tower, whose gates closed on him, yet not—this time—for ever.

With the fall of Alnwick only one fortress in the whole kingdom still resisted. The castle of Harlech, on the western sea, alone flaunted the Red Rose. Harlech stood a siege of seven years. When it surren- dered in 1468 there were found to be but fifty effective men in the garrison. With two exceptions, they were admitted to mercy. Among them was a child of twelve, who had survived the rigours of the long blockade. He was the nephew of Jasper, the grandson of Owen Tudor, and the future founder of the Tudor dynasty and system of govern- ment. His name was Richmond, later to become King Henry VII.

CHAPTER TWENTY-NINE

THE ADVENTURES OF EDWARD IV

KING EDWARD IV HAD MADE GOOD HIS RIGHT TO THE CROWN UPON the field. He was a soldier and a man of action; in the teeth of danger his quality was at its highest. In war nothing daunted or wearied him. Long marches, hazardous decisions, the marshalling of armies, the conduct of battles, seemed his natural sphere. The worse things got the better he became. But the opposite was also true. He was at this time a fighting man and little more, and when the fighting stopped he had no serious zest for sovereignty. The land was fair; the blood of youth coursed in his veins; all his blood debts were paid; with ease and goodwill he sheathed his sharp sword. It had won him his crown; now to enjoy life.

The successes of these difficult years had been gained for King Edward by the Neville family. Warwick or Montagu, now Earl of Northumberland, with George Neville, Archbishop of York, had the whole machinery of government in their hands. The King had been present only at some of the actions. He could even be reproached for his misguided clemency, which had opened up again the distresses of civil war. His magnanimity had been at length sternly repressed by his counsellors and generals. In the first part of his reign England was therefore ruled by the two brothers, Warwick and Northumberland. They believed they had put the King on the throne, and meant him to remain there while they governed. The King did not quarrel with this. In all his reign he never fought but when he was forced; then he was magnificent. History has scolded this prince of twenty-two for not possessing immediately the statecraft and addiction to business for which his office called. Edward united contrasting characters. He loved peace; he shone in war. But he loved peace for its indulgences rather than its dignity. His pursuit of women, in which he found no obstacles, combined with hunting, feasting, and drinking to fill his life. Were these not the rightful prizes of victory? Let Warwick and Northumberland and other anxious lords carry the burden of State, and let the King be merry. For a while this suited all parties. The victors divided the spoil; the King had his amusements, and his lords their power and policy.

Thus some years slipped by, while the King, although gripping from time to time the reins of authority, led in the main his life of pleasure. His mood towards men and women is described in the well-chosen words by the staid Hume:

"During the present interval of peace, he lived in the most familiar and sociable manner with his subjects, particularly with the Londoners; and the beauty of his person, as well as the gallantry of his address, which, even unassisted by his royal dignity, would have rendered him acceptable to the fair, facilitated all his applications for their favour. This easy and pleasurable course of life augmented every day his popularity among all ranks of men. He was the peculiar favourite of the young and gay of both sexes. The disposition of the English, little addicted to jealousy, kept them from taking umbrage at these liberties. And his indulgence in amusements, while it gratified his inclination, was thus become, without design, a means of supporting and securing his Government." After these comparatively mild censures the historian proceeds to deplore the weakness and imprudence which led the King to stray from the broad, sunlit glades of royal libertinage on to the perilous precipices of romance and marriage.

One day the King a-hunting was carried far by the chase. He rested for the night at a castle. In this castle a lady of quality, niece of the owner, had found shelter. Elizabeth Woodville, or Wydvil, was the widow of a Lancastrian knight, Sir John Grey, "in Margaret's battle at St. Albans slain." Her mother, Jacquetta of Luxemburg, had been the youthful wife of the famous John, Duke of Bedford, and after his death she had married his steward, Sir Richard Woodville, later created Earl Rivers. This condescension so far below her station caused offence to the aristocracy. She was fined £1,000 as a deterrent to others. Nevertheless she lived happily ever after, and bore her husband no fewer than thirteen children, of whom Elizabeth was one. There was high as well as ordinary blood in Elizabeth's veins; but she was an austere woman, upright, fearless, chaste and fruitful. She and her two sons were all under the ban of the attainder which disinherited the adherents of Lancaster. The chance of obtaining royal mercy could not be missed. The widow bowed in humble petition before the youthful conqueror, and, like the tanner's daughter of Falaise, made at first glance the sovereign her slave. Shakespeare's account, though somewhat crude, does not err in substance. The Lady Elizabeth observed the strictest self-restraint, which only enhanced the passion of the King. He gave her all his love, and when he found her obdurate he besought her to share his crown. He spurned the counsels of prudence and worldly wisdom. Why conquer in battles, why be a king, if not to gain one's heart's desire? But he was well aware of the dangers of his choice. His marriage in 1464 with Elizabeth Woodville was a secret guarded in deadly earnest. The statesmen at the head of the Government, while they smiled at what seemed an amorous frolic, never dreamed it was a solemn union, which must shake the land to its depths.

*   *   *   *   *

Warwick's plans for the King's future had been different. Isabella of the house of Spain, or preferably a French princess, were brides who might greatly forward the interests of England. A royal marriage in those days might be a bond of peace between neighbouring states or the means of successful war. Warwick used grave arguments and pressed the King to decide. Edward seemed strangely hesitant, and dwelt upon his objections until the Minister, who was also his master, became impatient. Then at last the truth was revealed: he had for five months been married to Elizabeth Woodville. Here then was the occasion which sundered him from the valiant King-maker, fourteen years older, but also in the prime of life. Warwick had deep roots in England, and his popularity, whetted by the lavish hospitality which he offered to all classes upon his many great estates, was unbounded. The Londoners looked to him. He held the power. But no one knew better than he that there slept in Edward a tremendous warrior, skilful, ruthless, and capable when roused of attempting and of doing all.

The King too, for his part, began to take more interest in affairs. Queen Elizabeth had five brothers, seven sisters, and two sons. By royal decree he raised them to high rank, or married them into the greatest families. He went so far as to marry his wife's fourth brother, at twenty, to the Dowager Duchess of Norfolk, aged eighty. Eight new peerages came into existence in the Queen's family: her father, five brothers-in-law, her son, and her brother Anthony. This was generally thought excessive. It must be remembered that at this time there were but sixty peers, of whom not more than fifty could ever be got to Parliament on one occasion. All these potentates were held in a tight and nicely calculated system. The arrival of a new nobility who had done nothing notable in the war and now surrounded the indolent King was not merely offensive, but politically dangerous to Warwick and his proud associates.

But the clash came over foreign policy. In this sad generation England, lately the master, had become the sport of neighbouring states. Her titled refugees, from one faction or the other, beset the Courts of Western Europe. The Duke of Burgundy had been shocked to learn one morning that a Duke of Exeter and several other high English nobles were actually begging their bread at the tail of one of his progresses. Ashamed to see such a slight upon his class, he provided them with modest dwellings and allowances. Similar charities were performed by Louis XI to the unhappy descendants of the victors of Agincourt. Margaret with her retinue of shadows was welcomed in her pauper stateliness both in Burgundy and in France. At any moment either Power, now become formidable as England had waned, might support the exiled faction in good earnest and pay back the debts of fifty years before by an invasion of England. It was the policy of Warwick and his connection to make friends with France, by far the stronger Power, and thus obtain effectual security. In this mood they hoped to make a French match for the King's sister. Edward took the opposite line. With the instinct which afterwards ruled our Island for so many centuries, he sought to base English policy upon the second strongest state in Western Europe. He could no doubt argue that to be the ally of France was to be in the power of France, but to be joined with Burgundy was to have the means of correcting if not of controlling French action. Amid his revelries and other hunting he nursed a conqueror's spirit. Never should England become a vassal state; instead of being divided by her neighbours, she would herself, by dividing them, maintain a balance. At this time these politics were new; but the stresses they wrought in the small but vehement world of English government can be readily understood nowadays.

The King therefore, to Warwick's chagrin and alarm, in 1468 married his sister Margaret to Charles the Bold, who had in 1467 succeeded as Duke of Burgundy. Thus not only did these great lords, who at the constant peril of their lives and by all their vast resources had placed him on the throne, suffer slights and material losses by the creation of a new nobility, but they had besides to stomach a foreign policy which they believed would be fatal to England, to the Yorkist party, and to themselves. What help could Burgundy give if France, joined to the house of Lancaster, invaded England? What would happen to them, their great estates, and all who depended upon them, in such a catastrophe? The quarrel between the King and Warwick, as head of the Nevilles, was not therefore petty, or even, as has often been suggested, entirely personal.

The offended chiefs took deep counsel together. Edward continued to enjoy his life with his Queen, and now and again, with others. His attention in public matters was occupied mainly with Lancastrian plots and movements, but underneath and behind him a far graver menace was preparing. The Nevilles were at length ready to try conclusions with him. Warwick's plan was singular in its skill. He had gained the King's brother, Clarence, to his side by whispering that but for this upstart brood of the Woodvilles he might succeed Edward as King. As bond it was secretly agreed that Clarence should marry Warwick's daughter Isabella.

When all was ready Warwick struck. A rising took place in the North. Thousands of men in Yorkshire under the leadership of various young lords complained in arms about taxation. The "thrave," a levy paid since the days of Athelstan, became suddenly obnoxious. But other grievances were urged, particularly that the King was swayed by "favourites." At the same time in London the House of Commons petitioned against lax and profuse administration. The King was now forced to go to the North. Except his small bodyguard he had no troops of his own, but he called upon his nobles to bring out their men. He advanced in July to Nottingham, and there awaited the Earls of Pembroke and Devon, both new creations of his own, who had marshalled the levies of Wales and the West. As soon as the King had been enticed northwards by the rebellion Warwick and Clarence, who had hitherto crouched at Calais, came to England with the Calais garrison. Warwick published a manifesto supporting the Northern rebels, "the King's true subjects" as he termed them, and urged them "with piteous lamentations to be the means to our Sovereign Lord the King of remedy and reformation." Warwick was joined by many thousands of Kentish men and was received with great respect in London. But before he and Clarence could bring their forces against the King's rear the event was decided. The Northern rebels, under "Robin of Redesdale," intercepted Pembroke and Devon, and at Edgcott, near Banbury, defeated them with a merciless slaughter, a hundred and sixty-eight knights, squires, and gentlemen either falling in the fight or being executed thereafter. Both Pembroke and later Devon were beheaded.

The King, trying to rally his scattered forces at Olney, in Buckinghamshire, found himself in the power of his great nobles. His brother, Richard of Gloucester, known to legend as "Crookback" because of his alleged deformity, seemed his only friend. At first he attempted to rally Warwick and Clarence to their duty, but in the course of conversation he was made to realise that he was their captive. With bows and ceremonies they explained that his future reign must be in accordance with their advice. He was conveyed to Warwick's castle at Middleham, and there kept in honourable but real restraint under the surveillance of the Archbishop of York. At this moment therefore Warwick the King-maker had actually the two rival Kings, Henry VI and Edward IV, both his prisoners, one in the Tower and the other at Middleham. This was a remarkable achievement for any subject. To make the lesson even plainer, Lord Rivers, the Queen's father, and John Woodville, her brother, were arrested and executed at Kenilworth without any pretence of trial. Thus did the older nobility deal with the new.

But the relations between Warwick and the King did not admit of such simple solutions. Warwick had struck with suddenness, and for a while no one realised what had happened. As the truth became known the Yorkist nobility viewed with astonishment and anger the detention of their brave, victorious sovereign, and the Lancastrians everywhere raised their heads in the hopes of profiting by the Yorkist feud. The King found it convenient in his turn to dissemble. He professed himself convinced that Warwick and Clarence were right. He undertook to amend his ways, and after he had signed free pardons to all who had been in arms against him he was liberated. Thus was a settlement reached between Warwick and the Crown. King Edward was soon again at the head of forces, defeating Lancastrian rebels and executing their leaders, while Warwick and all his powerful connections returned to their posts, proclaimed their allegiance, and apparently enjoyed royal favour. But all this was on the surface.

*　　*　　*　　*　　*

In March 1470, under the pretence of suppressing a rebellion in Lincolnshire, the King called his forces to arms. At Losecoat Field he defeated the insurgents, who promptly fled; and in the series of executions which had now become customary after every engagement he obtained a confession from Sir Robert Welles which accused both Warwick and Clarence of treason. The evidence is fairly convincing; for at this moment they were conspiring against Edward, and shortly afterwards refused to obey his express order to join him. The King, with troops fresh from victory, turned on them all of a sudden. He marched against them, and they fled, astounded that their own methods should be retorted upon themselves. They sought safety in Warwick's base at Calais; but Lord Wenlock, whom he had left as his deputy, refused to admit them. Even after they had bombarded the sea-front he made it a positive favour to send a few flagons of wine to Clarence's bride, who, on board ship, had just given birth to a son. The King-maker found himself by one sharp twist of fortune deprived of almost every resource he had counted upon as sure. He in his turn presented himself at the French Court as a suppliant.

But this was the best luck Louis XI had ever known. He must have rubbed his hands in the same glee as when he visited his former Minister, Cardinal Jean Balue, whom he kept imprisoned in an iron cage at Chinon because he had conspired with Charles the Bold. Two years earlier Edward as the ally of Burgundy had threatened him with war. Now here in France were the leaders of both the parties that had disputed England for so long. Margaret was dwelling in her father's Anjou. Warwick, friend of France, vanquished in his own country, had arrived at Honfleur. With gusto the stern, cynical, hard-pressed Louis set himself to the task of reconciling and combining these opposite forces. At Angers he confronted Margaret and her son, now a fine youth of seventeen, with Warwick and Clarence, and proposed brutally to them that they should join together with his support to overthrow Edward. At first both parties recoiled. Nor can we wonder. A river of blood flowed between them. All that they had fought for during these cruel years was defaced by their union. Warwick and Margaret had slain with deliberation each other's dearest friends and kin. She had beheaded his father Salisbury, slain his uncle York and his cousin Rutland. He for his part had executed the two Somersets, father and son, the Earl of Wiltshire, and many of her devoted adherents. The common people who had fallen in their quarrel, they were uncounted. In 1459 Margaret had declared Warwick attainted, a terrible outlawry. In 1460 he had branded her son as bastard or changeling. They had done each other the gravest human injuries. But they had one bond in common. They hated Edward and they wanted to win. They were the champions of a generation which could not accept defeat. And here, as indeed for a time it proved, appeared the means of speedy triumph.

Warwick had a fleet, commanded by his nephew, the bastard of Fauconberg. He had the sailors in all the seaports of the south coast. He knew he had but to go or send his summons to large parts of England for the people to take arms at his command. Margaret represented the beaten, disinherited, proscribed house of Lancaster, stubborn as ever. They agreed to forgive and unite. They took solemn oaths at Angers upon a fragment of the Holy Cross, which luckily was available. The confederacy was sealed by the betrothal of Margaret's son, the Prince of Wales, to Warwick's younger daughter, Anne. No one can blame Queen Margaret because in the ruin of her cause she reluctantly forgave injuries and welcomed the Kingmaker's invaluable help. She had never swerved from her faith. But for Warwick the transaction was unnatural, cynical and brutal.

Moreover, he overlooked the effect on Clarence of the new marriage he had arranged for his daughter Anne. A son born of this union would have had a great hope of uniting torn, tormented England. It was reasonable to expect the birth of an heir to these prospects. But Clarence had been swayed in his desertion of his brother by thoughts of the crown, and although he was now named as the next in succession after Margaret's son the value of his chance was no longer high. Edward had been staggered by his brother's conduct. He did not however allow his personal resentment to influence his action. A lady in attendance upon the new Duchess of Clarence proved to be a discreet and accomplished emissary of the King. She conveyed to Clarence soon after he fled from England that he had only to rejoin his brother for all to be pardoned and forgotten. The new agreement between Warwick and Margaret decided Clarence to avail himself of this fraternal offer, but not immediately. He must have been a great dissembler; for Warwick was no more able to forecast his actions in the future than his brother had been in the past.

King Edward was by now alarmed and vigilant, but he could scarcely foresee how many of his supporters would betray him. Warwick repeated the process he had used a year before. Fitzhugh, his cousin, started a new insurrection in Yorkshire. Edward gathered some forces and, making little of the affair, marched against the rebels. Warned by Charles of Burgundy, he even expressed his wish that Warwick would land. He seems to have been entirely confident. But never was there a more swift undeception. Warwick and Clarence landed at Dartmouth in September 1470. Kent and other southern

counties rose in his behalf. Warwick marched to London. He brought
the miserable Henry VI from his prison in the Tower, placed a crown
on his head, paraded him through the capital, and seated him upon
the throne.

At Nottingham Edward received alarming news. The major part
of his kingdom seemed to have turned against him. Suddenly he
learned that while the Northern rebels were moving down upon him
and cutting him from his Welsh succours, and while Warwick was
moving northward with strong forces, Northumberland, Warwick's
brother, hitherto faithful, had made his men throw up their caps for
King Henry. When Edward heard of Northumberland's desertion,
and also of rapid movements to secure his person, he deemed it his
sole hope to fly beyond the seas. He had but one refuge—the Court
of Burgundy; and with a handful of followers he cast himself upon his
brother-in-law. Charles the Bold was also cautious. He had to consider
the imminent danger of an attack by England and France united.
Until he was sure that this was inevitable he temporised with his royal
refugee relation. But when it became clear that the policy of Warwick
was undoubtedly to make war upon him in conjunction with Louis
XI he defended himself by an obvious manœuvre. He furnished King
Edward with about twelve hundred trustworthy Flemish and German
soldiers and the necessary ships and money for a descent. These forces
were collected secretly in the island of Walcheren.

*　　*　　*　　*　　*

Meanwhile the King-maker ruled England, and it seemed that he
might long continue to do so. He had King Henry VI a puppet in his
hand. The unhappy man, a breathing ruin sitting like a sack upon
the throne, with a crown on his head and a scepter in his hand,
received the fickle caresses of Fortune with the same mild endurance
which he had shown to her malignities. Statutes were passed in his
name which annihilated all the disinheritances and attainders of the
Yorkist Parliament. A third of the land of England returned to its old
possessors. The banished nobles or the heirs of the slain returned
from poverty and exile to their ancient seats. Meanwhile all preparations were made for a combined attack by England and France on
Burgundy, and war became imminent.

But while these violent transformations were comprehensible to the actors, and the drama proceeded with apparent success, the solid bulk of England on both sides was incapable of following such too-quick movements and reconciliations. Almost the whole population stood wherever it had stood before. Their leaders might have made new combinations, but ordinary men could not believe that the antagonism of the Red and the White Rose was ended. It needed but another shock to produce an entirely different scene. It is significant that, although repeatedly urged by Warwick to join him and her husband, King Henry, in London, and although possessed of effective forces, Margaret remained in France, and kept her son with her.

In March 1471 Edward landed with his small expedition at Ravenspur, a port in Yorkshire now washed away by the North Sea, but then still famous for the descent of Henry of Bolingbroke in 1399. The King, fighting for his life, was, as usual, at his best. York shut its gates in his face, but, like Bolingbroke, he declared he had only come to claim his private estates, and bade his troops declare themselves for King Henry VI. Accepted and nourished on these terms, he set forth on his march to London. Northumberland, with four times his numbers, approached to intercept him. Edward, by extraordinary marches, manœuvred past him. All Yorkist lords and adherents in the districts through which he passed joined his army. At Warwick he was strong enough to proclaim himself King again. The King-maker, disconcerted by the turn of events, sent repeated imperative requests to Margaret to come at once, and at Coventry stationed himself in King Edward's path. Meanwhile his brother Northumberland followed Edward southward, only two marches behind. In this dire strait Edward had a resource unsuspected by Warwick. He knew Clarence was his man. Clarence was moving from Gloucestershire with considerable forces, ostensibly to join Warwick; but Edward, slipping round Warwick's flank, as he had out-marched and out-witted Northumberland, placed himself between Warwick and London, and in the exact position where Clarence could make his junction with him.

Both sides now concentrated all their strength, and again large armies were seen in England. Edward entered London, and was cordially received by the bewildered citizens. Henry VI, who had actually been made to ride about the streets at the head of six hundred horsemen, was relieved from these exertions and taken back to his prison in the Tower. The decisive battle impended on the North Road, and at Barnet on April 14, 1471, Edward and the Yorkists faced Warwick and the house of Neville, with the new Duke of Somerset, second son of Edmund Beaufort, and important Lancastrian allies.

Throughout England no one could see clearly what was happening, and the Battle of Barnet, which resolved their doubts, was itself fought in a fog. The lines of battle overlapped; Warwick's right turned Edward's left flank, and *vice versa*. The King-maker, stung perhaps by imputations upon his physical courage, fought on foot. The new Lord Oxford, a prominent Lancastrian, whose father had been beheaded earlier in the reign, commanding the overlapping Lancastrian left, found himself successful in his charge, but lost in the mist. Little knowing that the whole of King Edward's rear was open to his attack, he tried to regain his own lines and arrived in the rear of Somerset's centre. The badge of a star and rays on his banners was mistaken by Warwick's troops for the sun and rays of King Edward. Warwick's archers loosed upon him. The mistake was discovered, but in those days of treason and changing sides it only led to another blunder. It was assumed that he had deserted. The cry of treason ran through Warwick's hosts. Oxford, in his uncertainty, rode off into the gloom. Somerset, on the other flank, had already been routed. Warwick, with the right wing, was attacked by the King and the main Yorkist power. Here indeed it was not worth while to ask for mercy. Warwick, outnumbered, his ranks broken, sought to reach his horse. He would have been wise in spite of taunts to have followed his usual custom of mounting again on the battle-day after walking along the lines; for had he escaped this zigzag story might have ended at the opposite point. But north of the town near which the main struggle was fought the King-maker, just as he was about to reach the necessary horse, was overtaken by the Yorkists and battered to death. He had been the foremost champion of the Yorkist cause. He had served King Edward well. He had received ill-usage from the youth he had placed and sustained upon the throne. By his depraved abandonment of all the causes for which he had sent so many men to their doom he had deserved death; and for his virtues, which were distinguished, it was fitting that it should come to him in honourable guise.

* * * * *

On the very day of Barnet Margaret at last landed in England. Somerset, the fourth Duke, with his father and his elder brother to avenge, fresh from the distaster at Barnet, met her and became her military commander. On learning that Warwick was slain and his army beaten and dispersed the hitherto indomitable Queen had her hour of despair. Sheltering in Cerne Abbey, near Weymouth, her thought was to return to France; but now her son, the Prince of Wales, nearly eighteen, in whose veins flowed the blood of Henry V, was for fighting for the crown or death. Margaret rallied her spirits and appeared once again unbroken by her life of disaster. Her only hope was to reach the Welsh border, where strong traditional Lancastrian forces were already in arms. The King-maker aberration had been excised. The struggle was once again between Lancaster and York. Edward, near London, held interior lines. He strove to cut Margaret off from Wales. Both armies marched incessantly. In their final march each covered forty miles in a single day. The Lancastrians succeeded in reaching the goal first, but only with their troops in a state of extreme exhaustion. Edward, close behind, pressed on, and on May 3 brought them to battle at Tewkesbury.

This battle was simple in its character. The two sides faced each other in the usual formation of three sectors, right, centre, and left. Somerset commanded Margaret's left, Lord Wenlock and the Prince of Wales the centre, and Devon her right. King Edward exercised a more general command. The Lancastrian position was strong; "in front of their field were so evil lanes, and deep dykes, so many hedges, trees, and bushes, that it was right hard to approach them here and come to hands."[1] Apparently the Lancastrian plan was to await the attack which the Yorkists were eager to deliver. However, Somerset saw an opportunity for using one of the "evil lanes" to pierce the Yorkist centre, and, either without consulting the other generals or in disagreement with them, he charged forward and gained a momentary success. But King Edward had foreseen his weakness in this quarter. He manfully withstood the irruption upon his main body, and two hundred spears he had thrown out wide as a flank guard fell upon Somerset at a decisive moment and from a deadly angle. The Lancastrians' wing recoiled in disorder. The Yorkists advanced all along the line. In their turn they fell upon their enemies' now unguarded flank, and the last army of the house of Lancaster broke into ruin. Somerset the Fourth evidently felt that he had not been supported at the critical moment. Before flying from the field he dashed out Wenlock's brains with his mace. This protest, while throwing a gleam upon the story of the battle, did not affect the result.

The Lancastrians were scattered or destroyed. Somerset and many other notables who thought themselves safe in sanctuary were dragged forth and decapitated. Margaret was captured. The Prince of Wales, fighting valiantly, was slain on the field, according to one chronicler, crying in vain for succour to his brother-in-law, the treacherous Clarence. Margaret was kept for a show, and also because women, especially when they happened to be queens, were not slaughtered in this fierce age.

Richard of Gloucester hastened to London. He had a task to do at the Tower. As long as the Prince of Wales lived King Henry's life had been safe, but with the death of the last hope of Lancaster his fate was sealed. On the night of May 21 the Duke of Gloucester visited the Tower with full authority from the King, where he probably supervised the murder of the melancholy spectator who had been the centre of fifty years of cruel contention.

When King Edward and his victorious army entered London, always their partisan, especially at such moments, the triumph of the Yorkist cause was complete.

> Once more we sit in England's royal throne,
> Re-purchas'd with the blood of enemies:
> What valiant foemen like to autumn's corn,
> Have we mow'd down, in tops of all their pride!
> Three Dukes of Somerset, threefold renown'd
> For hardy and undoubted champions;
> Two Cliffords, as the father and the son,

And two Northumberlands: two braver men
Ne'er spurr'd their coursers at the trumpet's sound;
With them, the two brave bears, Warwick and Montagu,
That in their chains fetter'd the kingly lion,
And made the forest tremble when they roar'd.
Thus have we swept suspicion from our seat,
And made our footstool of security.
Come hither, Bess, and let me kiss my boy.
Young Ned, for thee thine uncles and myself
Have in our armours watch'd the winter's night;
Went all a-foot in summer's scalding heat,
That thou might'st repossess the crown in peace;
And of our labours thou shalt reap the gain.

*   *   *   *   *

The rest of the reign of Edward IV may be told briefly. The King was now supreme. His foes and his patrons alike were dead. He was now a matured and disillusioned statesman. He had every means of remaining complete master of the realm while leading a jolly life. Even from the beginning of his reign he had been chary of calling Parliaments. They made trouble; but if money were needed they had to be called. Therefore the cry in those days which sobered all sovereigns was, "The King should live of his own." But this doctrine took no account of the increasing scope of government. How could the King from his paternal estates, together with certain tolls and tithes, fifteenths, and a few odd poundages, and the accidents of people dying intestate or without adult heirs, or treasure-trove and the like, maintain from these snips an administration equal to the requirements of an expanding society? Still less on this basis could full-blooded wars be waged against France as was expected. It was difficult indeed even to defend the Scottish Border. One had to make use of the warlike nobility of the North, whose hereditary profession was to keep the Marches. Money—above all, ready money. There was the hobble which cramped the medieval kings; and even now it counts somewhat.

Edward was resolved to have as little to do with Parliament as possible, and even as a boy of twenty in the stress of war he tried hard and faithfully to "live of his own." Now that he was victorious and unchallenged, he set himself to practise the utmost economy in everything except his personal expenses, and to avoid any policy of adventure abroad which might drive him to beg from Parliament. He had a new source of revenue in the estates of the attainted Lancastrians. The Crown had gained from the Wars of the Roses. Many were the new possessions which yielded their annual fruit. Thus so long as there was peace the King could pay his way. But the nobility and the nation sought more. They wanted to reconquer France. They mourned the loss of the French provinces. They looked back across their own miseries to the glories of Agincourt, Poitiers, and Crécy. The King, the proved warrior, was expected to produce results in this sphere. It was his intention to do the least possible. He had never liked war, and had had enough of it. Nevertheless he obtained from the Parliament considerable grants for a war in alliance with Burgundy against France.

In 1475 he invaded France, but advanced only as far as Picquigny, near Amiens. There he parleyed. Louis XI had the same outlook. He too saw that kings might grow strong and safe in peace, and would be the prey and tool of their subjects in war. The two kings sought peace and found it. Louis XI offered Edward IV a lump sum of 75,000 crowns, and a yearly tribute of 50,000. This was almost enough to balance the royal budget and make him independent of Parliament. Edward closed on the bargain, and signed the treaty of Picquigny. But Charles the Bold, his ally of Burgundy, took it amiss. At Péronne, in full assembly, with all the English captains gathered, he declared that he had been shamefully betrayed by his ally. A most painful impression was created; but the King put up with it. He went back home and drew for seven successive years this substantial payment for not harrying France, and at the same time he pocketed most of the moneys which Parliament had voted for harrying her.

At this date the interest of these transactions centres mainly upon the character of Edward IV, and we can see that though he had to strive through fierce deeds and slaughter to his throne he was at heart a Little-Englander and a lover of ease. It by no means follows that his policy was injurious to the realm. A long peace was needed for recovery from the horrible civil war. The French Government saw in him with terror all the qualities of Henry V. They paid heavily to hold them in abeyance. This suited the King. He made his administration live thriftily, and on his death he was the first King since Henry II to leave not debts but a fortune. He laboured to contain national pride within the smallest limits, but meanwhile he let the nation grow strong again. He who above all others was thought to be the spear-point became a pad; but at that time a good pad. It may well be, as has been written, that "his indolence and gaiety were mere veils beneath which Edward shrouded profound political ability."[2]

There came a day when he had to call Parliament together. This was not however to ask them for money. What with confiscations, the French tribute, and the profits of his private trading ventures, he could still make his way. His quarrel was with his brother Clarence. Although the compact made between these brothers before Barnet and Tewkesbury had been strictly kept, Edward never trusted Clarence again. Nothing could burn out from his mind the sense that Clarence was a traitor who had betrayed his cause and his family at one decisive moment and had been rebought at another. Clarence for his part knew that the wound although skinned over was unhealed; but he was a magnificent prince, and he sprawled buoyantly over the land. He flouted the King, defying the royal courts; he executed capital sentences upon persons who had offended him in private matters, and felt himself secure. He may have discovered the secret of Edward's alleged pre-contract of marriage with Eleanor Butler which Richard of Gloucester was later to use in justifying his usurpation. Certainly if Edward's marriage to Elizabeth Woodville were to be proved invalid for this reason Clarence was the next legitimate heir, and a source of danger to the King. When in January 1478 Edward's patience was exhausted he called the Parliament with no other business but to condemn Clarence. He adduced a formidable catalogue of crimes and affronts to the Throne, constituting treason. The Parliament, as might be expected, accepted the King's view. By a Bill of Attainder they adjudged Clarence worthy of death, left the execution in the hands of the King, and went home relieved at not having been asked to pay any more taxes.

Clarence was already in the Tower. How he died is much disputed. Some say the King gave him his choice of deaths. Certainly Edward did not intend to have a grisly public spectacle. According to Shakespeare the Duke was drowned in a butt of Malmsey wine. This was certainly the popular legend believed by the sixteenth century. Why should it not be true? At any rate no one has attempted to prove any different tale. "False, fleeting, perjured Clarence" passed out of the world astonished that his brother should have so long a memory and take things so seriously.

Other fortunes had attended Richard of Gloucester. Shortly after the death of Henry VI he got himself married to Anne, daughter of the dead King-maker and co-heiress to the vast Warwick estates. This union excited no enthusiasm; for Anne had been betrothed, if not indeed actually married, to the young Prince Edward, killed at Tewkesbury. Important interests were however combined.

Queen Elizabeth over the course of years had produced not only five daughters, but two fine boys, who were growing up. In 1483 one was twelve and the other nine. The succession to the Crown seemed plain and secure. The King himself was only forty. In another ten years the Yorkist triumph would have become permanent. But here Fate intervened, and with solemn hand reminded the pleasure-loving Edward that his account was closed. His main thought was set on securing the crown to his son, the unfledged Edward V; but in April 1483 death came so suddenly upon him that he had no time to take the necessary precautions. Although always devoted to Queen Elizabeth, he had lived promiscuously all his life. She was in the Midlands, when, after only ten days' illness, this strong King was cut down in his prime. The historians assure us that this was the penalty of debauchery. It may well have been appendicitis, an explanation as yet unknown. He died unprepared except by the Church, and his faithful brother Richard saw himself suddenly confronted with an entirely new view of his future.

CHAPTER THIRTY

RICHARD III

THE KING DIED SO SUDDENLY THAT ALL WERE CAUGHT BY SURPRISE. A tense crisis instantly arose. After Barnet and Tewkesbury the old nobility had had to swallow with such grace as they could muster the return of the surviving Woodvilles to the sunlight of power and favour. But throughout England the Queen's relations were viewed with resentment or disdain, while the King made merry with his beautiful, charming mistress, Jane Shore. Now death dissolved the royal authority by which alone so questionable a structure could be sustained. His eldest son, Edward, dwelt at Ludlow, on the Welsh border, under the care of his uncle, the second Lord Rivers. A Protectorate was inevitable. There could be no doubt about the Protector. Richard of Gloucester, the King's faithful brother, renowned in war, grave and competent in administration, enriched by Warwick's inheritance and many other great estates, in possession of all the chief military offices, stood forth without compare, and had been nominated by the late King himself. Around him gathered most of the old nobility. They viewed with general distaste the idea of a King whose grandfather, though a knight, had been a mere steward to one of their own order. They deplored a minority and thereafter the rule of an unproved, inexperienced boy-King. They were however bound by their oaths and by the succession in the Yorkist line that their own swords had established.

One thing at least they would not brook: Queen Elizabeth and her low-born relations should no longer have the ascendancy. On the other hand, Lord Rivers at Ludlow, with numerous adherents and family supporters, had possession of the new King. For three weeks both parties eyed one another and parleyed. It was agreed in April that the King should be crowned at the earliest moment, but that he should come to London attended by not more than two thousand horsemen. Accordingly this cavalcade, headed by Lord Rivers and his nephew, Grey, rode southward through Shrewsbury and Northampton. They had reached Stony Stratford when they learned that Gloucester and his ally, the Duke of Buckingham, coming to London from Yorkshire, were only ten miles behind them. They turned back to Northampton to greet the two Dukes, apparently suspecting no evil. Richard received them amicably; they dined together. But with the morning there was a change.

When he awoke Rivers found the doors of the inn locked. He asked the reason for this precaution. Gloucester and Buckingham met him with scowling gaze and accused him of "trying to set distance" between the King and them. He and Grey were immediately made prisoners. Richard then rode with his power to Stony Stratford, arrested the commanders of the two thousand horse, forced his way to the young King, and told him he had discovered a design on the part of Lord Rivers and others to seize the Government and oppress the old nobility. On this declaration Edward V took the only positive action recorded of his reign. He wept. Well he might.

The next morning Duke Richard presented himself again to Edward. He embraced him as an uncle; he bowed to him as a subject. He announced himself as Protector. He dismissed the two thousand horsemen to their homes; their services would not be needed. To London then! To the coronation! Thus this melancholy procession set out.

The Queen, who was already in London, had no illusions. She took sanctuary at once with her other children at Westminster, making a hole through the wall between the church and the palace to transport such personal belongings as she could gather.

The report that the King was in duress caused a commotion in the capital. "He was to be sent, no man wist whither, to be done with God wot what."[1] But Lord Hastings reassured the Council that all was well and that any disturbance would only delay the coronation, upon which the peace of the realm depended. The Archbishop of York, who was also Chancellor, tried to reassure the Queen. "Be of good cheer, madam," he said, "for if they crown any other than your son whom they now have with them, we shall on the morrow crown his brother whom you have with you here." He even gave her the Great Seal as a kind of guarantee. He was not in any plot, but only an old fool playing for safety first and peace at any price. Presently, frightened at what he had done, he managed to get the Great Seal back.

The King arrived in London only on May 4, and the coronation, which had been fixed for that date, was necessarily postponed. He was lodged at the Bishop of London's palace, where he received the fealty of all the lords, spiritual and temporal. But the Protector and his friends felt that it was hardly becoming that he should be the guest of an ecclesiastic, and when the Queen's friends suggested that he might reside at the Hospital of the Knights of St. John in Clerkenwell Richard argued that it would be more fitting to the royal dignity to dwell in one of his own castles and on his own ground. The Tower was a residence not only commodious but at the same time safe from any popular disorder. To this decision the lords of the Council gave united assent, it not being either easy or safe for the minority to disagree. With much ceremony and protestations of devotion the child of twelve was conducted to the Tower, and its gates closed behind him.

London was in a ferment, and the magnates gathered there gazed upon each other in doubt and fear. The next step in the tragedy concerned Lord Hastings. He had played a leading part in the closing years of Edward IV. After the King's death he had been strong against the Woodvilles; but he was the first to detach himself from Richard's proceedings. It did not suit him, nor some of the other magnates, that all power should rapidly be accumulating in Richard's hands. He began to be friendly with the Queen's party, still in the sanctuary of Westminster Abbey. Of what happened next all we really know is that Hastings was abruptly arrested in council at the Tower on June 13 and beheaded without trial on the same day. Sir Thomas More late in the next reign wrote his celebrated history. His book was based of course on information given him under the new and strongly established régime. His object seems to have been less to compose a factual narrative than a moralistic drama. In it Richard is evil incarnate, and Henry Tudor, the deliverer of the kingdom, all sweetness and light. The opposite view would have been treason. Not only is every possible crime attributed by More to Richard, and some impossible ones, but he is presented as a physical monster, crook-backed and withered of arm. No one in his lifetime seems to have remarked these deformities, but they are now very familiar to us through Shakespeare's play. Needless to say, as soon as the Tudor dynasty was laid to rest defenders of Richard fell to work, and they have been increasingly busy ever since.

More's tale however has priority. We have the famous scene at the Council in the Tower. It was Friday, June 13. Richard arrived in the Council chamber about nine, apparently in good humour. "My lord," he said to Bishop Morton, "you have very good strawberries in your garden at Holborn. I pray you let us have a mess of them." The Council began its business. Richard asked to be excused for a while; when he returned between ten and eleven his whole manner was changed. He frowned and glared upon the Council, and at the same time clusters of armed men gathered at the door. "What punishment do they deserve," demanded the Protector, "who conspire against the life of one so nearly related to the King as myself, and entrusted with the government of the realm?" There was general consternation. Hastings said at length that they deserved the punishment of traitors. "That sorceress my brother's wife," cried Richard, "and others with her—see how they have wasted my body with sorcery and witchcraft." So saying, he is supposed to have bared his arm and showed it to the Council, shrunk and withered as legend says it was. In furious terms he next referred to Jane Shore, with whom Hastings had formed an intimacy on the late King's death. Hastings, taken aback, replied, "Certainly if they have done so heinously they are worth a heinous punishment." "What?" cried Crookback. "Dost thou serve me with 'ifs' and 'ands?' I tell thee they have done it, and that I will make good upon thy body, traitor!" He struck the Council table with his fist, and at this signal the armed men ran in, crying "Treason!" and Hastings, Bishop Morton, and the Archbishop of York with some others were seized. Richard bade Hastings prepare for instant death. "I will not dine until I have his head." There was barely time to find a priest. Upon a log of wood which lay by chance in the Tower yard Hastings was decapitated. Terror reigned.

Richard had ordered his retainers in the North to come to London in arms under his trusted lieutenant, Sir Richard Ratcliffe. On the way south Ratcliffe collected Lords Rivers, Vaughan, Grey, and the commanders of the two thousand horse from the castles in which they were confined, and at Pomfret cut off their heads a few days after Hastings had suffered. Their executions are undisputed fact.

Meanwhile the Queen and her remaining son still sheltered in sanctuary. Richard felt that it would be more natural that the two brothers should be together under his care, and he moved the purged Council to request the Queen to give him up. The Council contemplated the use of force in the event of a refusal. Having no choice, the Queen submitted, and the little prince of nine was handed over in Westminster Hall to the Protector, who embraced him affectionately and conducted him to the Tower, which neither he nor his brother was ever to leave again. Richard's Northern bands were now approaching London in considerable numbers, many thousands being expected, and he felt strong enough to take his next step. The coronation of Edward V had been postponed several times. Now a preacher named Shaw, brother of the Lord Mayor of London, one of Richard's partisans, was engaged to preach a sermon at St. Paul's Cross. Taking his text from the Book of Wisdom, "Bastard slips shall not take deep root," he impugned Edward IV's marriage with Elizabeth Woodville upon a number of grounds, including sorcery, violation of the alleged previous betrothal to Eleanor Butler, and the assertion that the ceremony had been performed in an unconsecrated place. He argued from this that Edward's children were illegitimate and that the crown rightly belonged to Richard. The suggestion was even revived that Edward IV himself had not been his father's son. Richard now appeared, accompanied by Buckingham, evidently expecting to be publicly acclaimed; but, says More, "the people were so far from crying 'King Richard!' that they stood as if turned into stones for wonder of this shameful sermon." Two days later the Duke

of Buckingham tried his hand, and according to an eyewitness he was
so eloquent and well rehearsed that he did not even pause to spit; but
once again the people remained mute, and only some of the Duke's
servants threw up their caps, crying, "King Richard!"

Nevertheless on June 25 Parliament met, and after receiving a roll
declaring that the late King's marriage with Elizabeth was no marriage
at all and that Edward's children were bastard it petitioned Richard to
assume the crown. A deputation, headed by the Duke of Buckingham,
waited on Richard, who was staying at the house of his mother, whose
virtue he had aspersed. With becoming modesty Richard persistently
refused; but when Buckingham assured him of their determination
that the children of Edward should not rule and that if he would not
serve the country they would be forced to choose some other noble
he overcame his conscientious scruples at the call of public duty. The
next day he was enthroned, with much ceremony. At the same time
the forces which Ratcliffe had sent from the North were reviewed
in Finsbury Fields. They proved to be about five thousand strong,
"evil apparelled . . . in rusty harness neither defensible nor scoured."
The City was relieved to find that the reports of their strength and
numbers had been exaggerated.

The coronation of King Richard III was fixed for July 6, and
pageants and processions diverted the uneasy public. As an act of
clemency Richard released the Archbishop of York from arrest,
and transferred Bishop Morton of Ely to the easier custody of
Buckingham. The coronation was celebrated with all possible pomp
and splendour. Particular importance was attached to the religious
aspect. Archbishop Bourchier placed the crowns on the heads of
the King and Queen; they were anointed with oil; they received the
Sacrament in the presence of the assembly, and finally repaired to a
banquet in Westminster Hall. The King now had a title acknowledged
and confirmed by Parliament, and upon the theory of the bastardy
of Edward's children he was also the lineal successor in blood. Thus
the whole design seemed to have been accomplished. Yet from this
very moment there began that marked distrust and hostility of all
classes towards King Richard III which all his arts and competence
could not allay. "It followed," said the chronicler Fabyan, whose book

was published in 1516, "anon as this man had taken upon him, he fell in great hatred of the more part of the nobles of his realm, insomuch that such as before loved and praised him . . . now murmured and grudged against him in such wise that few or none favoured his party except it were for dread or for the great gifts they had received of him."

It is contended by the defenders of King Richard that the Tudor version of these events has prevailed. But the English people who lived at the time and learned of the events day by day formed their convictions two years before the Tudors gained power or were indeed a prominent factor. Richard III held the authority of government. He told his own story with what facilities were available, and he was spontaneously and almost universally disbelieved. Indeed, no fact stands forth more unchallengeable than that the overwhelming majority of the nation was convinced that Richard had used his power as Protector to usurp the crown and that the princes had disappeared in the Tower. It will take many ingenious books to raise this issue to the dignity of a historical controversy.

No man had done more to place Richard upon the throne than the Duke of Buckingham, and upon no one had the King bestowed greater gifts and favours. Yet during these first three months of Richard's reign Buckingham from being his chief supporter became his mortal foe. His motives are not clear. Perhaps he shrank from becoming the accomplice in what he foresaw would be the closing act of the usurpation. Perhaps he feared for his own safety, for was he not himself of royal blood? He was descended both through the Beauforts and Thomas of Woodstock from Edward III. It was believed that when the Beaufort family was legitimated by letters patent under King Richard II, confirmed by Henry IV, there had been a reservation rendering them incapable of inheriting the crown; but this reservation had not been a part of the original document, but had only been written in during the reign of Henry IV. The Duke of Buckingham, as a Beaufort on his mother's side, possessed the original letters patent under the Great Seal, confirmed in Parliament, in which no such bar was mentioned. Although he guarded this secret with all needful prudence he must now look upon himself as a potential claimant to the crown, and he must feel none the safer if Richard should so regard him. Buckingham's mind was troubled by the knowledge that all the ceremony and vigour with which Richard's ascent to the throne had been conducted did not affect the general feeling that he was a usurper. In his castle at Brecknock he began to talk moodily to his prisoner, Bishop Morton; and the Bishop, who was a master of the persuasive arts and a consummate politician, undoubtedly gained a great hold upon him.

*　　*　　*　　*　　*

Meanwhile King Richard began a progress from Oxford through the Midlands. At every city he laboured to make the best impression, righting wrongs, settling disputes, granting favours, and courting popularity. Yet he could not escape the sense that behind the displays of gratitude and loyalty which naturally surrounded him there lay an unspoken challenge to his Kingship. There was little concealment of this in the South. In London, Kent, Essex, and throughout the Home Counties feeling already ran high against him, and on all men's lips was the demand that the princes should be liberated. Richard did not as yet suspect Buckingham, who had parted from him at Gloucester, of any serious disaffection. But he was anxious for the safety of his crown. How could he maintain it while his nephews lived to provide a rallying point for any combination of hostile forces against him? So we come to the principal crime ever afterwards associated with Richard's name. His interest is plain. His character was ruthless. It is certain that the helpless children in the Tower were not seen again after the month of July 1483. Yet we are invited by some to believe that they languished in captivity, unnoticed and unrecorded, for another two years, only to be done to death by Henry Tudor.

According to Thomas More's story, Richard resolved in July to extirpate the menace to his peace and sovereignty presented by the princes. He sent a special messenger, by name John Green, to Brackenbury, the Constable of the Tower, with orders to make an end of them. Brackenbury refused to obey. "Whom should a man trust," exclaimed the King when Green returned with this report "when those who I thought would most surely serve at my command will do nothing for me?" A page who heard this outburst reminded his master that Sir James Tyrell, one of Richard's former companions in arms, was capable of anything. Tyrell was sent to London with a warrant authorising Brackenbury to deliver to him for one night all the keys of the Tower. Tyrell discharged his fell commission with all dispatch. One of the four gaolers in charge of the princes, Forest by name, was found willing, and with Dighton, Tyrell's own groom, did the deed. When the princes were asleep these two assassins pressed the pillows hard down upon their faces till they were suffocated, and their bodies were immured in some secret corner of the Tower. There is some proof that all three murderers were suitably rewarded by the King. But it was not until Henry VII's reign, when Tyrell was lying in the Tower under sentence of death for quite a separate crime, that he is alleged to have made a confession upon which, with much other circumstantial evidence, the story as we know it rests.

In the reign of Charles II, when in 1674 the staircase leading to the chapel in the White Tower was altered, the skeletons of two young lads, whose apparent ages fitted the two princes, were found buried under a mass of rubble. They were examined by the royal surgeon, and the antiquaries reported that they were undoubtedly the remains of Edward V and the Duke of York. Charles accepted this view, and the skeletons were reburied in Henry VII's Chapel at Westminster with a Latin inscription laying all blame upon their perfidious uncle "the usurper of the realm." This has not prevented various writers, among whom Horace Walpole is notable, from endeavouring to clear Richard of the crime, or from attempting to cast it, without any evidence beyond conjecture, upon Henry VII. However, in our own time an exhumation has confirmed the view of the disinterested authorities of King Charles's reign.

Buckingham had now become the centre of a conspiracy throughout the West and South of England against the King. He had reached a definite decision about his own claims to the crown. He seems to have assumed from his knowledge of Richard that the princes in the Tower were either dead or doomed. He met at this time Margaret, Countess of Richmond, survivor of the Beaufort line, and recognised that even if the house of York were altogether set aside both she and her son Henry Tudor, Earl of Richmond, stood between him and the crown. The Countess of Richmond, presuming him to be still Richard's right-hand man, asked him to win the King's consent to a marriage between her son Henry of Richmond and one of King Edward's daughters, Elizabeth, still in sanctuary with their mother at Westminster. Richard would never have entertained such a project, which was indeed the extreme opposite to his interests. But Buckingham saw that such a marriage would unite the claims of York and Lancaster, bridge the gulf that had parted England for so long, and enable a tremendous front to be immediately formed against the usurper.

The popular demand for the release of the princes was followed by a report of their death. When, how, and by whose hand the deed had been done was not known. But as the news spread like wildfire a kind of fury seized upon many people. Although accustomed to the brutalities of the long civil wars, the English people of those days still retained the faculty of horror; and once it was excited they did not soon forget. A modern dictator with the resources of science at his disposal can easily lead the public on from day to day, destroying all persistency of thought and aim, so that memory is blurred by the multiplicity of daily news and judgment baffled by its perversion. But in the fifteenth century the murder of the two young princes by the very man who had undertaken to protect them was regarded as an atrocious crime, never to be forgotten or forgiven. In September Richard in his progress reached York, and here he created his son Prince of Wales, thus in the eyes of his enemies giving confirmation to the darkest rumours.

All Buckingham's preparations were for a general rising on October 18. He would gather his Welsh forces at Brecknock; all the Southern and Western counties would take up arms; and Henry, Earl of Richmond, with the aid of the Duke of Brittany, would land with a force of five thousand men in Wales. But the anger of the people at the rumoured murder of the princes deranged this elaborate plan. In Kent, Wiltshire, Sussex, and Devonshire there were risings ten days before the appointed date; Henry of Richmond was forced to set sail from Brittany in foul weather on October 12, so that his fleet was dispersed; and when Buckingham unfurled his flag at Brecknock the elements took sides against him too. A terrific storm flooded the Severn valley, and he found himself penned on the Welsh border in a district which could not supply the needs of his army, and unable, as he had planned, to join the rebels in Devonshire.

King Richard acted with the utmost vigour. He had an army and he marched against rebellion. The sporadic risings in the South were suppressed. Buckingham's forces melted away, and he himself hid from vengeance. Richmond reached the English coast at last with only two ships, and sailed westwards towards Plymouth, waiting for a sign which never came. Such was the uncertainty at Plymouth that he warily made further inquiries, as a result of which he sailed back to Brittany. Buckingham, with a high price on his head, was betrayed to Richard, who lost not an hour in having him slaughtered. The usual crop of executions followed. Order was restored throughout the land, and the King seemed to have established himself securely upon his throne.

He proceeded in the new year to inaugurate a series of enlightened reforms in every sphere of Government. He revived the power of Parliament, which it had been the policy of Edward IV to reduce to nullity. He declared the practice of raising revenue by "benevolences" illegal. Parliament again legislated copiously after a long interval. Commerce was protected by a series of well-meant if ill-judged Acts, and a land law was passed to regulate "uses," or, as we should now say, trusts. Attempts were made to please the clergy by confirming their privileges, endowing new religious foundations, and extending the patronage of learning. Much care was taken over the shows of heraldry and pageantry; magnanimity was shown to fallen opponents, and petitioners in distress were treated with kindness. But all counted for nothing. The hatred which Richard's crime had roused against him throughout the land remained sullen and quenchless, and no benefits bestowed, no sagacious measures adopted, no administrative successes achieved, could avail the guilty monarch.

An impulsive gentleman, one Collingbourne, formerly Sheriff of Worcester, was so much incensed against the King that he had a doggerel rhyme he had composed nailed on the door of St. Paul's:

> The Catte, the Ratte, and Lovell our dogge
> Rulyth all Englande under a Hogge.

Catesby, Ratcliffe, Viscount Lovell, and Richard, whose badge was a boar, saw themselves affronted. But it was not only for this that Collingbourne suffered an agonising death at the end of a year. He was undoubtedly a rebel, actively engaged in conspiracy.

Even Richard's own soul rebelled against him. He was haunted by fears and dreams. He saw retribution awaiting him round every corner. "I have heard by creditable report," says Sir Thomas More, "of such as were secret with his chamberers, that after this abominable deed done he never had quiet in his mind, he never thought himself sure. Where he went abroad, his eyes whirled about, his body privily fenced, his hand ever on his dagger, his countenance and manner like one always ready to strike again. He took ill rest at nights, lay long waking and musing; sore wearied with care and watch, he rather slumbered than slept. Troubled with fearful dreams, suddenly sometimes started he up, leapt out of his bed and ran about the chamber. So was his restless heart continually tossed and tumbled with the tedious impression and stormy remembrance of his most abominable deed."

*　　*　　*　　*　　*

A terrible blow now fell upon the King. In April 1484 his only son, the Prince of Wales, died at Middleham, and his wife, Anne, the daughter of the King-maker, whose health was broken, could bear no more children. Henry Tudor, Earl of Richmond, now became obviously the rival claimant and successor to the throne. Richmond, "the nearest thing to royalty the Lancastrian party possessed," was a Welshman, whose grandfather, Owen Tudor, executed by the Yorkists in 1461, had married, if indeed he married, Henry V's widow, Catherine of France, and whose father Edmund had married the Lady Margaret Beaufort. Thus Richmond could trace his descent through his mother from Edward III, and on his father's side had French royal blood in his veins as well as a shadowy claim to descent from Cadwallader and the legendary ancient kings of Britain, including King Arthur. His life had been cast amid ceaseless trouble. For seven years of childhood he had been besieged in Harlech Castle. At the age of fourteen, on the defeat of the Lancastrians at Tewkesbury, he was forced to flee to Brittany. Thereafter exile and privation had been his lot. These trials had stamped themselves upon his character, rendering him crafty and suspicious. This, however, did not daunt a proud spirit, nor cloud a wise and commanding mind, nor cast a shadow over his countenance, which was, we are told, "smiling and amiable, especially in his communications."

All hopes in England were now turned towards Richmond, and it was apparent that the marriage which had been projected between him and Edward IV's eldest daughter Elizabeth offered a prospect of ending for ever the cruel dynastic strife of which the land was unutterably weary. After the failure of Buckingham's rebellion Richmond and his expedition had returned to Brittany. The Duke of Brittany, long friendly again accorded shelter and subsistence to the exile and his band of perhaps five hundred Englishmen of quality. But King Richard's diplomacy was active. He offered a large sum of money for the surrender of his rival. During the illness of the Duke of Brittany the Breton Minister, Landois, was disposed to sell the valuable refugee. Richmond however, suspecting the danger, escaped in the nick of time by galloping hell for leather into France, where, in accordance with the general policy of keeping English feuds alive, he was well received by the French regent, Anne. Meanwhile the Duke of Brittany, recovering, reproved his Minister and continued to harbour the English exiles. In France Richmond was joined by the Earl of Oxford, the leading survivor of the Lancastrian party, who had escaped from ten years' incarceration and plunged once again into the old struggle. As the months passed many prominent Englishmen, both Yorkist and Lancastrian, withdrew themselves from Richard's baleful presence, and made their way to Richmond, who from this time forth stood at the head of a combination which might well unite all England.

His great hope lay in the marriage with the Princess Elizabeth. But in this quarter Richard had not been idle. Before the rebellion he had taken steps to prevent Elizabeth slipping out of sanctuary and England. In March 1484 he made proposals to the Dowager Queen, Dame Elizabeth Grey as he called her, of reconciliation. The unhappy Queen did not reject his overtures. Richard promised in a solemn deed "on his honour as a King" to provide maintenance for the ex-Queen and to marry her daughters suitably to gentlemen. This remarkable document was witnessed not only by the Lords Spiritual and Temporal, but in addition by the Lord Mayor of London and the Aldermen. In spite of the past the Queen had to trust herself to this. She quitted sanctuary. She abandoned the match for her daughter with Richmond. She and the elder princesses were received at Richard's Court and treated with exceptional distinction. At the Christmas Court at Westminster in 1484 high revels were held. It was noticed that the changes of dress provided for Dame Elizabeth Grey and her daughters were almost royal in their style and richness. The stigma of bastardy so lately inflicted upon Edward's children, and the awful secret of the Tower, were banished. Although the threat of invasion was constant, gaiety and dancing ruled the hour. "Dame Elizabeth" even wrote to her son by her first marriage, the Marquis of Dorset, in Paris, to abandon Richmond and come home to share in the new-found favour. More surprising still, Princess Elizabeth seems to have been by no means hostile to the attentions of the usurper. In March 1485 Queen Anne died, probably from natural causes. Rumours were circulating that Richard intended to marry his niece himself, in order to keep her out of Richmond's way. This incestuous union could have been achieved by Papal dispensation, but Richard disavowed all intention of it, both in Council and in public. And it is indeed hard to see how his position could have been strengthened by marrying a princess whom he had declared illegitimate. However that may be, Richmond was thereby relieved of a great anxiety.

All through the summer Richmond's expedition was preparing at the mouth of the Seine, and the exodus from England of substantial people to join him was unceasing. The suspense was wearing to Richard. He felt he was surrounded by hatred and distrust, and that none served him but from fear, or hope of favour. His dogged, indomitable nature had determined him to make for his crown the greatest of all his fights. He fixed his headquarters in a good central position at Nottingham. Commissions of muster and array were ordered to call men to arms in almost every county. Departing perforce from the precepts he had set himself in the previous year, he asked for a "benevolence," or "malevolence" as it was described, of thirty thousand pounds. He set on foot a disciplined regular force. He stationed relays of horsemen every twenty miles permanently along the great roads to bring news and carry orders with an organised swiftness hitherto unknown in England. This important development in the postal system had been inaugurated by Edward IV. At the head of his troops he ceaselessly patrolled the Midland area, endeavouring by strength to overawe and by good government to placate his sullen subjects. He set forth his cause in a vehement proclamation, denouncing ". . . one, Henry Tydder, son of Edmund Tydder, son of Owen Tydder," of bastard blood both on his father's and mother's side, who of his ambition and covetousness pretended to the crown, "to the disinheriting and destruction of all the noble and worshipful blood of his realm for ever." But this fell cold.

On August 1 Richmond embarked at Harfleur with his Englishmen, Yorkist as well as Lancastrian, and a body of French troops. A fair wind bore him down the Channel. He evaded the squadrons of "Lovell our Dogge," doubled Land's End, and landed at Milford Haven on the 7th. Kneeling, he recited the psalm *Judica me, Deus, et decerne causam meam*. He kissed the ground, signed himself with the Cross, and gave the order to advance in the name of God and St. George. He had only two thousand men; but such were his assurances of support that he proclaimed Richard forthwith usurper and rebel against himself. The Welsh were gratified by the prospect of one of their race succeeding to the crown of mighty England. It had been for ages a national dream. The ancient Britons would come back into their own. Richard's principal chieftain and officer, Rhys ap Thomas, considered himself at first debarred by his oath of allegiance from aiding the invader. He had declared that no rebels should enter Wales, "except they should pass over his belly." He had however excused himself from sending his only son to Nottingham as a hostage, assuring Richard that nothing could bind him more strongly than his conscience. This now became an obstacle. However, the Bishop of St. David's offered to absolve him from his oath, and suggested that he might, if still disquieted, lay himself upon the ground before Richmond and let him actually step over his belly. A more dignified but equally satisfactory procedure was adopted. Rhys ap Thomas stood under the Molloch Bridge near Dale while Henry of Richmond walked over the top. Anything like a scandalous breach of faith was thus avoided. The Welsh gentry rallied in moderate numbers to Richmond, who displayed not only the standard of St. George, but the Red Dragon of Cadwallader. With five thousand men he now moved eastwards through Shrewsbury and Stafford.

*   *   *   *   *

For all his post-horses it was five days before the King heard of the landing. He gathered his army and marched to meet his foe. At this moment the attitude of the Stanleys became of decisive importance. They had been entrusted by the King with the duty of intercepting the rebels should they land in the West. Sir William Stanley, with some thousands of men, made no attempt to do so. Richard thereupon summoned Lord Stanley, the head of the house, to his Court, and when that potentate declared himself "ill of the sweating sickness" he seized Lord Strange, his eldest son, to hold him answerable with his life for his father's loyalty. This did not prevent Sir William Stanley with the Cheshire levies from making friendly contact with Richmond. But Lord Stanley, hoping to save his son, maintained till the last moment an uncertain demeanour.

The city of York on this occasion stood by the Yorkist cause. The Duke of Norfolk and Percy, Earl of Northumberland, were Richard's principal adherents. "The Catte and the Ratte" had no hope of life but in their master's victory. On August 17, thus attended, the King set forth towards Leicester at the head of his army. Their ordered ranks, four abreast, with the cavalry on both flanks and the King mounted on his great white charger in the centre, made a formidable impression upon beholders. And when on Sunday, the 21st, this whole array came out of Leicester to meet Richmond near the village of Market Bosworth it was certain that a decisive battle impended on the morrow.

Appearances favoured the King. He had ten thousand disciplined men under the royal authority against Richmond's hastily gathered five thousand rebels. But at some distance from the flanks of the main army, on opposite hill-tops, stood the respective forces, mainly from

Lancashire and Cheshire, of Sir William Stanley and Lord Stanley, the whole situation resembling, as has been said, four players in a game of cards. Richard, according to the Tudor historians, although confessing to a night of frightful dreams and demon-hauntings, harangued his captains in magnificent style. "Dismiss all fear. . . . Every one give but one sure stroke and the day is ours. What prevaileth a handful of men to a whole realm? As for me, I assure you this day I will triumph by glorious victory or suffer death for immortal fame." He then gave the signal for battle, and sent a message to Lord Stanley that if he did not fall on forthwith he would instantly decapitate his son. Stanley, forced to this bitter choice, answered proudly that he had other sons. The King gave orders for Strange's execution. But the officers so charged thought it prudent to hold the stroke in suspense till matters were clearer. "My lord, the enemy is past the marsh. After the battle let young Stanley die."

But even now Richmond was not sure what part Lord Stanley and his forces would play. When, after archery and cannonade, the lines were locked in battle all doubts were removed. The Earl of Northumberland, commanding Richard's left, stood idle at a distance. Lord Stanley's force joined Richmond. The King saw that all was lost, and, shouting "Treason! Treason!" hurled himself into the thickest of the fray in the desperate purpose of striking down Richmond with his own hand. He actually slew Sir William Brandon, Richmond's standard-bearer, and laid low Sir John Cheney, a warrior renowned for his bodily strength. He is said even to have reached Richmond and crossed swords with him. But at this moment Sir William Stanley's three thousand, "in coats as red as blood," fell upon the struggling Yorkists. The tides of conflict swept the principals asunder. Richmond was preserved, and the King, refusing to fly, was borne down and slaughtered as he deserved.

One foot I will never flee, while the breath is my breast within.
As he said, so did it he—if he lost his life he died a king.

Richard's crown, which he wore to the last, was picked out of a bush and placed upon the victor's head. The Duke of Norfolk was slain fighting bravely; his son, Lord Surrey, was taken prisoner; Ratcliffe was killed; Catesby, after being allowed to make his will, was executed on the field; and Henry Tudor became King of England. Richard's corpse, naked, and torn by wounds, was bound across a horse, with his head and long hair hanging down, bloody and hideous, and in this condition borne into Leicester for all men to see.

*   *   *   *   *

Bosworth Field may be taken as closing a long chapter in English history. Though risings and conspiracies continued throughout the next reign the strife of the Red and the White Rose had in the main come to an end. Neither won. A solution was reached in which the survivors of both causes could be reconciled. The marriage of Richmond with the adaptable Princess Elizabeth produced the Tudor line, in which both Yorkists and Lancastrians had a share. The revengeful ghosts of two mangled generations were laid for ever. Richard's death also ended the Plantagenet line. For over three hundred years this strong race of warrior and statesmen kings, whose gifts and vices were upon the highest scale, whose sense of authority and Empire had been persistently maintained, now vanished from the fortunes of the Island. The Plantagenets and the proud, exclusive nobility which their system evolved had torn themselves to pieces. The heads of most of the noble houses had been cut off, and their branches extirpated to the second and third generation. An oligarchy whose passions, loyalties, and crimes had for long written English history was subdued. Sprigs of female or bastard lines made disputable contacts with a departed age. As Cœur de Lion said of his house, "From the Devil we sprang and to the Devil we shall go."

At Bosworth the Wars of the Roses reached their final milestone. In the next century the subjects of the Tudors liked to consider that the Middle Ages too had come to a close in 1485, and that a new age had dawned with the accession of Henry Tudor. Modern historians prefer to point out that there are no sharp dividing lines in this period of our history, and that Henry VII carried on and consolidated much of the work of the Yorkist Kings. Certainly the prolongation of strife, waste, and insecurity in the fifteenth century had aroused in all classes an overpowering desire for strong, ordered government. The

Parliamentary conception which had prevailed under the house of Lancaster had gained many frontiers of constitutional rights. These were now to pass into long abeyance. Not until the seventeenth century were the old maxims, "Grievances before supply," "Responsibility of Ministers in accordance with the public will," "The Crown the servant and not the master of the State," brought again into the light, and, as it happened, the glare of a new day. The stir of the Renaissance, the storm of the Reformation, hurled their new problems on the bewildered but also reinspired mortals of the new age upon which England entered under the guidance of the wise, sad, careful monarch who inaugurated the Tudor dictatorship as King Henry VII.

ENDNOTES

CHAPTER I

[1] Cæsar, *The Conquest of Gaul,* translated by S. A. Handford, Penguin Classics, 1951.

[2] *History of England.*

[3] Collingwood and Myres, *Roman Britain.*

[4] *Op. cit.*

[5] Darby, *Historical Geography of England,* p. 42.

[6] *Antiquity,* vol. i, p. 189.

CHAPTER II

[1] Dio Cassius, chapter lx, pp. 19–20.

[2] *Ibid.*

[3] C. Suetonius Tranquillus, *The Lives of the Twelve Cæsars,* trans, by Alexander Thomson, revised by T. Forester.

[4] Extracts from Tacitus' *Annals* are from G. G. Ramsay's translation; passages from the *Agricola* come from the translation of Church and Brodribb.

[5] *History of England,* vol. i, p. 8.

CHAPTER III

[1] *An Economic Survey of Ancient Rome,* iii, 24.

[2] Written in 1939.

CHAPTER IV

[1] Constantine of Lyons, a near contemporary biographer of St. Germanus.

[2] See Sir Frank Stenton, *Anglo-Saxon England* (1943), p. 3: "The silence of Gildas may suggest that the Arthur of history was a less imposing figure than the Arthur of legend. But it should not be allowed to remove him from the sphere of history, for Gildas was curiously reluctant to introduce personal names into his writing."

[3] *Short History of the English People,* p. 4.

CHAPTER VI

[1] *Anglo-Saxon Chronicle,* AD 866.
[2] From *The Vikings and their Voyages,* by A. MacCallum Scott, "The Universal History of the World," ed. J. A. Hammerton, vol. iv.
[3] *History of the Anglo-Saxons,* vol. ii, p. 525.
[4] Quoted in Hodgkin, vol. II, p. 524.

CHAPTER VII

[1] Hodgkin, vol. ii, pp. 544–545.
[2] F. Stenton, *The Danes in England,* 1927, p. 13.
[3] Quoted in Hodgkin, *loc. cit.,* vol. ii, pp. 565–566.
[4] Quoted in Hodgkins, vol. II, p. 584.
[5] Quoted in Hodgkin, *History of the Anglo-Saxons,* p. 609.
[6] Ibid., p. 612.

CHAPTER VIII

[1] Kendrick's *History of the Vikings,* p. 259.
[2] *Ibid.*
[3] *History of England,* vol. i, p. 25.
[4] From the *Encomium Emma Regina,* in Langebek, *Scriptores Rerum Danicarum* (1773).
[5] From the *Heimskringla* of Snorre Sturlason.

CHAPTER IX

[1] From the *Heimskringla Saga,* by Snorre Sturlason.

CHAPTER X

[1] Written early in 1939.
[2] *Anglo-Saxon Chronicle,* in *English Historical Documents,* vol. ii. (Eyre and Spottiswoode, 1953.)

CHAPTER XI

[1] Douglas, *Age of the Normans,* p. 161.
[2] Translated from *Gesta Stephani,* ed. Howlett, p. 99.

CHAPTER XII

[1] Written in 1938.

CHAPTER XV

[1] *Taine.*

CHAPTER XXI

[1] Written in 1939.

CHAPTER XXV

[1] *Gesta Henrici V, English Historical Society,* ed. B. Williams.
[2] *Chronicles of London,* ed. C. L. Kingsford, p. 119.
[3] *History of England,* vol. i, p. 84.

CHAPTER XXVIII

[1] Gregory's *Chronicle.*

CHAPTER XXIX

[1] *The Arrival of Edward IV.*
[2] J. R. Green.

CHAPTER XXX

[1] More.

INDEX

SUGGESTED READING

◄╬►

ALDRITT, KEITH. *Churchill the Writer: His Life as a Man of Letters.* London: Hutchinson, 1992.

ASHLEY, MAURICE. *Churchill as Historian.* New York: Scribner, 1968.

CHURCHILL, WINSTON. *Lord Randolph Churchill.* London: Library of Imperial History, 1974.

——. *Marlborough: His Life and Times,* 2 vols. Chicago: University of Chicago Press, 2002.

——. *The Second World War,* 6 vols. Boston: Houghton Mifflin, 1985–86.

——. *The World Crisis and the Aftermath,* 5 vols. London: Odhams Press, 1923–31.

GILBERT, MARTIN. *Churchill: A Life.* New York: Holt, 1991.

——. *In Search of Churchill: A Historian's Journey.* Hoboken, NJ: John Wiley, 1997.

JACOB, ERNEST F. *Fifteenth Century, 1399–1485.* New York: Oxford University Press, 1961.

JENKINS, ROY. *Churchill: A Biography.* New York: Farrar, Straus & Giroux, 2001.

KEEGAN, JOHN. *Winston Churchill.* New York: Viking Books, 2002.

LUKACS, JOHN. *Churchill, Visionary, Statesman, Historian.* New Haven: Yale University Press, 2002.

MACAULAY, THOMAS BABINGTON. *The History of England.* Harmondsworth: Penguin Books, 1979.

MANCHESTER, WILLIAM. *The Last Lion: Winston Spencer Churchill,* 2 vols. Boston: Little Brown, 1983–88.

MCKISSACK, MAY. *Fourteenth Century, 1307–1399.* New York: Oxford University Press, 1959.

MULLER, JAMES W. *Churchill as Peacemaker.* Cambridge: Cambridge University Press, 2002.

MYRES, JOHN N. *English Settlements.* New York: Oxford University Press, 1989.

POOLE, AUSTIN LANE. *From Domesday Book to Magna Carta: 1087–1216.* New York: Oxford University Press, 1993.

POWICKE, SIR MAURICE. *The 13ᵗʰ Century (1216–1307): Oxford History of England.* Oxford: Clarendon Press, 1962.

ROSKILL, STEPHEN. *Churchill and the Admirals.* London: Pen and Sword, 1977.

SALWAY, PETER. *Roman Britain.* New York: Oxford University Press, 1981.

SCHAMA, SIMON. *A History of Britain: At the Edge of the World? 3600 BC–AD 1603.* New York: Hyperion, 2001.

SOAMES, MARY. *Winston Churchill: His Life as a Painter: A Memoir by His Daughter.* Boston: Houghton Mifflin, 1990.

STENTON, FRANK M. *Anglo-Saxon England.* Ed. George Clark. New York: Oxford University Press, 1971.

TREVELYAN, GEORGE MACAULEY. *A Shortened History of England.* Harmondsworth: Penguin Books, 1987.

Look for the following titles, available now from
The Barnes & Noble Library of Essential Reading.

Visit your Barnes & Noble bookstore,
or shop online at *www.bn.com/loer*

NONFICTION

Creative Evolution	Henri Bergson	0760765480
Critique of Judgment	Immanuel Kant	0760762023
Critique of Practical Reason	Immanuel Kant	0760760942
Critique of Pure Reason	Immanuel Kant	0760755949
Dark Night of the Soul, The	St. John of the Cross	0760765871
Democracy and Education	John Dewey	0760765863
Democracy in America	Alexis de Tocqueville	0760752303
Descent of Man and Selection in Relation to Sex, The	Charles Darwin	0760763119
Dialogues concerning Natural Religion	David Hume	0760777713
Discourse on Method	René Descartes	0760756023
Discourses on Livy	Niccolò Machiavelli	0760771731
Dolorous Passion of Our Lord Jesus Christ, The	Anne Catherine Emmerich	0760771715
Early History of Rome, The	Titus Livy	0760770239
Ecce Homo	Friedrich Nietzsche	0760777721
Edison: His Life and Inventions	Frank Lewis Dyer	0760765820
Egyptian Book of the Dead, The	E. A. Wallis Budge	0760768382
Elements, The	Euclid	0760763127
Emile	Jean-Jacques Rousseau	0760773513
Eminent Victorians	Lytton Strachey	0760749930
Encheiridion	Epictetus	0760770204
Enquiry concerning Human Understanding, An	David Hume	0760755922
Essay concerning Human Understanding, An	John Locke	0760760497
Essays, The	Francis Bacon	0760770182
Essence of Christianity, The	Ludwig Feuerbach	076075764X
Ethics and On the Improvement of the Understanding	Benedict de Spinoza	0760768374
Extraordinary Popular Delusions and the Madness of Crowds	Charles Mackay	0760755825
Fall of Troy, The	Quintus of Smyrna	0760768366
Fifteen Decisive Battles of the Western World	Edward Shepherd Creasy	0760754950
Florentine History	Niccolò Machiavelli	0760756015
From Manassas to Appomattox	James Longstreet	0760759200
From Ritual to Romance	Jessie L. Weston	0760773548
Great Democracies, The	Winston S. Churchill	0760768609
Guide for the Perplexed, The	Moses Maimonides	0760757577
Hannibal	Theodore Ayrault Dodge	076076896X
Happy Hunting-Grounds, The	Kermit Roosevelt	0760755817
History of Atlantis, The	Lewis Spence	076077045X

History of the Conquest of Mexico, The	William H. Prescott	0760759227
History of the Conquest of Peru, The	William H. Prescott	076076137X
History of the Donner Party, The	Charles F. McGlashan	0760752427
History of the English Church and People, The	Bede	0760765510
History of Wales, A	J. E. Lloyd	0760752419
How the Other Half Lives	Jacob A. Riis	0760755892
How to Sing	Lilli Lehmann	0760752311
How We Think	John Dewey	0760770387
Hunting the Grisly and Other Sketches	Theodore Roosevelt	0760752338
Imitation of Christ, The	Thomas À. Kempis	0760755914
In His Steps	Charles M. Sheldon	0760755779
Influence of Sea Power upon History, The, 1660–1783	Alfred Thayer Mahan	0760754993
Interesting Narrative of the Life of Olaudah Equiano, The	Olaudah Equiano	0760773505
Interior Castle, The	St. Teresa of Avila	0760770247
Introduction to Logic	Immanuel Kant	0760770409
Introduction to Mathematical Philosophy	Bertrand Russell	0760773408
Introduction to Mathematics	Alfred North Whitehead	076076588X
Investigation of the Laws of Thought, An	George Boole	0760765847
Kingdom of God is Within You, The	Leo Tolstoy	0760765529
Lady's Life in the Rockies, A	Isabella Bird	0760763135
Leonardo da Vinci and a Memory of His Childhood	Sigmund Freud	0760749922
Letters and Saying of Epicurus	Epicurus	0760763283
Leviathan, The	Thomas Hobbes	0760755930
Life of Johnson	James Boswell	0760773483
Lives of the Caesars, The	Suetonius	0760757585
Manners, Customs, and History of the Highlanders of Scotland	Walter Scott	0760758697
Meditations	Marcus Aurelius	076075229X
Memoirs	William T. Sherman	0760773688
Metaphysics	Aristotle	0760773637
Montcalm and Wolfe	Francis Parkman	0760768358
Montessori Method, The	Maria Montessori	0760749957
Mosby's Memoirs	John Singleton Mosby	0760773726

Tragic Sense of Life	Miguel de Unamuno	0760777764
Travels of Marco Polo, The	Marco Polo	0760765898
Treatise Concerning the Principles of Human Knowledge, A	George Berkeley	0760777691
Treatise of Human Nature, A	David Hume	0760771723
Trial and Death of Socrates, The	Plato	0760762007
Up From Slavery	Booker T. Washington	0760752346
Utilitarianism	William James	0760771758
Vindication of the Rights of Woman, A	Mary Wollstonecraft	0760754942
Violin Playing As I Teach It	Leopold Auer	0760749914
Voyage of the *Beagle*, The	Charles Darwin	0760754969
Wealth of Nations, The	Adam Smith	0760757615
Wilderness Hunter, The	Theodore Roosevelt	0760756031
Will to Believe and Human Immortality, The	William James	0760770190
Will to Power, The	Friedrich Nietzsche	0760777772
Worst Journey in the World, The	Aspley Cherry-Garrard	0760757593
You Know Me Al	Ring W. Lardner	0760758336

THE BARNES & NOBLE
LIBRARY OF ESSENTIAL READING

This newly developed series has been established to provide affordable access to books of literary, academic, and historic value—works of both well-known writers and those who deserve to be rediscovered. Selected and introduced by scholars and specialists with an intimate knowledge of the works, these volumes present complete, original texts in a modern, readable typeface— welcoming a new generation of readers to influential and important books of the past. With more than 100 titles already in print and more than 100 forthcoming, the Library of Essential Reading offers an unrivaled variety of thought, scholarship, and entertainment. Best of all, these handsome and durable paperbacks are priced to be exceptionally affordable. For a full list of titles, visit *www.bn.com/loer*.